The Individual
Income Tax

Studies of Government Finance

The Individual Income Tax

RICHARD GOODE

REVISED EDITION

Studies of Government Finance

THE BROOKINGS INSTITUTION

WASHINGTON, D.C.

Library of Congress Cataloging in Publication Data:
Goode, Richard.
　The individual income tax.
　(Studies of government finance)
　Includes bibliographical references.
　1. Income tax—United States.　I. Title.
II. Series.
HJ4652.G6　1976　　336.2′42′0973　　75-38735
ISBN 0-8157-3198-1
ISBN 0-8157-3197-3 pbk.

9 8 7 6 5 4 3 2 1

THE BROOKINGS INSTITUTION is an independent organization devoted to nonpartisan research, education, and publication in economics, government, foreign policy, and the social sciences generally. Its principal purposes are to aid in the development of sound public policies and to promote public understanding of issues of national importance.

The Institution was founded on December 8, 1927, to merge the activities of the Institute for Government Research, founded in 1916, the Institute of Economics, founded in 1922, and the Robert Brookings Graduate School of Economics and Government, founded in 1924.

The Board of Trustees is responsible for the general administration of the Institution, while the immediate direction of the policies, program, and staff is vested in the President, assisted by an advisory committee of the officers and staff. The bylaws of the Institution state: "It is the function of the Trustees to make possible the conduct of scientific research, and publication, under the most favorable conditions, and to safeguard the independence of the research staff in the pursuit of their studies and in the publication of the results of such studies. It is not a part of their function to determine, control, or influence the conduct of particular investigations or the conclusions reached."

The President bears final responsibility for the decision to publish a manuscript as a Brookings book. In reaching his judgment on the competence, accuracy, and objectivity of each study, the President is advised by the director of the appropriate research program and weighs the views of a panel of expert outside readers who report to him in confidence on the quality of the work. Publication of a work signifies that it is deemed a competent treatment worthy of public consideration but does not imply endorsement of conclusions or recommendations.

The Institution maintains its position of neutrality on issues of public policy in order to safeguard the intellectual freedom of the staff. Hence interpretations or conclusions in Brookings publications should be understood to be solely those of the authors and should not be attributed to the Institution, to its trustees, officers, or other staff members, or to the organizations that support its research.

Foreword

THE INDIVIDUAL INCOME TAX, the mainstay of the federal tax system of the United States, yielded 45 percent of all federal receipts in the past five fiscal years, dominating by a wide margin receipts from any other single source. Even though the minimum taxable level of income has been adjusted upward in recent years, a large majority of the nation's income recipients pay income tax. For more than sixty years, the levy has been a part of the nation's economic, political, and social landscape.

The extent of the nation's reliance on the individual income tax is not a measure of its popularity. Many, questioning the wisdom of progressive taxation, believe that too much reliance is placed on the income tax. Others believe that progression has not been carried far enough. Still others regard the tax, as it has developed in the United States, as too generous in permitting special exemptions, deductions, and exclusions for particular groups of taxpayers or activities.

Since the federal income tax was adopted in 1913, many changes in its structure have been made and others have been proposed. Alternatives, such as consumption and wealth taxes, have also been advocated. This study, an updated, thorough revision of the original book published by Brookings in 1964, is an evaluation of experience with the income tax, stressing the assessment of its equity and economic effects. It also analyzes suggested changes in the tax and considers the merits of other revenue sources. The author's comprehensive appraisal is intended as a contribution both to better public understanding of the problems of reforming the income tax and to better-informed policymaking.

Richard Goode, formerly a Brookings senior staff member, has been director of the Fiscal Affairs Department of the International Monetary Fund since 1965. He remains grateful for the criticism and suggestions received from members of the reading committee for the first edition, Douglas H. Eldridge, Lawrence H. Seltzer, Louis Shere, and Herbert Stein. Among the many others to whom he is indebted, he acknowledges especially the assistance he received from Joseph A. Pechman and Benjamin A. Okner. Herbert C. Morton edited the first edition and Richard Weintraub the revised edition. Evelyn P. Fisher verified the factual content of the manuscript. The index was prepared by Annette H. Braver, and the figures by Fred Powell.

This is the third publication in the Brookings Studies of Government Finance, second series, which is devoted to examining issues in taxation and public expenditure policy. The author's views are his own and should not be ascribed to the trustees, officers, or other staff members of the Brookings Institution or to the International Monetary Fund.

KERMIT GORDON
President

October 1975
Washington, D.C.

Contents

Text Tables

Text Figures

Appendix Tables

Appendix Figure

CHAPTER ONE

Introduction

ON FEBRUARY 25, 1913, the secretary of state certified the ratification of the Sixteenth Amendment to the Constitution, giving Congress "power to lay and collect taxes on incomes, from whatever source derived." This amendment, the first to be adopted in forty-three years, overturned a Supreme Court decision[1] that had blocked an individual income tax for almost two decades, and opened a new chapter in the fiscal history of the United States.

Within less than two months, the House Ways and Means Committee reported the bill that became the first permanent individual income tax law in the United States. The bill was approved October 3, 1913, and became effective March 1, 1913. At that time the income tax was already well established in Great Britain. Income taxes were also in use in Prussia, the Netherlands, the Swiss cantons, Australia, New Zealand, Japan, and other countries and in the state of Wisconsin.

The Ways and Means Committee described its 1913 income tax bill as a response to "the general demand for justice in taxation, and to the long-standing need of an elastic and productive system of rev-

1. *Pollock* v. *Farmers' Loan and Trust Company*, 157 U.S. 429 (1895), 158 U.S. 601 (1895). This decision declared unconstitutional an income tax law enacted in 1894. An income tax had been levied during the Civil War but was allowed to lapse in 1872.

enue." The committee made clear that it considered the income tax permanent and an important innovation. The report predicted that, once established, the tax would "meet with as much general satisfaction as any tax law" and—more sanguinely—that "all good citizens . . . will willingly and cheerfully support and sustain this, the fairest and cheapest of all taxes."[2]

Growth of the Income Tax

The act of 1913 set up an income tax system that remains in effect in the United States today, despite numerous revisions. It includes an individual income tax, applying to natural persons and trusts, and a corporation income tax. The individual tax is a global tax assessed against taxable income from all sources; however, long-term capital gains have been subject to special treatment since the Revenue Act of 1921 and earned income has been taxed at preferential rates at various times. Corporations are generally taxed as separate entities, and dividends received by shareholders are subject to the individual income tax. Unincorporated enterprises are generally not taxed as entities; their proprietors and partners pay the individual income tax on total profits regardless of whether those profits are withdrawn or retained in the business.[3]

The taxes on income fulfilled the expectation that they would be elastic and productive revenue sources, responding to both changes in tax rates and changes in national income. The individual income tax alone accounted for almost one-fifth of federal revenue during World War I. Its relative contribution rose in the 1920s, despite sharp rate

2. H. Rept. 5, 63 Cong. 1 sess. (1913), reprinted in U.S. Bureau of Internal Revenue, *Internal Revenue Bulletin,* Cumulative Bulletin 1939-1, pt. 2 (January–June 1939), pp. 1–3.

3. When certain conditions are met, closely held corporations may elect to be taxed as partnerships (Internal Revenue Code of 1954, as amended, secs. 1371–77), but only a small minority have chosen this option. My practice is to give citations of statutory provisions, regulations, and rulings that I judge not to be well known but to omit citations of familiar and easily accessible provisions. Readers whose needs are met by a reliable and rather detailed secondary source will find convenient the annual issues of Commerce Clearing House, *U.S. Master Tax Guide,* or Clarence F. McCarthy, *The Federal Income Tax: Its Sources and Applications* (Prentice-Hall, 1974). A good but now out-of-date reference is the World Tax Series volume of the Harvard Law School, *Taxation in the United States* (Commerce Clearing House, 1963).

reductions, and fell in the early 1930s, despite rate increases. In response to the fiscal demands of World War II, the income tax was transformed into a mass tax and became the federal government's leading revenue source. The yield increased spectacularly, and during World War II the individual income tax provided one-third of total cash receipts (including social insurance contributions and other nonbudget receipts). After the war, the proportion of revenue provided by the individual income tax continued to grow, reaching 45 percent in the fiscal years 1970–75 (appendix table A-2).[4]

The rise in yield of the income tax was made possible by rate increases far exceeding early expectations and by a great broadening of coverage. The 1913 act set rates ranging from 1 percent on the first $20,000 of taxable income to 7 percent on taxable income in excess of $500,000. The professor of public finance at Harvard found the maximum rates "clearly excessive" because Congress at one stroke had appropriated for the use of the federal government "about seventy percent of the total possible proceeds of direct taxation upon large incomes," which, "as the experience of all countries" showed, was subject to a safe limit of "probably ten percent" and certainly not more than 12 percent.[5] By 1917, the top rate had reached 67 percent. During World War II and most postwar years up to 1964, rates ranged from 20 percent or more in the first bracket to a maximum of more than 90 percent. Nominal rates now begin at 14 percent and rise to a top of 70 percent (appendix table A-10).

The 1913 act was expected to apply to only about 1 percent of the population, including taxpayers and their dependents,[6] and the actual number was smaller. As recently as 1939, only 5 percent of the population were subject to the income tax. In 1970, 81 percent of the population were covered (see table 1-1 and appendix table A-3).

By 1918, individual income tax liabilities surpassed $1 billion and approached 2 percent of total personal income. Twenty-seven years later, in another wartime year, the tax absorbed 10 percent of personal income (table 1-1). In 1970, the fraction was higher.

4. The World War I period is taken as fiscal years 1917–20, fiscal year 1920 being the year of peak revenue and reflecting the highest tax rates.

5. Charles J. Bullock, "The Federal Income Tax," in National Tax Association, *Proceedings of the Eighth Annual Conference, 1914* (1915), p. 277.

6. Derived from estimate of the House Ways and Means Committee (H. Rept. 5, reprint p. 3) on the assumption that the average number of persons covered on each taxable return was 2.5.

Table 1-1. Growth of the Federal Individual Income Tax, 1913–70

Year	Percentage of population covered	Tax as percentage of personal income
1913	Less than 1.0[a]	0.1[b]
1918	7.7	1.8[b]
1926	4.2	0.9
1939	5.0	1.2
1945	74.2	10.0
1950	58.9	8.1
1960	73.1	9.8
1970	80.8	10.4

Sources: Derived from the same sources as appendix tables A-3 and A-5.
a. Author's approximation.
b. The underlying personal income estimate for 1913 is the average for 1912–16; that for 1918 is the average for 1917–21.

Although most states use an individual income tax, it has never become as important a revenue source for the states as it is for the federal government. Until the mid-1930s, the tax spread rapidly among the states, and the movement was resumed during the 1960s, after a long interruption. By the end of 1971, forty of the fifty states had individual income taxes and these taxes had produced 19 percent of total state tax revenue in 1970, ranking second to state sales taxes, which produced 30 percent.[7]

Why Study the Income Tax?

The preeminence of the individual income tax in the federal revenue system reflects its productivity and, more basically, a widespread belief that it is the fairest means of meeting national government costs. Moreover, as the federal government has assumed greater responsibility for moderating economic fluctuations, the quick response of the income tax to changes in business activity has come to be considered a valuable stabilizing force as well as a fiscal convenience.

Opinions about the income tax, however, are sharply divided. Public opinion polls taken in 1972, 1973, and 1974 found that the federal income tax was regarded as the fairest of the major taxes used

7. Advisory Commission on Intergovernmental Relations, *State-Local Finances: Significant Features and Suggested Legislation, 1972 Edition* (ACIR, 1972), pp. 20, 171, 175. Four additional states imposed taxes on individual income from certain sources.

by the federal, state, and local governments but that it was considered the least fair by a large and growing minority of respondents.[8] Another poll, taken in mid-1973, found that 52 percent of respondents believed that the income tax was the fairest way of raising federal revenue but that 28 percent thought that a sales tax would be fairest.[9]

Criticisms of the income tax have persisted throughout its history. These criticisms differ in sophistication and vehemence and are advanced from various points of view. Some of the objections reflect simple dissatisfaction with heavy taxation of any kind and concentrate on reduction of tax rates. This dissatisfaction has been aggravated at times by the increases in income tax liabilities that automatically accompany rising incomes, whether a result of real growth or inflation. Many critics, however, believe the income tax is more objectionable than alternative taxes and should be partly or wholly replaced.

An income tax with high, graduated rates is said to inhibit private saving and investment and thus to slow capital formation and the rate of economic growth. It is also said to discourage initiative and enterprise in business ventures and to lessen the willingness to accept new and more responsible employment or to work long hours. Moreover, the income tax is alleged to cause business executives and individual investors to divert time and ingenuity from productive activities to tax compliance and minimization. Efforts to avoid taxation are thought to reduce economic efficiency because they distort decisions about forms of business organization, contracts, and portfolios. Critics note that the United States has been growing less rapidly than Germany, France, Italy, and Japan, which rely less heavily on income taxes and more heavily on indirect consumption taxes (see appendix table A-4).

Many supporters of the income tax have become less enthusiastic. They are disturbed by special provisions allowing much income to escape taxation, the ingenuity of taxpayers in finding loopholes, the reluctance of Congress to repair the erosion of the tax base, and incomplete compliance with the law. In 1970, for example, the amount

8. Opinion Research Corporation polls covering probability samples of the U.S. population aged eighteen and older; see Advisory Commission on Intergovernmental Relations, *Changing Public Attitudes on Governments and Taxes* (ACIR, 1974).

9. Harris Survey poll of "a nationwide cross section of 1,537 households" reported in *Washington Post,* July 24, 1973.

of income actually taxed equaled only about one-half of total personal income (figure 1-1). Economists have concluded that the income tax is less neutral in its effects than was often supposed in the past, and egalitarians ask whether progressive taxation of income is the best means of attaining their objectives. Suggestions for new forms of taxation have received far more attention from experts recently than they did twenty years ago.

Some of these criticisms reflect disillusionment with a revenue system which has moved in the direction many experts wished but which clearly is still far from ideal. Some tax experts are suffering from having got what they wanted, a fate that cynics assert is at least as sad as not getting what one wants. Other criticisms reflect renewed emphasis on the classical objective of growth and diminished interest in problems of income distribution.

Suggestions for improvement are numerous and varied. They call for actions ranging from minor technical amendments to abolition of the tax. A favorite program among supporters of the income tax includes broadening the base by ending unjustified omissions and deductions from taxable income and reducing nominally high tax rates to offset the revenue gained from base-broadening. As originally conceived, this approach was designed to maintain, or enhance, the role of the income tax in the federal revenue system. Base-broadening and rate adjustments, however, may be combined in a program that

Figure 1-1. Derivation of Individual Income Tax Base, 1970

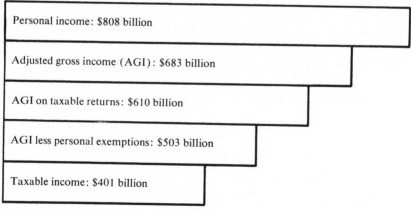

Personal income: $808 billion

Adjusted gross income (AGI): $683 billion

AGI on taxable returns: $610 billion

AGI less personal exemptions: $503 billion

Taxable income: $401 billion

Sources: Appendix tables A-6, A-7.

diminishes the percentage of total revenue obtained from the income tax.

Others suggest de-emphasis of the income tax and partial substitution of sales taxes and excises or other indirect taxes. These proposals usually are concerned more with tax rates than with structural reforms but often include some provisions of the latter kind. In the United States, they are sponsored mainly by business groups and conservatives; but in Sweden, Norway, and Denmark, Social Democratic or Labor governments have deliberately moved over the past two decades toward the greater use of sales or value-added taxes.[10]

More extreme programs would completely replace the income tax with a sales tax, turnover tax, or value-added tax. Usually these proposals are rooted in a persistent conservative opposition to progressive taxation. Paradoxically, the income tax is also disliked on the far left. In 1960, the Soviet Union adopted a program for eliminating the individual income tax over a period of years. Since the USSR had always relied mainly on turnover taxes, the program was less extreme than it would have been in the United States or most other Western countries; nevertheless, the Soviet government suspended the plan in 1962, assigning a higher priority to the need for revenue to strengthen defenses against "imperialists."[11]

Recently the range of alternatives for the U.S. system has been extended by suggestions for graduated taxes on personal consumption expenditures and on personal wealth as a major supplement to the income tax or as a complete substitute. Some economists think that the expenditure tax and the wealth tax would avoid the disadvantages of the income tax without sacrificing progressivity. Although personal taxes on consumption and wealth are not really new ideas, they have so far had only limited application and are novel elements in a program for action. The expenditure tax and the wealth tax merit attention because fresh proposals on taxation are scarce and because their analysis gives perspective on the income tax.

10. For an interesting account of the factors affecting Swedish policy in this respect, see Martin Norr and Nils G. Hornhammar, "The Value-Added Tax in Sweden," *Columbia Law Review*, vol. 70 (March 1970), pp. 382–87. See also an article by the Swedish Minister of Finance, G. E. Sträng, "Swedish Tax Policy," *European Taxation*, vol. 10 (August 1970), pp. I/190–92.

11. *Raising the Soviet Standard of Living*, Report by N. S. Khrushchev (Crosscurrents Press, 1960), pp. 19–33, 96–99; *Manchester Guardian Weekly*, vol. 87 (September 27, 1962), p. 7.

Scope of the Book

This book presents a general appraisal of the individual income tax and considers possible revisions of the tax. Emphasis is on the equity and economic effects of the income tax and alternative revenue sources, but attention is also given to administration and compliance and to certain other aspects of taxation. The focus is on the federal income tax in the United States, but many points that must be examined are relevant for state income taxes and for income taxes in other countries.

Only incidental references are made to the special problems of taxing business profits. Although technical provisions relating to the measurement of profits, such as depreciation and depletion allowances, generally apply to both the corporation income tax and the individual income tax, they can be more conveniently treated in connection with the taxation of corporations, which account for the major part of business profits in the United States. This book also omits the intricate questions arising from the relationship between the taxation of corporations and that of their shareholders.

The book appears soon after the sixtieth anniversary of the modern income tax in the United States. Sixty years may not seem a long time in the history of the republic or in the life of a form of taxation, but the period since 1913 has seen a huge increase in taxation and the development of new fiscal doctrines. Interesting and enlightening as it might be, a detailed history of the income tax is not presented.[12] The subject is the contemporary tax and the tax of the future. Where does the United States stand in income taxation after more than half a century of experience? Where should the country try to go in the years ahead?

The next chapter deals with the suitability of income as a tax base from the standpoints of fairness and practicality and examines the case for other tax bases. In chapters 3 and 4, the economic effects of the income tax are broadly compared with those of direct and indirect taxes on consumption and wealth. Three chapters on the definition and measurement of the income tax base follow. These treat certain costs of earning income that present special problems, income items

12. For historical reviews, see Roy G. Blakey and Gladys C. Blakey, *The Federal Income Tax* (Longmans, Green, 1940), and Randolph E. Paul, *Taxation in the United States* (Little, Brown, 1954).

that are excluded from taxable income, and personal deductions that are allowed even though they are not costs of obtaining income. A special effort is made to ascertain the influence of these provisions on the yield of the tax, its progressivity, and its influence on economic decisions. Capital gains and losses are the subject of a separate chapter because of their strategic importance and because of marked differences of opinion on the extent to which they should be reflected in taxable income and the tax rates that should apply to capital gains. Chapter 9 surveys topics relating to the level and structure of personal exemptions and income tax rates. The effects of the income tax on the distribution of income and wealth and on economic stability are examined in chapters 10 and 11. The book concludes with a chapter on income tax reform and the place of the individual income tax in the revenue system.

Taxes are never pleasant to those who pay them, and taxation seldom brings about an increase in production. If the benefits of government expenditures are ignored and only a particular tax or tax provision is considered, it is easy to find harmful economic effects or inequities. A grave shortcoming of this approach is the failure to take account of the undesirable consequences of other taxes that might be substituted for the one under consideration or of a budget deficit or reduction in government expenditures. An opposite error, occasionally encountered, is to excuse the defects of the income tax on the grounds that it finances essential government services, without considering the possibility of obtaining revenue from a revised income tax or from another source.

These biases cannot be wholly avoided but they can be minimized by frequent comparisons with alternative revenue sources and tax provisions. The comparative approach is followed to the extent feasible in a book on the individual income tax. No attempt is made to determine whether taxation is too heavy or too light relative to social needs or government expenditures. It is assumed in this study that any change in revenue resulting from income tax revision or the introduction of a new tax would not affect the government's total receipts because it either would be offset by changes in the rates of the income tax or other taxes or would prevent tax rate increases or decreases that would otherwise occur.

The object of the book is to increase understanding of the individual income tax and alternative taxes with the hope that in the long run this will help in policy formulation. On many economic issues—perhaps the majority of important questions—definitive conclusions cannot be provided. Theory and data are inadequate, and experts disagree. On other points, disagreements arise from conflicts of social values and political preferences. Nevertheless, progress toward a better public understanding of alternatives seems possible. I have not refrained from expressing opinions on controversial subjects but have tried to warn the reader of uncertainties and differences of opinion.

CHAPTER TWO

Income as a Tax Base

THE BELIEF that the individual income tax is the fairest of all taxes arises from the conviction that it accords best with ability to pay. Net income is a measure of a person's capacity to command economic resources, and, intuitively, it seems to be a good indicator of ability to help finance government.

The income tax has also gained approval because of its directness and adaptability to graduated rates. It is a direct tax in the sense that legislators expect those who pay it will be unable to shift it to others. A direct tax can take account of taxpayers' family circumstances and other individual conditions in a way that is not possible under a sales tax or other indirect tax which is collected from producers or distributors in the expectation that they will pass it on to customers. By providing for personal exemptions and graduated rates, the income tax may cause an individual's tax to increase faster than his income, with the result that the percentage of income absorbed by the tax rises with income. Because of this characteristic, the income tax is called a progressive tax, a term that should be understood in a technical rather than a political sense. The principle of tax progressivity has been accepted to some degree in nearly every country, and the income tax has won support as the primary instrument of progressivity.

The case for the income tax has elicited controversy as well as support. Ability to pay is subject to diverse interpretations; critics have called it a slogan rather than a principle. Progressivity has always been opposed by some; even its supporters disagree about its rationale. Income taxation, moreover, is not the only means of achieving progressivity. Taxes on estates, inheritance, and gifts contribute to progressivity, although their coverage is limited and it is doubtful that they could be made a major source of revenue. Direct, progressive taxes could also be assessed against personal consumption and wealth.

Whether personal income is indeed the fairest tax base and the best base for progressive taxation is ultimately a question of personal preference and political values. But this does not mean that the issues cannot be illuminated by analysis or that one set of preferences is as good as another. The implications of tax doctrines can be clarified and preferences examined for consistency with other values. The feasibility of correctly assessing alternative taxes can be considered. These questions are the subject of this chapter.

Fairness and Progressivity of Alternative Taxes

The significant alternatives to income as a basis of personal taxation are wealth and consumption. Taxes on personal wealth or net worth have been in effect for some time in Sweden, Denmark, Norway, the Netherlands, Germany, and a few other countries.[1] They are being introduced in the United Kingdom and Ireland. The yield of wealth taxes in these countries, however, is much lower than that of the income tax. The wealth taxes differ from the American general property tax in that they require the aggregation of all, or most, items of property owned by the individual and allow deductions for debts; personal exemptions are provided and rates may be graduated. There also has been discussion of a direct tax on personal consumption expenditures. Unlike sales taxes and excises, this tax would be assessed on the basis of individual returns, with provision for personal exemptions and graduated rates. Personal expenditure taxes were in-

1. See Noboru Tanabe, "The Taxation of Net Wealth," International Monetary Fund, *Staff Papers*, vol. 14 (March 1967), pp. 124–68; *Wealth Tax*, Presented to Parliament by the Chancellor of the Exchequer, Cmnd. 5704 (London: Her Majesty's Stationery Office, 1974); Department of the Treasury, *Net Wealth Taxes*, Treasury Taxation Paper 12 (Canberra: Australian Government Publishing Service, 1974).

troduced on a limited scale in India in 1957 and in Ceylon in 1959, but these taxes yielded little and have been rescinded.[2]

The U.S. Constitution may bar the federal government from imposing a wealth tax. Taxes on property have been held to be direct taxes which cannot be levied by Congress unless apportioned among the states according to population.[3] The status of an expenditure tax is also uncertain. It might be upheld as an income tax with a deduction for saving, or the courts might decide that it is not a direct tax within the meaning of the Constitution. Doubts about constitutionality, however, should not preclude the discussion of innovations. When the country was convinced that the income tax should be adopted, the Constitution was amended.

Definition of Income

Many American experts have accepted as the ideal starting point for tax purposes an income definition usually associated in the United States with the names of Haig and Simons but which was anticipated by Schanz in Germany and apparently also by David Davidson in Sweden.[4] In Haig's language, income is "the increase or accretion in one's power to satisfy his wants in a given period in so far as that power consists of (a) money itself, or, (b) anything susceptible of valuation in terms of money."[5] Simons equates personal income with the algebraic sum of consumption and change in net worth.[6]

2. Throughout this book, the terms "wealth tax" and "expenditure tax" refer to personal taxes of the kind just identified rather than to more familiar forms of taxation of property and consumption.

3. Art. 1, sec. 9; *Pollock* v. *Farmers' Loan and Trust Company,* 157 U.S. 429, 558 (1895); *Brushaber* v. *Union Pacific Railroad Company,* 240 U.S. 1, 14 (1916).

4. Georg Schanz, "Der Einkommensbegriff und die Einkommensteuergesetze," *Finanz-Archiv,* vol. 13, no. 1 (1896), pp. 1–87; Fritz Neumark, *Theorie und Praxis der modernen Einkommensbesteuerung* (Bern: A. Francke, 1947), pp. 34–50; Leif Mutén, *On the Development of Income Taxation Since World War I* (Amsterdam: International Bureau of Fiscal Documentation, 1967), pp. 24–34.

5. Robert Murray Haig, "The Concept of Income—Economic and Legal Aspects," in Haig, ed., *The Federal Income Tax* (Columbia University Press, 1921), p. 7, reprinted in Richard A. Musgrave and Carl S. Shoup, eds., *Readings in the Economics of Taxation* (Irwin for the American Economic Association, 1959), p. 59.

6. Henry C. Simons, *Personal Income Taxation: The Definition of Income as a Problem of Fiscal Policy* (University of Chicago Press, 1938), p. 50. Literally, Simons' definition applies to income net of the income tax and other direct personal taxes; however, it has generally been interpreted to mean income gross of personal taxes. See Henry Aaron, "What Is a Comprehensive Tax Base Anyway?" *National Tax Journal,* vol. 22 (December 1969), pp. 543–49.

Most experts believe, however, that it is not feasible to take into account all accrued changes in the value of assets and liabilities and that the income tax should be limited to realized income as reflected in transactions or conventional accounting statements.[7] Many think that it would not be desirable to tax unrealized capital gains even if it were feasible. A number of writers favor a definition of taxable income more restricted than that of Haig and Simons in other respects.

The U.S. statutes do not attempt a general definition of income; they rely mainly on the enumeration of items to be included, excluded, or deducted. However, the statutory listing is not exhaustive. The Internal Revenue Code, quoting the language of the Sixteenth Amendment, refers to income "from whatever source derived" and states that taxable income includes "but [is] not limited to" the enumerated items. The limits of the income concept have to be determined by administrators and the courts on a case-by-case basis. Although the courts have tended to become more permissive and to allow a broadening of the concept,[8] many important items that qualify as realized income are omitted from the tax base in the United States. Nevertheless, it will be convenient to compare income, consumption, and wealth as tax bases on the assumption that each is defined as comprehensively and accurately as would be feasible in a new system devised without regard to political commitments to the present income tax law or vested interests in its provisions.

Conceptual as well as practical difficulties are involved in applying the definition of income. One group of problems relates to the definition of personal consumption and turns mainly on the distinction between goods and services that yield direct satisfaction and intermediate goods and services that contribute to a final product. Other difficulties relate to measurement of change in net worth or capital gains and losses when the price level and interest rates vary.

The distinction between consumption and intermediate goods and services depends more on individual attitudes and convention than on physical characteristics. An automobile, a restaurant meal, or a scholarly book may be a source of personal gratification or a means of enabling its buyer to earn more income—or it may serve both pur-

---

7. Simons conceded this. See his book, published posthumously, *Federal Tax Reform* (University of Chicago Press, 1950), pp. 48, 74.

8. Harvard Law School, World Tax Series, *Taxation in the United States* (Commerce Clearing House, 1963), pp. 366–67.

poses. Simons acknowledges that the "measurement of consumption presents insuperable difficulties to achievement of a rigorous conception of personal income"[9] but concludes that, in practice, income can be measured well enough for tax purposes.

Nicholas Kaldor, on the other hand, gives little attention to the definition of consumption but stresses the difficulties of measuring changes in net worth. Because of these difficulties, Kaldor concludes that "the problem of *defining* individual Income, quite apart from any problem of practical measurement, appears in principle insoluble."[10] He then argues that consumption is a better measure of taxable capacity than income and recommends an expenditure tax as an important supplement to the income tax.

In Kaldor's view, "the ideal definition of Income, as a measure of taxable capacity, is to be thought of . . . as Consumption plus *Real* Capital Accumulation," and the insoluble problem is to distinguish between real and nominal capital accumulation. Real capital accumulation, he says, occurs when an individual secures "increased command over both consumption goods and income yielding resources."[11] Fictitious gains that are due merely to an increase in the price level can be approximately eliminated by deflating through the use of a consumer price index. But there is a second kind of rise in asset prices that Kaldor considers either fictitious or at least less valuable than other forms of capital increment and for which a proper correction cannot be made.

The value of income-yielding assets will rise if there is a general fall in interest rates. If, for example, the relevant interest rate falls from 5 percent to 4 percent, the capital value of a perpetual stream of income of $100 a year will rise from $2,000 to $2,500; the value of a twenty-year stream of $100 per year, from $1,246 to $1,359. Kaldor argues that this kind of appreciation is spurious because it does not make the investor better off relative to other capitalists and because it does not give him increased command over capital assets. He points out that a correction for changes in interest rates is not possible because the relevant interest rate cannot be inferred from the market; when share prices rise it is not possible to say how much of the rise is

9. *Personal Income Taxation,* p. 110.
10. Nicholas Kaldor, *An Expenditure Tax* (London: Allen and Unwin, 1955), pp. 54–78. The quotation is from p. 70.
11. Ibid., pp. 69–70.

due to a lower interest (capitalization) rate and how much to expectations of improved earnings.

Kaldor's criterion seems too exacting. Why should income be considered real only if it affords increased command over both consumption goods and capital assets; that is, increased power to consume now *and* in the future? Why not say that increased power to consume is a sufficient condition and that income accrues when an increase occurs regardless of whether the power is exercised? To be sure, an increase in capital values resulting from a fall in interest rates is less advantageous to a property owner than an increase resulting from the expectation of higher yields. If income is defined merely as an increase in the power to consume, this difference will not be taken into account immediately, but, if the expectation proves to be correct, the difference will be reflected in future income.[12] It is incorrect to say that an appreciation of asset values caused by a general decline in interest rates does not make the owners better off relative to other capitalists. Owners of long-term securities gain relative to holders of short-terms and cash and relative to those who aspire to accumulate wealth in the future. If income is interpreted each year as the power to command consumption goods, a consistent and logical pattern will emerge over the years.

It is debatable, moreover, whether the income tax would be fairer if all incomes were corrected for changes in the price level, a subject to be considered in the chapter on capital gains and losses.

Since the conceptual difficulties of defining income arise from ambiguities in the definitions of consumption and changes in net worth, replacement of the income tax by an expenditure tax *and* a wealth tax would resolve none of these difficulties. Substitution of one of the two alternative taxes would eliminate some of the conceptual problems. The literature on the definition of personal con-

---

12. For example, when a twenty-year income stream rises in market value from $1,246 to $1,359, the Haig-Simons definition indicates that $113 of income has accrued to the owner. If annual yield is the fixed amount of $100 per year, the capital appreciation is due to a fall in the interest rate from 5 percent to 4 percent. The total taxable income over twenty years is $113 + 20($100) = $2,113. If, on the other hand, the interest rate is constant at 5 percent, the capital appreciation reflects the expectation that the annual yield will rise from $100 to $109. If this expectation proves correct, the total taxable income, according to Haig-Simons, will be $113 + 20($109) = $2,293. It is true that the present value of the $2,293, discounted at 5 percent, is equal to the present value of the $2,113, discounted at 4 percent.

sumption and personal wealth is less extensive than that on the definition of income, and the problems of defining these items are less widely appreciated because the expenditure tax and the wealth tax have been used much less than the income tax.

Ability to Pay

Fairness is generally recognized as comprising equal treatment of equals and reasonable differences in the treatment of unequals. In regard to taxation, capacity or ability to pay is the relevant aspect of equality and inequality. Income and competing tax bases derive their appeal from their relation to capacity or ability to pay.

In the crudest sense, ability to pay means only the possession of resources that can be turned over to the state. A pauper can pay little in taxes whereas a millionaire can pay much. But the idea of ability to pay, if it has any value as a tax criterion, must convey something more.

The doctrine of ability to pay can be given meaning without reviving the pseudoscientific, and now discredited, interpretations that flourished in the past.[13] While the sacrifices of taxpayers cannot be precisely measured, as many earlier writers assumed, it is neither necessary nor wise to abandon the idea of appraising and comparing, in a rough way, the burdens that taxes impose.

Ability to pay taxes is the capacity for paying without undue hardship on the part of the person paying or an unacceptable degree of interference with objectives that are considered socially important by other members of the community. If A has more income than B, it seems reasonable to say that A has greater ability to pay taxes in the sense that the payment of a given amount will hurt A less and will be less likely to force a cut in socially desirable consumption. In judging what A and B will give up, one makes an estimate of what they would do and how they would feel if they were representative of others in similar circumstances. The doctrine of taxation according to ability to

13. For criticisms of the hedonistic interpretation of ability to pay, particularly of its use as an argument for progressive taxation, see Simons, *Personal Income Taxation*, pp. 5–19; Elmer D. Fagan, "Recent and Contemporary Theories of Progressive Taxation," *Journal of Political Economy*, vol. 46 (August 1938), pp. 457–98, reprinted in *Readings in the Economics of Taxation*, pp. 19–53; M. Slade Kendrick, "The Ability-to-Pay Theory of Taxation," *American Economic Review*, vol. 29 (March 1939), pp. 92–101; and Walter J. Blum and Harry Kalven, Jr., *The Uneasy Case for Progressive Taxation* (University of Chicago Press, 1953).

pay is not destroyed by the undoubted fact that others do not know how A and B actually feel as individuals. Debaters' points can easily be scored by supposing that, although A is a rich bachelor and B a poor widow, A is so sensitive that he will suffer more by forgoing an extra bottle of champagne than B will from giving up milk for her children. Most sensible people will consider this an implausible case and, if pressed, will say that, even in the assumed circumstances, milk for B's children should have priority over champagne for A.

The ability-to-pay principle supports progressive taxation only if taxpaying capacity increases faster than income, which is a stronger assertion than the general argument made above. The assertion has appeal because it is plausible to suppose that people first satisfy their most urgent needs and then use additional income to meet less urgent wants and because, in civilized communities, public or private assistance is given to those whose income is below a minimum level. Even severe critics of progression usually agree that people with income below a certain level should not be expected to pay taxes. Acceptance of a personal exemption necessarily implies at least a limited degree of progression, since tax liability will rise faster than income immediately above the exemption, even if rates are not graduated. In my judgment, the reasoning that approves this limited degree of progression can also justify much wider progressivity. To deny this would imply that there is a sharp discontinuity in the sacrifices made in paying taxes or in the social importance of successive increments of income, consumption, or wealth. It seems more plausible to suppose that the private and social importance of additional units diminishes gradually over a very wide range. This can be recognized by granting a variable exemption or, more effectively, by applying graduated tax rates.[14]

If this seems distressingly imprecise, it is because ability to pay is

14. Early in this century, Gustav Cassel proposed a progressive income tax consisting of a single statutory rate and personal exemptions that would increase with income but less rapidly than income. The exemptions were intended to cover the cost of "the necessaries of efficiency," which Cassel thought increased with income "but more slowly." "The Theory of Progressive Taxation," *Economic Journal,* vol. 11 (December 1901), pp. 481–91. The Carter Commission of Canada took a similar approach in 1966. It identified ability to pay with "discretionary" income and proposed a progressive rate schedule based on the idea of applying a proportional tax to the discretionary part of total income, which it assumed to be an ascending fraction of total income. See *Report of the Royal Commission on Taxation* (Ottawa: Queen's Printer, 1966), vol. 3, pp. 6–11.

being regarded as the name of a numerical formula rather than a term of ethics or politics, as it should be. Ability to pay is no more imprecise than concepts such as the national interest, general welfare, due process of law, morality, and duty. It is as susceptible to objective evaluation as are intelligence, social adjustment, prudence, and many other personal characteristics.

Basic ethical and political judgments can better be taken from political leaders or public consensus than from experts. The majority of citizens and legislators in the United States and other democratic countries appear to accept ability to pay as a guiding principle of taxation and to interpret it as justifying progressivity. They talk and act as if they believe that progressive taxation is needed both to maintain a proper relation between the sacrifices of individual taxpayers and to give recognition to social priorities in the use of income and wealth. Without assuming that some such beliefs are widely accepted, I find it hard to account for political discourse on taxation or for revenue legislation. Even if many participants in the debates use the language of ability to pay and progressivity as a cloak for personal or class interests, it is still significant that they think it advantageous to appeal to these ideas.

Generalizations about ability to pay provide no formula for tax allocation. In democratic countries, legislators are delegated the responsibility of choosing taxes and rate schedules in the light of their judgment about ability to pay and other criteria. Economists and sociologists can aid them by developing indirect measures of the consequences of unequal income distribution.[15]

Reduction of Economic Inequality

Critics of the ability-to-pay theory do not always reject progressive taxation. Many of them advocate progressivity but try to support it without resort to utilitarian arguments. They assert that progressive taxation is desirable because it will reduce economic inequality, which they treat as an objective in itself. Henry Simons, for example, urged that the discussion be reduced "frankly to the level of ethics or aesthetics" and, in a much-quoted sentence, said, "The case for

15. Fagan, in *Readings in the Economics of Taxation*, pp. 50–53; Robert J. Lampman, "Making Utility Predictions Verifiable," *Southern Economic Journal*, vol. 22 (January 1956), pp. 360–66; Harold M. Groves, "Toward a Social Theory of Progressive Taxation," *National Tax Journal*, vol. 9 (March 1956), pp. 27–34.

drastic progression in taxation must be rested on the case against inequality—on the ethical or aesthetic judgment that the prevailing
distribution of wealth and income reveals a degree (and/or kind) of
inequality which is distinctly evil or unlovely."[16]

The discard of pretensions to numerical exactness in the measurement of personal sacrifices and satisfactions is a step forward. It is
difficult, however, to accept the reduction of inequality as an ultimate
objective in the same sense that the minimization of sacrifices and the
maximization of happiness may be considered as ends.[17] To be sure,
the reduction of economic inequality or the prevention of excessive
growth of inequality has long been regarded as desirable as a means
of avoiding concentration of political power, envy, and unrest, but
much of the reasoning in support of this policy seems closely related
to the ability-to-pay theory.

Furthermore, Simons and others may go too far in rejecting the
possibilities of reasoned evaluation of taxes. They are open to the
interpretation that there are no objective standards for allocating
taxes, but only personal preference or caprice. To recognize the
element of ethics or aesthetics—or politics—is not to say that choices
do not also involve analytical issues. The ability-to-pay formulation
seems more fruitful than that of Simons because it suggests more lines
of inquiry concerning the consequences of different distributions of
taxes and disposable income. Finally, the reduction of inequality has
not received anything like the degree of popular support that has been
accorded ability to pay.

These considerations lead me to conclude that the reduction of
economic inequality is a valid objective of progressive taxation but
that it is secondary to the objective of allocating taxes according to
ability to pay.[18]

16. *Personal Income Taxation,* pp. 18–19.
17. Bertrand Russell took the position that, although "there are strong arguments for approximating to an even distribution" of material goods, "they are nevertheless arguments as to means," and an equal distribution should not be regarded
"as something having intrinsic value on its own account." See Russell, *Human Society
in Ethics and Politics,* rev. ed. (New American Library for World Literature, Mentor
Books, 1962), p. 109. See also Richard A. Musgrave, *The Theory of Public Finance*
(McGraw-Hill, 1959), p. 222.
18. For a recent attempt to relate tax principles to a rigorous theory of justice,
founded on the social contract idea, see John Rawls, *A Theory of Justice* (Belknap
Press of Harvard University Press, 1971), pp. 277–82.

Measures of Ability to Pay and Inequality

Income is an incomplete measure of the quantity of resources at the disposal of a person since it does not take account of wealth, which also represents command over resources. Wealth, to be sure, can be resolved into income because it arises either from the accumulation of past income or the expectation of future income. But this does not alter the fact that the possession of wealth gives economic power beyond that attributable to current income. A person with, say, an income of $5,000 a year and net worth of $100,000 is certainly better off than a person with the same income and no property.

Nevertheless, wealth can claim consideration only as a supplementary index of ability to pay. It does not rival income as the primary index principally because wealth, as usually defined, does not include the expectation of future income from personal effort. In modern legal and accounting systems, the capital value of personal earnings is not wealth because the right to receive all such income cannot be bought and sold; long-term labor contracts are commonly barred, and short-term contracts usually cannot be freely transferred. Wealth is a seriously incomplete index of taxable capacity because it takes no account of the economic resources of persons who depend on earnings from personal services.[19]

Consumption is a genuine rival to personal income as an index of ability to pay taxes and as a basis for the assessment of progressive taxes. Citing Thomas Hobbes, Kaldor contended that it may be just and expedient to tax people with reference to what they take out of the common pool (the national product) rather than what they contribute and suggested that consumption may be a better tax base than income.[20]

Although Kaldor's argument has merit, his metaphor is not very enlightening. Investment, no less than consumption, is a withdrawal

19. Earl R. Rolph and George F. Break suggest in *Public Finance* (Ronald Press, 1961), pp. 196–200, that human capital should be included in the base of a wealth tax, but I do not think that human capital can be measured with the degree of accuracy that is properly demanded for taxation. Furthermore, I see dangers of infringement on personal liberties in applying a tax on the present value of potential earnings: Would a person with great earning capacity who refused to work enough to earn the money to pay his tax be sent to jail?

20. *An Expenditure Tax*, p. 53.

from the common pool in that it is an exercise of a claim on the use of resources. In this respect, there is no difference between the purchase of, say, food-processing machinery and that of a household refrigerator. Taxes are levied because it is necessary to compel people to relinquish their claims on resources and thus allow the government to use them. Whether consumption claims or investment claims should give way is a question of policy.

The most important difference between income and consumption as tax bases resides in the differences in allocation of the base among individuals and over time for any one person. In the aggregate, the difference cannot be great because most disposable personal income is consumed. From 1950 to 1974, personal outlays (for consumption and interest paid by consumers) ranged between 92 percent and 95 percent of disposable income.[21]

Although the difference would be greater for particular families and individuals than for the aggregate, it appears that for a large percentage of the population lifetime disposable income and consumption are about equal. The majority have little opportunity to consume much more than their income over their lifetime because they start with little inherited wealth and cannot find creditors who will allow them to pile up large debts if they choose to borrow continually.[22] Furthermore, most people's lifetime savings seem to be small relative to their lifetime income; this is indicated by the small fraction who die with enough wealth to require an estate tax return and by other scattered information. At the end of 1962, for example, one-third of the consumer units with heads aged sixty-five and over had net worth of less than $5,000 and only one-fourth had more than $25,000; a survey indicated that only 4 percent of those in this age group mentioned the building of an estate as a motive for saving.[23]

For the majority whose lifetime consumption and disposable income are about equal, there are stages of the life cycle and occasional

21. *Economic Report of the President, February 1975*, p. 268.

22. This assertion is based on the Haig-Simons definition, which includes in income gifts received, social security and public assistance payments, and similar items which are often not regarded as income; if these items were excluded from income, the number with lifetime consumption in excess of income no doubt would be considerably increased.

23. Dorothy S. Projector and Gertrude S. Weiss, *Survey of Financial Characteristics of Consumers* (Board of Governors of the Federal Reserve System, 1966), pp. 97, 146.

years in which consumption is considerably more or less than disposable income. Young married couples and elderly persons can be expected to spend more than their current income, the young couples going into debt to cover the expenses of setting up households and rearing children and the elderly drawing down savings accumulated during more productive years. Statistical data seem to confirm these expectations,[24] though it is difficult to separate the influence of age from that of other factors. At any income or age level, consumption tends to exceed income in years of unemployment or illness of the wage earner, poor business conditions, or other adversity.

For the majority of the population, the substitution of an expenditure tax for an income tax would involve mainly a rearrangement of the timing of tax payment, with more taxes being paid in years of dissaving and less in years of saving. There seems to be no principle of justice, nor even any popular prejudice, holding that taxes should be relatively heavy in periods of youth and age and years of temporary adversity and relatively light at other times. Arguments have been advanced in favor of averaging out short-term fluctuations in the tax base and even variations over the life cycle, regardless of whether income or consumption is taxed. If averaging over a long period of time were allowed, the difference between an expenditure tax and an income tax would be greatly reduced.

There remains the difference in treatment of the relatively small number of people who build up or draw down their wealth by significant amounts over their lifetime. Under a flat-rate expenditure tax, Richard Spender and John Keeper would have the same total liability if their lifetime consumption were the same, even though Spender financed himself by using up inherited wealth while Keeper saved two-thirds of his income and built up a fortune. Under an income tax, Keeper would pay more tax than Spender.

Since the satisfaction obtained by Keeper and Spender cannot be directly measured, it is impossible to be sure whether they are equally well off and in a subjective sense have equal taxable capacity. If, however, a common standard of evaluation is used, Keeper clearly is better off because he enjoys the same amount of consumption as Spender plus whatever satisfaction is associated with adding to wealth. Spender is worse off, on these terms, because he enjoys no

24. Dorothy S. Projector, *Survey of Changes in Family Finances* (Board of Governors of the Federal Reserve System, 1968), pp. 13–15.

more consumption and suffers whatever pain is associated with giving up wealth. Consumption does not reflect these differences, but income does; income plus net worth, with some weighting, reflects them better. A person who could look into the psyches of the two might find that Keeper's low consumption ratio is due to poverty of imagination rather than to the positive attractions of wealth accumulation and that Spender attaches little significance to the dissipation of his wealth. But those who cannot do that kind of analysis must be content with the application of a common standard derived from general observation and market data—and from introspection. On that basis, the relation between the liabilities of Keeper and Spender seems more just under an income tax than under an expenditure tax.

When progressivity is viewed simply as a means of reducing economic inequality, personal income seems clearly superior to either consumption or wealth as a sole tax base. Economic inequality has two dimensions, differences in consumption and differences in power associated with the accumulation of wealth. Up to a high level, differences in consumption may be the most noticeable feature of inequality, but toward the top of the pyramid the accumulation of wealth has a more direct relation to the concentration of political influence and other forms of power. An income tax strikes accretions to economic power, whether devoted to consumption or other purposes. An expenditure tax is less effective than an income tax as a check on the accumulation of fortunes; a wealth tax does not affect consumption financed out of income from personal effort. A combination of an income tax and a wealth tax or a personal expenditure tax and a wealth tax might be superior to either the income tax or the expenditure tax alone as a means of reducing economic inequality. (This comparison is based on the assumption that the three taxes are equally well designed and administered—a condition that, as explained below, may be hard to satisfy.)

The superiority of the income tax over the expenditure tax is narrowed when the income tax applies to capital gains only as they are realized rather than to accrued but unrealized gains. A tax on realized income is less effective as a barrier to wealth concentration than a tax on accrued income but more effective than an expenditure tax.

The considerations that have convinced most experts that it would not be feasible to tax capital gains in advance of realization are equally relevant to a wealth tax. In the United States and other countries where a wealth tax is not levied, a tax on realized income of individuals is supplemented by taxes on corporate profits and on estates, inheritances, and gifts. This system, though less potent than a combination involving a wealth tax, can be an effective means of redistribution.

"Double Taxation of Saving"

A long-standing argument in favor of taxing consumption rather than income is the contention that a tax on income results in unfair double taxation of saving. John Stuart Mill asserted, "No income tax is really just from which savings are not exempted."[25] This amounts to saying that no income tax can be as fair as an expenditure tax. This view was endorsed by Marshall, Pigou, Einaudi, and other distinguished economists. Most of them, however, thought that a direct tax on consumption was not feasible and regarded the criticism as a theoretical nicety rather than as an argument for tax revision. Irving Fisher argued strongly for a direct tax on consumption in preference to a tax on personal income, although he confused the issue by insisting that the consumption tax should be called an income tax. He refused to concede that a direct tax on personal consumption (which he called income) was impracticable.[26]

Although it has been expressed with varying degrees of refinement, the double-taxation-of-saving argument is basically simple. Suppose that all income is taxed when it accrues. For the person who consumes his income that is the end of the story. But the saver must pay another tax on the return from his investments when that return accrues. He is taxed twice. Assume, for example, a proportional income tax of 50 percent and a market interest rate of 4 percent on safe investments. Suppose that John Keeper receives $100 of additional income, pays the tax on it, invests the remaining $50 in high-grade bonds, and thus obtains a gross annual yield of $2. His total taxes will be $50 in year 1 plus $1 a year in later years. Richard Spender, who also receives an

25. *Principles of Political Economy*, bk. 5, chap. 2, sec. 4 (London: Longmans, Green, 1929 edition, W. J. Ashley, ed.), p. 814.

26. Fisher's great theoretical work on income is *The Nature of Capital and Income*, originally published in 1906 by Macmillan; his views on taxation appear in "Income in Theory and Income Taxation in Practice," *Econometrica*, vol. 5 (January 1937), pp. 1–55, and in a book by him and Herbert W. Fisher, *Constructive Income Taxation: A Proposal for Reform* (Harper, 1942).

additional $100 of income, saves nothing and pays $50 of income tax. Under a flat-rate expenditure tax of 100 percent, Keeper would pay nothing in year 1 but would pay $2 a year in future years if he consumed the yield of his new investment. As under the income tax, Spender would pay $50 in year 1.[27]

While Keeper pays more income tax than Spender, this is not because Keeper is taxed on his saving as such but because he has more income. The income tax reaches the income from which saving is made and also investment yields, but the act of saving does not attract tax. A decision to save is not necessarily a decision to invest and hence not necessarily a decision to incur future income tax liabilities. If an investment is in fact made, its yield represents new income quite distinct from the income that was originally saved.

The income tax curtails opportunities to obtain additional income (power to consume) by investment or work. If the tax is uniform it curtails all such opportunities equally. An expenditure tax, on the other hand, applies to the exercise of power to consume rather than to its acquisition; if the tax is uniform, it applies equally to all consumption. The double-taxation-of-saving argument does not show that consumption is fairer than income as a basis for judging equal treatment. It is true that an income tax reduces the percentage gain in consumption that can be enjoyed by postponing consumption and investing one's savings, whereas an expenditure tax leaves the ratio between present and future consumption opportunities (but not the absolute amounts of consumption) the same as it would be with no tax. In my opinion, this characteristic does not pose a question of justice, but it does raise economic issues that will be considered in the next chapter.

Administration and Compliance

To assess a tax on accrued income in literal conformity with the Haig-Simons definition would require information on both personal consumption and net worth (wealth). An income tax administered in

27. On the assumption of a perpetual investment by Keeper and his heirs, and with a discount rate of 4 percent, the present value of the taxes payable by them is $75 under the income tax and $50 under the expenditure tax, whereas the present value of Spender's tax payments is $50 under both taxes (see A. C. Pigou, *A Study in Public Finance*, 3d ed. [Macmillan, 1949], pp. 118–19). It is doubtful, however, that the same discount rate should be applied under the two tax regimes.

this way would be more demanding than either an expenditure tax or a wealth tax, and if it were practicable to assess the income tax it would be easy to assess either of the other two taxes.

General Problems

The Haig-Simons definition is a conceptual guide rather than an assessment formula, and its authors did not suggest that taxable income actually be measured by adding together personal consumption and the change in the taxpayer's net worth. Nevertheless, the information required to assess a comprehensive tax on accrued income could also be used to assess taxes on wealth and personal consumption. Direct information on the value of capital assets would be necessary, and a figure for consumption could be derived indirectly, as the difference between income and net saving.

Even under an expenditure tax, direct measurement of personal consumption would be unnecessary. The usual proposal is that consumption be measured as a residual rather than by adding up its components: personal consumption expenditures would equal net income minus (positive or negative) additions to net worth or saving. This approach has been recommended because few families keep comprehensive records of consumption expenditures. If records were available they would be harder to verify than records of income receipts since most families have a larger number of consumption transactions than of income transactions and deal with more suppliers of consumer goods and services than payers of income. Accounting conventions and practices are concerned mainly with the measurement and reporting of income and net worth and only incidentally with consumption.

An income tax conforming to the Haig-Simons concept, which may be called a tax on accrued income, would be assessed on net income calculated as: gross current income *minus* costs of obtaining income *plus* realized net capital gains *plus* unrealized net capital gains (realized and unrealized capital losses being regarded as negative capital gains). Both gross income and costs would include cash items and certain imputed and accrued items. Conceptual and practical difficulties arise for each of the principal items entering into the assessment. What receipts should be included in gross income? How should costs of obtaining income be distinguished from personal consumption expenditures and from new investment? How should capital gains be measured? Must "true" gains and losses be distinguished from nominal gains and losses?

The peculiar difficulty with accrued but unrealized capital gains and losses is administrative. To take account of unrealized gains and losses would require the detailed listing of taxpayers' assets and liabilities and annual valuations. The lists would be long, and for many items market quotations would not be readily available. Considerable difficulty is encountered in valuing certain securities and many business properties for purposes of the estate tax, even though these valuations need to be made only once for each of a relatively small number of taxpayers. Most experts agree that annual appraisals would not be feasible under the income tax. Even if valuations were made somewhat less frequently, the accrual treatment seems impractical despite some offsetting gains in the form of simplification or elimination of certain complex features of the present income tax.[28]

The omission of accrued but unrealized capital gains and losses from the assessment results in what may be called a tax on realized income, even though its base includes certain accrued and imputed items. Efforts have been made to justify the omission on theoretical grounds by supporting a realization requirement, usually on the basis of a harvest analogy.[29] Income is likened to a fruit that cannot be enjoyed until it is severed from the tree. This line of argument is unconvincing for two reasons. First, the growth of unharvested fruits, or unrealized gains, surely constitutes an increase in economic power and is often a source of direct satisfaction, even though the accrued gain may be difficult to measure. Second, it seems inconsistent to require realization, in principle, for nonbusiness assets but to accept conventional acounting practices for depreciation and depletion and other accruals. On a less abstract level, it may be conceded that payment of a tax on accrued gains would be more inconvenient than payment only on realized gains, particularly for persons who hold

28. For contrary opinions, see Carl S. Shoup, *Public Finance* (Aldine, 1969), p. 324; and Boris I. Bittker, statement, in *General Tax Reform,* Panel Discussions before the House Committee on Ways and Means, 93 Cong. 1 sess. (1973), pt. 1, pp. 123–24.

29. On the legal and economic origins of the realization criterion, see Lawrence H. Seltzer, *The Nature and Tax Treatment of Capital Gains and Losses* (National Bureau of Economic Research, 1951), pp. 25–46; for critical comments on the criterion, see Simons, *Personal Income Taxation,* pp. 80–100.

illiquid assets such as real estate and unincorporated business enterprises.

The omission of accrued gains and losses makes the income tax a duller instrument than it would be if all gains and losses could be reliably determined and included as they accrue. But if provision is made for constructive realization of capital gains and losses when the taxpayer dies or gives away his property, this partly compensates for the failure to take account of the gains and losses as they accrue.

In practice, taxable income under U.S. law is not identical with realized net income, broadly defined. It does not include certain items of realized income, and in computing taxable income, some costs are not allowed as deductions and certain personal expenditures that are not costs of obtaining income are deducted. The consequences of the departures from a comprehensive measure of income will be considered in later chapters.

A tax on personal consumption could be assessed by subtracting net saving from realized income (or adding net dissaving to realized income). A country that levied an expenditure tax, while avoiding certain difficulties peculiar to the measurement of capital gains and losses, would encounter most of the conceptual and practical problems that are met in assessing a tax on realized income and the further problem of verifying net saving.

The measurement of net saving involves not only subtle theoretical issues relating to the definition of capital and capital maintenance— issues also encountered in the measurement of realized income—but major difficulties of administration. In practice, most of the subtleties probably would be disregarded under an expenditure tax, as they are under an income tax, but the administrative difficulties could not be avoided.

Saving could be measured on a flow basis as follows: outlays for capital assets *minus* proceeds of sales of capital assets *plus* repayment of debt *minus* proceeds of borrowing *plus* additions to bank accounts and other cash balances *minus* reductions in bank accounts and other cash balances. Or saving could be determined by comparing stocks at the beginning and end of the year and thus ascertaining the net increase in holdings of capital assets and cash balances and the reduction of indebtedness. All of the items, of course, can have negative or positive signs; the total of saving is the algebraic sum.

Both flow and stock information would be useful, but balance sheets would be needed to make sure that saving was properly measured. If complete balance sheets were not available, unscrupulous persons could evade the expenditure tax by failing to report proceeds from the disposal of assets and using the proceeds to finance consumption or to acquire items that are deductible as saving. They might also merely overstate their gross acquisitions of assets. This kind of evasion would be inhibited if a wealth tax were combined with the expenditure tax, but there still would be a need for balance sheets.[30]

Although complete balance sheets would be helpful for checking evasion of the income tax, they have not been generally demanded of individuals in the United States or other countries with well-developed income taxes. Balance sheets are less essential for enforcement of a tax on realized income than for assessment of a personal expenditure tax. Under the income tax, balance sheet data are useful for verifying capital gains and losses and for ascertaining whether changes in net worth are consistent with reported income. The latter purpose can be served only by reasonably complete balance sheets; the former requires information on the realization proceeds and acquisition costs of those assets that are likely to produce capital gains or losses. For income tax assessment, information is not essential on several items that are particularly hard to uncover and that seldom give rise to taxable gains or deductible losses, including cash balances, personal debt, jewelry, and consumer durables. For expenditure tax purposes, it is not necessary to know the original cost of old assets disposed of in the current year, but it is essential to know the realization proceeds of all disposals, the cost of all newly acquired assets, and changes in cash balances and debt. Omission or incorrect reporting of any of these capital items can affect the expenditure tax assessment by the

---

30. Nicholas Kaldor stresses the interlocking features of the expenditure tax and wealth tax in his *Indian Tax Reform, Report of a Survey* (New Delhi: Ministry of Finance, Government of India, 1956). For skeptical comments, see my paper "Taxation of Saving and Consumption in Underdeveloped Countries," *National Tax Journal,* vol. 14 (December 1961), pp. 305–22. William D. Andrews, taking a different approach from Kaldor and most other writers, argues that net saving could be satisfactorily measured solely on a cash flow basis ("A Consumption-Type or Cash Flow Personal Income Tax," *Harvard Law Review,* vol. 87 [April 1974], pp. 1113–88), but in my view there would be serious problems in applying his version of a personal consumption tax.

full amount of the error, whereas for income tax purposes only the gain or loss is at issue.[31]

Complete accounting for assets and liabilities would be indispensable for the administration of a wealth tax. Furthermore, current valuations would be highly desirable. If items were assessed at book value or original cost until a transaction occurred, as has been suggested,[32] the wealth tax would lose much of its advantage as a supplementary measure of economic capacity. Failure to take account of unrealized appreciation or decreases in the value of assets would be a more serious defect in a wealth tax than in an income tax. Any particular gain or loss affects wealth in all subsequent years but affects income of only one year; consequently later actual or constructive realization will do more to make up for the earlier omission of accrued gains and losses under the income tax than under the wealth tax. A wealth tax on book value, like a tax on realized income, imposes an additional liability when appreciated assets are sold and hence may deter economically desirable switches of investments.

American experience with the general property tax reveals grave difficulties in discovering and valuing intangibles and household property. Granted that the federal government might be more efficient than local assessors and that there would be advantages in linking wealth tax and income tax assessments, it still does not seem realistic to contemplate a wealth tax with low exemptions and broad coverage. A tax limited to a small number of rich persons might be feasible, and the tax could be extended to a somewhat larger group if it were thought to have great social and economic advantages. As an instrument for checking the concentration of wealth, however, an annual tax on net worth does not seem to have great advantages over an integrated system of income, estate, and gift taxes, and it would be easier to improve the existing income and transfer taxes than to introduce a new tax on wealth.

In summary, it seems that neither a tax on income including ac-

---

31. Richard E. Slitor, in a detailed paper, "Administrative Aspects of Expenditure Taxation" (in Richard A. Musgrave, ed., *Broad-Based Taxes, New Options and Sources* [Johns Hopkins University Press, 1973], pp. 227–63), reaches the "qualified conclusion" that an expenditure tax "probably is practicable within a relatively restricted scope of high-income, substantial-wealth taxpayers" (p. 257).

32. By Kaldor in his report on India (*Indian Tax Reform*, p. 25). The Indian statute, however, provides for annual valuations; see Harvard Law School, World Tax Series, *Taxation in India* (Little, Brown, 1960), pp. 411–12.

crued but unrealized capital gains nor a broad personal wealth tax could be successfully applied without extraordinary administrative cost. Of the two, the wealth tax would be more demanding because the exact timing of unrealized gains would have more influence on the cumulative amount of liability. A personal expenditure tax would be less difficult to administer than either a tax on accrued income or a personal wealth tax but more difficult than a tax on realized income. Assessment and enforcement of the expenditure tax would involve most of the steps necessary for the successful application of a tax on realized income and in addition the special problem of measuring net saving. The verification of net saving would require complete balance sheet data, including information on cash balances, personal debts, and other items that are particularly difficult to discover.[33]

American Experience with the Income Tax

The enforcement of the income tax has been greatly aided by withholding from wages and salaries. In the United States, the major portion of the total individual income tax is collected in this way. Withholding could be extended to dividends, interest, and certain other periodic income payments, as in many countries, but Congress has rejected proposals for doing so.

Although compliance with the income tax is incomplete, there is no evidence of widespread evasion in the United States. Comparison with national income estimates, which are derived mainly from data sources other than individual income tax returns, indicates that more than nine-tenths of estimated total adjusted gross income (AGI) appears on tax returns. (AGI is income net of business costs but

---

33. A more formal comparison of the items entering into the various tax bases can be presented as follows: Let G = gross income receipts, E = costs of obtaining income receipts, S = proceeds of sales of capital assets, P = purchases of capital assets, K = cost or other basis of capital assets sold, A = accrued but unrealized capital gains, B = cash balance, D = debt, T = personal taxes, and the subscripts 1 and 2 denote, respectively, the beginning and end of the year. Then accrued income is

$$G - E + S - K + A.$$

Realized income is

$$G - E + S - K.$$

Personal consumption is

$$G - E + S - P - (B_2 - B_1) - (D_1 - D_2) - T.$$

before personal deductions and personal exemptions.) Part of the remaining AGI belongs to persons who are not taxable because their income is less than their personal exemptions. In 1970, a sum equal to about 6.5 percent of total AGI apparently was illegally omitted from individual income tax returns owing to failure to file returns or understatement of AGI.[34] A further, unknown amount of income escaped taxation because of underreporting of capital gains and improper claims of personal exemptions and deductions not discovered by the Internal Revenue Service.

Administrative costs are moderate. In the fiscal year ended June 30, 1974, total administrative expenses of the Internal Revenue Service amounted to less than 0.6 percent of tax collections. An allocation of expenses among taxes is not available; however, even if extreme assumptions are made concerning other taxes, the expenses of administering the individual income tax were less than 1 percent of collections.[35]

Indirect Taxation

Excise taxes, sales taxes, and other indirect taxes still have an important role in the American federal-state-local revenue system as well as in other countries. Proposals are made from time to time for the adoption of a federal sales tax in the United States, most often in recent years in the form of a value-added tax. Indirect taxes, however, cannot be considered close substitutes for well-administered direct taxes on income or consumption since the former are ordinarily less broad in coverage, less easily adaptable to the individual circumstances of taxpayers, and usually lack progressivity. Do the indirect taxes nevertheless satisfy other tests of equity?

Aside from economic considerations, which are discussed later,

34. In 1970, 92.5 percent of estimated total AGI and 95 percent of the total population appeared on taxable and nontaxable returns (derived from appendix table A-7; U.S. Internal Revenue Service, *Statistics of Income—1970, Individual Income Tax Returns*, p. 91; and U.S. Bureau of the Census, *Statistical Abstract of the United States, 1974*, p. 5). Note that the percentage of the population covered by the income tax, as given in appendix table A-3, refers to taxable returns only. On various plausible assumptions, some 1 percent of total AGI may be assigned to nontaxable persons who were not covered by returns, leaving about 6.5 percent of AGI not accounted for and presumably illegally omitted from returns.

35. U.S. Internal Revenue Service, *Annual Report, 1974, Commissioner of Internal Revenue*, pp. 10, 109.

the main argument in favor of broad sales taxes or production taxes is that they would strike those who legally or illegally escape the income tax. Since the indirect taxes are simpler and require less information than the income tax, illegal evasion would be more difficult; furthermore, those who benefit from legal loopholes or other unjustifiable preferential treatment under the income tax would be reached by the sales tax. Partial substitution of a sales tax for an income tax, therefore, would transfer some of the tax load to those who successfully escape the income tax. Still, those who improperly escape the income levy would pay less taxes in the aggregate than other citizens, and the adoption of the sales tax would introduce new inequities. Might not justice be better served by devoting to the improvement of the income tax the political and administrative resources that would be required to adopt and collect a federal sales tax?

Where income tax evasion is more widespread than in the United States or where administrative capacity is limited, simplicity and enforceability may be overriding advantages of indirect taxation. Most of the underdeveloped countries cannot now successfully apply the income tax on a wide scale. The authorities cannot recruit either the technicians or the clerks that are needed. Modern acounting is not commonly practiced in business and the professions, many people are illiterate, and a large part of output originates in small-scale agriculture and shops. There is no tradition of voluntary compliance with tax laws. In these circumstances, an income tax may be so poorly and erratically applied that it lacks the characteristic advantages usually associated with it. Most countries in this position wish to make some use of the income tax in recognition of demands for social justice and in order to gain experience that will enable them to apply the tax more widely, but they cannot be expected to place primary reliance on the income tax in the near future. Indirect taxes are better suited to the environment.

In all countries, selective excises are regarded as appropriate for financing government services that specially benefit sections of the community but that cannot conveniently be sold to consumers. Gasoline taxes and other automotive taxes that are used to pay for highways are an important example. Excises also may be used to facilitate the regulation or discourage the production and consumption of goods that are thought to involve social costs not covered by market prices. Taxes on alcoholic beverages and tobacco are sometimes supported on this basis, but in practice these taxes ordinarily are not designed to carry out a coherent regulatory policy.

There is support for excises on luxuries or nonessentials on the grounds that consumption of these items is optional and indicates taxpaying ability. In fact, however, the excises with large yields are on commodities that are widely consumed and whose demand is relatively insensitive to price. If many consumers chose not to buy the taxed commodities, the yield would suffer. Economists have often condemned excises because they discriminate on the basis of taste. The popular emphasis on the voluntary character of excises on nonessentials, nevertheless, may not be completely unfounded. These taxes do allow consumers an additional dimension of flexibility in that a drastic reallocation of spending in response to illness or other emergencies can bring with it a reduction in the amount of taxes paid. The excises, however, seem a clumsy means of dealing with such situations compared with a deduction for medical expenditures under the income tax or other special allowances. A more important element in the public attitude may be what one writer has called a "perversion" that leads people to feel guilty about smoking, drinking, and luxurious spending and to think it right that they should be taxed on their indulgences.[36]

A more prosaic explanation of the continuation of the excises is that they have been used for a long time, and consumers seem to be less conscious and less resentful of them than they are of the income tax or a retail sales tax. Many do not know the excise tax rates, and others seem to have a kind of myopia that keeps them from seeing that small items in time add up to significant totals. Opinion leaders, whose income is usually above the average, may be less vexed by excises than by the progressive income tax.

These considerations may help explain the persistence of indirect taxes and cause one to doubt that they will be dispensed with in the foreseeable future. But I do not think they indicate that the American tax system could be made fairer by increasing the proportion of revenue obtained from indirect taxes.

36. David Walker, "Some Comments on the Taxation of Personal Income and Expenditure in the United Kingdom, 1945–53," *Public Finance*, vol. 9, no. 2 (1954), p. 206.

Conclusion

The income tax emerges well from this examination of the issues of equity and administration. Personal income seems to be the best single index of taxable capacity and the best single basis of progressive taxation. Income, however, is not a complete measure of ability to pay. There are strong arguments for supplementing an individual income tax with taxes on accumulated wealth in the form of estate and gift taxes; an annual tax on net worth also has appeal but may not be feasible unless narrowly limited in scope. A good case can be made for a few excise taxes.

CHAPTER THREE

Effects of Taxes on Income, Consumption, and Wealth

THE INCOME TAX, like other taxes, is intended to divert resources from private consumption and investment to public use. Taxation will also have the unintended effect of curtailing total output if it reduces investment and discourages work. An important question is how the income tax compares in this respect with alternative taxes. The comparison is important because it will help show whether the benefits of government expenditures could be obtained at less social cost by modifying the tax system.

In this chapter and the next one, the principal economic effects of the income tax and other taxes are compared on the assumption that the amount of revenue raised and the size and composition of government expenditures would be approximately the same under different tax systems. This assumption, though necessary, in my opinion, to allow isolation of questions of tax policy, is not free of ambiguities and difficulties. Alternative tax schemes that would yield equal revenues under certain economic conditions might yield unequal amounts under other conditions; there is no one set of equivalent-yield rates for the different taxes.[1] However, for analytical purposes it seems legitimate to defer for separate consideration the response of tax yields to fluctuations in business activity and to assume that tax rates would be adjusted from time to time as might be required to maintain equal revenues over longer periods of time.

Three analytical issues are involved in the comparison of taxes: (1) the significance of the choice of the tax base; (2) the influence of the degree of progressivity; and (3) the difference, if any, between direct and indirect or impersonal taxes, given the base and the degree of progressivity. To simplify presentation, I discuss the choice of the tax base in this chapter and combine the treatment of the other issues in chapter 4.

The analysis of different tax bases is conducted by comparing direct taxes on income, consumption, and wealth. Despite the practical difficulties in applying a direct expenditure tax and a wealth tax, a further analysis of them is useful because it may indicate whether a great effort to overcome the difficulties would be worthwhile and because it tells something about indirect and impersonal taxes on consumption and wealth. In an attempt to isolate the economic significance of the tax base, this chapter deals mainly with flat-rate taxes, with only passing attention to the effects of rate graduation. Although flat-rate taxes on consumption and wealth would not be proportional to income, owing to differences in the average ratios of consumption and wealth to income at high and low income levels, the analysis abstracts from possible differences in economic effects due solely to the distribution of the taxes among income groups.[2] The effects of rate graduation and of different distributions among income groups will be considered in chapter 4.

Influence on Saving

Much of the interest in the expenditure tax can be traced to a belief that its substitution for the income tax would favor saving and

---

1. Bent Hansen, *The Economic Theory of Fiscal Policy,* translated by P. E. Burke (Harvard University Press, 1958), pp. 34–37, 90–100.

2. This chapter draws on my papers "Income, Consumption, and Property as Bases of Taxation," in American Economic Association, *Papers and Proceedings of the Seventy-fourth Annual Meeting, 1961 (American Economic Review,* vol. 52, May 1962), pp. 327–34, and "Taxation of Saving and Consumption in Underdeveloped Countries," *National Tax Journal,* vol. 14 (December 1961), pp. 305–22.

therefore capital formation and growth. In examining this proposition, I shall consider first the influence of different forms of taxation on incentives and capacity to save, deferring to the next chapter comments on the relation between saving, capital formation, and growth.

Incentives to Save

Under an expenditure tax, a person who forgoes a given amount of present consumption and lends or invests his savings can enjoy a greater increase in future consumption than would be possible under an equal-yield income tax. The gain in future consumption may be regarded as a reward for saving or, more accurately, as a reward or incentive for saving-and-lending or saving-and-investing, since the gain is made possible by the interest obtained by lending or investing the savings.

Consider the alternatives open to a person subject to a 50 percent income tax or a 100 percent expenditure tax. If in year 1 he receives $100 of income he will be liable for $50 of tax under the income tax. He can either consume the remaining $50 immediately or save and invest it and, at a market rate of interest of 4 percent, realize a net return of $1 in one year ($2 gross return minus $1 of income tax). Thus, by giving up $50 of present consumption he can enjoy $1 of additional consumption each year in the future, or he can exchange $50 of present consumption for $51 of consumption one year later. Under the consumption tax, he can save and invest $100 in year 1 and obtain a yield of $4, which will allow him to consume an additional $2 a year, or he can exchange $50 of present consumption for $52 of consumption one year later. Under the expenditure tax, the interest reward for saving-and-investing—computed with respect to the amount of present consumption forgone—remains unimpaired at 4 percent, whereas the reward is cut in half by the 50 percent income tax.

The saver is better off under the expenditure tax because postponement of consumption also postpones tax payment, permitting him to earn interest on the postponed tax. In the illustrations above, the saver receives twice as large an increment to his future consumption power under the expenditure tax as under the income tax because he has twice as much to invest under the expenditure tax. By parallel reasoning, it can be shown that an expenditure tax increases the cost of anticipatory consumption financed by borrowing. Under the expenditure tax, advancing the date of consumption also advances the date of tax payment and requires additional borrowing, to cover the tax, and greater interest payments.

If aggregate net saving by taxpayers were zero each year, the opportunity for tax postponement by individual savers would not affect the yield of a flat-rate expenditure tax compared with that of a flat-rate income tax. In any year, savers would pay less than under an income tax but dissavers would pay more, and the negative and positive differences would be exactly offsetting. On the more realistic assumption that aggregate personal saving is positive, an allowance has to be made in setting equivalent-yield rates for the two taxes. For example, if personal saving equals 5 percent of total income, an expenditure tax of 111 percent would be required to yield as much revenue as a 50 percent income tax, whereas with zero aggregate saving a 100 percent expenditure tax would suffice.[3]

With a high expenditure tax rate, the absolute amount of consumption that one can enjoy immediately or in the future is smaller than with a low tax rate, but the relation between present and future consumption opportunities is not affected if the tax rate is uniform. Whatever the relation between the expenditure tax rate and the income tax rate, and regardless of whether the two taxes yield equivalent revenue, the interest reward for saving-and-investing always equals the market rate of interest under the expenditure tax; it is always less than the market rate of interest under the income tax. This is true if the reward is measured by relating the net increment in future consumption power to the amount of present consumption that the saver forgoes.[4]

A wealth tax, of course, falls directly on accumulated savings. It will more sharply restrict opportunities to add to future consumption by saving than will a general income tax of equal yield because the wealth tax is concentrated on recipients of property income, which constitutes only 15 to 20 percent of all personal income.[5] A comprehensive wealth tax will absorb five to seven times as great a fraction

3. Suppose income is 100 and income tax yield 50. With zero saving, consumption will be 50, and the required expenditure tax rate will be $50/50 = 100$ percent. With saving of 5, consumption will be 45 and the required expenditure tax rate $50/45 = 111$ percent. For a general statement concerning equivalent-yield rates of income tax and expenditure tax, see appendix B.

4. See appendix B.

5. Irving B. Kravis, "Relative Income Shares in Fact and Theory," *American Economic Review*, vol. 49 (December 1959), p. 933.

of property income as will an equal-yield general income tax (both taxes assumed to be nongraduated, to lack personal exemptions, and to be enforced equally). Since the average rate of return on total personal wealth usually does not exceed 4 to 5 percent,[6] a 1 percent general tax on wealth would take between one-fifth and one-fourth of all property income.

The rate of return on saving-and-investing will be higher under an expenditure tax than under an equal-yield income tax and much higher under either of these taxes than under an equal-yield wealth tax. There is, I think, a presumption that the propensity to save will respond to some degree to the rate of return and will therefore be highest under an expenditure tax, lowest under a wealth tax, and intermediate under an income tax.[7] Deductive reasoning does not indicate whether differences in thriftiness will be great or small, and the statistical evidence on the question is limited.[8]

In addition to the effects operating through the current rate of return, the taxes may influence the amount of wealth that people wish to hold in relation to income. Adoption of an expenditure tax will reduce the amount of real consumption that can be financed by using up a given amount of wealth and, in this sense, may be viewed as a capital levy on existing wealth held for future consumption. Wealth-holders may save more in an effort to restore the desired relation between wealth and income.[9] (Those who plan to accumulate in the future will not have to cut their consumption to build up additional wealth to cover the expenditure tax because the tax will be deferred until the wealth is used.) On the other hand, the payment of the expenditure tax may cause people who are already living off capital to use it up at a faster rate, which will partly offset any additional saving

6. This is an underestimate inasmuch as capital gains are not included in the return. For the derivation of the estimate, see appendix B.

7. This conclusion differs from the agnostic position that many economists have taken regarding the influence on thrift of a change in the interest rate and represents a revision of my own earlier position on the effect of different taxes. For an elaboration, see appendix B.

8. Colin Wright obtained estimates of about 0.2 for the interest elasticity of saving, with the influence of wealth and income statistically controlled. See Wright, "Some Evidence on the Interest Elasticity of Consumption," *American Economic Review*, vol. 57 (September 1967), pp. 850–55; and Wright, "Saving and the Rate of Interest," in Arnold C. Harberger and Martin J. Bailey, eds., *The Taxation of Income from Capital* (Brookings Institution, 1969), pp. 275–95.

9. Nicholas Kaldor, *An Expenditure Tax* (London: Allen and Unwin, 1955), p. 96.

undertaken by those who are anxious to build up their wealth. Since a wealth tax is an annual tax on past and future accumulations, rather than a one-time levy on wealth in existence at the time of its adoption, introduction of this tax seems more likely to cause a downward revision than an increase in the desired ratio of wealth to income.

Capacity to Save

Many popular discussions stress not the adverse effect of the income tax on incentives to save but its influence on the capacity to save. Income taxpayers simply have less left out of which they can save. Of course, any other tax of equal yield would take the same amount of resources from the private sector and would also tend to decrease private saving. The income tax can be said to reduce capacity to save more than other taxes of equal yield if those who pay the income tax are more disposed to save than those who bear the other taxes. The usual version of this argument depends on differences in progressivity, a subject which is discussed in chapter 4.

There is also a more subtle version of the capacity-to-save argument, which holds that aggregate saving can be increased by transferring taxation in each income class from those who are most inclined to save to those who are least inclined; the capacity to save is increased where the inclination to save is strongest. Furthermore, the argument does not require that the form of taxation influence attitudes toward present and future consumption or accumulation. The community's saving ratio can be raised without altering the ratio of saving to disposable income of any individual, provided high savers are given command over a larger fraction of the resources available to the private sector.

This reasoning suggests that an expenditure tax will be more favorable to private saving than an equal-yield tax on income because the expenditure tax will leave a larger proportion of real disposable income in the hands of those with higher-than-average saving rates. The implicit assumption is that people who have high ratios of total saving to total income will also save a large fraction of a small increment to their disposable income, that is, that a high marginal propensity to save is associated with a high average propensity to save. Although exceptions can be imagined, the assumption is plausible. Average saving ratios reflect age and family composition, tastes, habits, opportunities, and other factors which change slowly, and presumably these influences also determine marginal saving ratios.

It is nevertheless easy to form an exaggerated impression of what can be accomplished by reallocating taxes between high and low savers. Differences between the effects of alternative tax formulas will not be as great as differences between the marginal propensities to save of high and low savers, provided that the choice of tax formula does not itself influence individual propensities to save. This is true because all feasible measures impose taxes on both high and low savers; hence the effect on saving is a weighted average of high and low marginal propensities to save, depending on the amounts of tax paid.

To illustrate, consider A and B, who have equal incomes but different saving behavior. Assume that A's average and marginal propensities to save are zero and that B's are 20 percent and that these propensities are not affected by the form of taxation. If A is taxed while B goes free, private saving is unaffected; if B is taxed and A is not, saving is curtailed by 20 percent of the revenue. There is, however, no feasible and socially acceptable means of taxing A while exempting B, unless they differ in characteristics other than saving behavior. The alternatives are to tax both A and B on income, total consumption, selected items of consumption, or property. Under a general income tax A and B will pay equal amounts, and private saving will be reduced by 10 percent of the revenue. If A and B are subjected to a flat-rate expenditure tax, A will pay five-ninths of the aggregate tax and B four-ninths; private saving will be reduced by approximately 8.9 percent of the revenue.[10]

It is not clear whether the substitution of a wealth tax for an income tax or an expenditure tax (with rates set to distribute the total tax among income classes in the same proportions) would involve a reallocation of the tax load between persons with different saving propensities. The most widely accepted hypothesis is that saving is inversely related to the ratio of wealth to income because, as the ratio rises, further accumulation satisfies progressively less urgent wants. Even if this is true at a given time for any one individual, it is not necessarily a reliable indicator of differences between individuals. Wealthy persons may have relatively high propensities to save be-

10. If A and B each have income of 100, their consumption expenditures in the absence of tax will be 100 and 80 respectively. Their payments under a flat-rate expenditure tax will be divided in approximately the same proportions, with A paying $100/180 = 5/9$ and B paying the remaining $4/9$. The tax-induced reduction in private saving will be $(5/9 \times 0\%) + (4/9 \times 20\%) = 8.9\%$.

cause they have a taste for accumulation or at least have the habit of accumulation.

The factual evidence is mixed. Data on consumer budgets and balance sheets for 1962–63 offer some confirmation for the hypothesis that, given the income level, saving is inversely related to net worth; however, the statistical relationship is weak.[11] On the other hand, Morgan reports that his (earlier) studies indicate that high assets tend to be associated with high marginal propensities to save. He finds that high-asset families save more than other families at high income levels and less at low income levels and that, when the influence of income is statistically controlled, high-asset families save more when they have an increase in income and dissave more when they have a decrease in income than low-asset families experiencing similar changes in income. He attributes differences at lower income levels to the fact that assets facilitate dissaving and at higher incomes to the persistence of individual attitudes. Morgan concludes, "we can interpret public policy in terms of what it does to people who have many assets or few assets, on the general assumption that the people with large amounts of assets are the people who want to save, have always saved, will continue to do so, and are most likely to save any increments in income or assets."[12]

Conclusion about Saving

It appears that both incentives to save and capacity to save on the part of those who are most eager to do so will be greater under an expenditure tax than under an income tax and least under a wealth tax. To abstract from the difference in the distribution of these taxes among income classes, it follows that the propensity to save will be highest under an expenditure tax, intermediate under an income tax, and lowest under a wealth tax. The considerations on which this conclusion is based, however, neither reveal whether the range of differences in the propensity to save is wide or narrow nor allow a statement about the amount by which private saving will be affected by an increase or decrease in taxation.

11. Dorothy S. Projector, *Survey of Changes in Family Finances* (Board of Governors of the Federal Reserve System, 1968), pp. 87–88.

12. James Morgan, "The Motivations of Savers," in Walter W. Heller and others, eds., *Savings in the Modern Economy* (University of Minnesota Press, 1953), p. 214. See Morgan, "Analysis of Residuals from 'Normal' Regressions," in Lawrence R. Klein, ed., *Contributions of Survey Methods to Economics* (Columbia University Press, 1954), pp. 184–86.

A rise in the national propensity to save will contribute to growth only if accompanied by rising investment. The composition of investment, moreover, affects the growth rate and the social acceptability of any level of output. Consideration must be given to the influence of taxation on investment.

Influence on Investment

Advocates of the expenditure tax or indirect consumption taxes often imply that the rate of capital formation is limited by the propensity to save, but those who favor a wealth tax usually stress the inducement to invest as the limiting factor. Advocates of a wealth tax attach great importance to the fact that wealth tax liability is largely a fixed charge in the short run. Hoarders, bondholders, and owners of valuable works of art and furniture pay as much tax as equally wealthy investors in highly productive business ventures (provided all forms of wealth are taxed and are equally well assessed). Investment of cash balances, conversion of high-grade bonds into shares in risky enterprises, or borrowing in order to undertake a business venture increases wealth tax liability only if the yield is added to net worth. Income tax liability will be increased by any successful investment, and expenditure tax liability will go up if part of the yield is consumed.

As an illustration, consider the alternatives faced by a person with $1,000 cash at the beginning of the year under an income tax of 50 percent or a wealth tax of 2 percent. For simplicity, assume initially that he will not consume any additional income obtained by investing the cash and that the wealth tax is assessed on net worth at the end of the year. The results of hoarding and of investing in an asset with a gross yield of 4 percent will be as follows (in dollars):

	With income tax	*With wealth tax*
Hoarding		
Gross yield	0	0.00
Tax liability	0	20.00
Balance, end of year	1,000	980.00
Investment		
Gross yield	40	40.00
Tax liability	20	20.80
Balance, end of year	1,020	1,019.20
Net gain from investing	20	39.20

The wealth tax imposes an annual carrying charge on net assets and in a sense makes the financial yield of hoarding negative rather than zero. (This refers to the immediate financial yield; hoarders presumably derive other satisfaction from their cash balances or expect to obtain income from investing them in the future.) The gain from investing, with the wealth tax, is the difference between the balance that would be left at the end of the year if the owner hoarded and the balance he will have if he invests. In the above illustration, the net gain is the difference between a balance of $980.00 and one of $1,019.20. This gain falls short of the gross yield only by the amount of the wealth tax on the gross yield, which is assumed to be saved. Under the 50 percent income tax, the net yield is only half the gross yield. Paradoxically, the net gain from investing is greater under the wealth tax than under the income tax, even though the gross yield is the same and the wealth tax liability is greater than the income tax liability.

The difference between the wealth tax liability associated with a high-yield investment and that for a low-yield one is, at most, the wealth tax on the yield. There is no difference in wealth tax liability when the additional investment yield is consumed. Under an income tax, liability varies directly with investment yield, regardless of the proportion consumed. Since, for equal revenue, the wealth tax rate will be much lower than the income tax rate, the wealth tax always cuts much less deeply than the income tax into the gain that can be realized by choosing a high-yield investment rather than a low-yield one.

Expenditure tax liability, like wealth tax liability, depends on the proportion of investment yield which is consumed, but in this case the maximum tax liability occurs when the whole yield is consumed and no additional liability arises so long as none of the yield is consumed. The expenditure tax is more favorable than an income tax or wealth tax to those who strive for rapid accumulation by seeking high-yield investments. On the other hand, the expenditure tax offers less opportunity to increase current consumption by selecting high-yield assets. This is true for comparisons both with the wealth tax and with the income tax because, with tax rates yielding equal revenues, the expenditure tax will bear more heavily on a person who consumes all of his income than on the average person, who saves part of his income.

Before drawing conclusions about the influence of the different taxes on investment incentives, it is advisable to consider the function of high yields. The traditional view is that high yields—or, more accurately, prospects of high yields—are necessary to induce investment in especially risky enterprises. If the difference between high and low yields is narrowed by taxation, will not this result in a bias against venturesome investments, such as those associated with the introduction of new products, and in favor of conservative investments? And may not the tax discourage even conservative investments compared with hoarding? Contrary to first impressions, close analysis indicates that the answer to these questions is not clearly "yes" and may indeed be "no."

The key to the problem is the interpretation of the reward for risk. It seems that the reward should be measured, not in absolute amount nor in relation to the total investment, but in relation to the net amount of capital at risk. Now, the reward for assumption of risk will not be impaired relative to the net amount of capital at risk by a proportional income tax, provided all losses from unsuccessful investments can be fully offset against taxable income.[13] To illustrate, suppose that, in the absence of taxation, an investor is willing to commit $1,000 to a risky venture if he expects, in addition to the normal return on safe investments, a further 10 percent, or $100 a year, to compensate for the assumption of risk. A proportional income tax of 25 percent will reduce the risk premium to $75 after tax; but, if the loss can be fully offset against other taxable income in the event that the venture is wholly unsuccessful, the net amount at risk will be reduced to $750, and the risk premium will still be 10 percent of this sum. With no loss offset or an imperfect offset, the reward for risk assumption will be cut relatively more than the amount at risk, and the venture may become unacceptable.

Under the U.S. income tax, offsets are liberal for business operating losses but less so for losses on worthless securities. An operating loss of an unincorporated business may be deducted against any

---

13. The classic statement is that of Evsey D. Domar and Richard A. Musgrave in their paper "Proportional Income Taxation and Risk-Taking," *Quarterly Journal of Economics,* vol. 58 (May 1944), pp. 388–422, reprinted in Richard A. Musgrave and Carl S. Shoup, eds., *Readings in the Economics of Taxation* (Irwin, for the American Economic Association, 1959), pp. 493–524. See also Richard A. Musgrave, *The Theory of Public Finance* (McGraw-Hill, 1959), pp. 312–36.

other current income of the proprietor or partners; if the loss exceeds income, the deficit may be carried back and deducted against taxable income of the three preceding years, and any balance not offset in this way may be carried forward for five years. Capital losses are generally deductible only against capital gains, but adverse incentive effects are mitigated by the low tax rates on long-term gains and the option of timing realized gains to offset losses (chapter 8). Even for operating losses, offsets are imperfect, because sometimes losses are too large to be offset against income over a nine-year period and because tax rates are graduated. Under graduated rates, the reward for a successful investment tends to be taxed in a higher rate bracket than the income against which a loss is offset; hence possible rewards are cut more deeply than possible losses.

An expenditure tax allows no loss offset as such but permits the investor to set aside whatever premium he thinks appropriate to cover his risk and to recoup his investment as quickly as market conditions allow. The investor's own behavior, rather than formal accounting requirements and legal rules, defines the return that is subject to taxation. An expenditure tax, therefore, is more favorable to investment than an income tax that lacks loss offsets; the difference may be small, however, between an expenditure tax and an income tax incorporating loss offsets as liberal as those provided by the U.S. law.[14]

A wealth tax automatically allows losses to be offset against taxable wealth up to the full extent of the investor's net worth. Thus, within this limit, the tax does not alter the relation between the amount of resources that the investor risks and the gain that he may realize, even when the gain would all be added to taxable wealth.

Taxation, it seems, is much less damaging to the reward for risk-taking than it may appear when loss offsets are neglected. Indeed, a tax with full loss offsets may actually stimulate investors to be more venturesome than they would be in the absence of taxation. The tax will not cut the reward for risk in relation to the amount at risk but will cut investors' disposable income and may induce them to assume

---

14. E. Cary Brown is right, in my opinion, in criticizing Kaldor's treatment of risk. See "Mr. Kaldor on Taxation and Risk Bearing," *Review of Economic Studies,* vol. 25 (October 1957), pp. 49–52. Nevertheless, Kaldor's judgment that an expenditure tax is more favorable to risk bearing than an income tax may be correct when the comparison is between an expenditure tax and an income tax with seriously incomplete loss offsets. See his book, *An Expenditure Tax,* p. 121.

more risk in an effort to restore their income.[15] (On the other hand, feeling poorer, investors may consider a more conservative portfolio appropriate.)

This line of reasoning should not be pressed to the point of saying that investment incentives are immune to heavy taxation. Loss offsets are likely always to be less than perfect under the income tax, and their significance may not be fully appreciated by investors. The reward for assumption of risk is not the only socially necessary part of the return on investment. The prospective return must include compensation for the discovery and supervision of new investment opportunities. It must be more attractive than the nontaxable returns that can be obtained by purchasing art objects, furniture, automobiles, and other items that yield direct satisfaction to their owners.[16] (This competition increases the wider the range of imputed and monetary returns from property that are excluded from taxable income.) The existence of loss offsets does not prevent the income tax from encroaching on the part of ordinary investment returns that is necessary to overcome inertia and the attractions of owning property yielding nontaxable returns.

Furthermore, the separation of incentives for saving from incentives for investment, although analytically useful, may become misleading if too rigorously maintained. To the extent that saving is undertaken for the explicit purpose of financing a particular investment—say, an expansion of the saver's own business enterprise or the purchase of a house—the motives and incentives cannot be disentangled. The absolute amount of the possible net gain, not merely the reward for risk-taking, is relevant in such cases. The interaction of incentives for saving and investment can also be seen in connection with the wealth tax. Although a wealth tax is approximately neutral with respect to the form in which property is held, it is not neutral with respect to the amount of wealth held. A wealth tax would be more favorable to investment than a tax on property income, but it does not follow that it would be more favorable than a general income tax or general expenditure tax.

15. Domar and Musgrave, in *Readings in the Economics of Taxation*, pp. 513–15.

16. I am indebted to Leif Mutén for calling my attention to the competition between ordinary investment and the purchase of art objects and other personal property yielding direct satisfaction. The point is analogous to the effect of income taxation on the relative attractiveness of working for wages and of performing services for oneself discussed in chapter 6.

On balance, it seems that, of the three taxes, the expenditure tax is most conducive to private investment because it treats saving liberally and also infringes only slightly on the reward for risk-taking. The wealth tax is the least favorable to the growth of private capital but appears to have the minimum effect on the composition of financial portfolios and presumably also on the composition of real investment. The income tax seems to occupy an intermediate position. The margin of difference between the taxes is uncertain. It is important to remember that the attainment of a rapid rate of capital formation depends on monetary and fiscal policy and many other forces which, in the aggregate, are likely to be more influential than the form of taxation.

Factual Evidence on Investment Incentives

Doubts about the effect of the income tax on investment incentives unfortunately cannot be resolved by the simple procedure of asking investors how they feel. Investors do not necessarily analyze their own behavior clearly, and their self-interest disposes them to overstate the adverse effects of taxation. Nevertheless, carefully devised surveys may be worth something if the results are cautiously used.

An extensive survey of individual investors' attitudes was carried out by a Harvard Business School group in 1949.[17] They interviewed 746 "active investors," most of whom had large incomes. On the basis of explicit statements about taxation by the persons interviewed and the investigators' interpretation of the respondents' more general statements about their investments, the research group made the following findings about the influence of the income tax on investment decisions:

1. Whereas only about one-third of the whole sample group were influenced by the tax, the majority of those with incomes above $25,000 were influenced.

2. Among those whose decisions were influenced, 71 percent were induced to shift to more conservative investments and 29 percent to shift to more venturesome investments.

17. J. Keith Butters, Lawrence E. Thompson, and Lynn L. Bollinger, *Effects of Taxation: Investments by Individuals* (Harvard University, Graduate School of Business Administration, 1953).

3. Much of the shifting to more venturesome investments was motivated by a desire to take advantage of preferentially low tax rates on long-term capital gains.

4. The investors who were interviewed appeared to attach little significance to loss offsets; apparently the presence of loss offsets did not compensate in their minds for a reduction in after-tax yields and limitations on the deductibility of capital losses were not an important deterrent.[18]

The Survey of Financial Characteristics of Consumers conducted by the Board of Governors of the Federal Reserve System in 1963 found that, among respondents mentioning one or more investment objectives, 6 percent cited the minimizing of income taxes as an objective; 2 percent said it was their chief investment objective. In income classes between $25,000 and $100,000, 13 percent to 14 percent mentioned the objective of minimizing income taxes; at income levels above $100,000 this fraction rose to 27 percent. The particular assets that respondents most often associated with the objective of minimizing income taxes were real estate and corporate stocks (presumably growth stocks). Up to the $100,000 income level, however, there was no clear pattern of relationship between income size and the objective of capital appreciation, despite the favorable tax treatment of capital gains.[19] Another survey, carried out in 1964 by the University of Michigan Survey Research Center, revealed considerable tax consciousness among high income groups; nevertheless, more than one-fifth of those above the $10,000 level did not know their marginal income tax rate.[20]

Statistical data on the volume and composition of investment and investment yields shed little light on the effects of taxation on investment incentives because of the virtual impossibility of isolating taxation from the many other forces that influence investment and investment yields.

18. Ibid., especially pp. 36–43.

19. Dorothy S. Projector and Gertrude S. Weiss, *Survey of Financial Characteristics of Consumers* (Board of Governors of the Federal Reserve System, 1966), pp. 142–44. The sample was designed to be representative of all consumer units and at the same time to yield a sizable number of units in the upper income and wealth groups. There were 2,557 respondents; the refusal rate was much higher in upper-income strata than in lower-income strata (pp. 50, 52).

20. Robin Barlow, Harvey E. Brazer, and James N. Morgan, *Economic Behavior of the Affluent* (Brookings Institution, 1966), pp. 151–71.

Influence on Work

The income tax clearly reduces the net compensation for work; the expenditure tax does so only a little less obviously. Immediate or future consumption is presumably the principal reward that motivates work, insofar as economic considerations are controlling. The expenditure tax and the income tax will have the same kind of impact on current consumption capacity but, for equal revenues, the expenditure tax will fall somewhat more heavily on this part of the reward. Future consumption capacity is greater under the expenditure tax if part of the salary or wage is saved and invested, but it seems more meaningful to ascribe this gain to saving-and-investing than to count it as part of compensation for work. If a worker merely hoards his wages, the additional wealth he can build up under a flat-rate expenditure tax is illusory because it consists entirely of the postponed tax; future consumption capacity in this case is reduced as much as current capacity. Only to the extent that work is motivated by a desire to accumulate wealth for the sake of power and prestige rather than to augment consumption capacity can it be said that the expenditure tax infringes less than the income tax on rewards for working. The drive for accumulation may be significant for some business executives and professional persons.

A reduction in the net rate of compensation resulting from taxation does not necessarily cause people to work shorter hours, to retire earlier, or to refuse promotions. One reason is that much work, including a great part of the most highly paid, provides satisfaction in itself. Even for the more strictly economic side of working, the effect is uncertain. Taxation may cause some persons to work less owing to the cut in the economic reward, but it may cause others to work more in an effort to maintain or achieve a desired standard of living.[21] Deductive reasoning does not indicate which reaction will predominate. (As discussed in chapter 4, a judgment can be made about the influence of tax progressivity as distinguished from the average weight of taxation.)

The available evidence, though inconclusive and to some extent

21. Economists often call the negative influence the substitution effect and the positive influence the income effect. Theoretical analyses commonly run in terms of the substitution of leisure for income.

contradictory, offers more support for the hypothesis that the supply of labor as a whole is either insensitive or negatively related to the wage rate than for the hypothesis that there is a high positive response. Historically, the work week has shortened as real wages have risen; however, social and economic developments other than the improvement of wages may have been mainly responsible. A number of statistical studies have found inelastic or negatively sloping supply curves for labor in certain population groups or occupations.[22] Recent econometric investigations, concentrating on disaggregated data, indicate that the labor supply responses of adult males are less sensitive than those of married women to wage rates (and presumably also to income taxation), but differ considerably in their numerical estimates.[23] Potentially valuable information on the behavior of people with low incomes is provided by a unique experiment with a negative income tax (a scheme providing a minimum income for families by means of cash allowances that would be reduced by a fraction of the excess of income over the minimum) conducted in New Jersey and Pennsylvania between 1968 and 1972. The findings, however, are subject to different interpretations and cannot be directly applied to the regular income tax.[24]

Several interview studies dealing explicitly with the income tax have been made. Cautiously interpreted, these may be especially informative about the behavior of the self-employed and high-paid

22. For a tabular summary of the earlier studies, see George F. Break, "Income Taxes, Wage Rates, and the Incentive to Supply Labor Services," *National Tax Journal,* vol. 6 (December 1953), pp. 350–51. Break reviews later studies in "The Incidence and Economic Effects of Taxation," in Alan S. Blinder and others, *The Economics of Public Finance* (Brookings Institution, 1974), pp. 182–91. Mention should also be made of a field survey of 2,997 spending units in 1959 which found a negative relationship between hours of work and wage rates (James N. Morgan and others, *Income and Welfare in the United States* [McGraw-Hill, 1962], pp. 76–77, 450).

23. Marvin Kosters, "Effects of an Income Tax on Labor Supply," in Harberger and Bailey, eds., *The Taxation of Income from Capital,* pp. 301–24; Michael J. Boskin, "The Effects of Taxes on the Supply of Labor: With Special Reference to Income Maintenance Programs," in National Tax Association, *Proceedings of the Sixty-fourth Annual Conference on Taxation, 1971* (1972), pp. 684–98.

24. In the negative income tax, the substitution effect and the income effect both operate to reduce the amount of work done, instead of being offsetting as they are under the regular income tax. On the experiment, see Joseph A. Pechman and P. Michael Timpane, eds., *Work Incentives and Income Guarantees: The New Jersey Negative Income Tax Experiment* (Brookings Institution, 1975).

executives and professional persons. In most cases, the responses appear to apply to any kind of taxation that reduces real compensation rather than to special features of the income tax.

For a study completed in 1950, Sanders interviewed approximately 160 business executives and professional persons of the type who act as advisers or consultants to executives. He concluded that taxation had not caused a serious loss of executive services, except in certain areas. Taxes appeared to dispose executives to postpone retirement, but the effect was limited by formal retirement plans and other factors. Sanders found a considerable number of cases in which executives had refused promotions or offers from other companies when the change would have increased their work load without greatly increasing after-tax earnings. Withholding of effort for tax reasons appeared to occur chiefly among executives who were also owners of businesses and who were free of the demands of the corporate hierarchy.[25]

Another careful study of the influence of the income tax was conducted in England in 1956 by Break, who interviewed a sample of 306 solicitors and accountants—persons who should be more sensitive than most to taxation because they are self-employed, well informed about taxation, and subject to relatively high marginal tax rates. About half of the respondents indicated no tax influence on hours of work or date of retirement, and another one-quarter indicated only vague or remote influences. Among the others, whom Break classified as reporting definite tax effects, there was no clear preponderance of disincentives (13 percent) or incentives (10 percent). Break concluded:

> The fact that neither the qualitative nor the quantitative dimension of the problem can be measured with any precision . . . means that . . . any estimate of the magnitude of the net effect . . . is almost purely speculative. It can be stated with considerable certainty, nonetheless, that this net effect, be it disincentive or incentive, is not large enough to be of great economic or sociological significance.[26]

Break's study was essentially repeated by Fields and Stanbury

25. Thomas H. Sanders, *Effects of Taxation on Executives* (Harvard University, Graduate School of Business Administration, 1951).

26. George F. Break, "Income Taxes and Incentives to Work: An Empirical Study," *American Economic Review,* vol. 47 (September 1957), pp. 529–49 (quotation from p. 543).

using 285 interviews conducted in 1969. Although income tax rates had declined slightly in the United Kingdom after 1956, the proportion of solicitors and accountants experiencing net disincentive effects in 1969 (19 percent) was found to be somewhat higher than reported by Break for the earlier year and was significantly greater than the proportion found to be experiencing net incentive effects (11 percent).[27]

The University of Michigan Survey Research Center field study in 1964, referred to earlier in this chapter, provided information on a sample of 957 high-income persons (incomes of $10,000 or more in 1961) in the United States, nine-tenths of whom were in the labor force. When asked a direct question, one in eight said that the income tax discouraged work. The researchers, however, argued that this fraction considerably overstated the true extent of disincentives, noting that many of those who said that they were deterred by taxation had reported earlier in the interview that they had no opportunity to work longer and that this group worked about as many hours as the remaining seven-eighths. The University of Michigan study, unlike those of Sanders, Break, and Fields and Stanbury, found no evidence that taxation affected the age of retirement. The conclusion of the analysts was, "The implication of these findings is that the loss of annual output due to work disincentives caused by the progressive income tax is of negligible proportions."[28] This generalization refers to the length of time worked; the study did not deal with the possible influence of taxation on the willingness to assume responsibility or to move from one place to another.

The last interview study to be mentioned, by Holland, included lengthy interviews with 122 high-level American business executives in 1965–66. Unlike most of the other investigators, Holland asked straightforward questions about the effects of taxation, making no effort to approach the subject in a roundabout way. A unique feature of this study was an effort to separate the various effects of taxation by asking respondents to compare their behavior under the existing income tax with that under a hypothetical fixed tax based on "poten-

27. Donald B. Fields and W. T. Stanbury, "Incentives, Disincentives and the Income Tax: Further Empirical Evidence," *Public Finance*, vol. 25, no. 3 (1970), pp. 381–415.

28. Barlow, Brazer, and Morgan, *Economic Behavior of the Affluent*, pp. 3, 129–50.

tial" income which would not vary with changes in actual income. Holland found that most of the executives interviewed believed that even so revolutionary a change in the tax structure would not affect how hard they worked, the length of their vacation, or the date of their retirement.[29]

Theoretical considerations and the empirical evidence suggest three points worth emphasizing. First, the influence of taxation on the amount of work done is uncertain and may be weaker than popular discussions imply. Second, whatever the net influence is, it is likely to be much the same for the bulk of the labor force when the tax base is income as when it is consumption, provided the taxes yield equal revenue and are proportional or progressive to the same degree. Third, the allocation of labor among different kinds of employment may be more sensitive to taxation than the total labor supply is. A person who would work no less if real wages were generally reduced may change jobs in order to get a better wage. Even a carefully devised and fully enforced income tax or expenditure tax would not affect all kinds of employment equally because of differences in the degree to which total compensation consists of nonpecuniary advantages which are immune to both taxes. In addition to these unavoidable differences, there are also nonuniformities resulting from imperfections of tax law and varying opportunities for tax evasion. With high tax rates, labor can be expected to flow toward occupations and working arrangements that are subject to relatively light taxation and away from those subject to relatively heavy taxes. People may also be induced to do more house repairs, gardening, and other chores for themselves and less work for pay.[30]

Conclusion

Aside from any differences in progressivity or special features, the taxation of income seems likely to be less favorable to private saving and investment propensities than the taxation of consumption but more favorable than the taxation of personal wealth. Income taxes

29. Daniel M. Holland, "The Effect of Taxation on Effort: Some Results for Business Executives," in National Tax Association, *Proceedings of the Sixty-second Annual Conference on Taxation, 1969* (1970), pp. 428–517.

30. See my paper "The Income Tax and the Supply of Labor," *Journal of Political Economy*, vol. 57 (October 1949), pp. 428–37, reprinted in *Readings in the Economics of Taxation*, pp. 456–69.

and consumption taxes both reduce the reward for work, but it is uncertain whether, on balance, they increase or decrease the willingness to work. A wealth tax has no direct effect on earnings from personal effort and presumably has little if any influence on the supply of effort. Neither deductive reasoning nor the factual evidence now available clearly shows whether the economic differences among the three tax bases are great or small.

CHAPTER FOUR

Economic Effects of Progressivity

THE ECONOMIC ANALYSIS of tax progressivity can be conveniently combined with a comparison between direct and indirect taxes, since direct taxes are generally progressive and indirect taxes regressive or proportional. The income tax and the other direct personal taxes need not be progressive; if a consensus could be reached in favor of proportional or regressive taxation, it could be carried out more exactly by direct taxation than by indirect taxes. Prevailing sentiment, however, demands progressivity in direct taxes, for its own sake and as an offset to the regressivity of excises and other indirect taxes. Both supporters and opponents of progressivity rightly feel that their objective is associated with the extent to which revenue is raised by indirect taxes. Direct taxes on income, consumption, and wealth, moreover, are likely to differ in distribution among income classes and in progressivity, a point that was held to one side in the preceding chapter.

Progressivity is here measured with respect to income. A progressive tax or tax system takes a larger fraction of large incomes than of small incomes. A regressive tax or tax system takes a smaller fraction of large incomes than of small incomes, and a proportional one takes the same fraction of all incomes. Taxes that are progressive over certain ranges of income often are proportional or regressive over other ranges.[1]

Who Pays Indirect Taxes?

Indirect taxes are collected from producers or sellers in the expectation that they will be passed on to consumers as a separate charge or as an unidentified part of the price. Forward shifting is assumed to occur because, if it did not, producers would switch to untaxed activities. Even with full shifting to the consumer, some productive resources will be forced out of the industry because a smaller quantity of the taxed item will be consumed at the higher price.

Economists have always conceded that, in certain cases, producers may have to bear a large part of a new tax for a time because they are specialized in the production of the taxed item and cannot readily move to other industries. Some theorists go further, contending that absorption by the factors of production is the general rule even in the longer run. They argue that, when producers try to switch from taxed to nontaxed industries, earnings will be driven down in the latter. They conclude that factor incomes (wages, profits, interest, and rent) will be generally reduced and that the average price of goods will remain unchanged, with any rise in the prices of taxed goods being offset by a fall in the costs and prices of other goods.

The traditional theory does neglect some difficult points, particularly when applied to a sales tax, turnover tax, or other broad-based tax or to a large group of selective excises considered jointly. Since the taxed activities are a large part of the total, attempts by producers to move to untaxed fields are likely to have repercussions on factor incomes throughout the economy. Moreover, the prices of taxed goods can rise without a compensating fall in other prices only if total expenditures increase, which may be prevented by monetary restric-

1. Another usage is to define progressivity, regressivity, and proportionality with respect to the tax base rather than to income. The two usages may result in different classifications of taxes on consumption or wealth. My practice is to refer to consumption or wealth taxes that are proportional with respect to their bases as "flat-rate" taxes and taxes that are progressive with respect to their bases as "graduated" taxes.

tions or other conditions. The absolute price level is itself an influence on behavior rather than a neutral statistic.

Adjustment to a massive change in taxation is likely to be a more complex, time-consuming, and far-reaching process than the simple forward-shifting theory contemplates. Whatever happens to the general price level and to economic activity as a whole, however, the relative prices of goods that are subjected to sales or excise taxes can be expected to rise compared with other prices. In this sense, the taxes can be said to fall on buyers according to the part of their incomes that they spend for taxed items.

The hypothesis that excises and sales taxes are passed on to buyers seems the most plausible simple statement that can be made about the incidence of these taxes; nevertheless, I am not prepared to rule out the possibility of absorption by producers.[2] Later in this chapter, attention is given to statistical estimates based on the assumption that indirect taxes are fully passed on to buyers, but the implications of absorption by recipients of factor incomes are also noted. Since the indirect taxes are largely, although not exclusively, on consumer goods and services, the assumption of forward shifting treats them as general or selective consumption taxes. The alternative assumption equates the indirect taxes with taxes on income, which, in the absence of knowledge to the contrary about producers of a particular item, may be considered approximately proportional to factor income (personal income other than transfer payments).

The usual view is that direct taxes on personal income, consumption, or wealth cannot be shifted. While there are no doubt exceptional circumstances in which short-run shifting does occur, the assumption that, in general, the personal taxes rest on those who pay them seems reasonable.

Taxpayers are less aware of the amount paid in the form of many indirect taxes than they are of the income tax or other direct taxes.

2. For support of the forward-shifting hypothesis, see Richard A. Musgrave, "On Incidence," *Journal of Political Economy*, vol. 61 (August 1953), pp. 306–23, and Musgrave, *The Theory of Public Finance: A Study in Public Economy* (McGraw-Hill, 1959), pp. 211–31, 287–311. The hypothesis that indirect taxes are fully absorbed by the factors of production is developed by Earl R. Rolph, *The Theory of Fiscal Economics* (University of California Press, 1954), pp. 123–71. A succinct review of the controversy, with the conclusion that sales taxes fall mainly on consumers and are usually shifted through higher prices, can be found in John F. Due, "Sales Taxation and the Consumer," *American Economic Review*, vol. 53 (December 1963), pp. 1078–84.

Even when a sales tax or excise is quoted as a separate addition to commodity prices, as it customarily is when levied at the retail stage, consumers may underestimate the total that they pay in the course of a year. When the tax is absorbed by producers it is still harder to identify. Income tax withholding, however, reduces the difference in the degree to which people are aware of the amount they pay under that tax and under indirect taxes.

Tax consciousness may have important political implications, but it does not appear to condition the economic consequences of taxation to any great extent. Economists generally assume, for example, that a 1 percent tax on wages will have the same influence on labor supply and consumption as a 1 percent cut in the wage rate. Although organized labor might react differently in the short run, this simplification does not seem misleading as regards the more lasting effects of taxation.

More questionable is the assumption, also commonly made, that the effects of taxation depend mainly on changes in real income and relative prices rather than on money income and nominal prices. This means, for example, that workers will react in the same way to a reduction in money wages and to an equal cut in real wages caused by an increase in the prices of the things they buy. There is evidence that this is not true in the short run; a change in money income is more quickly felt than a change in the purchasing power of a constant income. People have an illusion about money that obscures changes in the real value of financial tokens. This illusion must have been weakened by the experience of rising prices, increased familiarity with price indexes, and the explicit introduction of the cost of living into wage negotiations. Adjustment lags caused by the money illusion are probably shorter than they formerly were, and in the long run the illusion does not seem significant.

If tax consciousness is economically unimportant and if the money illusion is weak and temporary, indirect taxes that raise the price of consumer goods will have approximately the same consequences as an expenditure tax that is distributed in the same way among population groups. Excises or sales taxes which were generally conceded to depress producers' earnings by a calculable amount would be equivalent to direct taxes on income, but, as argued below, the uncertainty of the incidence of the indirect taxes may condition their effects on business operations and investment.

Consumption and Wealth Tax Bases
in Relation to Income

The available information indicates that a tax on consumption—
either a flat-rate direct tax on expenditures or a fully shifted sales tax
—would be regressive with respect to income. A flat-rate tax on personal wealth or net worth apparently would be regressive with respect
to income over lower and middle income ranges and progressive over
high income ranges. This can be seen from figure 4-1, which shows,
for deciles of money income, the ratio of tax liability to income of
flat-rate taxes on consumption and wealth that would have yielded
about the same amount of revenue as the federal income tax in 1960–
62. A curve showing effective rates of the federal income tax (exclusive of the tax attributable to capital gains) is included for
comparison.

Figure 4-1. Ratios of Alternative Taxes to Money Income, 1960–62[a]

Percent of money income

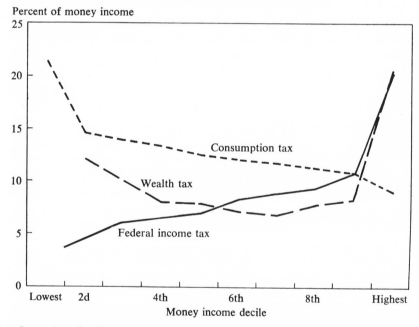

Source: Appendix table C-2.
a. Federal individual income tax (excluding tax attributable to net capital gains) compared with flat-rate
taxes of equal yield on wealth and personal consumption. See appendix C for further explanation.

The broadest retail sales taxes do not cover all consumption expenditures, and they usually apply to certain capital outlays and business expenses. A study based on 1950 expenditure patterns and state sales tax coverage indicated that the "typical retail sales tax" in the United States was slightly less regressive than a flat-rate tax on all consumption expenditures at lower income levels and that the two forms of tax would be almost equally regressive at higher income levels.[3] A later study based on 1960–61 data found the New Jersey state sales tax to be considerably less regressive with respect to income than a tax covering all consumption expenditures.[4] A value-added tax on the European Economic Community model may be regarded as an especially broad sales tax on consumption. It would cover most goods and services bought by consumers, with the significant exception of medical care. While the European value-added taxes generally do not apply to rents, and sales of houses are not taxed in some countries, the component materials and construction work for dwellings and public utility services are generally covered. The regressivity of a retail sales tax or a value-added tax can be greatly mitigated by the exemption of food and certain other items classified as essentials, or by granting a tax credit to people with low income as is done in a number of states in the United States.[5] Inequalities in taxation of people at the same income level would remain under any form of sales tax.

The statistics on the relation between consumption and income and net worth and income are unsatisfactory in several respects. The income and consumption data are thought to be less reliable for the lower and upper extremes of income than for the broad middle range.[6] Although the wealth data were collected by a careful survey that focused special attention on upper-income groups and the wealthy, the rate of response was much lower for the top income classes than

3. Reed R. Hansen, "An Empirical Analysis of the Retail Sales Tax with Policy Recommendations," *National Tax Journal*, vol. 15 (March 1962), pp. 1–13.

4. Jeffrey M. Schaefer, "Sales Tax Regressivity under Alternative Tax Bases and Income Concepts," *National Tax Journal*, vol. 22 (December 1969), pp. 516–27.

5. Hansen, "Empirical Analysis," p. 8; Schaefer, "Sales Tax Regressivity"; James A. Papke and Timothy G. Shahen, "Optimal Consumption-Base Taxes: The Equity Effects of Tax Credits," *National Tax Journal*, vol. 25 (September 1972), pp. 479–87; Charles L. Schultze and others, *Setting National Priorities: The 1973 Budget* (Brookings Institution, 1972), pp. 437–43.

6. U.S. Bureau of Labor Statistics, *Consumer Expenditures and Income, Total United States, Urban and Rural, 1960–61*, Report 237-93 (1965), p. 10.

for the whole sample.[7] The omission from the statistics underlying figure 4-1 of capital gains and losses and imputed rent of owner-occupied dwellings and other nonmonetary items of income and consumption further clouds the picture.[8]

Even if the statistics were highly accurate, their significance for tax policy would be debatable because they show a cross section for a single year rather than a continuous record, a snapshot instead of a moving picture. The high ratios of consumption to income and of net worth to income at the lower end of the income scale suggest that the current year's income may not be a good indicator of the longer-term economic status of families in these brackets. All budget surveys show consumption expenditures in excess of income in the lowest income classes, but it is hard to see how many families can go on spending more than their income for a long period of years (provided the measure of income includes public assistance payments and other transfers, as is the practice in most surveys). The high consumption ratio in the lowest income classes appears to be explained partly by the inclusion of families whose income is temporarily depressed and of retired persons whose previous income was greater. The high ratio of aggregate net worth to aggregate income in these classes may have a similar explanation, with retired persons exercising an especially great influence on the ratio. On the other hand, in high-income classes the ratios of aggregate consumption to aggregate income and of aggregate net worth to aggregate income may be held down by the presence of families whose incomes are higher than usual. Both low-income classes and high-income classes include families who are temporarily there, but the low-income classes include proportionately more of those whose income is below normal than of those whose income is above normal, whereas the reverse is true of high-income classes.

Statistics for any one year probably make a consumption tax appear more regressive with respect to income than would statistics in which the cumulative or average income and consumption for a period of several years, or for a lifetime, were compared. The cross-section statistics make a flat-rate tax on wealth appear more regres-

7. Dorothy S. Projector and Gertrude S. Weiss, *Survey of Financial Characteristics of Consumers* (Board of Governors of the Federal Reserve System, 1966), p. 52.

8. A major step toward improvement of the income distribution statistics has been taken by Joseph A. Pechman and Benjamin A. Okner; see their *Who Bears the Tax Burden?* (Brookings Institution, 1974).

sive in lower income classes and less progressive in higher income classes than would a longer-term comparison for identical families. Suitable data are not available to measure the difference between the two kinds of ratio. A hypothesis that has received attention from specialists in recent years is that the average ratio of consumption to families' normal or "permanent" income is the same at all income levels.[9] If this is true, a flat-rate tax on all consumption will be proportional with respect to normal or permanent income, although regressive with respect to current income in any one year.[10] I think, however, that this hypothesis goes much farther than is warranted.[11]

The most appropriate time period for judging progressivity or regressivity is not obvious. In general, short periods are subject to more erratic fluctuations than long periods. A day, a week, or a month seems too short to reveal significant relations, as in many respects is a year. But a long period of years, or a whole lifetime, is not necessarily ideal. Past prosperity mitigates the hardship of paying a tax that is high in relation to current income, and previous indigence helps excuse a low ratio of tax to current income, but there are limits to the degree to which the past should be allowed to dominate the present. The future, being unforeseeable in detail, simply cannot be brought into calculations of the tax burden.

Until better statistics are compiled, tax progressivity and regressivity can justifiably be measured on the basis of available single-year data, but with the qualification that the estimates for the lowest and highest incomes are probably less representative than those for a wide range of middle incomes.

9. Milton Friedman, *A Theory of the Consumption Function* (Princeton University Press for the National Bureau of Economic Research, 1957).

10. David G. Davies has made estimates suggesting that a general consumption tax would be proportional with respect to "permanent income" ("Progressiveness of a Sales Tax in Relation to Various Income Bases," *American Economic Review*, vol. 50 [December 1960], pp. 987–95, especially p. 993). These estimates, however, do not provide a test of the permanent income hypothesis but are illustrations of certain implications of Friedman's hypothesis, if valid. Lacking a direct observation of permanent income, Davies derived an estimate of permanent income in each measured income class by dividing mean measured consumption by a constant. This, of course, produces a constant ratio of consumption (and of a general consumption tax) to estimated permanent income.

11. Thomas Mayer concludes that the hypothesis is inconsistent with the statistical evidence. See *Permanent Income, Wealth, and Consumption: A Critique of the Permanent Income Theory, the Life-Cycle Hypothesis, and Related Theories* (University of California Press, 1972).

Impact on Saving

If high-income families tend to increase or decrease their saving by a larger fraction of any change in their disposable income than low-income families do—that is, if the marginal propensity to save increases with income—a progressive tax will be paid at the expense of private saving to a greater extent than a proportional or regressive tax. Although direct evidence on the marginal propensity to save in different income classes is not available, the marginal propensity can be approximated from statistics of disposable income and net saving. On the basis of such approximations, I have estimated the impact on net saving of the federal individual income tax in 1960–61 (exclusive of the tax attributable to net capital gains) and of a proportional income tax, a fully shifted flat-rate tax on consumption, and a flat-rate tax on net wealth that would have yielded enough revenue to replace the graduated income tax. The proportional income tax is included in order to show the influence of rate graduation and as a proxy for a sales tax that is fully absorbed by the factors of production. The estimates reflect solely the distribution of tax liability among income groups and do not allow for any differences in saving propensities under consumption taxes, wealth taxes, and income taxes.

The estimates for 1960–61 conditions, together with estimates for 1950 which were made for the original edition of this book, show that the proportion of revenue coming out of potential private saving would have been as follows (in percent):[12]

	1960–61	1950
Federal individual income tax	30	33
Proportional income tax	25	28
Flat-rate consumption tax	24	27
Flat-rate wealth tax	29	...

Taking account only of the distribution of the taxes among income classes and not allowing for any influence stemming from the form of taxation, the estimates indicate that the progressive income tax of 1960–61 (exclusive of the tax attributable to capital gains) had a slightly greater effect on private saving than would a flat-rate tax on

12. The 1960–61 figures are the average of two sets of estimates; their derivation is described in appendix C.

net wealth. They confirm the expectation that the progressive income tax falls more heavily on saving than would a proportional income tax or a flat-rate consumption tax, but the difference is smaller than many seem to imply.

For reasons mentioned in the discussion of progressivity and regressivity, cross-section budget data may not be a reliable indicator of the relation between income and expenditures of identical families for a period of years. If families determine their consumption partly with reference to their normal or permanent income rather than their current income, marginal propensities to save derived from cross-section data will overstate the impact on saving of a permanent tax.[13] This may help explain why marginal saving propensities derived from consumer budget studies often exceed statistical estimates based on time series. My cross-section estimates used here, however, imply marginal propensities to save and to consume fairly close to the time-series estimates used in the analysis of stabilization effects in chapter 11 and appendix E.[14] Estimates based on budget surveys for a single year may also exaggerate the difference between the effect of progressive and regressive taxes, but this is not necessarily true.[15]

Subject to the limitations of the data and methods, my estimates for 1960–61 indicate that the difference between the impact on saving of the progressive individual income tax and that of a flat-rate consumption tax is an unimpressive 6 percent of the yield (30 percent for the income tax compared with 24 percent for the consumption tax). On the assumption that this relationship was still applicable in 1970, replacement of the entire individual income tax by a flat-rate consumption tax would have increased private saving by about $5.0

---

13. Friedman, *Theory of the Consumption Function;* Franco Modigliani and Richard Brumberg, "Utility Analysis and the Consumption Function: An Interpretation of Cross-Section Data," in Kenneth K. Kurihara, ed., *Post Keynesian Economics* (Rutgers University Press, 1954), pp. 388–436.

14. One of my estimates of the impact on saving is based on a marginal propensity to save derived from a consumption function estimated from both time-series and cross-section data (Ralph D. Husby, "A Nonlinear Consumption Function Estimated from Time-Series and Cross-Section Data," *Review of Economics and Statistics,* vol. 53 [February 1971], pp. 76–79). However, the long-run version of the function, which I used, is similar to an estimate derived solely from cross-section data.

15. If the saving function were linear, the bias would cause the slope (the overall marginal propensity to save) to be overstated, but the marginal propensity to save would be the same at all income levels. For curvilinear functions, it is not certain what the effect will be.

billion. This sum is equal to about 9 percent of actual personal saving in 1970 and 10 percent of total net investment.[16] A comment on the possible contribution to growth of increased saving and investment appears at the end of the chapter.

Investment Incentives

Since investors in unincorporated enterprises and purchasers of corporate stock tend to have above-average incomes, they pay less under a proportional or regressive tax than under a progressive tax and have more resources to put into their own businesses or into the acquisition of shares. Furthermore, as explained in chapter 3, offsets of business losses may be more complete under a proportional or regressive tax than under a progressive one. In these respects, nonprogressive taxes are more favorable to business investment than a progressive income tax is.

Although indirect taxes ordinarily qualify as nonprogressive, they impose an obstacle to business operations and investment that is not raised by a net income tax. Producers and distributors must advance funds to cover taxes levied before the retail stage, which increases their working-capital requirements and exposes them to the risk that they may not be able to recover the advance if sales volume or prices prove to be lower than expected. Retail taxes are less troublesome but still must be paid on unprofitable sales as well as profitable ones. From the point of view of producers, the indirect taxes constitute an inescapable increase in the costs of doing business. In many industries, even a moderate-rate sales tax or excise will increase costs by an amount that is large relative to the margin of profit on sales. Even when they are generally reflected in higher prices, indirect taxes are not innocuous in their effect on investment.[17]

The actual volume of investment depends on both the willingness to invest under given market conditions and the expected state of demand for final output. If the substitution of indirect taxes for pro-

16. Individual income tax liability in 1970, after credits but *including* the tax on capital gains and the surcharge, was $83.8 billion (U.S. Internal Revenue Service, *Statistics of Income—1970, Individual Income Tax Returns*, p. 7). The estimates of personal saving and of investment are from *Economic Report of the President, February 1975*, pp. 265, 272.

17. I am indebted to Carl S. Shoup for calling my attention to the risk elements in indirect taxation.

gressive income taxes significantly narrowed the market for consumer goods, this would partly or wholly offset any beneficial effect on investment incentives. The foregoing analysis suggests that such a substitution would indeed reduce the propensity to consume but that the difference may not be great.

While, in my judgment, common opinion is probably correct in considering the present individual income tax more injurious to investment incentives than indirect taxes or a less progressive income tax would be, the extent of the difference is conjectural. Because of the large portion of private investment that is carried out by corporations, the corporation income tax probably influences investment decisions more than the individual income tax does.

Work Incentives

While the net influence of taxation is uncertain, it seems likely that people will choose to work more under a regressive or proportional tax system than under a progressive system. As pointed out in chapter 3, the net influence is the unpredictable result of two effects that are thought to be partly offsetting. One effect is a reduction in taxpayers' real disposable income, which tends to stimulate them to work more in an effort to restore their position. The other effect, which tends to discourage work, is a cut in net earnings per unit of work. Technically, the second effect is called the price or substitution effect, because economists view wages as the price of labor or a measure of the rate at which free time can be substituted for the goods and services purchasable with one's earnings. Regressive, proportional, and progressive taxes have similar income effects but different price or substitution effects.

To isolate the influence of progressivity, consider a person who would pay the same amount under alternative progressive, proportional, and regressive taxes, provided his money income was the same. The income effect of the three taxes will be the same, but the price effect will be different. Whereas the progressive tax reduces the net price received for successive units of free time, the proportional tax leaves the net earnings rate constant, and the regressive tax allows it to increase. Although the net balance remains uncertain, the price effect is clearly most adverse under the progressive tax. This conclusion is reinforced by the presumption that the attractiveness of free time increases relative to that of wage income as the work week lengthens and that a person who has control over the number of hours he works will insist on an increasing wage rate for hours above some minimum.

As an illustration, consider a person who is working 40 hours a week at an hourly rate of $3.00 and earning $120. A 10 percent proportional tax will reduce the net wage to $2.70; if hours of work are constant, income after tax will fall to $108. A progressive tax with an exemption of $60 per week and a rate of 20 percent on the first bracket of taxable income will also reduce the person's income to $108 after tax if his hours of work are unchanged, but the net wage rate will now be $3.00 for the first 20 hours and $2.40 for additional hours. Without knowing more about the person, we cannot predict whether he will try to maintain his after-tax income by working longer hours, but this course is clearly less feasible and less likely under the progressive tax. Under the proportional tax, income can be restored to the pretax level by working 4.44 hours more; under the progressive tax, 5.00 hours of additional work are required.

The force of this argument is diminished by the fact that most individuals do not have the opportunity of working exactly the number of hours they wish. Unless they are self-employed, they must conform to their employer's requirements. But there is flexibility through absenteeism, selection among jobs, and part-time supplementary jobs. Employers are likely to respond to the preferences of the majority of their workers; the length of the work week is a standard subject of collective bargaining.

Although the same difference between progressive taxes and proportional or regressive taxes exists for business executives, independent businessmen, and professional persons, the alternatives faced by such persons are more complex than those presented to wage earners. Power, prestige, interest in one's work, and nontaxable emoluments may be more important. The salary that the ABC Corporation must pay to entice an executive to work for it rather than the XYZ Corporation is surely much greater than the net compensation that society must offer to induce him to work as an executive rather than a clerk. Nevertheless, some persons may be discouraged from becoming executives or transferring to more responsible jobs because progressive taxation reduces the net earnings attainable by assuming responsibility.

A qualification that could be significant arises from the differences in amounts of tax payable by various social and economic groups under progressive, proportional, and regressive systems. High-income groups will pay more and low-income groups less under progressive rates than under the other systems. If it could be shown that high-income groups are less sensitive than low-income groups to a change in their marginal rate of compensation and more inclined to work more to try to make up for a cut in their average compensation rate, this would offset to some degree the greater discouragement to work offered by progressive tax rates. But this is a speculative matter on which it would be hard to obtain reliable information.

Cost of Tax Compliance—and Avoidance

A criticism of the income tax, which would apply with even greater force to the expenditure tax and the wealth tax, is that its complexity causes much time and energy to be diverted to the socially unproductive activity of complying with the tax. Individual investors and business executives give much attention to the income tax, with the aid of a large and talented group of tax lawyers and accountants. Surely, the argument runs, there are more useful things for these people to do.

Although the choice of word is a matter of semantics, most efforts seem to be devoted toward tax avoidance rather than compliance. A person who conducted his affairs without regard to opportunities for minimizing income tax would no doubt be somewhat inconvenienced by requirements for record-keeping and the filing of returns but would escape worry about many subtleties of law and accounting. It would be unrealistic, of course, to expect taxpayers to neglect possibilities of tax avoidance or to refrain from complaining about the trouble and expense to which they must go to take advantage of them.

A less conspicuous, but perhaps more important, form of economic waste is the alteration of investment and employment choices in order to avoid income taxes—the selection of investments whose before-tax yield is lower than that of others but whose after-tax yield is higher, the choice of jobs on the basis of the degree of tax shelter enjoyed by the compensation, and many other such decisions.

Although these are valid criticisms of the income tax or any other refined direct tax, something can be said on the other side. Many efforts at tax avoidance are provoked or invited by the existence of exclusions, deductions, and other provisions that are questionable from the standpoint of equity and social policy. Removal of these provisions would improve the equity of the income tax and at the same time lessen the waste and distortions attributable to it. Other complexities of the income tax are due to efforts to achieve equity and neutrality in a complex environment. If these refinements are not considered worth their cost in complexity and distortions, they could be eliminated within the income tax framework without going so far as to substitute indirect taxes for the income tax. Even though such a simplification of the income tax would sacrifice some of its characteristic advantages, the results might be preferable to those attributable to massive substitution of indirect taxes.

Although efforts at tax avoidance and complexities of the statutes, regulations, and administrative procedures depend to some extent on the height of tax rates, the exact relationship is unclear. Many of the practices that have grown up might not be eliminated or even greatly abated if income tax rates were simply reduced, without other reforms, and the revenue were replaced by indirect taxation.

Finally, indirect taxes are not without complications, and their effects on patterns of investment and production can be great. Selective excises will discourage production of the taxed items, to an extent depending on the elasticity of demand. Although the view that this inevitably results in a less efficient use of resources has been properly questioned, the probability that inefficiency will occur seems no less than it is for changes induced by the income tax.

Concluding Remarks

Many discussions have, I think, greatly exaggerated the possible differences in the influence of alternative taxes on work incentives, private saving, and investment. Careful theoretical analyses and factual evidence on the subject are inconclusive. Moreover, the contribution that additional saving and investment can make to the growth of an economy such as that of the United States may be less than is often supposed. According to Denison's estimates, net investment was responsible for only about one-fifth of the growth of potential national income over the period 1948–69—0.80 percentage point a year out of 4.02 percentage points.[18] If these estimates are combined with mine, it appears that even had the progressive income tax been replaced by a flat-rate tax on consumption, net saving in that period would have increased by an amount sufficient to have raised the annual growth rate by considerably less than 0.1 percentage point.[19] Some scholars attribute more of growth to capital formation than Denison does, mainly because they believe that technological progress must be "embodied" in new capital goods.[20] Their models allow more scope for stimulating growth by tax measures that increase saving.

A qualification of the remarks about the global estimates of the impact of taxation on saving is that alternative taxes are likely to have different effects on various forms of saving, or outlets for saving, owing to differences in asset preferences of savers. According to my estimates, the increase in total saving due to the substitution of a flat-rate consumption tax for the progressive income tax would accrue entirely to consumers in the top income decile; the saving of the remaining nine-tenths of families would decline.[21] As compared with others, the top income group holds a much larger fraction of its assets in the form of publicly traded corporate stock and equity in business and professions and a much smaller fraction in the form of equity in owner-occupied dwellings and of bank deposits and other liquid assets.[22] Presumably, therefore, the tax revision would not only raise total personal saving but would redirect it toward the former kinds of asset and away from the latter kinds. Insofar as the real investments that would be thus favored contribute more to innovation and growth

18. Edward F. Denison, *Accounting for United States Economic Growth, 1929–1969* (Brookings Institution, 1974), p. 127. In 1929–48 capital accounted for a much smaller fraction of total potential growth—0.13 percentage point out of 2.75 percentage points.

19. See appendix C.

20. See, for example, Robert M. Solow, "Technical Progress, Capital Formation, and Economic Growth," in American Economic Association, *Papers and Proceedings of the Seventy-fourth Annual Meeting, 1961 (American Economic Review,* vol. 52, May 1962), pp. 76–86. Comments by Denison appear in "The Unimportance of the Embodied Question," *American Economic Review,* vol. 54 (March 1964), pp. 90–94; and in *Accounting for Economic Growth,* pp. 55–56, 109–10, 133–35.

21. If the estimated change in aggregate saving is 100, the estimated change for the top decile is 178 and that for the other nine deciles is —78.

22. Projector and Weiss, *Survey of Financial Characteristics of Consumers,* pp. 110, 118.

than do other investments—as seems plausible—the effect of the reduction in tax progressivity would be greater than suggested by the global estimates.

A tax revision that would cause the number of hours worked to increase by x percent (with capital inputs constant) would increase total output much more than a revision that stimulated an x percent increase in the annual amount of new investment (with labor inputs constant). One reason is that the contribution of capital is made by the stock, of which new investment in any year is only a small fraction. Another reason is that the value of labor inputs—measured, as it must be, by labor's share of national income—is much greater than the value of capital inputs. But too little is known about the influence of taxation on work to allow an economist to confidently prescribe a tax system that would increase the amount of work done by x percent, even if he felt free to disregard other objectives.

The preceding remarks about saving are based on the tacit assumption that an increase in the propensity to save would immediately be translated into additional investment. The assumption implies that capital formation is limited by the propensity to save rather than by the willingness to invest. This may be true when final demand is buoyant and existing productive capacity is being used at a high rate, but it does not seem to have been true in the United States during the late 1950s and early 1960s or the early 1970s. During these periods the American economy appears to have suffered from a tendency toward a deficiency of aggregate demand. In these conditions, an attempt to save more may prove abortive and may depress income and output.

Predictions of demand over long periods of time are hazardous, and will not be attempted here. There is, however, no guarantee that demand will press so hard against productive capacity that an increased propensity to save will automatically increase private investment. In the formulation of a tax policy that will be conducive to sustained growth, consideration needs to be given to market adequacy and several other factors as well as to effects on saving.

CHAPTER FIVE

Treatment of Certain Costs of Earning Income

A NET INCOME TAX should allow the deduction from gross receipts of all costs of obtaining income. The U.S. tax makes adequate provision for the deduction of most business costs, as reflected in accounting statements, and for most costs of obtaining investment income. Provisions are less complete for deducting costs of earning income as a self-employed person or employee.

With respect to earned income, most of the obvious costs are deductible. A professional person or salesman, for example, can deduct all the usual expenses of maintaining an office, operating an automobile in connection with his work, and traveling away from home, as well as many outlays for entertaining clients and customers. An employed person is allowed to deduct nonreimbursed expenses of travel away from home in connection with his job, union and professional association dues, the cost of specialized work clothing and necessary tools, and other items.

The difficulties arise mainly in connection with items that may combine elements of consumption and cost. Items of this nature, which are considered in this chapter, include the expenses of traveling between home and place of employment, additional household expenses of working wives, educational expenses, and some travel and enter-tainment expenses. Also discussed is whether a depreciation or de-pletion allowance should be deducted to reflect the loss of earning capacity with the passage of time.

The American income tax is more generous than the British but less so than the Swedish and German taxes in allowing deductions by employed persons. In the United Kingdom, deductions from employ-ment income are limited to those that the person "is necessarily obliged to incur . . . wholly, exclusively, and necessarily in the per-formance" of his duties, and this rule is narrowly interpreted. Non-deductible items include expenses of obtaining employment and dues for membership in professional organizations.[1] The rules are more liberal for self-employed professional persons and appear to permit the deduction of most of the items that are deductible in the United States. In Sweden and the Federal Republic of Germany, permissible deductions appear to include most of the items allowed in the United States; however, in Sweden membership dues are generally not de-ductible even when they are necessary expenses, and practices may be more rigid than in the United States for entertainment expenses. Sweden and Germany both allow the deduction of commuting ex-penses within limits.[2]

As is shown in the discussion of individual items, there are no fully satisfactory criteria for distinguishing between consumption and costs of earning income. Although the distinction is customarily made in household budgets and the national income accounts, it is less firmly based than is usually supposed. In a sense, a large proportion of all consumption may be considered a cost of production—not only subsistence costs, but also conventional necessities and amenities, which vary greatly with occupation and social station. For example, a junior executive in a large firm who spent no more for clothing than is provided by the Bureau of Labor Statistics standard budget for a clerical worker might not keep his position very long. It is common-place for lawyers and brokers to meet prospective clients at the coun-try club. An acceptable address may be almost as important as re-

1. Harvard Law School, World Tax Series, *Taxation in the United Kingdom* (Little, Brown, 1957), p. 238.

2. Harvard Law School, World Tax Series, *Taxation in Sweden* (Little, Brown, 1959), pp. 314–19, and World Tax Series, *Taxation in the Federal Republic of Germany* (Commerce Clearing House, 1963), pp. 266–68, 401.

spectable conduct in gaining admittance to circles in which new clients can be found.

Property income is defined, generally and for the income tax, differently from income from personal effort. In principle, property income is measured net of all current costs of using the property and net of depreciation allowances covering the cost of capital assets whose value is exhausted with use or the passage of time.

It is unlikely that a rigorous measurement of net income from personal effort can be developed which is exactly comparable with net property income. Human beings cannot be treated merely as productive agents. Consumption is both the end of production and an intermediate good that induces further productive activity and makes it possible. All that can be hoped is that marginal refinements can be made in the measurement of taxable income, where this can be done without excessive burdens of compliance and administration.

Commuting and Moving Expenses

The costs of commuting to one's regular place of work are not deductible; deductions are allowed for travel to places of temporary employment away from home. Difficulties of interpretation arise in marginal cases with respect to the location of a person's home, the meaning of being away from home, and the distinction between temporary and indefinite periods of employment. These problems of tax administration are not at issue here. The question is whether the long-standing rule against the deduction of regular commuting expenses is proper. Some contend that commuting expenses are costs of employment and should be deducted if they can be properly identified and distinguished from other personal expenditures for local transportation.

In Sweden, costs of daily travel between home and place of work are deductible by an employee who lives far enough away to need transportation. Generally, the deduction covers only the cost of the cheapest means of transportation. Thus, a person who drives his car to work ordinarily may deduct the cost of bus or train transportation; however, if the saving in time resulting from the use of a private car is more than an hour and a half per day, a deduction may be taken for the cost of operating the car.[3]

3. *Taxation in Sweden*, p. 316.

It is true that, because of one's place of residence, commuting expenses may be necessary. But it does not follow that these expenses are primarily costs of earning income rather than consumption. A great part of commuting expenses may be regarded as the consequence of a consumption preference exercised in choosing a place of residence. Those who live in the suburbs because they like trees and grass clearly are making a consumption decision that entails commuting expenses as well as the costs of maintaining a lawn. Commuting expenses and housing expenses, moreover, are often close substitutes. Other things being equal, an easily accessible dwelling sells or rents for more than one in a remote location. A part of the difference in price reflects lower costs of commuting. If a person chooses to spend $100 a month traveling to and from his home in a distant suburb, this expenditure is similar to that of another who pays $100 a month more rent to live close to his place of work. While not everyone can live within walking distance of work, there is nearly always a wide range of choice of exact location.

The income tax already favors home-owning suburbanites over apartment-renting residents of central cities because of the treatment of owner-occupied dwellings; commuters by automobile are favored by the deductibility of state and local gasoline taxes. The addition of a deduction for ordinary commuting expenses would accentuate existing inequities, would mildly encourage further decentralization, and would stimulate extravagant means of travel. The rule against the deduction of commuting expenses seems justified.

The cost of moving to a new place of residence may be regarded as a consumer expenditure when the move reflects personal preference, or it may be considered a cost of earning income when it is dictated by employment requirements or opportunities. Often it is hard to classify moves objectively. The acceptance of a job in a new location is not enough to prove that the costs of moving were incurred primarily for the purpose of earning income. The change of jobs may well have been prompted by a desire to change residences. Motives may be mixed or obscure even to a person who moves.

Before the Revenue Act of 1964, no deduction was allowed for moving expenses; reimbursements for the cost of moving to a new place of work for the same employer were not included in adjusted gross income, but reimbursements received from a new employer were treated as income. The 1964 act granted a deduction for certain moving expenses, and this was broadened effective in 1970. An employee or a self-employed person may deduct moving expenses when the change of residence is incidental to commencing work in the new location. In order to qualify, the new place of employment must be at least fifty miles farther from the former place of residence than was the former place of employment.[4] Deductions are not available to persons who move in an unsuccessful effort to find a new job or to those who remain for only short periods at any one job location.

These provisions do not grant deductions for all moves motivated primarily by employment opportunities or deny deductions for all other moves. They appear to err more on the side of liberality since employed persons who move before retirement in order to enjoy a better climate or for any other reason can qualify. It can be argued that this is justifiable because an exact classification of moving expenses is not feasible and it is desirable to resolve doubts in favor of deductibility to encourage mobility.

Housekeeping and Child-Care Expenses

Persons who work outside the home often incur expenses for services that would otherwise be done at home. These are especially significant for working wives, although other employed people also incur additional expenses. The failure to allow the deduction of these costs in the computation of taxable income constitutes a bias against outside employment. To be sure, the tax system has not prevented a great increase in the proportion of married women in the labor force. But complaints are heard, particularly from upper-middle-class women who are articulate and tax conscious.

The absence of deductions for additional costs of working is a defect of the income tax that cannot be fully corrected. The costs in question are diverse and indistinguishable from ordinary consumption. They include the wages of domestic servants, additional expenditures for quickly prepared food and restaurant meals, and part of the

---

4. Moving expenses, like business expenses, are deductible in computing adjusted gross income. Several safeguards are specified including the following: (a) the deduction is limited to $2,500; and (b) an employee must work at the new location at least thirty-nine weeks during the first twelve months after the move and a self-employed person must work there at least seventy-eight weeks during the first twenty-four months after the move (Internal Revenue Code, sec. 217).

cost of clothes, personal care, and perhaps even household appliances. Outlays for all of these items also are incurred by families in which the wife does not work outside the home. It would be impossible to draw a satisfactory distinction between ordinary consumption and additional expenditures that are costs of earning income. Even if certain expenses could be identified as costs, a deduction for them would be unfair to families—usually those with low and low-middle incomes—in which the household work is done by the working wife or other family members in the evenings or on weekends compared with families that hire household help and enjoy more leisure. The practical effect of an allowance for expenses for household help would be discrimination in favor of upper-middle income groups.

These objections apply, but with less force, to the present limited deduction for child-care expenses (chapter 7).

The discrimination against working wives could be mitigated by a special earned income credit or a special minimum standard deduction (discussed in chapter 9). The credit or deduction would be allowed regardless of whether additional expenditures were actually made because of the wife's employment. This would be much simpler than a deduction for actual expenditures and more favorable to families that do the household work themselves instead of hiring others to do it or buying the services in the form of more highly processed goods. A minimum deduction would not satisfy professional women and others with above-average earnings, nor would an earned income credit unless it were a liberal one.

Educational Expenditures

Expenditures for education that increases earning capacity or is intended to do so are a strategically important cost of earning income but are deductible to only a limited extent.[5] Those who invest in themselves are discriminated against compared with persons who have spent little in preparation for their occupations. The tax provisions are paradoxical at a time when the country has become more aware

5. This section is based on my paper "Educational Expenditures and the Income Tax," in Selma J. Mushkin, ed., *Economics of Higher Education*, U.S. Department of Health, Education, and Welfare, Office of Education, Bulletin 1962, no. 5 (1962). For a general treatment of the economic aspects of education, see Theodore W. Schultz, *The Economic Value of Education* (Columbia University Press, 1963).

of the need for highly trained persons and of the contribution of education to economic progress.[6]

Present Regulations

Treasury regulations allow deductions for expenditures for education that

(1) Maintains or improves skills required by the individual in his employment or other trade or business, or

(2) Meets the express requirements of the individual's employer, or the requirements of applicable law or regulations, imposed as a condition to the retention by the individual of an established employment relationship, status, or rate of compensation.

However, even though education meets these tests, expenditures are not deductible if the education is required of the individual "to meet the minimum educational requirements for qualification in his employment or other trade or business" or if it is "part of a program of study . . . which will lead to qualifying him in a new trade or business." In either of the latter cases, the regulations hold that the outlays are "personal expenditures or constitute an inseparable aggregate of personal and capital expenditures" and are therefore nondeductible.[7]

A person who holds a job on a provisional or temporary basis, subject to the completion of certain educational requirements, may not deduct the cost of meeting these requirements, since this is a minimum condition of the employment. If, however, the requirements for the position are changed after the person has once fully qualified, the cost of meeting the new standard is deductible. For an employee, a change of duties does not involve a new trade or business if the employee continues in the same general type of work. The regulations state (sec. 1.162-5 [b] [i]) that for this purpose "all teaching and related duties shall be considered to involve the same general type of work."

Illustrating the application of the rules, the authors of the regulations mention the case of A, the holder of a bachelor's degree who is

---

6. Denison estimates that increased education was responsible for 12 percent of the growth of real national income in 1929–69 and 22 percent of the growth of real national income per person employed in that period. Edward F. Denison, *Accounting for United States Economic Growth, 1929–1969* (Brookings Institution, 1974), pp. 128, 136.

7. *Code of Federal Regulations,* Title 26, pt. 1 (1975), sec. 1.162-5 (issued 1967).

employed as a high school teacher in a state where a condition of continued employment is the completion of a fifth year of college within ten years after being hired. A completes the additional year of study and obtains a standard certificate. The cost is deductible inasmuch as the fifth year of training is not a minimum requirement of employment. B, who also holds a bachelor's degree, is temporarily employed as an instructor at a university while studying for an advanced degree. He may become a regular faculty member only if he obtains the graduate degree and may continue as an instructor only so long as he makes satisfactory progress toward obtaining the degree. The cost of the graduate studies is not deductible because they are part of the minimum requirements for qualification in B's trade or business. C, a self-employed accountant, attends law school at night and earns a law degree. The expenditures are not deductible because the course of study qualifies C for a new trade or business. D, a practicing psychiatrist, pursues a program of study and training at an accredited psychoanalytic institute which will lead to qualifying him to practice psychoanalysis. Expenditures for the program are deductible because it maintains or improves skills required by D in his trade or business and does not qualify him for a new trade or business.

The present regulations concerning educational expenditures were issued in 1967 to revise and clarify regulations issued in 1958. Both sets of regulations were prompted by court decisions holding that certain deductions for educational expenditures claimed by taxpayers but denied by the Internal Revenue Service were allowable as costs of earning income. The 1967 revision represents a degree of liberalization of the Treasury's previous position, particularly regarding expenditures by teachers and school administrators. Uncertainty remains, however, and some of the distinctions that are drawn in the regulations appear to be formalistic or arbitrary.

By denying deductions for the cost of education intended to meet the minimum requirements of obtaining employment or of qualifying for different work, the Treasury regulations exclude deductions for outlays that contribute to future earning capacity and that have great economic significance for the individual and the community. If a similar attitude were taken toward physical capital, deductions from taxable income presumably would be allowed for maintenance expenses and capital replacement costs, but would be denied for depreciation of capital used to establish new firms, to enlarge existing enterprises, or to introduce new products. The regulations concerning educational expenditures are less favorable to the young and the ambitious than to the established and the timeserver.

Unsatisfactory as the regulations may seem, the difficulties of devising better rules should not be underestimated. In many other countries, the tax treatment of educational expenses is less liberal than in the United States; however, university students often pay little or no tuition and, in certain European countries at least, may receive subsidies to cover living expenses. In Canada, students may deduct tuition fees in computing taxable income, subject to certain conditions; the deduction may be taken even when the fees are paid by parents or others (except the student's employer).

Possible Revisions

By analogy with the treatment of investment in physical capital, persons who make expenditures for education that increases their earning power, or is intended to do so, should be permitted to capitalize those outlays and write them off against taxable income through depreciation or amortization allowances. Income-producing educational expenditures are investments with a limited life and, if it is feasible, they should be given the same tax treatment as other investments. Failure to allow tax-free recovery of educational outlays means that the income tax falls in part on the return of capital rather than on net income.

To bring out significant issues, I shall attempt to give the broad outlines of a suitable plan. The suggestions are intended to serve as a basis for discussion rather than as recommendations for immediate legislation. The plan, in brief, is that part of the personal costs of college education and professional, technical, and vocational education should be capitalized and written off against the student's future earned income over a period of ten to twenty years or more. Minor costs of part-time study would be currently deducted. Provisions limiting deductions to expenses relating to the taxpayer's current position would be dropped.

If the amortization of educational expenditures is justified as a refinement in the definition of income, the deductions should be taken against the income attributable to the education. The deduction should be taken by the student rather than the parents, even when the latter pay the educational expenses. Expenditures by parents, relatives, or friends may be considered gifts. The student would be allowed to recover free of income tax the value of these gifts just as the cost of a depreciable asset acquired as a gift can be written off against the income of the recipient. The privilege of writing off the value of gifts in the form of education should not extend to scholarships and other aid received from educational institutions, governments, corporations, or other organized bodies.

The personal costs of education are far less than total costs because of heavy expenditures by governments and nonprofit institutions. Personal costs are those met by students, parents, and other private individuals. They include (1) money outlays for tuition and fees, books and supplies, and travel; (2) any additional living expenses of the student; and (3) earnings forgone while studying. Forgone earnings are by far the largest component of the costs of college and graduate education, and they constitute an important part of high school costs. This part of costs is already excluded from the tax base, and no special deduction is necessary or appropriate.[8] Although living expenses above those that would be incurred by a person who was not a student should be deductible, it would be difficult to distinguish these additional expenses from ordinary living costs; therefore, as a practical matter, no allowance is suggested for additional living expenses. The costs to be capitalized and amortized would be those listed under item 1 above.

In principle, expenditures for education should be classified as costs of earning income when incurred for that purpose, regardless of whether they could be shown to result in additional income. The taxpayer's intention is the dominant factor governing the distinction between other "ordinary and necessary" business and professional expenses and personal expenses. Mixed motives are especially common, however, with respect to education, and there are no account-

8. The freedom of forgone earnings from income tax is in some respects similar to rapid amortization of this part of students' investment. See Gary S. Becker, *Human Capital: A Theoretical and Empirical Analysis, with Special Reference to Education* (National Bureau of Economic Research, 1964), pp. 14–15, 149; J. Moreh, "Investment in Human Capital and the Income Tax," in M. Parkin and A. R. Nobay, eds., *Contemporary Issues in Economics,* Proceedings of the Conference of the Association of University Teachers of Economics (Manchester University Press, 1975), pp. 252–69.

ing and administrative rules to distinguish òne kind of educational outlay from another.

As a practical possibility, the current deduction or amortization of educational expenditures might be allowed for: (1) any course creditable toward a degree at an accredited college or university, regardless of whether a degree is earned; (2) vocational training at a recognized trade school, business college, or similar institution; and (3) a supplementary, continuation, or refresher course of a predominantly professional or vocational nature taken at a recognized or accredited institution. Part-time studies and correspondence courses as well as full-time resident study should be eligible. Expenditures for ordinary high school studies and elementary school would be classified as personal expenses rather than costs of earning income.

For college and university studies, this plan would err on the side of liberality, because it would cover some educational expenditures that are predominantly consumption, as judged by presumed motivation or apparent influence on income. Most college and university education, however, seems to add to earning capacity, and it is difficult to rule out the possibility of economic motivation in connection with any part of it. With all private costs, including forgone earnings, treated as investment, the rate of private return has been estimated at about 15 percent a year for both college education and graduate instruction and research.[9] If a large fraction of the costs were classified as consumption expenditures, the calculated rate of return on the remaining outlays would be high indeed. The imperfections resulting from a liberal allowance for college costs seem less objectionable than the present practice of permitting virtually none of these expenditures to be charged against taxable income.

The diversity of trade schools, business colleges, and similar insti-

9. For a summary and comments on the various studies see Theodore W. Schultz, "Human Capital: Policy Issues and Research Opportunities," in National Bureau of Economic Research, *Human Resources,* Fiftieth Anniversary Colloquium VI (Columbia University Press for NBER, 1972), pp. 28–34. According to Richard Freeman and J. Herbert Hollomon ("The Declining Value of College Going," *Change,* vol. 7 [September 1975], p. 25), the rate of return on college education declined sharply between 1969 and 1974 and was 7 to 8 percent in 1974. It is unclear, however, to what extent these estimates reflect permanent changes as distinguished from cyclical movements and inflation.

tutions and the absence of a comprehensive accrediting system for them would complicate the application of administrative checks to ensure that the expenses of study at these institutions were legitimate educational expenditures. A difficulty in connection with supplementary training and continuation or refresher courses would be to identify vocational courses. Many extension courses, evening classes, and correspondence courses are almost entirely consumption, dealing with subjects such as hobbies, arts and crafts, current events, and music appreciation. Courses cannot always be distinguished on the basis of their content. A music course, for example, may be vocational training for one person but avocational for another. It seems that the best rule would be to allow current deductions or amortization charges only for expenses relating to education which the taxpayer represents as being primarily vocational or professional and which the authorities consider reasonably related to his occupation or occupational plans. This standard would be harder to apply than the present rule on education but little if any more difficult than the rules on a number of other deductions. The amounts involved may be smaller and many may feel that it is sound public policy to be more liberal about educational expenses than about some of the items now deductible.

The suggestion that no income tax allowance be made for ordinary high school education is debatable. There is considerable overlap between high school courses and the training offered by trade schools and business colleges, on the one hand, and by liberal arts colleges, on the other. For pupils in public high schools, however, the amount that could be written off would be small. Since most young people now go to high school, the principal effect of an income tax allowance for the personal costs of secondary education would be to encourage attendance at private schools.

It would seem reasonable to limit the deductions or amortization charges to taxable earned income, without insisting that a direct link be shown between the education and the taxpayer's occupation. Although education may make one a better investor, the relation between property income and education is tenuous. If educational expenditures could be written off against property income, persons with inherited wealth might gain an undue advantage. Even with the earned-income limitation, the applicable marginal tax rate, and hence the value of the deduction, would be influenced by the amount of property income received.

The requirement that deductions or amortization charges be taken only against taxable earned income would disqualify housewives when they were not working outside the home.[10] This would not be as unfair as it may seem. Although a housewife's services have economic value and her contribution to the family's economic welfare is enhanced by her education, the value of her services does not enter into taxable income. Hence denial of a writeoff for educational costs that qualify the housewife to perform her services at home more effectively cannot be regarded as discriminatory in the same way as failure to take account of costs of earning a taxable income.

By analogy with physical assets, educational expenditures should be capitalized and written off against taxable income over the period in which they contribute to earnings—ordinarily the whole working life of the person. This approach, however, might be cumbersome for major expenditures and ridiculous for small items. A practical procedure would be to allow persons incurring large educational expenses to capitalize them and amortize them over a fixed period of, say, ten or twenty years, or the period ending at the age of sixty-five if that is shorter. Students could be permitted to begin amortization immediately or to postpone it until they are established in their occupations. Taxpayers incurring minor educational expenses might be given the option of capitalizing their outlays or deducting them currently.

Persons who become totally and permanently disabled and the estates of those who die before completing the amortization of their educational expenses might appropriately be allowed to deduct the unamortized balance in the last taxable year and be granted a carryback of net loss and refund of prior-year taxes if the deduction reduced the last year's income below zero. Similar treatment might be urged for women who withdraw from the labor force after marriage, but this would be questionable since many of these women later resume outside employment.

10. The attribution to a wife of part of the earnings of her husband under a state community property law should be disregarded in determining qualification for the deduction.

Consequences of Revised Treatment

Expenditures of college and university students for tuition and fees, books and supplies, and travel have been growing rapidly and for 1969–70 are estimated at $5.9 billion compared with $1.6 billion a decade earlier (table 5-1). Comparable information is not available for trade schools, correspondence schools, and other institutions offering courses that would give rise to expenditures that might be amortized or deducted.

If the 1969–70 expenditures shown in table 5-1 had been currently deductible or amortizable, the ultimate revenue loss would have been about $1.2 billion.[11] This loss would occur only over a period of ten or twenty years if the suggestions made above concerning amortization were adopted. After introduction of the plan, the annual revenue loss would increase yearly as successive groups began to claim deductions or amortization allowances. If students' expenditures remained constant at the 1969–70 level, the annual revenue loss would stabilize at approximately $1.2 billion after ten or twenty years. Educational expenditures, however, can be expected to continue to increase with increases in enrollment, tuition charges, and the price level, though enrollment probably will grow less rapidly than in the past. On the basis of increased enrollment projected by the U.S. Office of Education and on the assumption that expenditures per student will rise at the same rate as in the period 1959–60 to 1969–70, amortizable or deductible expenditures in 1979–80 may be estimated at approximately $12.4 billion.[12] The ultimate revenue loss related to the expenditures of that year might amount to $2.5 billion, spread over one or two decades. These rough estimates make no allowance for any increase in taxable income due to a stimulus to education provided by tax revision.

Regardless of its merits as a refinement of income measurement,

11. Based on the assumption that 90 percent of eligible expenditures would be deducted and that the average marginal rate of those claiming the deductions would be 22 percent (which is the rate that applies to taxable income of $8,000 to $12,000 for married couples).

12. Total enrollment is projected to increase by 28 percent between fall 1969 and fall 1979; estimated expenditures per student increased by 65 percent from 1959–60 to 1969–70. The enrollment figure for 1979 was derived by interpolation from the projections given in U.S. Bureau of the Census, *Statistical Abstract of the United States, 1974*, p. 134.

Table 5-1. Selected Expenditures of College and University Students, 1953–54, 1959–60, and 1969–70

Millions of dollars

	Academic year		
Expenditure	*1953–54*	*1959–60*	*1969–70*
Tuition and fees	508	1,075	4,420
Books and supplies	129	214	620
Travel[a]	190	313	880
Total	827	1,602	5,920

Sources: Estimates for 1953–54 from Richard Goode, "Educational Expenditures and the Income Tax," in Selma J. Mushkin, ed., *Economics of Higher Education*, U.S. Department of Health, Education, and Welfare, Office of Education, Bulletin 1962, no. 5 (1962), p. 294; 1959–60, estimates made in the same way as the estimates for 1953–54; 1969–70, tuition and fees, from U.S. Bureau of the Census, *Statistical Abstract of the United States, 1973*, p. 135; other items projected from the 1959–60 estimates on the basis of total enrollment in institutions of higher education (Department of Health, Education, and Welfare, *Digest of Educational Statistics, 1972 Edition*, p. 74; *Statistical Abstract, 1973*, p. 132) and the movement of the consumer price indexes for reading and recreation and for transportation from 1960 to 1970 (*Statistical Abstract, 1973*, p. 354).

a. Travel between home and a college or university located in another place; excludes local travel between college address and campus and other travel.

adoption of a plan for amortization of educational expenditures would be unlikely to have a great influence on the total investment in education and on the choice among occupations requiring different amounts of such investment. The role of economic calculations in educational and occupational choices is uncertain, and the tax benefits of an amortization plan would equal only a small proportion of the total personal costs of college and university education. Forgone earnings of college and university students, which are a part of personal costs but which would not be amortizable, are much larger in the aggregate than expenditures for items that might properly be subject to amortization (tuition and fees, books and supplies, and travel). In the academic year 1959–60, the amortizable items accounted for only about 17 percent of estimated total personal costs of college and university education, exclusive of any additional living expenses of students; the remaining 83 percent of personal costs consisted of forgone earnings.[13]

On the assumption of a marginal tax rate of 20 to 25 percent, the tax saving attributable to amortization of educational expenditures

13. The estimated total personal costs were $9.5 billion, consisting of $1.6 billion for tuition and fees, books and supplies, and travel (table 5-1) and $7.9 billion of forgone earnings. The estimate of forgone earnings was made by the method of Theodore W. Schultz, "Capital Formation by Education," *Journal of Political Economy*, vol. 68 (December 1960), p. 580.

would have equaled only about 3 to 4 percent of total personal costs of college and university education under conditions prevailing in 1959–60. This figure should be discounted because of the distribution of the tax saving over a period of years. An item as small as this can hardly be a strong influence on the amount of educational expenditures or on occupational choice.

The tax benefits from amortization would not represent a major fraction of personal costs of even the most expensive kinds of education. Although students' outlays for tuition and fees and other expenses at certain prestige colleges and at professional schools of private universities are much larger than average expenditures for all college and university students, forgone earnings are still the largest item of personal education costs.[14]

The most important incentive effects of the amortization plan might be a contribution toward overcoming reluctance to lend and to borrow for educational purposes. With better credit facilities and the amortization plan, much could be said for tuition charges high enough to cover the full marginal costs of instruction in vocational or professional courses, especially in fields such as medicine, where educational costs and earnings are much above the average.

Objections Considered

Two objections to the amortization plan can be raised—one relating to its claim to be a refinement of the income measure and the other to its efficiency as an aid to education. The first, and more weighty, objection is that part of the educational expenses that would be deductible or amortizable are really consumption rather than costs of earning income. Although this is undoubtedly true, it is also true that part of the expenses are costs. I know of no evidence that the consumption component is greater than the cost element, and I believe that it is good social policy to resolve doubts in favor of more liberal writeoffs.

A different kind of objection is that the amortization plan would offer less effective help to education than an immediate deduction for parents of students, as provided in many bills that have been introduced in Congress. However, a deduction for parents would be quite different in principle from the proposed deduction for students and

14. See, for example, my estimates of the cost of medical education, in "Educational Expenditures and the Income Tax," p. 298.

should be evaluated by different standards. A deduction for parents could not be justified as a refinement in the measurement of the parents' earnings. The general rule is that costs, including investment outlays, are properly chargeable against the gross income that they generate, and neither the Internal Revenue Code nor popular opinion treats parents and their adult sons and daughters as a single economic unit.

A deduction for parents of college students would be subject to the objection that it would give the greatest amount of assistance to families with the largest incomes and no assistance to those with very small incomes; it would resemble a federal scholarship that increases as the parents' means increase. The tax value of deductions for students would also increase with the size of their income, but this is not a valid criticism of deductions for genuine costs of earning taxable income.

Proposals to allow parents to deduct tuition payments and other educational expenses call for a subsidy or special encouragement of a socially desirable form of expenditure and should meet the exacting standards that are properly applicable to such subsidies. In particular, the efficiency and equity of the deduction should be compared with that of additional government expenditures to aid education. Although this kind of comparison is not wholly extraneous to the evaluation of the proposal for amortization of educational expenses against students' income, it is less significant. Under the net income tax, there is a presumption in favor of the deduction of costs against the gross income to which they relate, but other deductions require special justification. Few would argue that depreciation allowances for each kind of physical capital should be allowed or denied on the basis of a judgment whether the government could do more to promote capital formation by denying the deduction and spending more for direct government investment or by allowing the deduction and relying on private investors.

Conclusions about Educational Expenditures

Current and deferred deductions for students who are pursuing education that increases their earning capacity are consistent with income tax principles. A suitable plan would allow a refinement of the income definition, would improve equity, and would have incidental consequences of a desirable character. The particular plan outlined here is intended only as a basis for discussion; further consideration might indicate that different provisions should be adopted for eligible expenditures and the amortization period. The essential point is that the deductions should be limited to actual expenditures and should be available to students rather than parents. Although the adoption of the amortization plan would stimulate educational investment to some extent, this effect probably would not be great because forgone earnings, which would not be amortizable, are the major component of costs of education beyond high school. Nevertheless, the recognition for tax purposes that certain educational expenditures are investments would help establish an important principle that may be overlooked in personal and public decisions.

Depreciation of Earning Capacity?

From time to time, the comment is heard that the income tax, to be fair, should allow individuals to deduct from gross income a depreciation or depletion allowance to reflect the loss of their earning capacity with the passage of time. The argument is that an annual deduction for depreciation or depletion is as appropriate in the measurement of net income from personal effort as in the determination of net profits of business enterprise, since a person's productive life, like that of a machine or mineral deposit, is limited.

Although superficially plausible, this argument rests on a misunderstanding of the nature of depreciation allowances and, if literally followed, would lead to absurd conclusions. Depreciation allowances are intended to cover the cost of capital goods (usually measured on a historical basis but also measurable on the basis of estimated replacement cost). Depreciation is equal to the loss of earning capacity when the cost of a capital good equals the discounted present value of its expected future earnings, the normal situation in competitive equilibrium, but is greater or less than the loss of earning capacity when cost exceeds or falls short of the present value of expected future earnings. If an investor is fortunate enough to own a well-located building or an unusually productive piece of equipment, the depreciation allowances to which he is entitled may well be smaller than the loss of earning capacity during the year. The same is true of cost depletion for mineral deposits. On this basis, allowances would be designed to permit tax-free recovery of the cost of the deposit and working machinery, which would be substantially lower than the earning capacity of the property in the case of a lucky discovery. The opportunity of obtaining percentage depletion allowances in excess of costs actually incurred in acquiring and developing mineral properties is widely regarded as an inequitable feature of the U.S. income tax.

In principle, net income from personal effort should be calculated with an allowance for the amortization of the costs of education or other investments in earning capacity, but no deduction should be made for the exhaustion of earning capacity due to innate ability, luck, or opportunities acquired without cost. To grant the latter deduction would be as inequitable as percentage depletion[15] and would cost far more revenue. Indeed, an exactly computed allowance would virtually eliminate the taxation of earned income, for during the course of a year a person irretrievably loses whatever capacity he has to earn income during that year. Consider, as an illustration, the outlook on January 1 for an employee who faces compulsory retirement on December 31. He can look forward to one year's salary and to the disappearance over the twelve months of his expectation of receiving the salary; if he were allowed to treat the exhaustion of his earning capacity as a cost, the deduction would wipe out the salary—surely an absurd result.

Travel and Entertainment Expenses

Like educational expenditures, travel and entertainment expenses include both consumption and cost elements but have received far more liberal treatment under the income tax than educational expenditures. Deductions have been allowed for the costs of transportation, meals, and lodging while away from home on business trips, and business purposes have been broadly construed in deciding whether travel qualifies. Many kinds of expenditures for entertaining customers and clients, actual and prospective, have been ruled deductible, including expenses for meals, attendance at theaters and sporting events, club dues, the operation of hunting lodges and yachts. In the past, many gifts to business associates and customers

15. William Vickrey, *Agenda for Progressive Taxation* (Ronald Press, 1947), pp. 50–51.

were deductible, though not classified as taxable income of the recipients; however, deductions for gifts were limited by law in 1962.

Three kinds of tax avoidance have arisen. First, self-employed persons and officers of closely held corporations have deducted from taxable income outlays covering ordinary living expenses, vacations, and entertainment of personal friends. Second, employees have received nontaxable compensation in the form of travel and expense-account perquisites. Third, customers and clients and their employees have received nontaxable income in the form of entertainment and business gifts.

It is especially hard to determine whether travel and entertainment expenses are necessary business or professional costs and reasonable in amount. The question whether a particular trip or entertainment activity is required by business or professional considerations, though subject to some objective tests, is largely a matter of judgment. This is also true of the amount spent. Travel to conventions, entertainment for the purpose of creating goodwill, and other activities that are not intimately associated with ordinary business or professional transactions raise particularly close questions.

Most travel and entertainment expenses are for items that, unless for a business or professional purpose, would be classified as personal consumption. Even when the activity serves a business or professional purpose, the self-employed person or employee may receive personal benefits. For persons subject to high tax rates, there is a great advantage in treating personal expenses as deductible costs and hence a temptation to decide close questions in their own favor. The difficulty of auditing a claimed deduction is accentuated by the subjectivity of the distinction between necessary costs and personal consumption. Whether a trip to a resort area or attendance at a musical comedy is a pleasure or a duty depends on individual taste and the novelty of the experience. Luncheons that appear lavish to some may be routine for others.

Successive commissioners of internal revenue in the 1950s expressed concern about improper deductions for travel and entertainment, and special efforts were made to improve taxpayers' records and compliance and to examine these items. However, the administrative efforts were only partly successful owing to the unique character of travel and entertainment expenses, and by 1961 the Treasury Department had concluded that administrative measures were inadequate to cope with the problem.[16] The President called for legislation to limit the deductibility of entertainment expenses and business gifts, to establish fixed maximums for deductions for meals and the cost of food and lodging while traveling, and to require additional records for these items.[17]

Congress accepted the substance of the administration's recommendation on business gifts by including in the Revenue Act of 1962 a provision barring deductions for gifts in excess of $25 a year to any one individual (or husband and wife), but did not go nearly as far as recommended for other items. The act and regulations issued under it imposed some restrictions on the deduction of entertainment expenses and strengthened requirements for substantiation and record-keeping.

All deductions for travel and entertainment expenses are subject to the conditions that they be "ordinary and necessary" for carrying on a trade, business, or profession and not be "lavish or extravagant." These standards, together with some more specific statutory requirements, are insufficient in practice to prevent all improper deductions of travel and entertainment expenses. Since individual determinations of the propriety of claimed deductions are difficult, the most promising approach may be the denial of deductions for whole categories of entertainment expense and the establishment of maximum allowances for meals and lodging, as suggested by the Treasury Department in 1961. A narrower definition of business travel and more stringent provisions for allocating travel costs between business and personal purposes seem justifiable.

Admittedly, such rules would deny the deduction of some genuine costs of earning income and doubtless would seem harsh to many businessmen. However, the extent to which entertainment expenses are actually "ordinary and necessary" for any one firm greatly depends on the practices of its competitors. If the disallowance of deductions curtailed business entertainment generally, the effect on

16. U.S. Treasury Department, "Study on Entertainment Expenses," in *Revenue Act of 1962*, Hearings before the Senate Committee on Finance, 87 Cong. 2 sess. (1962), pt. 1, pp. 267–351, especially pp. 270–77. This study includes a review of administrative experience, an analysis of court decisions, and a compilation of comments in newspapers and magazines.

17. *President's Tax Message Along with Principal Statement, Detailed Explanation, and Supporting Exhibits and Documents*, H. Doc. 140, 87 Cong. 1 sess. (1961), pp. 10–11, 38–40, 198–207.

sales might be small. Finally, it should be recognized that the deduct-ibility issue relates to the definition of taxable income, not to the freedom to spend as one pleases, as some comments on past proposals seem to imply. The question is whether certain expenditures shall be met out of after-tax income or shall be deducted from gross income.

Conclusion

Although a net income tax should allow deductions for all costs of earning income, this principle is hard to apply because of the difficulty of distinguishing between costs and personal consumption. Among doubtful items, a strong case can be made for more liberal deductions for educational expenditures that increase earning capacity. A gen-eral allowance for the depreciation or depletion of earning capacity, however, cannot be justified by analogy with the assessment of busi-ness income.

Proposed deductions for commuting expenses and additional household and personal expenses of working wives would be unde-sirable because the expenditures seem to be predominantly consump-tion or a reflection of personal preferences in regard to living arrange-ments. Nevertheless, a small, special standard deduction for working wives or for all employed persons would be defensible in recognition of the existence of costs that cannot be accurately measured.

Present rules and procedures covering travel and entertainment expenses do not succeed in limiting deductions to necessary costs of earning income. Stricter standards are needed to check tax avoid-ance.

CHAPTER SIX

Exclusions from Taxable Income

WHEN NET INCOME is taxed, there is a presumption that all of its components should be taken into account in assessing the tax. This is not to say that all net income should actually be taxed; personal exemptions and certain personal deductions are quite proper. Rather the presumption is that the assessment should begin with a comprehensive definition of income. In technical language, adjusted gross income should be an inclusive aggregate.

The primary justification for a broad definition is that taxpaying capacity can be better measured by total net income than by the sum of certain of its components. When important items are excluded, statutory tax rates must be increased to raise the same amount of revenue. Since the omitted items are not evenly distributed, some people gain while others lose. The effects on true tax rates are not widely appreciated and often are hard to ascertain. Moreover, efforts to obtain nontaxed income lead to changes in the use of resources that may impair economic efficiency.

The exclusion of a particular item from taxable income, nevertheless, is justifiable when it serves an important social or economic purpose that could not be so well served by other means. Exclusions are also appropriate when they obviate excessive costs of administration and compliance.

In this study, an "exclusion" is an item that appears to constitute income as defined by Haig, Simons, and other scholars but which is omitted from adjusted gross income (AGI) as defined in the Internal Revenue Code.[1] The Haig-Simons definition, it will be recalled, equates personal income with the algebraic sum of consumption and changes in net worth.

The exclusions discussed in this chapter are known to be large, although the size of some of them cannot be closely estimated. In 1970, items included in personal income, as estimated by the Bureau of Economic Analysis of the Department of Commerce, but not in AGI equaled about one-fourth of AGI.[2] Reliable information is unavailable on items included in Haig-Simons income but not in personal income or AGI—gifts and inheritances, unrealized capital gains, and consumption treated as business costs.

Gifts and Inheritances

Receipts of gifts and inheritances fall within the Haig-Simons definition because they allow the recipients to consume more or to increase their net worth. These items are not included in taxable income in the United States, but special taxes are imposed on persons making certain gifts and on estates of deceased persons. Many states tax inheritances.

The Internal Revenue Code specifically excludes from AGI "the value of property acquired by gift, bequest, devise, or inheritance" (section 102) but does not define these terms. A rigorous definition of *gift* is hard to draw, since the essential distinction between gifts and other transfers turns on the intention of the parties. Generally, transfers made to discharge legal or moral obligations are not regarded as gifts; tips, bonuses, severance pay, and other voluntary pay-

1. Often the omitted items are referred to as tax-exempt income, but it is preferable to reserve the term "exemption" for the personal exemptions. In deference to long-established usage, however, interest on state and local government securities will be called tax-exempt income.

2. Estimated total AGI is $683 billion; items included in personal income but not in AGI total $173 billion (table A-6); however, $6.5 billion of the latter sum (fiduciary income not distributed to individuals and property income of nonprofit organizations) is not properly includable in individual income.

ments by employers to employees are included in taxable compensation. But business gifts to customers and prospective customers are not regarded as income to the recipients, though their cost is deductible by the giver, subject to a limit of $25 per recipient per year. Doubtful items are classified as gifts or income payments on a case-by-case basis.

Here I wish to consider neither the treatment of business gifts nor the niceties of definition but the treatment of transfers between family members or friends, which are generally acknowledged to be gifts.

Faithful to his general definition, Simons insisted that gifts, as well as bequests and inheritances, should be taxed as income to recipients. He also argued that, in general, gifts should be regarded as a form of consumption by donors and hence should not be deductible by them.[3] Only a few writers have followed Simons. A Canadian royal commission (the Carter Commission) recommended in 1966 that gifts received be included in taxable income,[4] but the government did not agree.

Contrary to the opinions of Simons and the Carter Commission, I believe that there are good reasons for continuing to exclude non-business gifts from AGI. Transfers between living persons—which the word "gift" is intended to mean in the present context—may be regarded in many cases as a sharing of the giver's income rather than the creation of new income. This characterization seems particularly appropriate for gifts to dependents or other close relatives, which must represent a large part of the total of such transfers. Many transfers of money and other property between close relatives seem essentially similar to benefits enjoyed from living in a common household, which is a clear case of income sharing.

Simons' contention that giving is a form of consumption is not persuasive. It seems more realistic to say that consumption is pooled for members of any one household and that gifts to persons who are not members of the household are voluntary transfers of consumption power. When A gives money to his married daughter, who promptly spends it to meet the expenses of her separate household, is total consumption greater than if A had kept the money and spent it himself?

3. Henry C. Simons, *Personal Income Taxation: The Definition of Income as a Problem of Fiscal Policy* (University of Chicago Press, 1938), pp. 125–47.

4. *Report of the Royal Commission on Taxation* (Ottawa: Queen's Printer, 1966), vol. 3, chap. 17, pp. 465–519.

Consumption is increased if A obtains a quid pro quo, but to ask whether he does is merely to repeat the question. If one concludes that most such cases represent sharing of income, there is still a choice between taxing the income to the donor or to the donee. Taxation to the donor seems preferable because, as Simons recognized, the alternative would undermine the progressivity of the income tax by allowing the rich to split income with relatives and others without transferring the corpus of their wealth.

Even if the principle of treating gifts as income to the recipient were conceded, the problem of administration would be difficult. It would be impracticable to include small items such as most Christmas and birthday presents and ordinary hospitality; valuation of gifts often would be difficult, and many problems would arise because the recipient of a gift often does not control its form, value, or timing. Consider, for example, the embarrassment of the impecunious young couple who had to choose between rejecting a costly portrait of a rich uncle and paying income tax on its value.

Transfers at death and large, nonrecurrent gifts or systematic transfers made by living persons over a period of time may be distinguished from other gifts. The tax system of the United States, like most other systems, reflects the view that these transfers are best regarded as the division of an income source, rather than the sharing of income. Estate, gift, and inheritance taxes have been specially devised to tax such transfers and seem better suited to the purpose than the income tax.

Selected Government Transfer Payments

An important and rapidly growing group of nontaxable items consists of government transfer payments for public assistance, veterans' benefits, unemployment insurance benefits, and old-age retirement, survivors', and disability benefits (table 6-1). From 1950 to 1970, these items grew more than twice as fast as the gross national product.

Public Assistance, Veterans' Benefits,
and Unemployment Insurance

Public assistance and the part of veterans' benefits that covers pensions for non-service-connected disability are payable only to persons

Table 6-1. Government Transfer Payments, Selected Programs, 1950, 1960, and 1970

Millions of dollars

Program	1950	1960	1970
Public assistance[a]	2,456	3,785	14,467
Veterans' benefits[b]	2,224	3,438	5,480
Unemployment insurance benefits[c]	1,468	3,025	4,173
Old-age retirement benefits[d]	828	8,790	22,188
Disability benefits[d,e]	77	715	3,286
Survivors' benefits[d,f]	321	2,517	7,852
Total	7,374	22,270	57,446

Sources: U.S. Bureau of the Census, *Statistical Abstract of the United States, 1963*, p. 286; ibid., *1973*, pp. 290, 308 (referred to in other tables in this chapter as *Statistical Abstract*, followed by the year).

a. Old-age assistance, medical assistance, aid to families with dependent children, aid to the blind, aid to the permanently and totally disabled, general assistance, and emergency assistance.

b. Retirement, disability, and monthly survivors' benefits paid by the Veterans Administration. Excludes lump-sum survivors' benefits and retirement and disability pay by Department of Defense.

c. State unemployment compensation, railroad unemployment benefits, federal employee program, and veterans' programs. Excludes training allowances.

d. Payments under old-age, survivors, disability, and health insurance (OASDHI) and railroad retirement.

e. Excludes temporary disability insurance under railroad retirement and state systems.

f. Monthly benefits; excludes lump-sum payments.

who qualify under a needs test. Public assistance has been provided by state and local governments, according to varying standards, with the aid of substantial federal grants. Beginning in 1974, assistance for the aged, the blind, and the permanently and totally disabled has been paid under a federal program according to nationally uniform standards for eligibility and amounts, which may be increased by state supplements. Other forms of public assistance continue to be a responsibility of state and local governments with differing eligibility requirements and amounts.

Veterans' benefits for service-connected disability or death and unemployment insurance are intended to compensate in part for loss of earnings, but payments are made without regard to the amount of income that beneficiaries may receive from property, their wealth, or the economic situation of other family members.[5] As an adjustment to presumed need, the veterans' benefits are varied according to the degree of disability and the number of dependents. Under most state unemployment compensation plans, benefits depend only on the worker's previous wage, subject to a rather low maximum, but in

5. Except for surviving parents of deceased veterans who qualify only if their income does not exceed specified levels. U.S. Department of Health, Education, and Welfare, Social Security Administration, *Social Security Programs in the United States* (1973), p. 126.

ten states and the District of Columbia dependency allowances are paid in addition to the basic benefit.[6]

There has been little public discussion of the merits of excluding from AGI public assistance, veterans' benefits, and unemployment insurance benefits. Perhaps most legislators and others who have considered the subject have felt that the tax immunity is obviously warranted because of the hardships suffered by the recipients and their need for aid. Scholars and official and unofficial groups who have examined the income-maintenance programs have not thought it necessary to defend the tax-free status of the transfer payments but have sometimes allowed for it in appraising their adequacy. Occasionally the assertion has been made that payments would have to be increased if they were subjected to income tax and that the main result would be merely to transfer money from one government account to another.

A few tax experts have argued that all transfer payments should be included in AGI.[7] They concede that the recipients may be needy by certain standards but contend that the personal exemptions set general standards for taxpaying ability under the income tax. Under present arrangements, many persons who receive the transfer payments, either throughout the year or for a shorter period, pay less tax than others with the same amount of income from wages or other taxable sources. This, the critics say, is inequitable. They suggest that, if the personal exemptions are considered too low, they should be increased for everyone. The critics argue, furthermore, that exclusions are an inefficient means of helping the needy whatever the level of the personal exemptions. The exclusions do not benefit those with the lowest incomes, who would not be liable for tax even if the transfer payments were counted as part of AGI, and are most advantageous to recipients who have enough income from other sources to use up their personal exemptions.

The great merit of this position is that it affords a general view of an area often seen only in detail and shows that provisions which may

---

6. As of January 1, 1973 (ibid., p. 61).

7. For example, Joseph A. Pechman, "What Would a Comprehensive Individual Income Tax Yield?" in *Tax Revision Compendium,* Papers Submitted to the House Committee on Ways and Means (1959), vol. 1, pp. 260–61; Melvin I. White, "Consistent Treatment of Items Excluded and Omitted from the Individual Income Tax Base," in ibid., pp. 319–20, 321, 326.

appear quite reasonable can result in inequities. Its major weakness is the questionable assumption that the personal exemptions under the income tax reflect a deliberate community decision concerning the socially acceptable minimum standard of living, and that the decision embodied in the tax law should override other standards.

My view is that the case is persuasive for excluding from taxable income payments made only on the basis of need as indicated by a means test; for the other payments, the case is much weaker. For veterans' benefits, however, the inclusion in AGI of compensation and pensions for service-connected disability would have the anomalous result of taxing some recipients who could pass the needs test and be eligible for non-service-connected disability benefits. On the whole, it seems better to continue the exclusion for all veterans' benefits. Since the tax-free minimum income level has been increased substantially in recent years by raising exemptions and instituting the low-income allowance, it seems justifiable to end tax immunity for unemployment compensation benefits.

Social Security and Railroad Retirement

By 1970, old-age, survivors, disability, and health insurance (OASDHI) and the railroad retirement system covered almost 90 percent of all employed persons, including the self-employed, and their dependents.[8] Benefits are financed by contributions of employees, employers, and the self-employed and by interest on accumulated trust funds.

All benefit payments under OASDHI and railroad retirement are excluded from AGI. The exclusion of OASDHI benefits was granted by administrative ruling[9] in 1941 and has never been confirmed by statute, not even when the Internal Revenue Code was rewritten in 1954. Railroad retirement benefits are excluded by the Railroad Retirement Act of 1937.[10]

Both OASDHI and railroad retirement benefits are paid to eligible persons without demonstration of individual need, and the system is

8. U.S. Bureau of the Census, *Statistical Abstract of the United States, 1973*, p. 291 (hereafter *Statistical Abstract,* followed by the year).

9. I.T. (income tax ruling) 3447, 1941-1 C.B. (*Internal Revenue Cumulative Bulletin*) 191; see also Revenue Ruling 70-217, 1970-1 C.B. 12; Rev. Rul. 70-341, 1970-2 C.B. 31.

10. 50 Stat. 316, 45 U.S.C. 228*l*.

not confined to low-income groups. The broad coverage and contributions by workers sharply distinguish OASDHI from old-age assistance and other income-maintenance programs.

Often OASDHI and railroad retirement benefits are spoken of as earned benefits and compared with private pensions and annuities. There are, however, important differences. Workers do not have property rights in social security benefits, and Congress may reduce or withdraw benefits at any time.[11] The benefit formulas give preferential treatment to workers who were already employed when the system was adopted or extended and to low-paid workers. Benefits are paid for dependents and survivors, although contribution rates and primary benefits do not vary with the number of dependents of the covered worker. Self-employed persons receive the same benefits as employed persons, although their contribution rate is in general only three-fourths of the combined rate paid by employees and employers. Finally, benefits are reduced or denied to persons over the retirement age but under seventy-two who earn more than a certain amount.

The omission of social insurance benefits from taxable income cannot be justified on the same grounds as the exclusion of the transfer payments discussed in the preceding section, and the existence of an inequity has been widely recognized. Congress attempted to mitigate the discrimination in 1954 by introducing a credit for persons receiving retirement income from sources other than OASDHI and railroad retirement, but this is an unsatisfactory solution, and ending the exclusion of OASDHI and railroad retirement benefits has been suggested.

It would be unfair to include all social insurance benefits in AGI because a substantial part of the benefits represents the return of the earlier contribution of the covered worker, which was included in his AGI when the contribution was made. This situation exists also under private pension plans, and an obvious possibility would be to treat OASDHI and railroad retirement like the private plans. The rule for the private plans is that a retired person is allowed to recover his

---

11. *Flemming* v. *Nestor,* 363 U.S. 603 (1960). This was a five-to-four decision of the Supreme Court; however, it appears that only two of the dissenters (Justices Hugo L. Black and William O. Douglas) disagreed with the majority concerning the nature of the right to social security benefits.

aggregate contributions free of tax over the period of his life expectancy and is required to include the remainder of benefits in AGI.

There would be technical difficulties, however, in applying the general rule for private pensions to social insurance benefits owing to the lack of vested property rights in social insurance benefits and the failure to follow actuarial principles. At the date of retirement, for example, it is not possible to determine the actuarial value of expected social insurance benefits in the same way that the value of a private pension can be calculated because the social insurance beneficiary may be disqualified if his earnings exceed the allowable minimum and because the amount of his benefits will depend on the number of his dependents. It would be possible, though cumbersome, to require each retired person to amortize his individual contributions over his life expectancy.

A more serious objection is that the application of the rule for private pensions would achieve results that seem to conflict with the priorities that govern the benefit formulas. The proportion of benefits to be included in AGI would be highest for those who are most favored under the benefit formulas, that is, for those whose contributions pay for the smallest fraction of their benefits. Thus, the fraction of benefits included in AGI would be relatively large for low-paid workers and those with several dependents and relatively small for high-paid workers and those with no dependents. While these results are defensible from the standpoint of income theory, they are questionable from the viewpoint of probable need.

A more acceptable rule, which has been suggested, would be to require that recipients of pensions from OASDHI or railroad retirement insurance include one-half of their benefits in AGI. The fraction one-half is plausible because employee and employer contributions are equal, but this justification is superficial because of wide variations in the relation between benefits and contributions and because of interest accruals on the trust funds. The merit of a uniform fraction is its simplicity. Insured persons with high earnings would be treated less favorably for taxation, as well as for benefits, than lower-paid persons; however, under present OASDHI benefit formulas and scheduled contribution rates, a factor of one-half would not require even the most highly paid persons to include more in AGI than they would if social insurance old-age benefits were treated like a private pension.[12] One reason for the liberal results with a factor of one-half is the failure to allow for interest accruals. Another and more important reason is the periodic improvement of benefits—by legislation and, in the future, by operation of an automatic adjustment for inflation—relative to the past earnings history of covered workers and retired persons.

The discrimination in favor of social insurance beneficiaries is much less for disability and survivorship benefits than for old-age retirement benefits. Provisions governing the taxation of disability and survivorship benefits under private plans are complex, but generally more lenient than those applicable to retirement annuities. Disability benefits in many cases may be excluded from AGI as workmen's compensation or health and accident insurance benefits or as sick pay. Life insurance proceeds, under either group term policies or individual policies, which are paid by reason of the death of the insured, are excludable. Part of the death benefits paid under private pension and profit-sharing plans also qualify for this exclusion. However, when a retired person dies after his pension has begun and payments are continued to his spouse or other survivor, the receipts are includable in AGI to the same extent that the annuity was during the lifetime of the retired worker.[13]

Unless the provisions governing benefits under private plans are changed, it would be unfair to apply the one-half-inclusion rule to disability and survivorship benefits under the social insurance programs. Application of the rule only to old-age retirement benefits would have increased AGI by $11.1 billion in 1970; application to

12. To verify this point, computations were made on the following assumptions: (1) the benefit formula and tax provisions of 1974 continue unchanged (with allowance for a scheduled increase in the year 2011 of the contribution rate payable by employees but without allowance for inflation-adjustment increases of taxable earnings and benefits); and (2) the person works continuously in covered employment from 1974 to 2018, receiving each year the maximum taxable earnings ($13,200), and then retires at the age of sixty-five. Application of the same rule as for private annuities would allow a retired male with this earnings history to exclude from AGI 36 percent of social security retirement benefits if he had worked as an employee or 49 percent if he had worked as a self-employed person (and paid the higher contribution rate of the self-employed). The exclusion ratios would be lower for women because their life expectancy is greater and lower for persons retiring with dependents because their annual benefits would be larger relative to past contributions.

13. *Code of Federal Regulations*, Title 26, pt. 1 (1975), secs 1.72-2, 1.402(a)(1).

disability benefits as well would have raised the figure to $12.7 billion. (See table 6-1.)

An alternative approach would be to allow employees and the self-employed to deduct their social insurance contributions from taxable income and to include all social insurance benefits in AGI when received. This seems inferior to the present rule and to the alternative of partial inclusion of benefits with no deduction of contributions. The deduction of social insurance contributions would be used as an argument for allowing deduction of contributions under private plans and perhaps of other forms of saving. Since persons over sixty-five now enjoy extra personal exemptions and are likely to be subject to lower marginal tax rates after retirement than during their working years, the inclusion of all benefits in AGI would not make up for the deduction of contributions. Some beneficiaries, nevertheless, might find it inconvenient to be required to include the full amount received in AGI after retirement.

If a satisfactory method of taxing OASDHI and railroad retirement benefits were adopted, elimination of the retirement income credit, which was adopted in 1954 to alleviate discrimination against recipients of taxable pensions, would be fully justified. The credit is a complex measure which has partly accomplished its purpose, but it does not touch the broader inequities in the treatment of retired persons.

Workmen's Compensation, Health Insurance, and Sick Pay

Also excluded from AGI are several kinds of payments received as compensation for loss of income because of sickness or injury. These items are: (1) workmen's compensation benefits, which arise from work-related injuries; (2) amounts received by an individual under an accident or health insurance policy that he himself purchased; (3) amounts received by an employee under an accident or health insurance plan to the extent that the plan is supported by employee contributions; and (4) certain "sick pay" under employer-financed plans. Statistics on these items appear in table 6-2.

Workmen's compensation payments are stipulated by law rather than being the choice of the employer. Sick pay is much broader. It consists of amounts received from an employer as wages or pay-

Table 6-2. Selected Health and Welfare Benefits, 1950, 1960, and 1970
Millions of dollars

Benefit	*1950*	*1960*	*1970*
Workmen's compensation: disability	360	755	1,664
Workmen's compensation: survivor	55	105	205
Cash sickness benefits under group and public plans	294	810	1,854
Individual health insurance[a]	153	393	694
Excludable sick pay[b]	...	675	768
Total[b]	862	2,738	5,185

Sources: *Statistical Abstract, 1973*, pp. 302, 306; U.S. Internal Revenue Service, *Statistics of Income— 1960, Individual Income Tax Returns*, p. 4, and *1970*, p. 17.
a. Income-maintenance payments only; does not include reimbursement of medical expenses.
b. There is an unknown amount of double counting in the total since part of cash sickness benefits under group plans and public plans qualify as excludable sick pay.

ments in lieu of wages while absent from work because of any injury or illness. The part of sick pay that is excludable from AGI is determined by rather complex rules. If sick pay is more than 75 percent of regular wages, no exclusion is allowed for the first thirty calendar days of absence; thereafter, sick pay up to $100 a week may be excluded. If, however, sick pay is less than 75 percent of regular wages, the employee may exclude up to $75 a week, from the first day of absence if he is hospitalized for at least one day, or after seven days of absence if he is not hospitalized. After thirty days the ceiling rises to $100 a week. As noted above, the sick-pay exclusion applies to disability pensions as well as to payments received during short-term illness.

The sick-pay exclusion is questionable. Generally, those who receive sick pay are better protected against economic loss from temporary disability than those who are not covered by such plans. In some cases the provision allows a person to receive more take-home pay while he is absent from work than when he is working. In evaluating the sick-pay exclusion, it is necessary to remember that persons who are absent from work save on work-related expenses and benefit from the personal deduction for medical expenses.

Cash benefits under health insurance are excluded from AGI only when they are paid for by the beneficiaries. It would be unfair to include the benefits in AGI unless a deduction were allowed for premium payment. While that approach has a certain appeal,[14] it would

14. William Vickrey, *Agenda for Progressive Taxation* (Ronald Press, 1947), p. 63.

have the questionable result of increasing insured persons' income tax liability in years in which they were sick or injured relative to their tax in other years. The total tax base would be decreased, since aggregate insurance benefits fall short of premiums by a wide margin representing company expenses, taxes, and profits.[15]

Private and Government-Employee Retirement Plans

The treatment of private pension plans and plans for civilian government employees and career military personnel raises a question of income timing. The subject is considered here because it is related to the taxation of social insurance benefits and because timing of taxable income may be regarded as a matter of exclusion or inclusion in AGI in any one year.

Under most plans, employees are not taxable until they receive pensions or other benefits. Beneficiaries include in AGI all of the pension except the part that represents the return of any contribution that they have made toward the financing. Thus employer contributions and interest earned on pension reserves are taxable to beneficiaries when received as retirement income rather than when added to pension funds. Benefits from plans financed jointly by employers and employees are divided between the excludable contribution of the employee and the taxable remainder on the basis of actuarial calculations which allow recovery of the employee's contribution over the period of his life expectancy.[16]

If a pension or profit-sharing plan covers a large proportion of employees, is nondiscriminatory, provides for minimum vested, or nonforfeitable, rights to employees, and meets certain other requirements, it is a "qualified" plan and is exempt from income tax on the

---

15. In the decade 1952–61, premiums on individual income-replacement insurance policies exceeded benefit payments by $3.3 billion, or 110 percent. Alfred M. Skolnik, "Income-Loss Protection Against Short-Term Sickness 1948–61," *Social Security Bulletin*, vol. 26 (January 1963), p. 12.

16. If the amount that the retired employee will receive during the first three years in which payments are made exceeds his total contribution, the life-expectancy rule does not apply; in that case, all receipts are excludable until the full amount of the employee's contribution is recovered, and thereafter all receipts are includable in AGI. In 1970, 64 percent of all persons reporting income from contributory pensions and annuities used the three-year rule. *Statistics of Income—1970, Individual Income Tax Returns*, pp. 88–89.

return earned on its reserves. Employers may deduct from taxable income their contributions to qualified plans but can deduct contributions to other plans only if employees' benefit rights are fully vested at the time of the contribution. Since employees having vested rights under a nonqualified plan are currently taxable on their employer's contributions, nonqualified plans have tax disadvantages for either the employer or employees.

Benefit payments under private plans and public-employee plans grew at the rapid rate of 14.2 percent a year between 1960 and 1970 but were still smaller than social insurance retirement benefits in 1970 (tables 6-1 and 6-3). Partly because the plans were expanding so rapidly, employer contributions to private pension funds were much greater than current benefits.

Those who question the present rule about the timing of income from pension and profit-sharing plans argue that the plans provide supplementary compensation for employees that should be reflected in AGI before the date of retirement. Everyone would agree that if an employer deposited part of an employee's salary to his credit in a

Table 6-3. Benefit Payments under Public and Private Retirement Plans, and Contributions under Private Plans, 1950, 1960, and 1970[a]

Millions of dollars

Type of program	1950	1960	1970
Benefit payments			
Private plans[b]	370	1,720	7,360
Federal government plans			
Civilian[c]	485	1,582	6,051
Military[d]	219	693	2,853
State and local government plans[e]	300	1,015	3,135
Total benefits	1,374	5,010	19,399
Contributions			
Private plans			
Employer	1,750	4,710	12,580
Employee	330	780	1,420

Sources: Military, 1950, *Retirement Policy for Federal Personnel*, S. Doc. 89, 83 Cong. 2 sess. (1954), pt. 2, pp. 66–67; 1960, *The Budget of the United States Government for the Fiscal Year Ending June 30, 1962*, p. 498; 1970, *The Budget ... 1972, Appendix*, p. 288; all other, *Statistical Abstract, 1963*, pp. 286, 295, and *1973*, pp. 290, 298.

  a. Includes retirement, disability, and survivor benefit plans.

  b. Includes refunds to employees and their survivors and lump sums under deferred profit-sharing plans.

  c. Excludes lump-sum payments.

  d. For fiscal years ended June 30; payments by Department of Defense in 1960 and 1970 and by Army, Navy, Air Force, and Marine Corps in 1950; excludes pensions paid by Veterans Administration.

savings account, where it remained until the employee retired, this would not be a sufficient reason for omitting that part of the salary from current taxable income. The situation is not so simple when the deposits are placed with a trustee or insurance company under a formal retirement plan, but in some respects these plans are similar to savings accounts.

Postponement of taxation is advantageous to employees in two ways. First, deferment allows interest to accrue on money that otherwise would have been paid in taxes. To illustrate, suppose $100 is deposited each year in a fund earning 5 percent, compounded annually. At the end of forty years, the amount accumulated will be $12,080. Taxed at the rate of 25 percent, it will be reduced to $9,060. Alternatively, suppose a 25 percent tax is deducted annually from the deposit and the interest earnings. Then the accumulated amount after forty years will total only $6,722, one-fourth less than the net amount when tax is deferred. Second, employees are likely to have smaller incomes after they retire than while they are working, and hence to be subject to a lower marginal tax rate.

The tax advantages of private pension plans are widely appreciated, not only by highly paid executives but also by labor unions. Tax considerations may well have had something to do with the rapid growth of such plans. Self-employed persons long contended that they were being discriminated against, and they finally persuaded Congress in 1962 to extend to them some of the deferment privileges enjoyed by those who are covered by pension plans. Tax-deferred individual retirement savings plans were sanctioned in 1974 for persons with earned income not covered by an employer plan or a plan for the self-employed.

A possible alternative to present rules would be to require that employees include employer contributions and interest earned on pension reserves in AGI and to allow them to exclude pensions received. This seems fair and feasible with respect to employees' vested rights to future benefits but much less reasonable with respect to rights that are not vested. Although the expectation of benefits is worth something in the latter case, it cannot be valued with the precision that is usually demanded for tax purposes. Until 1974, qualified plans usually were not required to provide vested rights to employees before the normal retirement age, and many of them did not do so. Legislation enacted in 1974 prescribes either full vesting after ten years of service or graduated vesting over a period of years beginning after five years of service.[17]

Despite its appeal as an improvement in the measurement of taxable income, a requirement that employees include in current AGI employer contributions and interest accruals pertaining to vested benefit rights—but not other contributions and interest accruals—could result in arbitrary distinctions where the difference between vested and nonvested rights is more formal than real. It might also discourage the introduction of more liberal vesting provisions. This would be an undesirable side effect since vesting reduces an impediment to labor mobility.

Judged strictly, the present method of taxing pensions is inequitable. Congress tacitly recognized this in 1974 but reacted as it has in other cases: it attempted to balance the advantages of tax deferral enjoyed by those covered by employer pension and profit-sharing plans by liberalizing and extending deferral benefits for others (see below). The result is not likely to prove satisfactory for long, and the question whether tax deferral for retirement saving should be narrowed or broadened will have to be debated further.

Retirement Savings of the Self-Employed and Other Individuals

Persons not covered by employer pension plans may obtain certain tax postponement benefits under retirement plans for the self-employed or individual retirement savings plans. The Self-Employed Individuals Tax Retirement Act of 1962 allows self-employed persons to set up retirement plans and to deduct from current income their contributions. The deducted contributions and accumulated interest are includable in AGI when received later as distributions from the retirement plan.

Almost all self-employed business or professional individuals and partners are eligible, provided they perform personal services. Any full-time employees with three years or more of service must also be covered on a nondiscriminatory basis and, in general, contributions made on their behalf must be vested.

17. The Employee Retirement Income Security Act of 1974 (P.L. 93-406) requires that a qualified plan meet one of three minimum vesting schedules.

After the 1974 liberalization, the limit on contributions by a self-employed person on his own behalf is $7,500 a year or 15 percent of earned income, whichever is less.[18] Contributions must be set aside in a separate fund, which cannot be intermingled with other resources of the self-employed person; however, he may control the investment of the fund. Benefit payments may not begin before the age of fifty-nine and a half, except in cases of disability or death, or later than seventy and a half; penalties are prescribed for premature distribution. Benefits received in the form of annuities are subject to the general rules applicable to annuities or pensions, which in this case allow the beneficiary to recover tax-free the portion of his contributions that he did not previously deduct from taxable income and which require him to include in AGI benefits representing previously deducted contributions and earnings of the fund. When a lump-sum distribution is made in a single year, the income tax is limited to five times the increase in liability resulting from including one-fifth of the distribution in AGI in the year in which it occurs.

The 1962 act, approved after proposals had been pending in Congress for ten years, was adopted because officials and legislators recognized that there was indefensible discrimination against self-employed persons. Moreover, the discrimination applied erratically. Business proprietors could qualify for pension plans by incorporating their businesses and putting themselves on salaries, but professional persons often were barred from this course because they could not incorporate under state laws. Many state laws were amended to allow professional persons to incorporate so that they could set up pension plans qualifying under the old law. The provisions for the self-employed as originally enacted were much narrower than had been proposed and were liberalized effective in 1968 and again in a 1974 act.

The Employee Retirement Income Security Act of 1974 authorized a new form of individual retirement savings account effective as of 1975. Persons not covered by either an employer plan or a self-employed individuals' retirement plan may set up an individual retirement account and make tax-deductible contributions to it equal to 15

18. Earned income includes professional fees and other compensation for personal services. It also includes gains of authors, composers, and inventors from the sale of their works. Where both personal services and capital are material income-producing factors, the full net profits are treated as earned income.

percent of their compensation or earned income, up to a maximum of $1,500 a year. (Contributions may be deducted from gross income regardless of whether the individual itemizes personal deductions or elects the standard deduction.) The account may be funded by organizing it as a domestic trust, with a bank as trustee. Alternative possibilities include the purchase of an individual annuity contract from a life insurance company and investment in special U.S. bonds. The return obtained from the accumulated fund is not currently taxed. As with plans of the self-employed, distribution must begin between the ages of fifty-nine and a half and seventy and a half. Tax-free changes in the form of investment of the accumulations in the account ("rollovers") may be made, subject to certain conditions.

Although both the 1962 plan for the self-employed and the 1974 addition are called "retirement" plans, beneficiaries are not required to retire from employment. In this respect the legal position is the same as that of employer-financed pension plans, which are not subject to a statutory provision limiting their benefits to persons who have actually retired. In practice, however, the employer plans ordinarily pay benefits only after retirement.

The plans for the self-employed and other individuals do lessen discrimination against them as compared with beneficiaries of qualified employer pension and profit-sharing plans. However, a closer approach to equality of treatment is desirable, either by limiting the extent of tax deferral under employer plans or by widening tax deferral possibilities under individual plans. The former method would be more consistent with income tax principles, though it appears to be less attractive to Congress.

Fringe Benefits

Many employees receive fringe benefits, such as life insurance coverage and hospitalization and medical insurance, that are economically equivalent to supplementary compensation. They also may benefit from amenities, such as air conditioning and recorded music, that are generally considered incidental conditions of employment, rather than compensation, even when designed to attract workers. Less easily classified are discounts on merchandise, meals and living quarters provided free or at less than market prices, parking spaces, company recreational facilities, liberal travel and expense allowances, special clothing, and insurance against occupational hazards. Other items that are often called fringe benefits, such as paid vacations and holidays and bonuses, raise no special tax problem because for tax purposes they are treated as salaries and wages.

Contributions of employers in the private nonfarm sector for life, accident, and health insurance plans in 1970 may be estimated at approximately $12.3 billion.[19] Comprehensive information is not available on the value of other fringe benefits.

The general rule now is that an employee receives income for tax purposes when his employer pays any of his "personal expenses." But there are major exceptions to this rule, and it seems likely that most fringe benefits are not included in AGI.[20] Specifically excluded are premiums paid by employers under group term life insurance policies for individual coverage up to $50,000;[21] premiums for medical and hospitalization insurance; and the value of meals and lodging furnished on the employer's business premises for the convenience of the employer, provided the employee is required to accept the lodging as a condition of employment. Also excluded in practice are "courtesy" discounts when relatively small in amount and the value of most of the services under employee recreation and welfare plans.

The tax-free status of fringe benefits encourages this form of compensation. Employees and employers may be led to prefer a form of compensation and a consumption pattern different from those they would choose if the income tax applied equally to all compensation. For example, an employee who is subject to a 20 percent marginal rate of income tax would rationally prefer tax-free insurance coverage worth only $81 to him to an additional $100 of taxable salary. Economists classify such modifications of individual preferences as

19. According to a sample survey by the U.S. Bureau of Labor Statistics, these contributions equaled 2.9 percent of wages and salaries in this sector (calculated from *Statistical Abstract, 1973,* p. 246); total wages and salaries in this sector are estimated at $423.4 billion by the Bureau of Economic Analysis, U.S. Department of Commerce, in *Survey of Current Business,* vol. 53 (July 1973), table 6.2, p. 41.

20. For critical reviews and suggestions, see Joseph H. Guttentag, E. Deane Leonard, and William Y. Rodewald, "Federal Income Taxation of Fringe Benefits: A Specific Proposal," *National Tax Journal,* vol. 6 (September 1953), pp. 250–72, and Hugh H. Macaulay, Jr., *Fringe Benefits and Their Federal Tax Treatment* (Columbia University Press, 1959).

21. Group term life insurance has no current cash surrender value; employees are taxable on employer payments of premiums of other life insurance when the proceeds of the policy are payable to the employee's estate or beneficiary.

distortions which result in a loss of economic efficiency, unless the tax-induced change reflects an overriding social preference.

Support for the exclusion of employer contributions for group life insurance and for hospitalization and medical insurance can be mustered on the basis of the public interest in the promotion of family security and good health. But is it clear that the insurance plans merit just the degree of encouragement that is provided by the exclusion? Protection can be provided by individual insurance as well as group insurance and by other means. The health insurance plans rarely cover the cost of ordinary preventive care, much less the cost of good nutrition and other items that contribute to health. The group plans often do not cover retired workers and, of course, do not extend to the self-employed.

In my judgment, the advantages of economic neutrality and tax equity are great enough to justify the termination of the exclusion of employer contributions for life insurance coverage and insurance against hospital and medical expenses. The best general rule, in my opinion, would be to include the contributions in current taxable salaries and wages but to continue to exclude benefit payments from employees' AGI. While compliance would be somewhat inconvenient for employers, they could allocate their contributions among employees on the basis of standard tables (similar to those provided by the Revenue Act of 1964 for life insurance policies of more than $50,000). When the amount allocable to an individual fell below a certain minimum, it might be appropriate to continue the exclusion.[22]

The inclusion in AGI of fringe benefits in the form of discounts on purchases and participation in welfare and recreation programs would involve acute difficulties of valuation and verification of compliance. Probably not much can be done to improve the present situation, in which the Internal Revenue Service has the right to assess tax when the amounts involved are important but does not attempt to take account of minor sums.

For meals and lodging, the convenience-of-the-employer and business-premises tests do not adequately distinguish compensation from

22. It appears that the amounts to be allocated to individual employees would be small in most cases but not trivial. The average amount of employer contributions in 1970 was a little over $200 per employee in the private nonfarm sector, computed from the estimate of $12.3 billion of total contributions given above and the average number of full-time and part-time employees in this sector from *Survey of Current Business* (July 1973), p. 41.

incidental conditions of employment. Like incidental conditions of employment, meals and lodging affect the attractiveness of a job; however, they seem to be a more direct substitute for ordinary compensation because they consist of goods and services that employees would often buy for themselves and because the consumption of individual employees can be measured, which is not generally true of incidental conditions of employment. Where the value of meals and lodging is significant, it could appropriately be included in AGI, conservatively appraised to allow for the lack of free choice. Any extra costs arising from a remote location or other unusual conditions should be omitted on the ground that they are special costs of employment. It seems expedient to continue to overlook minor amounts of compensation in the form of subsidized meals in company cafeterias and dining rooms.

Work clothes provided by employers ordinarily involve elements of compensation—because they relieve employees of expenses even when the clothes are used only on the job—but also substitute for costs that would otherwise be deductible by the employees. The amounts of compensation appear to be small enough in most cases to justify overlooking them for income tax purposes.

Imputed Rent of Owner-Occupied Dwellings

A person who resides in his own house or apartment obtains an income in the form of consumer services. This imputed return is classified as personal income in national income and product accounts, and individuals often recognize that homeownership is an alternative to other income-yielding investments.[23]

Homeowners are often puzzled by economists' assertions that they derive an income from their houses; these owners look on their houses as a source of expense rather than income. They are right in insisting that homeownership entails expense, but they overlook the fact that part of their shelter cost is covered by the imputed return on their equity. A homeowner is an investor who takes his return in the form of services. If he wishes, he can convert his imputed return to cash by moving and renting his house.

23. For a more detailed treatment, see my paper "Imputed Rent of Owner-Occupied Dwellings Under the Income Tax," *Journal of Finance,* vol. 15 (December 1960), pp. 504–30.

Imputed rent of owner-occupied dwellings is taxable in a number of countries, but is not included in AGI in the United States. The United Kingdom taxed imputed rent from the beginning of the income tax early in the nineteenth century but allowed the provision to become ineffective after World War II, owing to obsolete assessments, and dropped it in 1963.[24]

Under a net income tax, the item to be included in income would be imputed net rent, defined as gross rental value minus necessary expenses of ownership. The expenses consist of interest on mortgage debt, property taxes, depreciation, repairs and maintenance, and casualty insurance. Homeowners may now deduct interest and taxes, even though imputed rent is not included in AGI. The taxation of imputed net rent, therefore, would involve an addition to taxable income equal to gross rent minus expenses other than interest and taxes. This increase in the tax base would equal the sum of imputed net rent and the personal deductions now allowed for mortgage interest and property taxes on owner-occupied dwellings. Merely to increase the tax base by the amount of net rent would imply double deductions for interest and property taxes, one set in the form of the personal deductions now granted and a second set in the computation of net rent.

Estimates of imputed net rent, mortgage interest, and property taxes in selected years appear in table 6-4. These items have been growing rapidly. From 1950 to 1970 their annual rate of increase was 9.4 percent, while the growth rate of total personal outlays was 6.1 percent (in current prices).

The omission of imputed net rent from AGI and the personal deductions for mortgage interest and property taxes discriminate in favor of homeowners compared with renters and with other investors. Homeowners obtain a tax-free return on their investment and at the same time are allowed to deduct important items of housing costs that tenants also pay as part of their rent but without obtaining a tax deduction.

---

24. In April 1962, Selwyn Lloyd, then Chancellor of the Exchequer, announced the intention of making the change, mentioning the great increase in tax that would occur when pending revaluations of properties were completed and terming imputed rent "notional income." *The Economist* (London) characterized Mr. Lloyd's statement as "near double talk" (vol. 203, April 14, 1962, p. 168). In 1955, the Royal Commission on the Taxation of Profits and Income had supported the continued taxation of imputed rent. See its *Final Report,* Cmd. 9474 (London: Her Majesty's Stationery Office, 1955), pp. 249–51.

Table 6-4. Imputed Net Rent, Mortgage Interest, and Property Taxes on Owner-Occupied Nonfarm Dwellings, 1950, 1960, and 1970

Billions of dollars

Item	1950	1960	1970
Imputed net rent	3.9	8.9	13.9
Mortgage interest	1.6	6.5	16.9
Property taxes	1.7	5.4	12.6
Total	7.2	20.8	43.4

Sources: U.S. Department of Commerce, *The National Income and Product Accounts of the United States, 1929–1965: Statistical Tables* (1966), pp. 152–53; Department of Commerce, *Survey of Current Business,* vol. 53 (July 1973), p. 47.

The size of the discrimination is substantial. In 1970, net rent, mortgage interest, and property taxes amounted to 73 percent of the gross rental value of owner-occupied nonfarm dwellings.[25] The aggregate tax saving equaled about 15 percent of homeowners' housing costs, but it differed widely among families. The saving rises with income and tax rates. At the $50,000 income level, it amounts to about one-third of housing costs for a married couple, and at the maximum it covers half or more of these costs.

According to a study by Aaron, about half of the total tax benefits in 1966 accrued to families with incomes between $7,000 and $15,000 though the benefits were relatively greater in higher income brackets.[26] Treasury Department estimates for 1971 indicate that tax benefits from homeownership were concentrated to a greater extent above the $15,000 income level,[27] reflecting, at least in part, rising incomes and changes in the standard deduction. These figures demonstrate that the exclusion and deductions reduce the progressivity of the income tax.

If imputed net rent had been taxable in 1970, the federal income tax liabilities of owner-occupants of nonfarm dwellings would have been increased by roughly $8.9 billion—$3.2 billion of tax on imputed net rent proper and $5.7 billion from eliminating the personal deductions for mortgage interest and property taxes.[28]

25. *Survey of Current Business* (July 1973), p. 47.

26. Henry J. Aaron, *Shelter and Subsidies: Who Benefits from Federal Housing Policies?* (Brookings Institution, 1972), pp. 58, 223, 224.

27. See table A-13.

28. The estimates for the elimination of the deductions are by the U.S. Treasury Department: *General Tax Reform,* panel discussions before the House Committee on Ways and Means, 93 Cong. 1 sess. (1973), pt. 1, p. 29. The estimate for imputed net rent proper was made by applying to it the mean marginal tax rate implied in the Treasury Department estimate for the property tax deduction, 23.0 percent.

The tax saving resulting from the exclusion and deductions may be viewed as a reduction in the effective price of housing services or— looked at from another angle—as an increase in the rate of return on owner-occupants' investment in their houses. This is fully valid, however, only if, as implicitly assumed above, the existence of the tax benefits has no effect on the market price of houses and on rents. I shall return to this important point shortly.

The influence on the consumption of housing services depends on the elasticity of demand with respect to price. Statistical estimates of elasticity differ considerably, but a value on the order of -1 appears plausible.[29] This means that a small percentage reduction in price will be accompanied by an equal percentage increase in the quantity consumed. If this is correct (and any effect on the market price of houses is not taken into account), the income tax advantages of homeowners were responsible for additional consumption of housing services of about $9 billion in 1970, or about 10 percent of the total housing consumption of homeowners and tenants.[30] Presumably the effect is greatest for higher-priced units, which are likely to be occupied by the persons who gain most from the exclusion and personal deductions.

The income tax probably has more influence on the choice between homeowning and renting than on the total amount of housing services consumed. The price difference that will induce a shift from renting to owning is doubtless much smaller than that required to divert expenditure from other goods and services to housing. There was a sharp increase in homeownership between 1940 and 1960, from 44 percent of all units to 62 percent, but in the next decade the fraction of owner-occupied units grew only slightly, to 63 percent.[31] Nontax factors must have been important in the trend toward homeownership after World War II. Among these were the rise in real

29. Richard F. Muth, "The Demand for Non-Farm Housing," in Arnold C. Harberger, ed., *The Demand for Durable Goods* (University of Chicago Press, 1960), pp. 29–96; Margaret G. Reid, *Housing and Income* (University of Chicago Press, 1962), p. 381; Frank de Leeuw, "The Demand for Housing: A Review of Cross-Section Evidence," *Review of Economics and Statistics,* vol. 53 (February 1971), pp. 8–9; Sherman J. Maisel, James B. Burnham, and John S. Austin, "The Demand for Housing: A Comment," *Review of Economics and Statistics,* vol. 53 (November 1971), pp. 410–13.

30. Derived from *Survey of Current Business* (July 1973), table 2.5, p. 29.

31. *Statistical Abstract, 1973,* p. 689.

income, the movement to the suburbs, the increased availability of mortgage loans, and the gains realizable by debtors in a period of inflation.

As noted above, the analysis has been based on the assumption that preferential treatment of owner-occupied dwellings under the income tax has no effect on the market price of houses and market rents. If the stock of houses suitable for owner occupancy were fixed or if it could be increased only at sharply rising unit costs, this assumption would be unrealistic; in these circumstances, the price of the houses could be expected to rise and to offset part of the income tax advantages. But units can be converted from rental to owner occupancy and additional units can be constructed. While in the short run the construction industry probably is subject to steeply rising unit costs, there seems no reason to suppose that this is true over a period of several years. Some rise in site values might occur as a consequence of increased demand for housing and the amounts of land required for owner-occupied units. This reasoning suggests that any price increases resulting from the preferential income tax treatment should be transitory or small.

Although there is no direct evidence on the influence of the income tax provisions on the market price of houses, indirect evidence can be obtained by examining the imputed rate of return on homeowners' equity. This return appears to be consistently and surprisingly low. According to my estimates, the average rate of return on owner-occupants' equity in nonfarm dwellings was 3.3 percent in 1950–51, 3.7 percent in 1956–57, 3.2 percent in 1960–61, and 3.0 percent in 1970–71.[32] These rates were lower than the dividend yield of common stocks in all of the years except 1960–61 and were lower than the yield of high-grade tax-exempt bonds in 1960–61 and 1970–71.[33] While the estimates are no doubt subject to a fairly wide margin

32. Based on estimates by the Bureau of Economic Analysis of imputed net rent and estimates of owners' equity derived from the following sources: value in four benchmark years, from John C. Musgrave, "New Estimates of Residential Capital in the United States, 1925–73," *Survey of Current Business,* vol. 54 (October 1974), p. 34; home mortgage debt, from Board of Governors of the Federal Reserve System, "Flow of Funds Accounts, 1945–1972" (1973; processed), pp. 83–84. The equity estimates are for the end of calendar years; they are related to averages of estimated net rent for that year and the next year.

33. Averages of calendar years, Standard & Poor's statistics from *Economic Report of the President, February 1975,* pp. 317, 342.

of error, they support the conclusion that the average price of owner-occupied dwellings is high relative to the net value of their rental services.[34] It is fruitless to speculate to what extent this is due to the capitalization in house prices of the value of the preferential tax treatment, as distinguished from other influences on housing demand and prices. The evidence, however, is consistent with the hypothesis that, contrary to the deductive arguments stated above, the potential benefits to homeowners have been offset in part by a rise in house prices resulting from their efforts to take advantage of the income tax benefits.

If house prices have increased in response to the income tax provisions, the benefits to homeowners as a group have been reduced and the stimulus to housing consumption has been lessened, but discrimination has not been eliminated. Homeowners with large incomes and high marginal tax rates will still benefit relative to families with smaller incomes and lower tax rates. Tenants will have to pay more rent without being able to write off any of their housing expenses against taxable income.

There is no evidence that the present income tax treatment of owner-occupied houses was deliberately devised to promote housing and homeownership. The personal deductions for interest and tax payments and the omission of imputed income are general provisions.

In retrospect, however, the present treatment has been supported as a means of fostering homeownership and the civic virtues associated with it. While homeownership does seem to enjoy wide public esteem, the social advantages claimed for it are somewhat vague. A possible disadvantage is that homeownership decreases mobility. Furthermore, if housing is like most other industries, landlords, being specialists, can provide services at lower cost than owner-occupants.

Like other special provisions, the treatment of imputed rent involves a conflict between the objective of encouraging a particular kind of behavior and the goal of equal taxation. And, as always, it is reasonable to ask whether the tax provision is more effective, relative to cost, than other government programs designed to accomplish the same social purpose. The effectiveness of the present provisions may be impaired by an increase in the price of houses. Whatever assistance

---

34. An alternative possibility is that the Bureau of Economic Analysis estimates of net rent are too low; see Henry Aaron, "Income Taxes and Housing," *American Economic Review*, vol. 60 (December 1970), p. 791.

is afforded for housing and homeownership varies directly with the family's taxable income and marginal tax rate, which seems unfair and inefficient. The loss of tax revenue is large relative to the cost of other federal government programs for housing, including low-rent public housing, rent supplements, direct homeownership assistance through subsidized mortgages, and mortgage insurance.[35] There seems to have been no systematic comparison of the merits of aiding housing and homeownership by the present income tax provisions and by direct government expenditures.

A possible defense of the federal income tax provisions covering owner-occupied dwellings is that they are justified as an offset to property taxes imposed by state and local governments. Property taxes are much heavier on housing than on other goods and services.[36] The amount of property taxes paid by nonfarm homeowners is substantially greater than their special income tax benefits—in 1970, $12.6 billion as against $8.9 billion. A weakness of this argument is that rental housing is also subject to property taxes, but tenants receive no income tax concession. The property tax on all housing, moreover, is partly a payment for services that specially benefit local residents. If the tax system as a whole is to be evaluated, it should be noted also that another major form of taxation, federal and state corporate profits taxes, affects housing less than most other industries.[37]

The only method of eliminating discrimination between persons and forms of investment arising from the present treatment of owner-occupied dwellings would be to require that the net rental value of

35. *The Budget of the United States Government, Fiscal Year 1975*, p. 326; Aaron, *Shelter and Subsidies*, p. 162.

36. If property taxes on owner-occupied nonfarm dwellings had been no higher in relation to gross national product originating in that sector in 1970 than in the remainder of the economy, they would have amounted to about $1.4 billion rather than $12.6 billion, as derived from *Survey of Current Business* (July 1973), tables 3.3 and 7.3, pp. 31, 47.

37. Leonard G. Rosenberg found that in 1953–59 corporate profits taxes and property taxes together equaled 28 percent of income from capital invested in nonfarm residences as compared with 40 percent in all other nonfinancial industries. "Taxation of Income from Capital, by Industry Group," in Arnold C. Harberger and Martin J. Bailey, eds., *The Taxation of Income from Capital* (Brookings Institution, 1969), pp. 174–77. Under the federal income tax, depreciation allowances are now more liberal for rental housing than for other real estate but no more liberal than for other forms of investment.

these dwellings be included in adjusted gross income for tax purposes. Owing to the novelty of this solution in the United States and the undoubted difficulties of administration and compliance, the suggestion has been made that the discrimination between owners and tenants be attacked either by disallowing personal deductions for mortgage interest and property taxes or by allowing tenants to deduct rental payments. Inasmuch as the personal deductions for mortgage interest and property taxes on owner-occupied houses are considerably larger than the estimated net rent of these dwellings, the elimination of the personal deductions would accomplish a substantial part of the objective of taxation of imputed net rent. The disallowance, nevertheless, would be an incomplete solution. The elimination of the interest deduction, for example, would have no effect on persons who own their dwellings free of mortgage debt and hence would do nothing to reduce the discrimination between this group and tenants. Among homeowners, denial of the interest deduction would remove a difference in the taxable income of those with and without mortgages which corresponds to a difference in economic income. From the standpoint of equity, the case for eliminating the property tax deduction is stronger (see chapter 7).

Under the Civil War income tax in the United States, tenants were allowed to deduct rental payments on their residences in computing taxable income. If this precedent were followed, the present discrimination against renters would be replaced by a discrimination in their favor, since the sum of the deductions and exclusion now allowed owner-occupants is less than gross rent. In the aggregate, rough equality could be achieved by allowing a deduction equal to about three-fourths of rental payments. The deduction, however, would increase the favoritism for housing consumption over other goods and services and would further narrow the tax base.

The administrative problems in taxing imputed net rent, which would be substantial, would turn mainly on the establishment of rental value, by direct estimation or by taking a conventional percentage of capital value or owner's equity. The valuation difficulties would not be novel, since appraisals are frequently made for mortgage loans and property tax assessments. However, higher standards of accuracy have customarily been demanded in the measurement of taxable income than in the establishment of values for the other purposes. Property tax assessments have been poor in many areas but fairly good in others. Federal administrators could derive assistance from assessment records of governmental units with good administration, whereas in other areas the availabilty of federal income tax valuation data might help improve local property tax assessments.

The gains in tax equity, economic efficiency, and federal revenue seem to be great enough to justify the effort required to take account of imputed net rent in the assessment of the individual income tax. This tax reform merits serious consideration.

Life Insurance

Most life insurance policies combine pure insurance and saving features. The pure insurance is the protection against the risk of economic loss caused by premature death. The savings take the form of reserves accumulated out of premium payments, which earn interest for the benefit of the insured. The pure insurance protection afforded by a policy at any time is the difference between the face amount and the reserve. Policies combine pure insurance and saving in varying proportions. A one-year term policy involves almost no saving; an endowment policy may be mainly a saving instrument.[38]

Both pure insurance proceeds and interest earned on savings accumulated under life insurance policies may be provisionally regarded as income in the broad sense. Yet pure insurance proceeds are never included in AGI, and it appears that only a minor part of interest obtained by individuals through life insurance is included.

Under U.S. tax law, death benefits from life insurance policies are wholly excluded from the income of the insured person and of the beneficiary (but are included in the taxable estate of the deceased). No distinction is drawn between the components of death benefits, which comprise pure insurance proceeds, the return of the insured person's savings, and interest earned on the savings. When the proceeds of a life insurance contract are paid for reasons other than the death of the insured—on account of surrender or maturity—an attempt is made to take account of interest income for tax purposes. As shown below, however, the provision is defective and allows a large part of the interest to escape the individual income tax.

38. Calculations are made for large classes of policyholders rather than for individual policies; and assumptions about mortality, interest earnings, and expenses are not always realized.

The large size of life insurance benefits and of interest earnings on individual saving through life insurance makes the tax treatment of these items important. The subject, nevertheless, has received little attention.[39] In the following pages, pure insurance proceeds and interest income will be separately treated, although the two elements are usually combined in an insurance policy.

Pure Insurance Proceeds

Pure life insurance proceeds are death benefits other than the return of the policyholder's accumulated savings and the distribution of interest income. These proceeds represent an increase in net worth of the beneficiary and are income according to the Haig-Simons definition. Life insurance is intended to replace part of the income that the insured person would have earned if he had continued at work, and the earned income would have been included in AGI.

An objection to including life insurance proceeds in taxable income is that they resemble bequests, which are not included. Actually, however, the close parallel is between a bequest and the return of the insured person's own contribution, not between a bequest and pure insurance proceeds. A bequest consists of property accumulated out of income by the deceased or an earlier owner; when originally received it was exposed to tax to the same degree as other income arising at that time from the same source. The pure insurance proceeds, on the other hand, are a new income item which partly replaces expected future earnings.

Nevertheless, there are good reasons for the continued exclusion of pure insurance proceeds from AGI. The death of the insured is often a time of economic loss for the family and therefore an inconvenient moment for paying an additional income tax. Application of graduated income tax rates to lump-sum insurance settlements would be harsh unless relief were granted, and the usual income-averaging plans might not be suitable for this purpose. There is, moreover, a social interest in encouraging individual efforts to provide for one's dependents. No close substitute exists for the pure insurance element

---

39. It is well analyzed by William Vickrey in "Insurance Under the Federal Income Tax," *Yale Law Journal*, vol. 52 (June 1943), pp. 554–85, and Vickrey, *Agenda for Progressive Taxation*, pp. 64–75. My own views are more fully stated in my paper "Policyholders' Interest Income from Life Insurance under the Income Tax," *Vanderbilt Law Review*, vol. 16 (December 1962), pp. 33–55.

of life insurance policies as a means for safeguarding dependents. In several countries, public approval of life insurance is expressed, not only by excluding pure insurance proceeds from taxable income, but also by allowing a deduction for a limited amount of insurance premiums.

Interest Income

Interest on personal savings built up through life insurance policies differs in an important respect from pure insurance proceeds. The interest income is related to the saving-investment features of insurance policies rather than their protective features.

The nature of personal saving through life insurance and the interest income from it can be clarified by an examination of different policies. An ordinary life policy, the most popular form of individual life insurance contract, calls for a constant annual premium and matures only at the death of the insured. In the earlier years of the contract, the annual premiums are much greater than the current cost of insurance, and savings are accumulated in a reserve fund, which is invested by the company and which earns interest. Limited-payment whole life policies also mature only at the death of the insured, but premium payments end after a stated number of years. Compared with an ordinary life policy, the limited-payment policies provide for heavier annual premiums, more rapid accumulation of savings, and greater interest earnings. A single-premium policy is the extreme form. Under this contract, the investment of the original premium yields an interest return which covers the cost of insurance and adds to the reserve. Endowment policies, in contrast to the whole life policies, mature either at the death of the insured or after a stated number of years, whichever is earlier.

Illustrative figures for the first twenty years for four insurance policies of $1,000 issued at the age of forty-five are shown in table 6-5. Although the policies have the same face value, the limited-payment and endowment policies provide less insurance protection (measured by the difference between the face amount and the reserve) on the average than the ordinary life policy. The premiums given in the table are net of the loading charges that are always added to cover company expenses. Because these charges vary among companies, they are omitted here for simplicity. The terminal reserve, which embodies the policyholder's accumulated savings at the end of the pe-

Table 6-5. Illustrative Figures for First Twenty Years for Four Life Insurance Policies of $1,000 Issued at Age 45[a]

Dollars

Description	Ordinary life	20-payment life	Single-premium life	20-year endowment
Total net premiums	600	776	551	919
Total cost of insurance	271	207	122	154
Total interest earned	123	185	324	235
Terminal reserve	451	754	754	1,000

a. Commissioners 1941 Standard Ordinary Mortality Table with interest of 2.5 percent. Line 4 = line 1 − line 2 + line 3, but figures may not check exactly because of rounding.

riod, equals net premiums minus the cost of insurance plus interest earned.

The question at issue is whether the interest earned on life insurance saving can be and should be included in individual income for tax purposes. Under present law, the interest is not taken into income as it accrues, and it is never included if the policy is paid because of the death of the insured. As the figures in table 6-5 illustrate, the interest element would constitute a large fraction of the sum received by the beneficiary if the insured died at the end of twenty years (but just before the maturity of the endowment policy).

If the insured survived, he could surrender the whole life policies for cash settlements approximately equal to the terminal reserves and could collect the face amount of the endowment policy. Under present law, he would then be required to report as income only the excess, if any, of the proceeds over the premiums paid. On the assumption that the proceeds would equal the terminal reserve, no income would have to be reported on the surrender of the ordinary life and twenty-payment life policies, and the amount to be reported for the other policies would be far less than the interest earned. In practice, the reportable income would be even smaller than the excess of the terminal reserves over the aggregate net premiums because the insured is allowed to deduct aggregate gross premiums, which exceed net premiums by the amount of the loading charge. The rule for determining income takes no account of the cost of insurance protection while the contract was in force. Interest earnings are included in AGI only to the extent that they exceed the cost of insurance and loading; in effect, personal insurance expenses are charged against interest income.

A different tax result would be obtained if the insured purchased protection in the form of a series of one-year policies, which, like the typical fire insurance or other casualty policy, involve virtually no saving, and invested his savings in other assets. He would then be currently taxable on the interest earned on the savings. The contrast is most marked in the case of the single-premium policy but exists for the other policies as well. Channeling the saving through a life insurance company allows a large part of the return to escape individual income tax and postpones the taxation of the remainder.

Although the interest earned is not currently paid to the policyholder, it is used for his benefit. The policyholder, moreover, has access to his savings and accumulated interest. He can realize the savings prior to the maturity of the policy by surrendering it for cash or by converting it to a paid-up policy or extended-term policy. He can also use the savings as collateral for a loan. Minimum surrender values, as provided by state laws, are somewhat less than policy reserves, but companies often offer more liberal surrender values.

The arguments that justify the exclusion of pure insurance proceeds from taxable income do not apply to interest on policy reserves. The interest income accrues as savings build up, not just at the time of family misfortune. Whereas no close substitutes for life insurance are available to an individual as a means of protecting his dependents against the risk of premature loss of his earning capacity, the saving provisions of insurance contracts are only one of a wide range of investment media. The benefit to a policyholder from the preferential treatment of interest on life insurance reserves depends on the extent to which he uses insurance as an investment rather than on the amount of pure insurance coverage for his dependents he carries.

The net interest earned on life insurance policy reserves has been growing as the result of increases in outstanding reserves and rising interest rates (table 6-6). In 1970, the exclusion of this item from adjusted gross income reduced the federal income tax liabilities of policyholders by about $1 billion.[40] Treasury Department estimates indicate that the tax benefit is heavily concentrated in upper income classes (table A-13), but these estimates—and indeed the estimate of the total tax reduction due to the exclusion—may be viewed some-

---

40. Treasury Department estimate, *General Tax Reform,* Panel Discussions, pt. 1, p. 30.

Table 6-6. Life Insurance Reserves Attributable to Individual Policyholders, and Interest Earned on the Reserves, 1950, 1960, and 1970

Amounts in billions of dollars

Description	1950	1960	1970
Reserves[a]	48.3	67.6	96.1
Net rate of interest earned (percent)[b]	3.13	4.11	5.30
Interest earned on reserves	1.5	2.8	5.1

Sources: Reserves, Board of Governors of the Federal Reserve System, "Flow of Funds Accounts, 1945–1972" (1973; processed), pp. 83–84, 100–02; rate of interest, Institute of Life Insurance, *1971 Life Insurance Fact Book* (1971), p. 63.

a. Average of amounts at beginning and end of year; derived by allocating total for households, personal trusts, and nonprofit organizations between life insurance reserves and other reserves (excluded here) in proportion to outstanding reserves of life insurance companies for life insurance and for pension funds. May be overstated because it is not clear that reserves for health insurance and certain other purposes are excluded.

b. Net rate of interest earned on invested funds, U.S. life insurance companies.

what skeptically because of the paucity of reliable data on the distribution of policyholders' equity.[41]

The preferential tax treatment of interest earned on policy reserves makes possible a larger net yield on saving through life insurance than could be obtained if this interest were taxed in the same way as other investment income. Savers who wish to avail themselves of the tax shelter, however, must incur costs for insurance protection and loading charges. This may not be a disadvantage for those who desire life insurance for its own sake, especially since saving and insurance can be combined in widely different proportions. It may, however, diminish the attractiveness of the tax shelter to wealthy people, who have less need for life insurance protection than people who depend mainly on earned income. Among investors, moreover, the management skill and guaranteed minimum return associated with a life insurance policy are more attractive to people of moderate means than to those with large resources. For those in high tax brackets, municipal bonds offer tax exemption without the necessity of paying for life insurance company services. The net rate of interest earned by life insurance companies was higher than the yield of high-grade

41. In the Survey of Financial Characteristics of Consumers for 1962, which is the best source of information on the distribution of wealth, policyholders' equity in life insurance was omitted from the basic tables owing to the incomplete and inconsistent nature of the responses concerning this item; the data obtained were presented in a separate table. See Dorothy S. Projector and Gertrude S. Weiss, *Survey of Financial Characteristics of Consumers* (Board of Governors of the Federal Reserve System, 1966), pp. 48–49, 147.

tax-exempt securities in 1950 and 1960, but in 1970 this relationship was reversed.[42]

The favored tax treatment of the interest return on life insurance savings could be expected to have its greatest influence on the decisions of people in upper-middle income groups, particularly those who depend mainly on salaries or professional fees. There is some information that tends to confirm this expectation, at least so far as it relates to the reliance on life insurance in different income classes, but there is little evidence of awareness of the tax advantages of saving through life insurance.[43]

Aggregate statistics do not reveal any tendency for the special tax status of life insurance to result in a disproportionate attraction of savings. Over the two decades 1950 to 1970, households' equity in life insurance reserves grew much less rapidly than their total net financial assets.[44]

The case for ending the privileged tax status of savings through life insurance appears to be much more a matter of equity than of the desirability of correcting a distortion in the use of saving. Equal treatment of life insurance savings and fully taxable savings outlets would require that the accrued interest on life insurance policy reserves be allocated annually to policyholders and included in their AGI, even though the interest was not currently received in cash. The procedures necessary to carry out this revision would be bothersome for the government, insurance companies, and policyholders.

The insurance companies do not routinely allocate interest earnings to individual policies; their calculations relate to large classes of policies and policyholders. The companies would have to be required to make individual allocations. For participating policies, which are eligible to share in surplus earnings through dividends and which account for three-fifths of total life insurance, the allocation could

42. Standard & Poor's yield on high-grade municipal bonds; *Economic Report of the President, January 1973,* p. 260.

43. Projector and Weiss, *Survey of Financial Characteristics of Consumers,* p. 147; J. Keith Butters, Lawrence E. Thompson, and Lynn L. Bollinger, *Effects of Taxation: Investments by Individuals* (Harvard University, Graduate School of Business Administration, 1953), pp. 316–26; Robin Barlow, Harvey E. Brazer, and James N. Morgan, *Economic Behavior of the Affluent* (Brookings Institution, 1966), pp. 56–59, 163–64. In the survey reported in the last cited work, only 1 percent of respondents said that tax considerations made life insurance a good way to save.

44. Federal Reserve System, "Flow of Funds Accounts, 1945–1972," pp. 83–84.

appropriately be made by applying the actual earned interest rate to the average policy reserve. The interest rate would be net of investment expenses and company taxes. Policy dividends would be treated as a reduction of premium and excluded from AGI, as they now are. For nonparticipating policies, the allocation would be made at the guaranteed rate provided in the policy.

An alternative procedure, which would be simpler but less satisfactory, would be to allocate to each policyholder an amount equal to the increase in the cash surrender value of his policy during the year, minus the premium paid.[45] This procedure is similar to the rule now followed when the proceeds are paid for reasons other than death, with the important modification that the income would be reportable annually. As explained above, the cost of current insurance protection would, in effect, be charged against interest earnings, with the result that the greater part of this income would continue to escape tax.

Allocation of interest to individual policies and company reporting to policyholders and the Internal Revenue Service would not ensure that all of the income would appear on tax returns. Special collection procedures might be needed. For participating policies, the companies might be required to withhold tax from policy dividends, but this procedure would be inapplicable to nonparticipating policies and unsuitable for participating policies when interest earnings exceeded policy dividends. "Withholding" by the companies might have to take the form of collecting an addition to the annual premium which would be remitted to the Internal Revenue Service and credited to the policyholder.

Further study would be required to ascertain whether the inconvenience and expense for the insurance companies and the government would be as great as they at first appear to be. Consideration should be given to the possibilities of using automatic data processing, which has been installed by the large insurance companies and by the Internal Revenue Service. Consideration might also be given to an exemption from current reporting requirements for policies with small reserves, thus eliminating many small items.

An alternative approach would be to defer reporting and taxation of interest income until it is realized through loan, surrender or ma-

45. Suggested by Joseph A. Pechman in *Tax Revision Compendium,* vol. 1, p. 263.

turity of the policy, or death of the insured. This would allow tax deferral but would eliminate the permanent exclusion of a large part of interest on policy reserves. The approach would be subject to the same charge of harshness and inconvenience to taxpayers as mentioned in the comments on pure insurance proceeds. It might be acceptable, nevertheless, if applied only to new policies, inasmuch as the policyholders would have been placed on notice about their future liabilities.

In light of the objections to the methods of taxing policyholders' interest income considered above, it is not clear what, if any, revision of the law should be adopted. The proven adaptability of the income tax to complex situations, however, encourages the hope that a way of improving the present situation can be discovered. The effectiveness of any plan for the taxation of policyholders' interest income would be enhanced if interest on state and local government securities were also taxed. Otherwise, savers could continue to avoid tax on interest income by switching from life insurance to tax-exempt bonds.[46]

Interest on State and Local Securities

Of all the omissions from taxable income, the exclusion of interest on state and local government securities has attracted the most attention.[47] It has been attacked by many writers on taxation and by several secretaries of the treasury but vigorously defended by state

46. The Carter Commission of Canada in 1966 recommended that investment income accumulated in life insurance policy reserves be allocated annually to policyholders and included in their taxable income and also that dividends on participating policies be included in taxable income and that mortality gains and losses be taken into account in computing taxable income at the time of maturity of a policy. The government did not accept these recommendations but proposed a two-part plan (enacted in 1969) comprising (a) the taxation of the net proceeds of matured policies according to a rule similar to that followed in the United States and (b) a 15 percent tax on the investment income of life insurance companies in lieu of taxation of policyholders on this income. See *Report of the Royal Commission on Taxation* (Ottawa: Queen's Printer, 1966), vol. 3, pp. 441–55, 585–90; George E. Lent, "Taxation of Financial Intermediaries," *National Tax Journal,* vol. 22 (March 1969), pp. 149–50; and William M. Carlyle, "Taxation of Life Insurance Proceeds," *Canadian Tax Journal,* vol. 17 (September–October 1969), pp. 321–30.

47. For a convenient review of the facts and issues, see David J. Ott and Allan H. Meltzer, *Federal Tax Treatment of State and Local Securities* (Brookings Institution, 1963).

and local officials and by securities dealers. The question whether the Constitution allows the federal government to tax this interest has been extensively debated but never resolved because the statutes have provided for the exclusion since 1913. Although the constitutional question will not be considered here, authoritative opinion has tended toward the position that Congress could end the exclusion if it wished.

Statistics on interest payments by state and local governments and estimates of the amount received by individuals appear in table 6-7. The estimated amount of tax-exempt interest received by individuals grew at the rapid rate of 13.9 percent a year between 1950 and 1960, but the annual rate of growth declined to 7.0 percent between 1960 and 1970 owing to a slower rate of increase in state and local borrowing and interest payments and to a fall in the proportion of tax-exempt securities held by individuals.

The tax immunity of interest on state and local securities brings out in acute form the issues posed by other exclusions. Because state and local securities can be freely bought and sold with little expense and little risk and without the necessity of buying consumer services at the same time, they are ideal for persons who wish to avoid high rates of income tax. A tax-free return is available without the inconvenience and expense associated with homeownership or life insurance. It is true that the market for state and local securities is less fluid than that for many other securities, but state-local bonds are more liquid than houses.

Reliable current information is not available on the distribution of holdings of state and local government securities and of interest received from them by individuals classified by size of income. Statistics from federal estate tax returns and deductive reasoning indicate, however, that, among individuals, ownership is heavily concentrated in the hands of the wealthy. Treasury Department estimates, which

Table 6-7. Interest Paid by State and Local Governments and Estimated Amount Received by Individuals, 1950, 1960, 1970, and 1971

Millions of dollars

Description	1950	1960	1970	1971
Total interest paid	613	2,028	5,123	5,904
Estimated amount received by individuals	235	864	1,693	1,745

Sources: First row, *Statistical Abstract, 1973*, p. 419; second row, total amount of interest paid by state and local governments allocated between individuals and others in proportion to holdings of state and local obligations by households, personal trusts, and nonprofit organizations and by all others (average of beginning and end of year) as estimated in Federal Reserve System, "Flow of Funds Accounts, 1945–1972," pp. 83–84, 88–90.

are subject to a considerable margin of error, place the federal income tax value of the exclusion of interest on individual holdings at $800 million in 1971, of which virtually all is allocated to holders with incomes above $15,000 and four-fifths to holders above the $50,000 income level.[48]

Many comments exaggerate the effect of the exclusion on the equity and progressivity of the income tax because they take no account of the compensating reduction in market yields of tax-exempt securities. If, for example, all holders of the securities were subject to a marginal tax rate of 50 percent and if yields on state-local securities were only half those on comparable taxable securities, the tax advantage would be fully discounted in the market. Although state and local governments would still gain from the tax immunity, the choice between state-local securities and other securities would be a matter of indifference to high-income investors. In these circumstances, the effective rate of income tax would seem less progressive than it would without the exclusion; however, the distribution of income would not be affected, and investors in state-local securities would receive no unfair advantage.

Questions of income distribution and equity arise because investors are subject to various tax rates and because the market does not fully discount the tax advantages of state and local securities for holders as a group. Even if yields on tax-exempt securities were half those on other securities, the holders of tax-exempts who were subject to marginal rates above 50 percent would gain an advantage. For example, a person subject to a marginal tax rate of 70 percent would have no preference between a taxable security yielding 4.0 percent and a comparable tax-exempt security yielding 1.2 percent, whereas the market yield on the tax-exempt would be 2.0 percent.

There is reason to believe, moreover, that the yield differential is smaller than that which would be necessary to bring about an exact equivalence for the weighted average of all holders. The yield differential is almost certainly less than that required to compensate for the tax advantages enjoyed by individual holders as a group and probably less than the tax advantages of corporate and individual holders taken together. This is true because yields must be high enough to attract marginal investors, who are subject to tax rates lower than the weighted average for all holders, and to induce high-income

48. *General Tax Reform,* Panel Discussions, pt. 1, p. 34.

buyers to acquire more of the securities than they would if the differential exactly equaled the tax advantage. Prudent investors will insist on a margin as insurance against a future reduction of tax rates. In 1970 the market yield of high-grade corporate bonds was 24 percent greater than the yield of high-grade tax-exempt bonds, and in 1971 the yield differential was 30 percent.[49] Treasury Department estimates imply weighted marginal rates of federal income tax for all (individual and corporate) holders of tax-exempt securities of some 45 percent in these years.[50] These figures suggest that the interest saving realized by state and local governments was only half to two-thirds the cost to the federal government of the exclusion. This can be regarded as only a rough approximation; a refined estimate would require much more elaborate calculations taking account of lower grade securities and the repercussions of the changes in investment patterns and market yields that would occur if the tax exemption were ended.[51]

The exclusion of interest on state-local securities is economically objectionable because it diverts high-income investors from stocks and other risky private investments to government securities, and thus reduces risk-taking and innovation. This objection, however, seems to have been overrated in many past discussions. At the end of 1970, the state-local security holdings of households, personal trusts, and nonprofit institutions accounted for only 2.4 percent of the total financial assets of this sector.[52] Another objection to the exclusion is that choices between investment in the public sector and investment in the private sector are biased. This criticism is hard to evaluate because it is uncertain whether the interest rate significantly affects the amount of borrowing and spending by state and local governments.

49. The comparison is between Moody's Aaa corporate bonds and Standard & Poor's high-grade municipals, as reported in *Economic Report of the President, January 1973*, p. 260.

50. Derived from Treasury Department estimates published in *General Tax Reform*, Panel Discussions, pt. 1, p. 29, and total interest payments of state and local governments as shown in table 6-7.

51. See Ott and Meltzer, *Tax Treatment of State and Local Securities;* Harvey Galper and John Petersen, "An Analysis of Subsidy Plans to Support State and Local Borrowing," *National Tax Journal*, vol. 24 (June 1971), pp. 205–34; Peter Fortune, "The Impact of Taxable Municipal Bonds: Policy Simulations with a Large Econometric Model," *National Tax Journal*, vol. 26 (March 1973), pp. 29–42.

52. Federal Reserve System, "Flow of Funds Accounts, 1945–1972," pp. 83–84.

The exclusion of interest on state-local securities has been defended as a necessary or desirable feature of federalism, regardless of constitutional requirements. The historic doctrine that each level of government should be completely immune from taxation by the other level, however, seemingly is being superseded by the opinion that a successful federal system requires only that each level be protected from discriminatory, and hence possibly destructive, impositions. Federal and state salaries have been taxable by both levels of government for the past thirty-five years with no apparent harm to the federal system. If the federal government were to tax interest on state-local securities, it is generally agreed that Congress should make clear that there would be no objection to nondiscriminatory state taxes on the interest on federal securities.

Although the tax immunity of interest on state and local government securities has resulted in inequities, it would be unfair simply to withdraw the exemption from outstanding issues. Investors have bought the securities at prices and yields reflecting the expectation of continued tax exemption and would suffer capital losses if the interest were made taxable. Withdrawal of the exemption only for interest on future issues would not immediately end the problem—indeed, it would result in windfall gains for holders of outstanding issues which would acquire a scarcity value—but it would stop the growth of tax-exempt interest.

The failure to win acceptance for proposals to tax interest on future issues, together with increased sensitivity to the financial problems of state and local governments, has stimulated interest in proposals that the federal government pay a direct subsidy to state and local governments which elect to issue taxable securities. Since the revenue loss to the federal government due to tax exemption appears to exceed the interest saving to state and local governments, it should be possible to select a subsidy rate (applicable to interest payments) that would be advantageous to both levels of government and would encourage the voluntary relinquishment of the tax-exempt status of state-local issues.[53] It would be necessary to revise the subsidy from time to time to take account of changing conditions in financial

---

53. See Galper and Petersen, "Analysis of Subsidy Plans"; Fortune, "Impact of Taxable Municipal Bonds"; Robert P. Huefner, "Municipal Bonds: The Costs and Benefits of an Alternative," *National Tax Journal,* vol. 23 (December 1970), pp. 407–16.

markets. This approach could greatly reduce existing inequities, but it seems unlikely that it would entirely eliminate tax-exempt issues. As state and local borrowing was diverted to taxable issues, the supply of tax-exempt issues would shrink relative to demand, and yields on both outstanding issues and new issues would decline. Unless the federal subsidy were repeatedly raised and finally brought to a very high level, it would always be possible for some governments to borrow more cheaply by issuing tax-exempt securities than by issuing subsidized taxable securities. As a means of assisting state and local governments, the explicit subsidy would be more efficient than the tax exemption, but the allocation of benefits among state and local governments would not conform closely to need as measured by the standards usually adopted or proposed for grants-in-aid.

The ending of the tax immunity of future issues of state-local securities would be desirable from the standpoint of equity and economic efficiency and, in my judgment, would not pose a threat to a healthy federal system. Short of this, the adoption of an explicit subsidy plan that would induce state and local governments to reduce their reliance on tax-exempt securities voluntarily would be a step forward.

Excluded Dividends

Individual stockholders are allowed to exclude the first $100 of dividends received from domestic corporations; husbands and wives filing joint returns may exclude $200. Until 1964, the exclusion was equal to half these amounts. The exclusion and a 4 percent credit for dividends received were adopted in 1954 as a means of reducing the so-called double taxation of distributed corporate profits and encouraging corporations to finance themselves by stock issues rather than borrowing. The President recommended in 1961 and again in 1963 that both the exclusion and the credit be repealed on the grounds that they were inequitable and ineffective. Congress agreed to drop the credit but doubled the exclusion.

Regardless of the merits of the controversy about the taxation of corporate profits, the dividend exclusion is an inequitable and ineffective means of reducing the differential tax on dividend income. While it is true that the exclusion eliminates double taxation on small dividends received by stockholders who are subject to individual income tax, this hardly justifies the provision. If double taxation of small amounts of dividends is objectionable, is it not also objectionable for large amounts? More fundamentally, double taxation in the literal sense is not the real problem posed by the lack of integration of the corporate and individual income taxes. The problem is one of overtaxation and undertaxation of corporate profits compared with other income. The equalization of taxes cannot be accomplished by excluding part of dividends received, because the corporate and individual income tax rates differ in all brackets except one.

In 1970, the dividend exclusion reported on individual tax returns totaled $1.2 billion, or 7 percent of all dividends reported on these returns.[54] Forty-two percent of the total was on returns with income above $15,000. The estimated revenue cost of the exclusion was $280 million (table A-12).

Miscellaneous Items of Imputed Income

There are certain miscellaneous items of imputed income that have always been excluded from taxable income in all countries. Among these are the return from ownership of consumer durable equipment, part of the return on cash balances, and personal services performed for oneself. The value of farm-produced-and-consumed food and fuel is often omitted but is taxed in some countries, usually on the basis of an arbitrary valuation. No serious consideration seems to have been given to the possibility of taxing most of these items because legislators do not think of them as income. The virtual impossibility of assessing the items has convinced most specialists that the exclusions must continue, even though certain inequities and economic distortions may result.

I agree that the inclusion of these items in taxable income would be impracticable. The purpose of the following remarks is to consider whether the exclusions seriously impair the income tax.

Consumer Durable Equipment

Ownership of consumer durable equipment such as furniture, appliances, and automobiles is similar to homeownership. Much the same argument can be made for including the net service value of

54. *Statistics of Income—1970, Individual Income Tax Returns*, p. 54.

the durable equipment in AGI as for taking account of the net rent of owner-occupied dwellings. At the end of 1968, consumers' equity in durable equipment was about 45 percent as large as their equity in owner-occupied dwellings.[55] The net yield on the equity in durables may have been a larger fraction of that from houses since it is unlikely that the rate of return on them has been depressed by higher prices in the same way as may have occurred for houses. The opinion that consumer durables yield little net return because of their short average life is incorrect.[56] A short life means that depreciation is heavy relative to original cost, or service value, but does not imply that the net rate of return on the equity is small. With respect to business assets, it is well recognized that the gross yield of a short-lived item should exceed that of a long-lived one by a margin wide enough to cover the additional depreciation allowance on the less durable asset and to permit approximately equal net rates of return. The same principle seems applicable to consumer investments in equipment and houses.

Because the renting of consumer durables is less prevalent than the renting of dwellings, discrimination between renters and owners seems less acute for durables than for houses. In addition to renters, however, there are many consumers who buy services similar to those provided by consumer-owned durables. The patrons of commercial laundries and public transportation, for example, pay the whole cost of the services in cash, whereas owners of home laundry equipment and automobiles meet part of the cost of the services with the tax-free imputed net return on their investment in the equipment. The difference in tax treatment is similar to the difference between the taxation of tenants and homeowners.[57]

Experience with the general property tax indicates that tax officials could not discover and value household goods or impute net income

55. The estimated equity was $176 billion in consumer durables and $393 billion in owner-occupied nonfarm dwellings. The estimate of the equity in consumer durables was derived by deducting from the total value of the stock consumer installment debt in the form of automobile paper and other consumer-goods paper (*Statistical Abstract, 1973,* pp. 343, 455). The estimate of owners' equity in nonfarm dwellings is a rough approximation obtained by capitalizing estimated net rent, as shown in the national income and product accounts, at a rate of 3 percent (see p. 121).

56. I believe that Henry Simons' comments are incorrect or, at least, ambiguous. See *Personal Income Taxation,* pp. 118–19.

57. C. Harry Kahn, *Personal Deductions in the Federal Income Tax* (Princeton University Press for the National Bureau of Economic Research, 1960), pp. 118–19.

to their owners. The omission of imputed income from consumer durables is a shortcoming of the income tax which must be accepted. The failure to take account of the yield of durables, however, does not justify the continued exclusion of net rent of owner-occupied houses. Probably the ownership of durable equipment and houses is positively correlated. If so, the effects of omitting imputed returns on both kinds of investment are cumulative rather than offsetting.

Cash Balances

Large cash balances are convenient; they enable one to make advantageous purchases and, when held in checking accounts, to avoid bank service charges. The return on business balances is reflected in taxable business income, but this is not true of individual balances held for convenience in making consumption payments. Although direct evidence is not available on the point, it seems likely that the greater part of individual balances is intended to allow the holders to take advantage of investment opportunities or to avoid the necessity of borrowing and paying interest. If these purposes are actually realized, taxable income of the holders will be increased by virtue of larger investment income or smaller deductions for interest payments. Even if investments are not made, the sacrifice of interest on the cash balances may be regarded as a cost of seeking income. I conclude that the amount of income that ideally should be attributed to holders of cash balances is small and that the failure to take account of this item is not a significant defect of the income tax.

Farm-Produced-and-Consumed Food and Fuel

Another item that is omitted from gross income for tax purposes is the value of farm families' consumption of their own output. Although the imputed net income attributable to this consumption is less than the value of the products by an amount equal to the cost of supplies, depreciation, and other expenses properly assignable to the production of the home-consumed items, it seems likely that AGI is understated by the full value of the products. This will be true if, as seems to be the common practice, farmers deduct the full amount of their operating expenses and capital costs in arriving at AGI.

For the great majority of farmers, it does not seem to be practicable to ascertain the value of the home-consumed items or even to allocate costs between marketed and nonmarketed output. With the growth of specialized farming, the problem is becoming less important. According to estimates of the Department of Commerce, the value of farm-produced-and-consumed food and fuel has been declining in recent years, and in relation to the total value of farm output it has fallen sharply. Estimates spanning two decades are as follows:[58]

Year	*Value* *(billions of dollars)*	*Percentage of* *total farm output*
1950	2.1	6.3
1960	1.2	3.3
1970	0.7	1.4

Personal Services

The consumption of one's own services is a form of income. Housekeeping, dressmaking, painting, carpentry, and gardening are examples of services that may be either done by family members or purchased. The performance of these chores, moreover, often competes for time with work for wages and salaries. Because it takes account of the salaries and wages, but not the value of services performed for oneself, the income tax results in inequities and penalizes specialization. If a homeowner takes time off from his regular job and repaints his house, his taxable income is reduced by much more than his real income. The most important case is that of housewives; the value of their services at home is excluded from taxable income, but any earnings that they obtain by taking a job away from home are taxable.

Any attempt to value the services performed within the household, however, would immediately come up against insurmountable obstacles of both a theoretical and practical nature. It would be impossible to distinguish activities that produce valuable services from relaxation or to separate the commercial from the noncommercial, the significant from the trivial. As Henry Simons points out, "if the value of goods and services produced within the household are to be accounted for, one must face, first of all, the necessity of stopping somewhere; and no convenient stopping-place is discernible. Shall

58. U.S. Department of Commerce, *The National Income and Product Accounts of the United States, 1929–1965: Statistical Tables* (1966), p. 29; *Survey of Current Business* (July 1973), p. 24.

one include the value of shaves? of instruction to children? of a mother's services as a nurse?"[59]

The exclusion of the value of services performed for oneself is less unfair than it may seem because to a great extent the performance of these services competes with leisure, which is another form of consumption, and hence a part of income, which escapes taxation. Between the suburbanite who spends weekends tending his garden and his neighbor who goes golfing, there is no tax inequity. There is an inequity, and possibly a perverse economic effect, in the treatment of these two compared with that of a third person who works overtime at his regular job on weekends.

General Remarks

The treatment of the miscellaneous items of imputed income is a matter of concern only when viewed in the light of the high standards of equity and neutrality that are properly demanded of the personal income tax. Under indirect taxes, such questions do not arise, not because they are resolved but simply because they are not considered. The personal expenditure tax, which aspires to the same degree of refinement as the income tax, would encounter most of the same problems as the income tax. I conclude that, though the income tax has unavoidable shortcomings in the treatment of imputed income, these weaknesses are not serious enough, or easily enough circumvented, to affect the ranking of the income tax and alternative taxes.

Recapitulation

Of the items discussed in this chapter, I consider it desirable and quite feasible to include in AGI the following: unemployment insurance benefits; one-half of OASDHI and railroad retirement, old-age, and disability benefits; excludable sick pay; interest on new issues of state and local government securities; and the part of dividends now excluded from AGI. Also justifiable and probably feasible is the inclusion of employer contributions to the cost of life, accident, health, and medical insurance for employees and imputed net rent of owner-occupied dwellings (together with the elimination of the deductions

59. *Personal Income Taxation*, p. 110.

for mortgage interest and property taxes on these dwellings). In 1970, these items, including interest received by individuals on outstanding state-local securities, totaled $76 billion. Part of social insurance survivorship benefits (total $7.9 billion in 1970), but less than one-half, could also appropriately be included in AGI. Policyholders' interest income from life insurance reserves ($5.1 billion) could justifiably be included in AGI, but there would be difficulties in devising a fair and practicable plan for doing so. All of these items (counting the full amount of social insurance retirement and disability benefits) constitute about one-half of the individual income items that are included in personal income for the national income and product accounts, but not in AGI. They equal 13 percent of total AGI of taxable and nontaxable individuals, and their inclusion in AGI would increase taxable income by substantially more than this fraction.

In principle, AGI should also include the value of farm-produced-and-consumed food and fuel, employee meals in private industry, and employee discounts, but it would not be worthwhile to attempt to assess these items except in the few cases in which amounts enjoyed by individuals are large. Although a good argument can be made for currently including in employees' AGI the amount of employers' contributions to private pension and deferred profit-sharing plans, I think it expedient to continue to reflect the value of these contributions mainly at the time benefits are received rather than when contributions are made.

It would not be desirable, in my opinion, to include public assistance, veterans' benefits, and individual health insurance benefits in AGI; these items amounted to $20.7 billion in 1970. Also, I think it undesirable or impracticable to attempt to include in AGI unrealized capital gains, gifts and inheritances, life insurance death benefits other than the part attributable to interest on policyholders' savings, the service value of consumer durables, imputed interest on cash balances, and the value of personal services performed for oneself or family. The total of these items is not known.

CHAPTER SEVEN

Personal Deductions

PERSONAL DEDUCTIONS are expenses that are subtracted from adjusted gross income (AGI) in arriving at taxable income. They cover living expenses and certain costs of obtaining income that do not qualify as business expenses, which are subtracted from gross receipts in computing AGI. The major items are interest paid, medical expenses, philanthropic contributions, and taxes paid. Minor items include uninsured casualty losses, child-care expenses, and miscellaneous deductions. Taxpayers may elect a limited standard deduction in lieu of itemized personal deductions.

Growth of Deductions and Their Distribution

The personal deductions have been growing rapidly, increasing from 9 percent to 17 percent of AGI between 1940 and 1970 (table 7-1). From 1940 to 1950, the increase in relation to income seems to have been due to a new deduction for medical expenses and the introduction of the optional standard deduction; the other deductions grew much less than income. Thereafter the traditional itemized deductions for interest paid, contributions, and taxes grew more rapidly than income.

Because of the existence of the standard deduction, the deduction shown in table 7-1 for a particular item is an incomplete report of

Table 7-1. Personal Deductions on Taxable Individual Income Tax Returns, 1940, 1950, 1960, and 1970

Type of deduction	1940	1950	1960	1970
	Percent of adjusted gross income			
Interest paid	1.8	0.9	2.7	3.8
Medical expenses	. . .	0.8	1.5	1.5
Contributions	2.2	1.3	2.2	2.0
Taxes paid	3.5	1.3	3.4	5.1
Other itemized deductions	1.5	1.4	1.3	1.3
Standard deduction	. . .	6.4	3.9	3.0
Total deductions	9.0	12.0	15.0	16.8
	Percent of total deductions			
Interest paid	20.2	7.2	17.8	22.4
Medical expenses	. . .	6.6	10.0	9.1
Contributions	24.6	11.1	14.4	12.2
Taxes paid	38.9	10.8	22.5	30.4
Other itemized deductions	16.3	11.4	9.2	8.0
Standard deduction	. . .	52.9	26.2	18.0
Total deductions	100.0	100.0	100.0	100.0

Sources: 1940 and 1950, C. Harry Kahn, *Personal Deductions in the Federal Income Tax* (Princeton University Press for the National Bureau of Economic Research, 1960), p. 36; 1960 and 1970, U.S. Internal Revenue Service, *Statistics of Income—1960, Individual Income Tax Returns*, pp. 55, 66, and *1970*, pp. 9, 120, 131 (referred to in later tables as *Statistics of Income*, followed by the year). Figures are rounded.

taxpayers' outlays for it. Changes over time in the amount deducted are due to both the trend of outlays for the item and the extent to which taxpayers choose itemization rather than the standard deduction. Thus the decline in the ratio of itemized deductions to income between 1940 and 1950 was in part a consequence of the introduction of the standard deduction, while the increase in the ratios for particular items from 1950 to 1970 was partly caused by the growing tendency to itemize deductions.

Relative to income, the personal deductions are greatest in the lowest and highest income classes, dipping somewhat in a wide intermediate range (table 7-2). The high ratio to income in the lowest income classes is due entirely to the standard deduction and particularly to the low-income allowance which is the predominant form of the standard deduction in AGI classes below $5,000.[1] The low-income allowance, though an alternative to other personal deductions, may be regarded as equivalent to a form of personal exemption.

1. U.S. Internal Revenue Service, *Statistics of Income—1970, Individual Income Tax Returns*, p. 103 (hereafter *Statistics of Income*, followed by the year).

Table 7-2. Distribution of Personal Deductions on Taxable Individual Income Tax Returns, by Adjusted Gross Income (AGI) Class, 1970

AGI class (thousands of dollars)	Percent of total deductions	Deductions as percent of AGI
Under 2	1.1	50.8
2–3	2.7	30.0
3–5	6.0	17.3
5–10	26.3	16.5
10–25	48.7	16.2
25–50	8.5	15.9
50–100	3.7	16.4
100–500	2.4	20.7
500 and over	0.7	27.0
All classes	100.0	16.8

Source: *Statistics of Income—1970*, p. 9. Figures are rounded.

Views on the Role of Deductions

The personal deductions have been increasingly questioned. When taxes were raised during World War II, suggestions were made for curtailing personal deductions. The adoption of the predecessor of the standard deduction in 1941 seems to have been motivated partly by doubts about the desirability of itemized deductions, the attitude being that the standard allowance wiped out certain unjustified differences in tax resulting from itemized deductions. More recently, many critics have come to regard personal deductions as a cause of the erosion of the tax base and have suggested that they be restricted.

While a skeptical attitude toward personal deductions is justified, it should be recognized that properly limited deductions have advantages in adapting the income tax to individual circumstances and in advancing socially important objectives. The identification of such possibilities requires an examination of particular items. Congress may be more receptive to a critique of particular items than to a general attack on the deductions. It has declined to act on proposals for a blanket restriction on itemized deductions, but in 1964 and 1969 it limited certain deductions while liberalizing others.

The original reasons for allowing some of the personal deductions are not clear; however, the deductions now seem to have four main purposes: (1) to allow the deduction of certain items that are costs of obtaining nonbusiness income or that are hard to distinguish from such costs; (2) to relieve hardships that would arise from strict application of a tax on economic income; (3) to encourage voluntary support of certain socially desirable activities; and (4) to promote intergovernmental comity in a federal system.[2] The allowance of costs of obtaining income appears to be the dominant reason for the deductions for interest paid, child-care expenses, and most of the miscellaneous minor deductions.[3] The deductions for medical expenses and casualty losses are intended to relieve hardship. That for philanthropic contributions is thought of primarily as an incentive to voluntary support of certain socially desirable institutions and their activities. The personal deduction for state and local taxes may be classified as a means of easing friction in a federal system. The optional standard deduction is a surrogate for the itemized deductions, and in the lowest brackets is equivalent to a supplementary personal exemption.

Interest Paid

The deduction for interest paid, which goes back to 1913, has grown rapidly and among itemized deductions in 1970 was second only to taxes paid. The interest deduction is most important for the debt-laden middle classes. In 1970, the proportion of taxpayers with itemized deductions who claimed the interest deduction was greater in the middle brackets than at either lower or higher income levels (appendix table A-8). Interest payments also were a larger fraction of total itemized deductions in the middle brackets than in other brackets. The ratio of the deduction to AGI was highest in the $5,000 to $10,000 income class but varied somewhat erratically at other income levels (appendix table A-9).

A justification for the deduction of interest payments may begin with the proposition that the net return from assets can be determined

2. See the discussion in C. Harry Kahn, *Personal Deductions in the Federal Income Tax* (Princeton University Press for the National Bureau of Economic Research, 1960), pp. 12–16.

3. The items classified as "other itemized deductions" in table 7-1 include certain employee business expenses, educational expense, certain costs of obtaining investment income, child-care expense, casualty losses, and alimony and separate maintenance payments. Separate information is available on only one of these items, child-care expense, which in 1970 amounted to only 0.3 percent of total itemized deductions on taxable returns.

only after subtracting interest paid on any indebtedness that allows the owner to hold the assets. This is generally recognized for business firms; there is an important sense in which the proposition also applies to people who are not in business. When the gross return on property is taken into account for tax purposes, failure to allow the deduction of interest on a debt incurred to carry it will result in an overstatement of net income. This is less obvious but may also be true when there is no formal link between the asset and the liability. For example, if a person owns securities and owes a debt to a bank, the debt helps finance the security holdings even though the securities are not the collateral for the loan and the debt was not incurred for the explicit purpose of buying the securities. If the loan were called or fell due, the investor might well have to reduce his portfolio. Also, he would have an incentive to dispose of securities and pay off the bank loan if the interest deduction were disallowed while the return on the securities remained taxable.

This justification does not apply, however, when the return on assets is excluded from gross income for tax purposes, as is true of owner-occupied dwellings and consumer durable equipment. In these cases, the allowance of an interest deduction results in an understatement of income and a bias in favor of investment in the tax-sheltered kinds of property.

It is true that, regardless of the taxability of the yield of assets financed by the borrowing, the payment of interest is a negative item in economic income. As pointed out in the discussion of owner-occupied dwellings, a homeowner who has a mortgage has a smaller economic income, other things being equal, than a person who owns his house free of debt. Similar statements can be made about owners of consumer durable equipment. The allowance of an interest deduction differentiates between debtors and nondebtors and therefore may be defended as a means of recognizing real differences in income and taxpaying capacity, even when certain kinds of property income are excluded from AGI.[4]

---

4. This seems to be the position of White; see Melvin I. White, "Deductions for Nonbusiness Expenses and an Economic Concept of Net Income," in Joint Committee on the Economic Report, *Federal Tax Policy for Economic Growth and Stability*, 84 Cong. 1 sess. (1955), pp. 357–60; and White, "Proper Income Tax Treatment of Deductions for Personal Expense," in *Tax Revision Compendium*, Papers submitted to the House Committee on Ways and Means (1959), vol. 1, pp. 365–66.

The rebuttal to this argument is that the interest deduction not only recognizes real differences but creates differences in taxable income that do not correspond to any difference in economic income. To illustrate, consider three individuals, A, B, and C, each of whom receives a salary of $20,000 a year and no other income that is includable in AGI. Suppose that A and B own and occupy houses worth $40,000; A's house is subject to a $20,000 mortgage on which he pays interest of $1,400 a year, whereas B owns his house clear of debt. C is a tenant. Although A's interest deduction reflects a difference between his economic income and B's, it distorts the relation between A and C. While A's economic income is greater than C's by the amount of any imputed net return that A obtains on his equity in his house, the interest deduction makes A's taxable income $1,400 less than C's (other things being equal).

No manipulation of the interest deduction can establish a relationship among the taxable incomes of A, B, and C corresponding to their economic incomes. The question is whether the relation between A and B or that between A and C is more important. Partly this depends on the number of people in the groups that A, B, and C represent; the amounts of interest payments are also relevant, although it is hard to say how they should be weighted.[5] A judgment that the inequity between A and C that is created by the interest deduction is more serious than the inequity between A and B that is prevented by the deduction might be defended on the grounds that, even without an interest deduction, A will be treated better than C so long as imputed rent is excluded from AGI. One might also argue that the difference between A and B may be ignored because the exclusion of imputed rent indicates a legislative decision to disregard this item in measuring taxable capacity.

The fundamental difficulty arises from the omission from AGI of the imputed return on owner-occupied houses and consumer durables. With the yield on these items excluded and all interest payments deductible, the taxable income of the owner is understated by the amount of the net yield plus interest paid on debt related to the property. Congress has recognized the inconsistency in the case of tax-exempt securities, and has attempted to deny the deduction of inter-

5. For a suggestive but inconclusive treatment, see Shirley B. Johnson and Thomas Mayer, "An Extension of Sidgwick's Equity Principle," *Quarterly Journal of Economics*, vol. 76 (August 1962), pp. 454–63.

est paid on debt incurred to finance holdings of these securities, but has not dealt with the general problem. If the gross yield of consumer capital were taken into account in computing taxable income, it would be quite proper to allow a deduction for interest payments— as a cost of obtaining income.

The deduction of interest paid on a home mortgage may seem questionable, even if imputed rent were included in gross income, because the payment appears to be a consumption expenditure. This objection, however, is unwarranted. A homeowner acts in a dual capacity—as an investor and as a consumer. As an investor he is, in effect, a landlord; as a consumer, he is his own tenant. He takes the interest deduction in his capacity as a landlord, not as a tenant. That this is not a sophistry can be seen by noting that, if imputed rent were taxed, the homeowner's tax position would not be altered if he moved to another city, leased his house, and rented a similar one in the new location. Under present law, these transactions would increase his taxable income.

Although existing inequities cannot be completely eliminated so long as substantial amounts of monetary or imputed property income are excluded from AGI, an improvement could be made by allowing interest payments to be deducted only to the extent that they are costs of obtaining taxable income. One way of applying this principle would be to restrict the deduction to interest paid on debts contracted for business or professional purposes or for the carrying of taxable securities, denying the deduction for interest on consumer debt and for interest on home mortgages so long as imputed rent is not taxable. This is the rule in Canada.

This procedure, however, is open to criticism on theoretical and practical grounds owing to the difficulty of pairing particular debts and assets.[6] Since all of a person's debts and assets have to be consolidated in order to ascertain his financial position, any interest paid can be regarded as a cost of obtaining any property income received by the individual. This suggests that an appropriate procedure for tax purposes would be to pool all property income and interest payments and to allow the deduction of the latter from the former. Interest payments could be deductible up to the full amount of receipts of taxable

6. Gordon Bale finds the Canadian rule unsatisfactory conceptually and practically; see "The Interest Deduction Dilemma," *Canadian Tax Journal*, vol. 21 (July– August 1973), pp. 317–36.

income from property but not beyond, or could be allocated between taxable and nontaxable income according to a general rule.

Either the matching or the pooling procedure would eliminate the bulk of personal interest deductions (interest deductions claimed against AGI as distinguished from interest payments taken into account in arriving at AGI).

About one-fourth of personal interest deductions in 1970 was on returns reporting income only from salaries and wages (table 7-3) and hence could not have been a cost of obtaining property income in that year.[7] A large part of the remainder was claimed by persons whose interest deductions exceeded their taxable income from sources other than salaries and wages. If individuals had been allowed to deduct interest payments only up to the amount of their taxable income from property, two-thirds or more of the interest deductions actually taken in 1970 would have been ruled out. These are minimum fractions because in table 7-3 all income from unincorporated business enterprises, which includes a substantial amount of labor income, is treated as if it were property income. Middle- and low-income taxpayers would be much more affected than those with high incomes, but this is not a valid objection if the interest deduction is regarded as an allowance for a cost of obtaining income.

The interest deduction, in my opinion, should be limited to payments related to the production of taxable income, as determined by the pooling procedure described above or, less satisfactorily, by direct matching.[8] Students' payments of interest on debts contracted to finance education intended to increase their earning power should be classified as costs related to the production of their earned income and should be deductible against that income. A special carryover or averaging provision might be appropriate for persons with fluctuating income or interest payments.

_____

7. But some of these interest payments may have related to taxable property income of prior or future years or to debt contracted to pay for expenditures on education that added to earnings.

8. In the Tax Reform Act of 1969 Congress imposed, effective in 1972, a mild limitation on the deduction of interest payments. This is addressed, not to the general problem discussed in the text, but to an abuse consisting of deducting against ordinary income large amounts of interest paid on funds borrowed to buy or carry assets that yield their return in the form of long-term capital gains. See Internal Revenue Code, sec. 163(d); *Tax Reform Act of 1969*, H. Rept. 91-413, 91 Cong. 1 sess. (1969), pt. 1, pp. 72–73.

Table 7-3. Distribution of Itemized Personal Deductions on Individual Income Tax Returns for Interest Paid and Relation to Nonwage Income, by Adjusted Gross Income (AGI) Class, 1970[a]

		Percent of interest deductions in AGI class	
AGI class (thousands of dollars)	Percent of total interest deductions	On returns with no nonwage income[b]	"Excess" deductions on other returns[c]
Under 2	*	1	41
2–3	*	21	38
3–5	3	37	28
5–10	23	41	33
10–25	56	27	46
25–50	10	3	35
50–100	4	*	17
100–500	2	*	13
500 and over	1	0	6
All classes	100	27	39

Source: Brookings 1970 Tax File. Figures are rounded.
* Less than 0.5.
a. Taxable and nontaxable returns with itemized deductions.
b. Percent of interest deductions in the AGI class claimed on returns reporting income only from salaries and wages.
c. Computed as ratio of (1) excess of interest deductions on returns with nonwage income over nonwage income on these returns (negative nonwage income being treated as zero) to (2) total interest deductions in the AGI class.

Casualty Losses

The Internal Revenue Code allows a deduction for "losses of property not connected with a trade or business, if such losses arise from fire, storm, shipwreck, or other casualty, or from theft." The amount deductible is the excess of the loss over $100 for any one occurrence. Since the deduction cannot exceed the cost or other basis of the property, the disappearance of unrealized capital gains does not give rise to a deduction. Furthermore, in computing the deduction, the recognized loss is reduced by any insurance or other compensation received.

The limitation of the deduction to losses exceeding $100 was introduced in the Revenue Act of 1964. In adopting this clause, Congress made clear that it regarded the casualty-loss deduction as a hardship provision rather than a refinement of the income definition. The House Ways and Means Committee stated that its intention was "to allow the deduction only of those losses which may be considered extraordinary, nonrecurring losses, and which go beyond the average or usual losses incurred by most taxpayers in day-to-day living" and which are "sufficient in size to have a significant effect upon an individual's ability to pay Federal income taxes."[9]

The case for the casualty-loss deduction as a means of relieving hardship is weak. For this purpose, a floor related to income, as for the medical-expense deduction, would be more appropriate than the present provision, since a $100 loss is not as great a hardship for a person with a high income as for one with a low income.

A more important objection is that persons who wish protection can insure themselves against most of the casualties. Since uninsured losses are deductible but insurance premiums are not, the income tax discriminates against those who carry insurance and favors those who do not.[10] Through the casualty-loss deduction, the government in effect acts as a coinsurer, with its participation varying according to the taxpayer's marginal rate.

The bias extends also to measures to care for property. For example, a householder who does not take the trouble to protect his shrubbery from a quick freeze or sudden drought may experience a deductible casualty loss. Expenditures incurred to care for the shrubs, of course, would be nondeductible personal expenses. Nor would a deduction be allowed if a loss was suffered because of neglect extending over a long period of time.

While uninsured casualty losses might be appropriate deductions for a tax assessed on accrued income comprehensively defined, their allowance is questionable so long as important items of imputed income and accrued capital gains are not taken into account. In my judgment, the casualty-loss deduction should be confined to uninsured losses on property yielding taxable income, and premiums paid on insurance against losses on such property should also be deductible. The reasoning is that the losses or insurance premiums are properly viewed as costs of obtaining the services of capital goods and

9. *Revenue Act of 1963,* H. Rept. 749, 88 Cong. 1 sess. (1963), p. 52. The same language appears in *Revenue Act of 1964,* S. Rept. 830, 88 Cong. 2 sess. (1964), p. 57. The President had recommended that nonbusiness casualty losses be allowed only to the extent that they exceeded 4 percent of AGI. *President's 1963 Tax Message Along with Principal Statement, Technical Explanation, and Supporting Exhibits and Documents Submitted by Secretary of the Treasury,* House Ways and Means Committee Print (1963), pp. 15–16.

10. William Vickrey, *Agenda for Progressive Taxation* (Ronald Press, 1947), pp. 60–62.

should be charged against the yield of these goods. When the yield is taxable, the costs are properly deductible in computing taxable income; when the yield is not taxable, the deduction is inequitable for the same reason that a deduction for interest payments is inappropriate.

Child Care and Disabled-Dependent Care

A deduction of expenses for the care of children and disabled dependents or spouses was adopted in 1954 and has been subsequently liberalized. The deduction covers not only direct expenses for the care of children or disabled persons in the taxpayer's household and the care of children outside the household but payments for necessary domestic help. It is available to married persons who were employed on a substantially full-time basis during the period in which the expenses were incurred and to single persons who maintain a household that includes one or more qualifying individuals but only if care was provided for the purpose of enabling the taxpayer (and spouse, if married) to be gainfully employed. Qualifying individuals are dependents under the age of fifteen, other dependents who are physically or mentally incapable of self-care, and a spouse who is physically or mentally incapable of self-care.[11]

The deduction is limited to a maximum of $400 a month. When the taxpayer's adjusted gross income (combined with the AGI of the spouse in the case of married persons) exceeds $35,000 in the year, the deduction is reduced by one-half of the amount over $35,000. Thus no deduction is allowed for persons with AGI above $44,600. These income limits apply to years beginning after March 29, 1975, the effective date of the Tax Reduction Act of 1975; the previous limits were $18,000 and $27,600, respectively. The estimated revenue cost of the deduction is about $300 million.[12]

Congressional committee reports and the language of the statute make clear that the primary purpose of the deduction is to cover

11. Within the technical meaning of the Internal Revenue Code, one's spouse is never a dependent, but a "taxpayer" regardless of whether he or she receives a separate income.

12. Estimate for calendar year 1975 income level, derived from *Special Analyses, Budget of the United States Government, Fiscal Year 1976*, p. 108; and *Summary of the Major Provisions of Public Law 94-12, Tax Reduction Act of 1975*, prepared by the House Committee on Ways and Means, 94 Cong. 1 sess. (1975), p. 17.

certain costs of earning income. The deduction, nevertheless, is an itemized personal deduction rather than an expense that may be taken into account in computing AGI. The amount of the deduction is not explicitly related to the amount earned from employment and can exceed that amount. However, the Treasury Department states, "Generally, if your employment-related expenses exceed your earnings for the same period, it would cast doubt on whether the purpose is to enable you to be *gainfully* employed."[13]

As a refinement of the definition of income, the deduction is a partial and imperfect solution of a general problem. It is too narrow in that it does not cover all kinds of work-related expenses and is not granted to all who incur additional expenses to enable them to work outside the home. At the same time, the deduction extends to some expenses that by ordinary standards would be considered personal consumption rather than costs of obtaining income. The income limitation suggests that Congress regards the relief of hardship as a secondary objective of the deduction. Viewed from this standpoint, it is questionable on the grounds that the amount of the benefit bears no clear relation to need and that the income limitation is high.

On balance, the deduction appears to offer too generous treatment in circumstances that are too restrictively specified. Before proposing further revisions, however, it seems advisable to wait a few years in order to obtain information on the extent to which the present provision is used and on possible abuses and complexities.

Medical Expenses

The deduction for medical expenses was introduced in 1942. It applies to expenditures for medical and dental care, hospitalization, drugs and medicines, certain related goods and services, and health and accident insurance. The deduction is intended to cover only expenses that are extraordinarily large in relation to income.[14] It has always been restricted to expenses in excess of a certain minimum percentage of income and in the past it was subject to a dollar limit. The floor at present is 3 percent of AGI, but for drugs and medi-

---

13. Internal Revenue Service, *Your Federal Income Tax, 1974 Edition,* p. 97.
14. According to the House Ways and Means Committee, "generally only what are considered abnormal medical expenses are deductible" (*Revenue Act of 1963,* H. Rept. 749, p. 56).

cines only amounts spent in excess of 1 percent of income may be included. Up to $150 of payments for medical insurance may be deducted without regard to the 3 percent floor, and the remainder may be added to other medical expenses which are deductible subject to the floor. A dollar ceiling on the medical-expense deduction was eliminated effective in 1967.

The 3 percent floor does not seem highly restrictive. In 1970, consumers' expenditures for medical care averaged 5.9 percent of personal income.[15] Seventy-seven percent of all taxpayers who itemized deductions were able to claim a deduction for medical expenses in 1970 (table A-8).

When the deduction was first adopted in 1942, total medical expenses equaled 3 percent of personal income, and the deduction was allowed only for expenses in excess of 5 percent of income. Thereafter, medical expenses grew more rapidly than personal income and the limitation was liberalized. These factors, together with the increased frequency of itemization of personal deductions, resulted in a rise in the proportion of estimated total medical expenses that was deducted on tax returns, from 18 percent in 1942 and 1950 to 27 percent in 1960. This trend was then reversed, and in 1970 the amount deducted on tax returns was equal to 22 percent of estimated total medical expenses of consumers.[16]

More than other major itemized deductions, that for medical expenses tends to decline as a fraction of income as income rises (table A-9). Nevertheless, a large part of the deduction and of the tax saving resulting from it—estimated at $1.7 billion in 1970—accrues to middle- and high-income persons, and the majority of high-income taxpayers qualify (tables A-8, A-12, A-13).

The medical-expense deduction has been widely approved, even by some who are critical of other personal deductions. The attitude

15. U.S. Department of Commerce, *Survey of Current Business,* vol. 53 (July 1973), pp. 27, 29. This estimate of medical expenditures includes some items that are not eligible for deduction but excludes other items that are eligible. See Kahn, *Personal Deductions,* pp. 136–37, note 19.

16. Derived from estimates of total personal consumption expenditures for medical care in U.S. Department of Commerce, *The National Income and Product Accounts of the United States, 1929–1965: Statistical Tables* (1966), pp. 44–45, and *Survey of Current Business* (July 1973), p. 29. Deductions for medical expenses shown on taxable and nontaxable returns are from Kahn, *Personal Deductions,* p. 137; *Statistics of Income—1960,* p. 55, and *1970,* p. 120.

seems to be that a person has little control over the amount of his medical expenses and that these expenses are unforeseeable and sometimes catastrophically large. Above a certain normal level, medical expenses are regarded as a reduction of an individual's freely disposable income and hence a reduction in his ability to pay taxes relative to others with the same income.

This attitude reflects the high regard in which medical care is held and the faith that is placed in its efficacy. In view of prevailing values, it is plausible. Yet the attitude does understate the voluntary element in medical expenditures and the consumption component of these outlays. Surely the difference between the cost of a private suite in a proprietary hospital and a bed in a voluntary hospital is to a large extent a living expense rather than a medical expense; nevertheless, the whole cost of both accommodations is deductible.

The difficulty in distinguishing between ordinary consumption and medical expenses is reflected in numerous rulings and court decisions. The most troublesome items relate to travel, food and lodging, education and training, and consumer durables. The cost of necessary transportation, both local and away from home, for the purpose of obtaining medical care qualifies. This extends to travel to a warmer climate when prescribed by a physician, but generally not to the cost of food and lodging while away from home. A taxpayer wintering in Florida on the advice of his doctor was allowed to deduct the cost of preparing salt-free food and of taxi rides to restaurants serving it— but not the cost of the food itself. Expenditures for special food or beverages prescribed by a physician solely for the alleviation or treatment of an illness qualify, provided they are additional to the normal diet and not a substitute for items ordinarily consumed. As examples, the Internal Revenue Service mentions as deductible the cost of two ounces of whiskey taken twice a day for the relief of angina pain (by a nondrinker?) but as nondeductible the cost of a special diet prescribed for an ulcer patient.

When a person is in a nursing home because of his physical condition and the availability of medical care, the entire cost, including the cost of meals and lodging, is deductible; however, if he is in such an institution "primarily for personal or family reasons" only the portion of the charge attributable to medical or nursing care qualifies. In one case, the cost of sending a child with psychological problems to a special school was held deductible on the grounds that education was only incidental to the function of medical care, but in another case the tax court held nondeductible the cost of sending a child with emotional problems to a school emphasizing corrective and remedial reading on the grounds that education was the primary function of the school. Dancing lessons did not qualify, even when recommended by a physician to a person who had undergone abdominal surgery and psychiatric treatment. However, the cost of a clarinet and of lessons in playing it was deductible when the taxpayer's son had a tooth defect that allegedly was helped by playing the instrument. The installation of elevators, air conditioners, and other home improvements may give rise to deductible expenditures but only to the extent that they do not increase the value of the property. Finally, funeral expenses do not qualify.[17]

Despite the inclusion of medical insurance premiums in expenses for purposes of the deduction, those with insurance are less favorably treated than others. The expenditures of a person with insurance against catastrophic medical expenses are more regular than those of an uninsured person and hence less likely to exceed the floor in any one year. If the floor were equal to the average annual ratio of medical expense to income, a representative taxpayer with insurance or a prepayment arrangement covering all medical bills would never be able to claim a deduction. Anyone who carries no insurance makes the government a coinsurer against extraordinary medical expenses. In this respect, the medical deduction resembles the casualty loss deduction but is less discriminatory. The discrimination is real enough, nevertheless, to raise the question whether it is good public policy to offer a tax preference to those who choose not to carry insurance.

To carry out the intention of limiting the deduction to abnormal expenses, the floor should be raised to at least 5 percent or 6 percent of income. Still more effective as a means of aiding persons with extraordinary expenses would be to convert the deduction into a tax credit; that is, to allow all or part of eligible expenditures to be subtracted from tax liability rather than from taxable income. Many variations of the floor and the deduction or credit would be possible,

17. *Code of Federal Regulations*, Title 26, pt. 1 (1975), sec. 1.213-1; *Your Federal Income Tax, 1974 Edition*, pp. 85–89; *Prentice-Hall Federal Taxes, 1975* (Prentice-Hall, 1975), vol. 2, par. 16,390–16,437.

with the total amount of aid being more or less than that now provided by the deduction.[18] A disadvantage of proposals that would
offer a full tax credit or a large percentage credit is that they, like
comparable medical insurance plans, would further diminish the
interest of individuals in keeping down costs and would tend to stimulate nonessential expenditures. There would be merit in defining
extraordinary medical expenses for tax purposes by reference to
average income and expenditures over a period of several years rather
than the current year only; however, the added complexity probably
would outweigh any gain in equity.

Finally, proposals for a system of national health insurance have
been widely discussed in recent years. If a comprehensive plan is
adopted, consideration should be given to eliminating the medical
expense deduction.

Philanthropic Contributions

A personal deduction for philanthropic contributions was proposed but rejected in 1913, when the first income tax bill after the
Sixteenth Amendment was under consideration. The deduction was
adopted in 1917 in response to the fear that high tax rates would
cause contributions to decline.[19] The deduction is now allowed for
contributions to religious, charitable, scientific, literary, and educational organizations and organizations for the prevention of cruelty
to children and animals. These organizations must meet three tests:
no part of their net earnings, if any, may be used for the benefit of
private shareholders or individuals; "no substantial part" of their
activities may consist of "carrying on propaganda, or otherwise, at-
tempting to influence legislation"; and they may not "participate in,
or intervene in" a political campaign on behalf of a candidate for
public office. Also eligible for deduction are contributions to the
federal government, state and local governments, veterans' organizations, and nonprofit cemetery companies. Contributions to foreign
organizations (except certain Canadian charities) do not qualify;
however, funds contributed to U.S. organizations may be transferred
to foreign organizations provided the U.S. organization retains con-

18. See Edward R. Fried and others, *Setting National Priorities: The 1974
Budget* (Brookings Institution, 1973), pp. 118–20.
19. Kahn, *Personal Deductions,* pp. 6–7, 46–47.

trol over their use. Gifts to individuals are not deductible. With a minor exception, the deduction has always been subject to a limit related to the taxpayer's income.[20]

According to the available estimates, total contributions from living individual donors have amounted to something less than 2 percent of personal income in the years since 1940.[21] In 1970 almost nine-tenths of the estimated total contributions were claimed as itemized deductions on taxable and nontaxable individual income tax returns.

The deduction for philanthropic contributions is relatively more important in the top income brackets than any of the other personal deductions. A curve relating contributions to income of taxpayers with itemized deductions would be U-shaped, with higher ratios at the two extremes than in the middle brackets (appendix table A-9). In this respect it would be the opposite of the curve for the interest deduction.

The justification for deduction of philanthropic contributions is usually stated as the encouragement or reward of socially desirable activity, rather than the refinement of the income definition or allowance for differences in taxable capacity. Occasionally, efforts have been made to justify the deduction on the grounds that contributions divest the taxpayer of income, but this reasoning has not been widely accepted in the United States. In the United Kingdom, on the other hand, contributors can obtain tax relief only because of the general doctrine allowing avoidance of tax on assigned income, and the conditions are much more restrictive than in the United States.[22]

Contributions finance educational, cultural, religious, and welfare

20. Formerly no limit was imposed when a person's contributions plus his income tax exceeded 90 percent of taxable income for the current year and eight of the preceding ten years. This provision was ended by the Tax Reform Act of 1969 and was phased out over the five years 1970–74.

21. For the period before 1960, the estimates of total contributions are from Frank G. Dickinson, *The Changing Position of Philanthropy in the American Economy*, Occasional Paper 110 (Columbia University Press for the National Bureau of Economic Research, 1970), p. 41; for later years the estimates are those of the American Association of Fund-Raising Counsel, Inc., from U.S. Bureau of the Census, *Statistical Abstract of the United States, 1973*, p. 314. Estimates of personal income and disposable income are those of the Bureau of Economic Analysis, U.S. Department of Commerce.

22. Royal Commission on the Taxation of Profits and Income, *Final Report*, Cmd. 9474 (London: Her Majesty's Stationery Office, 1955), pp. 58–60.

activities, which are highly important but which are not adequately provided by a market economy. The cost of many of these activities would be assumed by the state if they were not covered by contributions, and to the extent that the deduction stimulates their voluntary support it helps relieve pressure on the budget.

But many of the organizations and activities would not be supported by taxation or would be financed less liberally if they were no longer financed by contributions. This is the basis of a strong criticism of the deduction. The taxpayer, by making a deductible contribution, forces the government, in effect, to make a partially matching grant for a purpose of his own choosing and to an organization whose operations are not subject to government review or control. Sectarian, provincial, eccentric, or frivolous uses of money may be aided along with the most worthy. Public money would not be appropriated for the religious functions of churches, which are major recipients of deductible contributions, or for many other activities that benefit from the deduction.

This criticism can be met on its own terms by arguing that the lack of government control is a positive advantage. Granted a consensus on the general desirability of the purposes that are aided, the absence of detailed legislative specifications concerning eligibility for assistance allows divisive controversy about the relations of church and state to be avoided. An atheist can tolerate deductions for gifts to churches if he knows that he can deduct contributions to causes that he espouses.

For educational, scientific, and cultural activities, voluntary support helps maintain diversity and independence. In my judgment, it is fortunate that Congress does not feel it necessary to scrutinize deductions for contributions as regularly and carefully as it examines appropriations or to attach the same conditions to the two. The appropriations process is not well suited to the nourishment of new or unpopular ideas or minority tastes; the usual procedures for handling public funds would often be cumbersome or worse in this area. Despite occasional agitation for stricter limitations, Congress, in addition to denying deductions for contributions to organizations that attempt to influence legislation or support a candidate for public office, has placed only one further political or ideological control on the deductibility of contributions: its denial for contributions to registered communist-action organizations or to organizations that have been directed to register as such by the Subversive Activities Control Board.[23] A considerable amount of waste and personal gratification of donors to questionable philanthropies may not be too high a price to pay for decentralized control and flexible operations of the worthy organizations and activities. I think it unlikely that a system of matching government grants to charitable organizations that receive gifts from taxpayers, which has been proposed as a substitute for the deduction,[24] would be as free of undesirable controls or would serve the values of pluralism as well.

A real issue remains concerning the effectiveness of the deduction as an incentive to giving. Even if the arguments in favor of the deduction are conceded to be qualitatively valid, they would not establish a case for its continuance if it could be shown that the amount of giving stimulated by the deduction is very small relative to the revenue loss. The loss of government revenue requires either that tax rates be raised or that public expenditures be curtailed.

The revenue cost of the deduction is substantial. According to Kahn's estimates, it amounted to one-third or more of total contributions by living donors in 1954.[25] The comparable figure for 1970 was about 26 percent.[26]

It is difficult to judge how contributors are influenced by the tax saving and how much weight they attach to the opportunity of turning over to the recipient organization an amount exceeding their own sacrifice of disposable income. The introduction of the optional standard deduction in the early 1940s, which removed the tax incentive for contributions by persons using it, appears not to have diminished the share of income devoted to philanthropy.[27] A study by Taussig concluded that the incentive effect of the deduction is weak and

23. Internal Security Act of 1950, sec. 11(a) (64 Stat. 996; 50 U.S.C. 790). The courts and the Internal Revenue Service have denied deductions for contributions to schools and social organizations that maintain racial segregation. For a review of this and other constitutional questions related to the deduction, see Stanley S. Surrey and others, *Federal Income Taxation: Cases and Materials* (Foundation Press, 1972), vol. 1, pp. 585–601.

24. Paul R. McDaniel, "An Alternative to the Federal Income Tax Deduction in Support of Private Philanthropy," in *Tax Impacts on Philanthropy,* Symposium Conducted by the Tax Institute of America (TIA, 1972), pp. 171–209.

25. *Personal Deductions,* p. 72.

26. Derived from a Treasury Department estimate of the revenue cost of the deduction (table A-12) and the estimate of contributions cited in footnote 21 above.

27. Kahn, *Personal Deductions,* p. 72.

attributable almost entirely to the reaction of the very high income group. The author cautioned, however, that his findings had only weak statistical reliability and were subject to serious qualifications.[28] In the light of later research, Taussig appears to have underestimated the incentive effect. A study by Schwartz, using different statistics and methods, indicates that the response is much greater at all income levels than Taussig reported, though it agrees with him that the revenue loss from the deduction exceeds the amount of contributions that it stimulates.[29] Feldstein, in a recent study, finds that the deduction increases contributions by somewhat more than it reduces the Treasury's revenue.[30] While these later estimates seem to meet higher technical standards of statistical significance than those of Taussig, both Schwartz and Feldstein caution about problems in their reliability and interpretation.

Contrary to the suppositions of informed observers,[31] Schwartz and Feldstein find that, in relation to the amount of tax saved by virtue of the deduction, low- and middle-income givers are at least as responsive as those with large incomes and high marginal tax rates. Nevertheless, with allowance for the greater tax value per dollar of deduction in the high-income classes, it is true that the amount given by high-income persons is more affected. This is significant because of differences in the kind of gifts made by donors in different income groups. Small givers contribute mainly to religious organizations, whereas large givers offer more support to educational institutions, hospitals, and foundations.[32] For example, in 1962, among taxpayers who itemized deductions, donors with adjusted gross income below $15,000 gave 69 percent of their contributions to religious organizations and accounted for 80 percent of the amount given to these

28. Michael K. Taussig, "Economic Aspects of the Personal Income Tax Treatment of Charitable Contributions," *National Tax Journal*, vol. 20 (March 1967), pp. 1–19.

29. Robert A. Schwartz, "Personal Philanthropic Contributions," *Journal of Political Economy*, vol. 78 (November–December 1970), pp. 1264–91.

30. Martin Feldstein, "The Income Tax and Charitable Contributions: Part 1— Aggregate and Distributional Effects," *National Tax Journal*, vol. 28 (March 1975), pp. 81–100.

31. Kahn, *Personal Deductions*, p. 72; William S. Vickrey, "One Economist's View of Philanthropy," in Frank G. Dickinson, ed., *Philanthropy and Public Policy* (National Bureau of Economic Research, 1962), p. 54.

32. See F. Emerson Andrews, *Philanthropic Giving* (Russell Sage Foundation, 1950), p. 56; Kahn, *Personal Deductions*, pp. 81–82.

organizations. Donors with AGI above $15,000 diversified their gifts to a greater extent; they contributed 79 percent of the amount given to educational institutions and hospitals.[33]

A better balance between revenue cost and incentive effects might be struck by limiting the deduction for contributions to persons whose gifts exceed a certain percentage of income. Contributions, like medical expenses, would become a factor in determining income tax liability only when they rose above a routine level. The objective would be to focus the reward or incentive more sharply by withdrawing the deduction from persons whose contributions are small relative to income while continuing it for heavier contributions. Those whose gifts were close to the floor would find that an increase in contributions would qualify them for the deduction and thereby reduce the cost to them of the additional contributions.

Consideration might be given to a floor of about 3 percent of AGI. This figure is a little higher than the average for all returns with itemized deductions in 1970 but is considerably below the average for high-income classes (table A-9). In 1970, only one-third of the individual returns that claimed deductions for charitable contributions reported amounts over 3 percent of AGI, but this group accounted for two-thirds of the total deductions.[34]

Introduction of the floor would cause the disallowance of a large number of small contributions, which are almost impossible for the Internal Revenue Service to verify and which may not be accurately reported. It might be advisable—though a complication—to require some kind of averaging of income and contributions over a period of years to prevent taxpayers from bunching their contributions with a view to minimizing the effect of the floor. Such manipulation of the floor for the deduction of medical expenditures is also possible but is less easy.

The rationale for a ceiling on deductions for contributions is not obvious and the ceiling is now complex in form. In general, the deduction is limited to 50 percent of adjusted gross income, computed without regard to the net operating loss carry-back. However, for contributions to certain private nonoperating foundations, veterans' organizations, fraternal societies, and cemetery organizations, the

33. *Statistics of Income—1962*, p. 6. The percentages relate only to itemized deductions on taxable individual returns.
34. *Statistics of Income—1970*, p. 128.

limit is 20 percent. A 30 percent limit applies to certain gifts of so-called capital gains property (see below). Contributions in excess of the 50 percent limit may be carried over and deducted in the next five years.

The 50 percent ceiling may reflect the view that beyond this point the revenue needs of the government should have priority over the admittedly worthwhile activities supported by contributions that qualify for the maximum deduction. This line of reasoning, however, seems to be related more to aggregate deductions than to the contributions of the small number of individuals who will be subject to the ceiling. The lower limit for private nonoperating foundations apparently was motivated by skepticism about the value of the programs of some of these organizations and concern about abuses in their operations. Other provisions of the Tax Reform Act of 1969 attack these problems more directly and would seem to be more effective.[35] Although the 50 percent ceiling does not appear to be very restrictive, consideration might be given to lifting it if the treatment of gifts of appreciated property were simultaneously revised.

Gifts of property as well as money are deductible, but contributions of one's own services are not deductible. The latter provision is reasonable, although at first it may seem discriminatory. If one contributes $100 of his current earnings to charity, he will still be taxed on that sum unless a deduction is allowed. If he does unpaid work worth $100, no deduction is needed to remove the contribution from his taxable income.

Before 1970, writers or artists could circumvent this provision by contributing their own literary or artistic works and obtaining a deduction for their full fair market value. This opportunity was eliminated by legislation enacted in 1969. A provision aimed at political figures also ended the possibility of claiming a deduction for the value of letters or memoranda produced by the donor or by other persons for him.

Gifts of appreciated property of a kind that would result in a capital gain if sold are accorded especially favorable treatment. Subject to certain conditions, a person who gives capital gains property—

---

35. See Francis M. Gregory, Jr., "The Congress and Private Foundations—Will the Patient Survive the Operation?" in National Tax Association, *Proceedings of the Sixty-fourth Annual Conference on Taxation, 1971* (1972), pp. 179–206; Robert Anthoine, "Effect on Donors," in *Tax Impacts on Philanthropy*, pp. 60–63.

for instance, securities, real estate, or works of art—to an organization that qualifies for the 50 percent ceiling is entitled to deduct the full current market value.[36] When the current value exceeds the original cost, he obtains a deduction for gains that have never entered into taxable income. It is advantageous to give appreciated property directly instead of selling it and contributing the proceeds. If the property were sold, the realized capital gain would be included in income and offset by the deduction. But if the property is given directly, no gain is taken into account, and the deduction applies against other income.

A donor who gives appreciated property makes a smaller sacrifice, relative to what he could obtain from a sale, than one who makes another gift. If, for example, two art collectors who are both subject to a 60 percent marginal tax rate each give a museum a painting worth $10,000, the deduction will save each of them $6,000 of tax. If one collector had bought his painting many years earlier for $1,000, he would have had to pay $2,250 of capital gains tax if he had sold it (25 percent of a $9,000 capital gain) and would have realized $7,750. Compared with selling, the net financial cost of the gift is $1,750 ($7,750 − $6,000). If the other collector bought his painting recently at a price equal to its current value, he could sell without paying a capital gains tax; the net financial cost of his contribution would be $4,000 ($10,000 − $6,000), which is the same as the cost of a $10,000 cash contribution.[37]

There seems to be no good reason for favoring those who contribute appreciated property over those who give other property or cash. The present provision, moreover, gives rise to difficulties in valuing gifts of art objects, books and manuscripts, and other items and apparently tempts some donors to place excessive values on their gifts, occasionally with the collusion of recipient institutions. The inequalities and administrative difficulties could be avoided by limiting deductions for gifts of property to an amount equal to the cost (or other basis). Another approach, which would be less simple but which

36. This does not apply to items produced by oneself, inventory, or items held less than six months. If tangible personal property is contributed and it is not for the use of the recipient organization in its tax-exempt function, the deduction is reduced by one-half of the appreciation. A similar reduction applies to gifts to private foundations.

37. The illustration assumes that the first collector qualifies for the 25 percent alternative tax on capital gains. See p. 176.

would deal with the inequities and abuses and lessen the valuation problems, would be to treat a gift as a constructive realization of a capital gain for tax purposes (see chapter 8). Either of these reforms would reduce the special tax incentives for making gifts of appreciated property but would leave unimpaired the general incentives for contributions.

Taxes

The deduction for taxes paid covers state and local taxes on property, income, gasoline, and other motor fuels and state and local general sales taxes. Other state and local taxes and federal taxes are usually deductible only if incurred in business or the production of income. Foreign taxes on real property and income are deductible, but other foreign taxes are not deductible unless connected with trade or business or the production of income. Subject to certain conditions, taxpayers may credit foreign income taxes against their U.S. tax instead of deducting them from gross income, and this option is ordinarily chosen.

The personal deduction for taxes paid has been curtailed over the years. Originally, most taxes that were legally imposed on a person, including the federal income tax itself, were deductible. (The deduction of the income tax did not require the solution of simultaneous equations; payments were then made in the year after the accrual of liability, and a taxpayer on a cash basis deducted the amount paid during the year rather than the liability on the current year's income.) The deduction of the federal income tax was eliminated in 1917, and that of federal excise taxes was dropped in 1943. In 1964, the deduction was ended for state and local taxes on tobacco and alcoholic beverages, automobile and drivers' licenses, and other state-local selective excises except gasoline taxes. Death and gift taxes are also nondeductible; however, a special credit for state death taxes is allowed against the federal estate tax.

In 1970 about 44 percent of total state and local taxes qualified as personal deductions, and some seven-tenths of the eligible amount was claimed on returns with itemized deductions.[38] Most of the re-

38. Estimated from state and local tax receipts as shown in the national income and product accounts (*Survey of Current Business*, July 1973, tables 3.3, 7.3), and personal deductions reported in *Statistics of Income—1970*, p. 123. Deductible taxes include personal income taxes, general sales taxes, personal property taxes, property

Table 7-4. Personal Deductions for Taxes Paid on Taxable Individual Income Tax
Returns with Itemized Deductions, by Adjusted Gross Income (AGI) Class and
Type of Tax, 1970

AGI class (thousands of dollars)	Tax as percent of AGI					
	All	Real estate	Sales	Income[a]	Gasoline[a]	Other
Under 3[b]	11.1	5.7	2.3	0.9	1.6	0.6
3–5	8.3	3.4	2.1	1.0	1.3	0.5
5–10	7.2	2.7	1.8	1.3	1.0	0.4
10–25	6.9	2.7	1.5	1.8	0.6	0.3
25–50	7.1	2.5	1.1	3.0	0.3	0.2
50–100	7.0	2.0	0.7	3.8	0.1	0.2
100–500	7.3	1.6	0.5	4.8	0.1	0.3
500 and over	5.9	0.8	0.2	4.4	*	0.5
All classes	7.1	2.6	1.4	2.0	0.6	0.3

Source: *Statistics of Income—1970*, p. 123. Figures are rounded.
* Less than 0.05.
a. State and local taxes.
b. Statistics shown relate to returns with AGI above $1,000; returns with AGI under $1,000 are omitted here because of high sampling variability but are included in the totals.

maining state and local taxes probably were deductible as business
expenses.[39]

Almost everyone who itemizes deductions reports tax payments
(table A-8). In relation to AGI, total deductions for taxes are
roughly constant over a wide income range (table 7-4). As would
be expected, real estate, sales, and gasoline taxes decline in relation
to income whereas state and local income taxes are progressive. The
high ratio of tax deductions in the income classes below $5,000
should not be taken as representative of the impact of the state-local
tax system inasmuch as the statistics relate only to the small minority
of taxpayers in these classes who itemized their deductions.

An argument in favor of the personal deduction for taxes that
formerly attracted popular support is that the failure to allow the
deduction would result in a particularly objectionable form of double
taxation, involving "a tax on a tax." Congress rejected this rationale

taxes on owner-occupied nonfarm dwellings, and part of gasoline taxes. Gasoline
taxes were allocated between consumers and business users by reference to estimated
total consumer expenditures for gasoline and the average state-local gasoline tax
rate (Bureau of the Census, *Statistical Abstract, 1973*, pp. 550, 551, 658; *Survey of
Current Business,* July 1973, table 2.5).

39. James A. Maxwell, *Tax Credits and Intergovernmental Relations* (Brookings
Institution, 1962), pp. 107, 187–98.

when it ended the deductibility of federal excises and certain state-local taxes.

The most widely accepted reason for deducting state and local taxes is to aid in fiscal coordination in a federal system. A common version of this argument is that a deduction is needed to prevent confiscation. The danger that marginal tax rates will approach or exceed 100 percent is greatest for income taxes, and many commentators have concluded that the deduction should be allowed only for state and local income taxes. Another view is that confiscation in the literal sense is merely an extreme example of injustices that may occur when two levels of government tax independently. The federal government, because of its greater financial strength and wider jurisdiction, is better able than the states to grant relief from burdens caused by overlapping taxes.

By offering a deduction for state-local taxes, the federal government also aids the other governments. The state and local governments are given more scope for taxation; the impact of tax increases on their citizens is lessened, and governing bodies are likely to feel less worried about the risk of losing population and business to places with lower taxes. The state and local governments, therefore, may be enabled to finance more adequately the important public services that are their primary responsibility. Deductibility, however, should not be overrated. It stops far short of removing the differences between high and low taxes and between progressive and regressive taxes. When federal income tax rates are reduced, the significance of deductibility diminishes.

An objection that is sometimes made to the deductibility of state and local taxes, particularly income taxes, is that it reduces the progressivity of the federal income tax. This is correct[40] but not very significant for tax policy. If, as seems likely, deductibility induces state and local governments to rely less on regressive taxes and to impose more progressive income taxes, the progressivity of the combined federal, state, and local tax system will be increased, or its regressivity decreased.

In my judgment, the best balance between considerations of equity and intergovernmental fiscal coordination would be struck by con-

---

40. See Benjamin Bridges, Jr., "Deductibility of State and Local Nonbusiness Taxes under the Federal Individual Income Tax," *National Tax Journal,* vol. 19 (March 1966), pp. 7–8, 15.

tinuing the personal deduction for state and local income taxes and broad sales and use taxes while eliminating it for property taxes and gasoline taxes. Taxes other than income taxes and general sales and use taxes would be deductible only as costs of obtaining taxable income. By allowing both income taxes and sales taxes to be deducted, the federal government would lessen inhibitions on the use of the former without exerting pressure on states to choose one or the other revenue source. Payments of income tax and sales taxes depend less on individual tastes and living arrangements than other tax payments and are less often used to finance services that especially benefit those who pay the taxes. The amount of income tax paid is easily ascertained; and, with the development by the Internal Revenue Service of tables showing standard amounts of deductions for sales tax in the various states, reporting and auditing of this item have been simplified.

The elimination of the personal deduction for gasoline taxes is justified because most of the proceeds of these taxes are used for the special benefit of those who pay them. Acting as a subsidy for commuting and other travel by automobile, this deduction makes its own small contribution to congestion and smog.

The property tax is a doubtful item. Although it has special-benefit aspects, the tax is a major source of general revenue for local governments and may be sensitive to political pressures and competition between jurisdictions. Since the deduction is available only to homeowners, however, it gravely discriminates against renters, who bear a large part of the property tax on their dwellings. This inequity, in my opinion, outweighs the advantages of property-tax deductibility as a coordination measure. Others may think differently.[41] If imputed rent of owner-occupied dwellings were included in gross income, property taxes as well as other costs of ownership should be deductible.

Political Campaign Contributions

The Revenue Act of 1971 introduced a limited personal deduction and an alternative tax credit for contributions to political candidates

41. Maxwell believes that the rationale for deductibility of property taxes, income taxes, and sales taxes is "much superior" to that for deductibility of excises that are levied on a benefit basis or that serve sumptuary purposes (*Tax Credits,* pp. 97–100).

or campaign committees, provided the contribution is used in connection with candidacy for public office. Effective in 1975 the original limits were doubled. The maximum deduction became $100 ($200 on a joint return of husband and wife). The credit, which may be elected in lieu of the deduction, is equal to one-half of the contribution, subject to a maximum of $25 ($50 on a joint return). In addition, a taxpayer may designate $1 of his payment ($2 on a joint return) to be applied toward a Presidential Election Campaign Fund.

These provisions are interesting as a new instance of an attempted use of the income tax to promote voluntary financial support of a public or quasi-public purpose. The alternative of the credit, set at a high level for small contributions, suggests that Congress was sensitive to the argument—which has been advanced also about charitable contributions—that deductions of this kind favor high-income persons. It is too early to evaluate the deduction and credit as means of broadening the basis of financing election campaigns.

Standard Deduction or Floor for Deductions

There are two possible methods of limiting the use of itemized personal deductions which are superficially quite different but actually rather similar. One is an optional standard deduction, which allows a person to deduct a certain percentage of his income or a fixed sum in lieu of itemized deductions. This method has been used in the United States for more than three decades. The other method is a provision, considered but not accepted in 1963–64, that would allow itemized deductions only to the extent that the total reported by a taxpayer exceeded a certain percentage of his AGI.[42] The latter idea is somewhat misleadingly called a "floor" for deductions, and I shall follow that usage.

The basic similarity between the optional standard deduction and a floor for itemized deductions is that both would lessen the extent to which income tax liability depends on expenditures for deductible items. Both measures are based on the belief that small expenditures for deductible items should not influence tax liability, either because the deductions are really unjustifiable but politically entrenched or because the deductions are best regarded as a form of special relief or incentive for people who incur unusually large expenditures for

42. *President's 1963 Tax Message*, pp. 14–15, 42–44, 98–99.

deductible items. A particular reason for disregarding small itemized deductions may be the belief that these are inaccurately reported and often are a means of petty cheating.

A difference between the standard deduction and the floor is that the former may require higher marginal tax rates than the latter to raise the same amount of revenue. Part of the difference in rates may be only nominal. For example, a rate of 20 percent on AGI minus a 15 percent standard deduction is really the same as a rate of 17 percent with no deductions. But once the standard deduction was exceeded, the marginal rate under the former would be higher than that under the latter. In practice, furthermore, the floor would be more likely to affect high-income persons than is the standard deduction.

On equity grounds, it is hard to put forward a positive case for either a standard deduction or a general floor. Neither device can distinguish between desirable and undesirable deductions. An express disallowance is necessary to eliminate unjustifiable items. There seems to be no good reason for making the deductibility of interest on a mortgage on an owner-occupied house, for example, turn on its ratio to the taxpayer's income. A homeowner with an unusually expensive house, a heavy mortgage, and a high interest rate seems no more deserving of relief than an average homeowner; both have voluntarily chosen their consumption patterns and financial arrangements. On the other hand, smallness is not a good reason for denying a deduction for interest paid on a debt relating to the production of taxable income. As argued above, separate floors can be rationalized for medical expenses (because the deduction is a form of government insurance against unusually heavy expenses) and for contributions (as a means of sharpening the incentive effects of the deduction). These considerations do not support a general floor.

The standard deduction, nevertheless, is well established and does simplify tax compliance and auditing. Simplification was the principal objective when the standard deduction was introduced in rudimentary form in 1941 and further developed in 1944. The minimum standard deduction, introduced in 1964 and later substantially increased, is equivalent to a selective increase in personal exemptions (see chapter 9).

The standard deduction, which may be taken in lieu of all itemized personal deductions, is equal to the greater of (1) a percentage deduction of 15 percent of AGI up to a maximum of $2,000, or (2) a low-income allowance of $1,300.[43] Thus up to an AGI of $8,667 the low-income allowance applies, and the full 15 percent percentage deduction is available only from that level up to $13,333.[44]

The standard deduction no doubt greatly facilitated the extension of the income tax during World War II to millions of persons who had not previously filed returns. While the number of taxable individual returns increased tenfold from 1939 to 1944, the number of returns with itemized personal deductions only doubled.[45] In 1944, more than four-fifths of all taxpayers elected the standard deduction, and this ratio was approximately maintained in the early postwar years. By 1970, however, the proportion using the standard deduction had fallen to 43 percent.[46]

The 1970 statistics on the standard deduction give no indication of its frequency of use or the amount of the standard deduction in later years since both the percentage standard deduction and the low-income allowance have been greatly increased.[47]

Conclusion

On the basis of the review of individual items, it seems that a substantial curtailment of personal deductions would be justifiable but that a large part of the deductions should be continued. The major restrictions that seem appropriate are (1) limiting the deductions for interest and casualty losses to items associated with the production of

43. When married persons file separate returns, the maximum amount of the percentage standard deduction or low-income allowance that either may take is cut in half. When a child under nineteen or a student who qualifies as a dependent of his parents files a separate return, the percentage standard deduction applies only to his earned income and the low-income allowance, if applicable, is limited to the amount of his earned income.

44. For the single year 1975, the percentage standard deduction has been raised to 16 percent up to a maximum of $2,300 for single persons and $2,600 for married persons filing joint returns. The low-income allowance (minimum standard deduction) for 1975 is $1,600 for single persons and $1,900 for married persons filing joint returns.

45. Number of taxable returns from U.S. Bureau of the Census, *Historical Statistics of the United States, Colonial Times to 1957* (1960), pp. 714–15; number of taxable returns with itemized deductions based on data in Kahn, *Personal Deductions*, p. 163.

46. *Statistics of Income—1970*, pp. 108, 131.

47. In 1970 the percentage standard deduction was 10 percent of AGI, subject to a maximum of $1,000. The low-income allowance was determined by the number of dependents and AGI and was subject to a ceiling of $1,100.

taxable income; (2) restricting the deduction for taxes to income taxes and broad sales taxes and to liabilities relating to the production of taxable income; (3) raising the floor for the medical expense deduction to at least 5 percent of AGI; and (4) introducing a floor of, say, 3 percent of AGI for the deduction for contributions. If these provisions had been in effect in 1970 they would have eliminated about $43 billion of deductions, or about one-half of all itemized deductions.[48]

Any significant curtailment of the itemized deductions would make appropriate a cut in the percentage standard deduction, but not in the low-income allowance. The revisions would allow a reduction in tax rates without loss of revenue and would bring about a reapportionment of taxes among individuals.

48. The estimate reflects the assumption that the following would have been eliminated: 66 percent of the personal deduction for interest paid; all personal deductions for real estate taxes, personal property taxes, and gasoline taxes; 67 percent of the medical expense deduction; and 33 percent of the deduction for contributions. Data on the deductions in 1970 are from *Statistics of Income—1970,* pp. 120, 123. The amount of deductions for taxes that would be disallowed probably is overstated, since some of the taxes no doubt were associated with the production of taxable income. On the other hand, the proportion of interest payments that would be disallowed probably is understated, and no figure is available for casualty loss deductions in 1970.

CHAPTER EIGHT

Capital Gains and Losses

THE TAX TREATMENT of capital gains and losses has undergone several sweeping revisions since 1913. The present provisions have been vehemently attacked as too lenient and as too strict, which unfortunately does not imply that they are close to the golden mean.

Present Treatment

Capital gains and losses are those realized on the sale or exchange of "capital assets," which, according to the Internal Revenue Code, constitute all property except stock in trade or other items held primarily for sale to customers in the ordinary course of trade, depreciable property and land used in business, copyrights, and certain other enumerated items. Gains realized on capital assets held six months or less are taxed as ordinary income, whereas only one-half of gains on assets held longer than six months, so-called long-term gains, is included in taxable income. The maximum rate on the first $50,000 of an individual's net long-term gain (the first $25,000 for a married person filing a separate return) is 25 percent.[1] Capital

---

1. On this amount of gain the rate is thus one-half that on ordinary income or 25 percent, whichever is less. The excluded half of the net capital gain is included in the base of the 10 percent tax on preference items (see pp. 242–43). With a top rate of 70 percent on ordinary income, the maximum tax rate on capital gains is

$$0.70 \times 0.50 + 0.10 [(1 - 0.70) 0.50] = 36.5 \text{ percent.}$$

losses may be offset against capital gains in full; against other income the maximum offset is $1,000 in any one year, and for this purpose only one-half of a net long-term capital loss may be counted. Any loss not offset in the year in which it occurs may be carried forward for an unlimited number of years.

Capital gains and losses are taken into account only when they are realized by sale or exchange. Gifts are not considered realizations, and the recipient takes over the basis of the donor for the computation of capital gains. (The "basis" of a capital asset is usually, though not always, the cost; it is subtracted from the amount realized from a sale or exchange to compute the gain or loss.) The rule for gifts means that when the recipient sells the asset his taxable gain is the difference between the cost or other basis of the previous owner and the selling price, not the difference between the value at the time of the gift and the selling price. For computing a capital loss, the recipient's basis is the value at the time of transfer or the donor's basis, whichever is lower. For property passing at death by bequest or inheritance, no gain is considered to be realized by the decedent or the estate, and the heir takes as his basis the value at the date of death (or, in some cases, six months later). Thus any unrealized gain or loss that had accrued between the time of acquisition by the decedent and his death is never brought to account under the income tax.

Special treatment is accorded to a capital gain on the sale of a taxpayer's principal residence. Generally, recognition and taxation of the gain are deferred if another principal residence of equal or greater value is bought and occupied within eighteen months before or after the sale. The period for occupancy is increased to two years after the sale if the new residence is constructed or reconstructed by the taxpayer. If the cost of the new house or apartment is less than the sales proceeds from the old, tax is currently payable on a fraction of the gain equal to the ratio of the value of the new residence to the value of the old. The basis of the new residence is reduced by the amount of unrecognized gain on the sale of the old house. Hence, if the homeowner sells and does not replace within the time limit, he is taxable on the cumulative amount of deferred gains on past residences as well as any gain on the most recent one. A person who is sixty-five or older may exclude from adjusted gross income (AGI) any capital gain attributable to the first $20,000 of the sale price of his personal residence. When the price exceeds $20,000, the gain is apportioned.[2]

A few other special provisions should be noted. Although depreciable property and land used in business are not classified as capital assets, gains from their sale may be taxed as capital gains,[3] whereas losses are treated as ordinary losses and are deductible from income without regard to the limitation that applies to capital losses. The same is true of livestock held for breeding, dairy, or draft purposes and unharvested crops. Certain kinds of income that do not arise from the transfer of capital assets are taxed at the capital gains rates. These pseudo-capital gains include: income from cutting or disposal of timber, coal royalties, iron ore royalties, certain lump-sum distributions from retirement plans, certain lump-sum employment-termination payments, and gains associated with qualified employee stock-option plans. Proceeds of the sale of patents are classified as long-term capital gains regardless of the form in which payment is received, whereas capital gains treatment is expressly denied for the sale of copyrights and literary, musical, and artistic compositions held by the person who created them.[4]

The origins and apparent purposes of the special provisions will not be reviewed in detail here. The provisions applying to the lump-sum payments may have been intended as a crude substitute for averaging income that accrues over several years and that might be subject to unfairly high rates if taxed at ordinary graduated rates in one year; however, the special provisions were not repealed when a general averaging plan was adopted in 1964. Capital gains treatment for income from cutting timber and coal and iron ore royalties might

2. This exclusion, which was adopted in 1964, is available only once and is subject to certain other conditions; when property is owned jointly by a husband and wife, only one of them is required to be over sixty-five.

3. Gains on sales of depreciable personal property are classified as ordinary income to the extent to which depreciation has been allowed since January 1, 1962, while any remaining gain is treated as a capital gain (Internal Revenue Code of 1954, as amended, sec. 1245 [added in 1962]). Gains on depreciable real property are treated as ordinary income only to the extent that depreciation allowances in excess of straight-line depreciation have been taken since January 1, 1964 (ibid., sec. 1250 [added in 1964]).

4. The statutory provisions covering capital gains and losses, and judicial interpretations of them, are complex. A number of refinements and qualifications which may be important in particular cases have not been included in the summary given in the text.

be rationalized on the grounds that this treatment could be gained by selling the standing timber or deposit and that without the special provision uneconomic sales would be stimulated. This argument, however, would be equally applicable to other mineral deposits and perhaps also to buildings and other long-lived properties and would not support special treatment for coal, iron ore, and timber. The special treatment of depreciable property does not seem to conform to any clear principle; it may be characterized as an incentive scheme or as special-interest legislation, depending on one's point of view. The distinction between patents and copyrights may reflect the relative standing of technicians and artists and writers in American society.[5]

The following discussion concerns the general provisions for capital gains and losses of individuals, but toward the end of the chapter further comments will be made about the special provisions.

Capital Gains and the Income Definition

The definition of income that was endorsed in chapter 2 makes no distinction for tax purposes between capital appreciation and other sources of power to consume. Adherents to a broad definition have conceded that it may be necessary to confine the income tax to realized gains and have recognized that, under a graduated tax, this may give rise to inequities unless relief is granted for gains on assets held for more than one year. Others, who do not accept the Haig-Simons definition, have vigorously contended that capital gains and losses are basically different from ordinary income and losses and that they cannot fairly be subjected to the general income tax even if allowance is made for spreading them over the period during which they accrued or otherwise tempering the graduated rates. The question of tax justice will be examined in the next few pages; then attention will be turned to economic and administrative problems.

5. There were, however, special circumstances leading up to the statutory formalization of the different treatments of patents and copyrights and literary, musical, and artistic creations. See Peter Miller, "Capital Gains Taxation of the Fruits of Personal Effort: Before and under the 1954 Code," *Yale Law Journal,* vol. 64 (November 1954), pp. 8–13; and Dan Throop Smith, *Federal Tax Reform: The Issues and a Program* (McGraw-Hill, 1961), p. 139.

The Nature of Capital Gains

One line of thinking, more common in Great Britain than in the United States, is that capital gains are not income—or at least are not income of the kind that the income tax is intended to reach—because of their casual and nonrecurrent nature. According to this approach, which has had a profound influence on the income tax of several countries, income must come from a continuing source, as fruit from a tree. This attitude originated in a predominantly agricultural economy in which landed property was the chief form of wealth and in which entailed estates were an important means of preserving family riches and power. Life-tenants and trustees could dispose of the annual harvest but were not allowed to sell the land. This mode of thinking continued to influence trust law and practice after the growth of wealth in the form of securities and other intangibles. In the income tax field, it was held that a distinction should be made between trading and other transactions entered into for profit, which result in taxable income, and changes in investments, which are not taxable events unless frequent enough to constitute a trading activity.[6] This treatment was consistent with the schedular system of income taxation (a group of separate taxes on income from different sources), which was the original form of the tax in the United Kingdom and several other European countries. In principle, capital gains were not taxable in the United Kingdom, and capital losses were not deductible, until 1962, when "speculative," short-term gains were made taxable. Long-term gains became taxable in 1965. In Canada, the taxation of capital gains was introduced in 1972. Capital gains are still not generally taxable in many countries, including Belgium, France, the Federal Republic of Germany, Japan, and Australia.

American thinking on the nature of income has differed from that in Great Britain and many other countries. In the American environment, actual and prospective appreciation in the selling value

6. Lawrence H. Seltzer, *The Nature and Tax Treatment of Capital Gains and Losses* (National Bureau of Economic Research, 1951), pp. 25–108; *Report of the Royal Commission on the Income Tax*, Cmd. 615 (London: His Majesty's Stationery Office, 1920), par. 90–91; Royal Commission on the Taxation of Profits and Income, *Final Report*, Cmd. 9474 (London: Her Majesty's Stationery Office, 1955), pp. 27–28.

of land, structures, and securities has always attracted much attention. This attitude, together with the unitary approach to income
taxation in the United States, has influenced the tax treatment of
capital gains. From the beginning of the modern income tax they have
always been subject to tax. In the years 1913 through 1921, including
a period of high wartime tax rates, capital gains were taxed as ordinary
income; the treatment of capital losses varied from no provision for
their deduction (1913–16), to offsetting against capital gains (1916–
18), to full offsetting against ordinary income (1918–23). Since
1922, important categories of capital gains have been subject to lower
tax rates than ordinary income. And since 1924, there have been
limitations on the deductibility of capital losses against ordinary income.[7]

In a modern economy, it is impossible to draw a clear distinction
between capital gains and other income from property. There is no
fundamental difference between the yield of a bond or note that is
originally issued at a discount—for example, a U.S. Treasury bill or
savings bond—and a coupon bond. The difference is at most a matter
of the timing of the yield. If the discount appears in the market after
a security has been issued, it is an integral part of the yield for a
prospective buyer and is equivalent to an additional final coupon.
Investors in corporate shares and real estate act as if the prospect of
selling the property for more than they paid for it is as important as
dividends or rent in their decisions. The excess of the yield of bonds
over that of shares, which has been characteristic of U.S. financial
markets since the late 1950s, implies that buyers of shares are counting on capital appreciation as part of their return.[8] Investment companies are ready to assume responsibility for the selection of securities
that promise to rise in value and to distribute realized gains to individual investors in the convenient form of capital gains dividends
(which are taxed to shareholders as long-term capital gains). The
list of instances in which capital appreciation is a form of investment
yield could easily be extended. Other kinds of income, including

7. See Anita Wells, "Legislative History of Treatment of Capital Gains under the
Federal Income Tax, 1913–1948," *National Tax Journal*, vol. 2 (March 1949), pp.
12–32.

8. In 1957–74 the annual average yield of medium-grade corporate bonds
(Moody's Baa) was continuously above the dividend yield of common stocks (Stan-
dard & Poor's 500 stocks), in the later part of the period by a wide margin. See
Economic Report of the President, February 1975, pp. 317, 342.

certain labor income, can be converted into capital gains to obtain a tax advantage. United States law explicitly denies capital gains treatment to original-issue discount on bonds,[9] but market discount is eligible for the preferential tax rate as are other types of capital gain that are economically indistinguishable from fully taxed income.

The expected or unexpected character of the receipt does not afford a basis for a useful distinction. A large part of capital gains consists of the capitalization of reinvested corporate profits and other investment returns that are deliberately sought. Other capital gains are windfalls or casual income, but it is hard to see that this provides any guidance for tax policy. There is no way of discovering whether a particular gain is a windfall, and windfalls may take the form of dividends as well as capital appreciation. Nor is it clear that true windfalls, if identifiable, should be taxed more lightly than other income; heavier taxation seems at least as appropriate. Predictability and regularity of recurrence are not criteria of taxability in the American system, and—to American writers—they have no intuitive appeal as possible standards.

This line of reasoning indicates that investment and so-called speculation cannot be clearly separated. Virtually all investors are speculators in the sense that they risk their wealth in accordance with their expectations of future prices and yields. Speculative gains and losses are commonly associated with changes in asset prices but these reflect changes in yields; speculative gains and losses can be experienced without a sale.

Double Taxation?

Since capital values reflect expected earnings, an increase in the market value of an asset indicates that its yield is expected to rise in the future (on the assumption of a constant rate of discount or capitalization). To illustrate, suppose an investor owns 100 shares of stock on which current and expected annual dividends are $1 per share and the market value $16 per share. Suddenly the expected annual dividends increase to $2 per share and the market price of a share rises to $32. The investor has an accrued capital gain of $1,600, and if the expectation about yields proves correct he will receive $100 more in dividends each year for as long as he continues to hold the

9. Internal Revenue Code, sec. 1232. There was doubt about the exact status of original-issue discount before 1954.

shares. Would it be unjust double taxation to tax both the accrued capital gain and the additional dividends? Will the answer be different if capital gains are taxed only at the time of realization?

Even though the appreciation of the shares is due solely to the expectation of increased dividends, the capital gain and the receipt of the additional dividends, in my view, may justifiably be regarded as separate taxable events. The appreciation represents an immediate increase of consumption power, resulting either from the retention of past corporate profits or from improved earnings prospects, and the receipt of the dividends represents a further gain of consumption power.[10] There is no injustice in taxing both accretions to consumption power; failure to tax the capital gain will mean omitting part of the investor's income. The reasoning in this case is analogous to that applicable to the so-called double taxation of saving (chapter 2). Fundamentally, whether capital gains are taxed as accrued or only at realization is irrelevant to the double-taxation point. However, when gains are taxed only at realization, even the appearance of double taxation is dispelled because it is then clear that the appreciation of the value of the asset and the additional earnings are separable. If realized gains were not taxed, an investor who sold his shares immediately after the rise in their market value and consumed the proceeds would never be taxed on the increase in his consumption power.

The argument that preferential treatment of capital gains is justifiable as a means of abating the so-called double taxation of corporate profits is also unpersuasive. Although corporate shares are an important source of capital gains, they are not the only source. Among stocks, the greatest capital gains tend to be realized on issues of corporations that retain the largest fraction of their profits and whose earnings hence are least exposed to any double taxation resulting from the application of the corporation income tax and the individual income tax on dividend income.

Price-Level Changes

Several writers who agree that certain capital gains are equivalent to ordinary investment income argue that a large proportion of

10. When an appreciation is due merely to the expectation of a nonrecurrent dividend or other distribution, the market value of the shares will decline after the distribution. In this case, accrued net capital gains over the whole period will be zero.

nominal gains are spurious, being attributable to changes in interest rates or the price level. The point about changes in interest rates was examined in chapter 2, where it was concluded that a rise in market value resulting from a decline in the relevant rate of interest represents a real gain to the investor and that no injustice is done in taxing him on it. The question of price-level changes was left for consideration here.

Appreciation in the price of an asset that reflects only a general rise in prices is a fictitious gain because it gives the investor no increased command over goods and services. Other income items are also affected, though in differing degrees. To illustrate, suppose the consumer price index, annual wages, dividends, and the average market price of common stocks all rise by the same percentage. Both wage earners and share holders experience a nominal increase in current income receipts but no increase in real income; the shareholders also have an accrued nominal capital gain. So long as the shareholders refrain from realizing their nominal capital gain, their taxable income will be overstated no more than that of the wage earners. If, however, the shareholders sell some of their stock, their taxable income will be further increased unless a correction for inflation is made. Under a strictly proportional tax (a flat rate with no personal exemptions) the real tax burden would not be increased on wages or dividends, but a tax would be imposed on realized capital gains solely from the inflation. With personal exemptions and graduated rates, recipients of all kinds of income will face rising effective rates of taxation during inflation unless adjustments are made to prevent this, but the impact will be heavier on realized capital gains.

The best way of removing inflation-induced capital gains from the tax base would be to calculate taxable gain as the difference between the amount realized from sale or other disposal of an asset and an adjusted basis determined by writing up the basis by a factor reflecting the increase in the price level over the holding period. An alternative procedure would be to deflate the realization proceeds by the price factor and to include in taxable income the excess of this deflated value over the basis. The latter procedure, however, would be less satisfactory because it would convert the proceeds from disposal of capital assets into the prices of an earlier period, while other receipts would be measured in current prices.[11] The appropriate price

11. For assets whose value had risen at the same rate as the price level, the two methods would produce the same zero value for the corrected capital gain; for assets

index would be one of consumer goods and services or of all goods and services, rather than an index of the prices of capital assets, because adjustment by the latter index would eliminate genuine gains associated with increases in earnings and relative prices of capital assets. The Internal Revenue Service could publish a table of index numbers annually.

The results obtained by either of the two correction methods described above could not be approximated, even in a rough way, by two other techniques that are sometimes considered: deflation of the nominal realized gain by a price index or exclusion from taxable income of a percentage of realized gains that would increase with the length of time the asset had been held or with the size of the increase in the price level over the holding period.[12] Both of these techniques would leave part of nominal realized gains subject to taxation but would relieve of taxation part of real gains realized on assets that had appreciated in value more than the price level had risen. They would favor the taxpayers who had the most lucrative investments and, among them, those subject to the highest marginal tax rates.[13]

A proposal to correct capital gains for inflation raises questions of

---

whose value had risen more than the price level, the first method would produce a larger corrected gain; for assets whose value had risen less than the price level, both methods would produce a corrected negative figure (that is, a loss), and the first method would produce a larger corrected loss. Algebraically, if S is the realization proceeds, B the basis, and P the ratio of the price level at the time of realization to the price level at the time of acquisition of the asset $(P > 1)$, the corrected gain calculated by the first method would be $S - BP$, and the gain calculated by the second method would be $(S/P - B)$. When $S/B = P$,

$$(S - BP) = (S/P - B) = 0.$$

When $S/B > P$,

$$(S - BP) > (S/P - B) > 0.$$

When $S/B < P$,

$$(S - BP) < (S/P - B) < 0.$$

For proof, rearrange and substitute BS/B for S:

$$B(S/B - P) - 1/P[B(S/B - P)] \gtreqless 0.$$

The three cases are

$$(S/B - P) = 0; (S/B - P) > 0; (S/B - P) < 0.$$

12. The two techniques would yield the same result when the exclusion ratio equaled $(1 - 1/P)$.

13. For a general treatment, see Roger Brinner, "Inflation, Deferral and the Neutral Taxation of Capital Gains," *National Tax Journal*, vol. 26 (December 1973), pp. 565–73; Roger Brinner and Alicia Munnell, "Taxation of Capital Gains: Inflation and Other Problems," *New England Economic Review* (September–October 1974), pp. 3–21.

fairness, administration, and economic policy. In a period of rising prices, the correction would reduce the amount of taxes paid by owners of corporate stock, unincorporated business enterprises, real estate, and other equities relative to the taxes paid by other members of the community. The persons who would obtain tax relief usually fare better during inflation than do recipients of fixed incomes and holders of money claims. Furthermore, the opportunity of deferring tax on capital gains by postponing their realization, always advantageous, becomes particularly so during inflation because payment is made in depreciated money.

Special problems would arise in the treatment of losses. Symmetrical application of the procedure for adjusting the basis of assets for inflation would turn some nominal gains into losses and would increase nominal losses realized when prices were rising. If the price level should decline—admittedly a contingency that seems far less likely than in the past—some nominal losses would be converted into gains. Such adjustments would attach even greater significance than at present to the definition and timing of realization. For example, a literal application would mean that the maturity of a bond or certificate of deposit would be the occasion for an inflation adjustment, whereas the drawing down of a savings deposit or checking account would not be. Furthermore, the logic of applying a correction to assets but not to liabilities, or to investment accounts but not to business operating accounts, is doubtful. Clearly, the adjustment of all items in balance sheets, as would be necessary to achieve fully consistent results, would be difficult, if not wholly impracticable. From the standpoint of macroeconomic policy, application of a correction for inflation to capital gains, or more broadly, would be questionable because, by reducing tax liabilities in periods of rising prices, it might lessen the stabilizing power of the income tax.

My conclusion is that under conditions of moderate inflation, such as has been experienced in the United States up to now, the adoption of a provision for correcting nominal capital gains and losses for price-level changes would be undesirable. With more extreme inflation, however, it would become expedient at some point to adapt many features of the income tax to take account of the declining value of money. In these circumstances, the measurement of capital gains as well as income from other sources should be adjusted, together with rate schedules and personal exemptions.

Implications for Equity, Progressivity, and Administration

In the 1950s and 1960s the estimated tax on net capital gains ranged between some 2.5 percent and 9 percent of total individual income tax; the average figure was about 5 percent.[14] These percentages would have been substantially increased (but less than doubled) if capital gains had been taxed at the same rates as ordinary income.

The treatment of capital gains is far more significant for the income tax than these statistics may suggest. The progressivity and equity of the tax are greatly affected because of the concentration of gains in the hands of high-income groups and because of variations in the amounts of gains realized by persons in the same income class. The close relation of capital gains to the ownership of corporate stock and other business assets gives them strategic economic importance.

Information on the distribution of net capital gains in 1968, a year of large gains, and for 1970, a year of much smaller gains, is summarized in table 8-1. The table shows that realized capital gains were a major source of income in high brackets but a minor income source in middle and low brackets. Almost half of all reported net gains appeared on returns with AGI of $50,000 or more, which represented only 0.5 percent and 0.6 percent of all returns in 1968 and 1970, respectively. Since these returns reported only 8 percent and 6 percent of all gross income, capital gains were much more concentrated than total income.

Owing to the distribution of capital gains, the preferential tax rates for them have little effect on average effective tax rates in lower brackets but substantially reduce average effective rates at the top, thereby lessening progressivity. Statistics relating to the influence on effective rates are given in chapter 9 (figure 9-1) and appendix A (table A-11). Of course, particular individuals are affected more or less than the average for their income class depending on the composition of their income.

14. Treasury Department estimates for the years through 1968, from Joseph A. Pechman, *Federal Tax Policy,* rev. ed. (Brookings Institution, 1971), p. 301. The average is the unweighted arithmetic mean of the annual percentages.

Table 8-1. Net Capital Gains as Percent of Gross Income and Their Distribution, by Adjusted Gross Income (AGI) Class, 1968 and 1970[a]

AGI class (thousands of dollars)	Net capital gains as percent of gross income		Cumulative percent of net capital gains	
	1968[b]	1970	1968[b]	1970
Under 5	3.2	2.2	6.9	9.2
5–10	1.7	0.9	15.6	18.2
10–15	2.0	0.7	24.3	25.7
15–20	3.8	1.0	31.5	31.8
20–25	6.5	1.9	36.6	37.0
25–50	11.7	3.9	51.7	51.0
50–100	20.3	8.4	64.9	63.7
100–200	35.0	20.0	75.1	75.1
200–500	56.4	39.2	85.3	86.3
500–1,000	71.5	54.9	91.0	91.8
1,000 and over	80.8	62.4	100.0	100.0
All classes	6.0	2.5	...	...

Sources: Derived from U.S. Internal Revenue Service, *Statistics of Income—1968, Individual Income Tax Returns* (1970), pp. 7, 34–35; ibid., *1970* (1972), pp. 9, 74–75.

a. Taxable and nontaxable individual returns. Net capital gains are the full amount of gains minus current-year capital losses, without regard to the statutory limitations on the amount of gains and losses taken into account for tax purposes. Capital loss carry-forward from prior years is not deducted from current-year gains. Gross income is adjusted gross income plus the part of net capital gains not included in AGI.

b. For AGI classes above $15,000, includes only taxable returns.

Low rates on capital gains are favorable to investors; however, since 1924, the low rates have been accompanied by an unfavorable provision consisting of limitations on the deductibility of capital losses from ordinary income. The intention apparently is to prevent investors from timing their gains and losses so that the losses are off-set against ordinary income, which is subject to higher tax rates than capital gains. Successful use of this technique would mean that the net tax attributable to the cumulative amount of net capital gains (gains minus losses) over a period of years would be even lower than the nominal rate on capital gains. The limitations, however, may work hardships on those whose gains and losses occur irregularly. These investors may be taxed on gains in certain years without ever being able to fully deduct losses incurred in other years. (Skillful investors with diversified portfolios can avoid this by careful timing of gains and losses.) A limitation on the deductibility of losses is not a suitable averaging device to correct for possible anomalies under graduated rates; the purpose of averaging would be to allow more liberal treatment than would be accorded by full deductibility in a single year.

To the extent that losses are experienced by persons who never realize equivalent gains, the favorable taxation of gains can hardly be regarded as an offset to the restrictions on loss deductibility. In the absence of continuous records of the investment experience of a representative sample of identical persons, it is not clear to what extent gains and losses are realized by different persons. Within any one year, it is usual for certain individuals to have losses far in excess of their gains.

Even if capital gains were taxed as heavily as ordinary income, Congress, fearing manipulation, might hesitate to allow full deduction of capital losses. Full deductibility would surely encourage the realization of accrued losses. Persons with diversified portfolios might be able to schedule transactions so as to minimize their exposure to higher-bracket tax rates. But if capital losses are indeed negative income items, the chief objection to this practice is that such persons would have especially good opportunities for averaging taxable income—not a grave inequity if all capital gains, including those accrued at death, were included in gross income. Full deductibility would offer an additional incentive to claim artificial losses, but the problem of auditing such claims would not be wholly new and seems unlikely to be very difficult.

A consequence of the present tax treatment of capital gains that is not widely appreciated is that it inhibits other tax reforms. An illustration is percentage depletion. Supporters of percentage depletion argue that little would be accomplished by restricting depletion allowances to the recovery of actual costs because this would merely encourage owners of mineral deposits to sell in order to take advantage of the capital gains tax rate. Percentage depletion allowances may amount to as much as 50 percent of net taxable income from the mineral property (computed without allowance for depletion), and in extreme cases, where cost depletion would be negligible, income tax liability is virtually halved. Under present capital gains provisions, if percentage depletion were eliminated, the owner of the deposit could sell at a price reflecting the present value of expected future net production[15] and be taxed at the preferential capital gains

15. That is, the discounted value of output less production costs other than depletion and less income tax.

rates. The new owner could claim cost depletion on the basis of his purchase price. With accurate foresight and a fairly active market for mineral properties, present owners could escape much of the possible effect of eliminating percentage depletion unless capital gains provisions were simultaneously tightened.[16] Percentage depletion was eliminated effective in 1975 for major producers of oil and gas, previously the largest users—without changing the capital gains provisions—but is still available to small producers of oil and gas and to producers of other minerals.

Another objection to the capital gains provisions is that they allow conversion of ordinary income into capital gains in order to take advantage of the lower rate. Income from personal effort, profits from the active conduct of a business enterprise, and returns from passive investments can all be turned into capital gains in certain circumstances, but in general the ease with which the conversion can be made varies in inverse order to this listing. The history of the income tax discloses many ingenious schemes, which led to preventive legislation, which in turn prompted new efforts to qualify for long-term capital gains treatment.[17] Several of the more transparent schemes are no longer allowed, but it will never be possible to preclude all conversions.

The fundamental method, which is perfectly legal, is to reinvest profits in a corporate business and later sell the shares at a price that reflects the earning power of accumulated profits or, better still, pass on the shares to one's heirs. This technique is suitable mainly for closely held corporations, but it can also be adapted to publicly held companies. For the latter it is facilitated by the periodic issuance of small nontaxable stock dividends.

An aspect of the capital gains problem that has received less attention than it deserves is the complexities of law, administration, and compliance that are attributable to the preferential treatment of long-term capital gains. When the tax rates applicable to one form of income differ widely from those on other income, it must be expected

16. So long as new owners were allowed to take cost depletion on the basis of their purchase price, the elimination of percentage depletion would not depress the value of a mineral property to prospective buyers since cost depletion would ordinarily be more advantageous to them in any case. See Stephen L. McDonald, *Federal Tax Treatment of Income from Oil and Gas* (Brookings Institution, 1963), pp. 92–100.

17. Seltzer, *Capital Gains and Losses,* pp. 211–53.

that taxpayers will make great efforts to bring their income receipts within the preferred area while tax administrators try to protect the revenues by resisting these efforts.

One expert has summarized his views as follows:

The income tax provisions of the 1954 Internal Revenue Code [most of which are still in effect] represent probably the most complex revenue law ever enacted in the fiscal history of any country. The subject singly responsible for the largest amount of complexity is the treatment of capital gains and losses. And the factor in that treatment which is accountable for the resulting complexity is the definition of capital gain and of capital loss.[18]

He sees no escape from difficulties "formidable almost beyond belief" so long as there is a large difference between tax rates on capital gains and ordinary income, the refined and intricate definitions of the present code are followed, and Congress continues to grant relief from ordinary income tax rates by bestowing capital gains status on certain kinds of income.[19] The exclusion of capital gains from taxable income would not obliterate definitional problems, but would intensify them because it would increase the difference between the tax on capital gains and other income.

A New Method of Taxing Capital Gains and Losses

The arguments so far examined point to the conclusion that capital gains should be taxed like other income, except for a provision to alleviate the effect of the application in one year of graduated tax rates to gains that have accrued over several years. Equity also seems to call for full deductibility of capital losses from taxable income, again with a provision for correcting the effect of bunching. Bunching occurs because gains and losses are taken into account only when realized; it is in principle distinguishable from irregularities in the rate at which capital gains and losses accrue over the years.

Even the case for relief from discrimination arising from bunching of realized gains and losses is weaker than is sometimes implied. The

18. Stanley S. Surrey, "Definitional Problems in Capital Gains Taxation," in *Tax Revision Compendium,* Papers Submitted to House Committee on Ways and Means (1959), vol. 2, p. 1203; for an earlier version of this paper with the same title, see *Harvard Law Review,* vol. 69 (April 1956), pp. 985–1019.

19. Surrey, "Definitional Problems," pp. 1228–29.

discrimination is partly or wholly offset by the advantages of post-poning tax until the gain is realized. Tax postponement allows the investor to earn a return on the amount that will later be paid in tax. Bunching, moreover, increases the tax only when the investor moves into a higher tax bracket than he would occupy if the gains were distributed over the years during which they accrued. Movements between brackets may not occur when the gain is small relative to taxable income. If gains on different assets are realized in more or less equal amounts each year, no discrimination occurs even if gains are bunched on each asset and are large relative to total income.

Some method of alleviating the effects of progressive tax rates on recipients of large and irregular capital gains or losses would never-theless be desirable. One approach would be a proration plan for gains or losses realized on assets held longer than one year. The objective would be to approximate the tax result that would have occurred if the gain or loss had been realized in equal installments over the period during which the investor held the asset. Basically, the method would be to prorate the gain or loss and to determine the tax rate applicable to the whole gain or loss by regarding the pro rata amount as a marginal addition to, or deduction from, current-year ordinary income. The total tax would be the sum of the tax on ordinary income and the (positive or negative) tax on the capital gain or loss. Where only a few transactions were involved, it might be feasible to prorate gains or losses separately for each transaction by dividing by the number of years the asset was held; but this would not be practicable for large portfolios. It would be much simpler and almost equally effective to prorate by dividing the aggregate net long-term gain or loss by an arbitrary factor of, say, 3 or 5. This would have the effect of widening the tax brackets for long-term capital gains or losses by a multiple equal to the proration factor.[20]

Full taxation of capital gains and full deductibility of capital losses, with proration, would substantially increase the tax on income from this source and would significantly increase the progressivity of the income tax as a whole. Computations for 1970 show that, with a proration factor of 5, the tax on net gains would have been more than

20. For further details, see the first edition of this book, pp. 199–204; Martin David, *Alternative Approaches to Capital Gains Taxation* (Brookings Institution, 1968), pp. 103–06, 166–72, 218–19.

doubled, provided that the amount realized was not affected; results with proration factors of 3 and 8 would have been similar.

A proration plan along the lines set out above was recommended in the first edition of this book; however, further consideration leads me to conclude that bunching, though conceptually different from the general problem of the appropriate treatment of fluctuating incomes, could be dealt with as well—or better—in the framework of general averaging. A limited averaging plan was adopted in 1964 and liberalized effective in 1970, when it was extended to capital gains. This plan has shortcomings (see chapter 9), but it would be reasonably adequate for the taxation of long-term capital gains, provided they were included in full in taxable income. Compared with proration, full taxation with averaging would not benefit investors whose total income, including realized capital gains, was stable from year to year, and it would avoid certain anomalies that could arise under the proration plan when realized gains were large relative to ordinary income.[21] In its present form, the averaging plan would do nothing to improve the treatment of capital losses, but the allowance of full deductibility, even without correction for bunching, would be a major liberalization.

Full taxation of capital gains, with proration or averaging, would increase the yield and progressivity of the income tax. If the additional revenue were not desired, statutory tax rates could be cut either by the same number of percentage points or the same fraction in each bracket, which would leave the tax more progressive, or by greater amounts in the higher brackets, which would leave both yield and the average degree of progressivity unchanged but would effect a redistribution of tax between recipients of capital gains and others in each bracket.

Admittedly, either a proration plan for capital gains and losses or wider application of income averaging would be complex. Capital gain or loss transactions were reported in 1970 on more than one-tenth of all individual returns, taxable and nontaxable. However, for

---

21. Under proration a variation in the taxpayer's ordinary income could affect the marginal rate applicable to a large capital gain enough to cause total after-tax income to move in the opposite direction, which would imply a marginal tax rate in excess of 100 percent. See David, *Alternative Approaches to Capital Gains Taxation,* p. 170.

a large proportion of these returns the amount of gain or loss was too small to affect tax liability under a proration plan or averaging. Sixty percent of the persons with net gains reported less than $1,000.[22] Many of those who realized larger gains received amounts that were small relative to their ordinary income or average income. It would be possible to exclude from the proration or averaging plan a large number of persons who would not benefit significantly from it and to devise a return form that would allow them to omit the computations required for proration or averaging.

The effect of proration or averaging could not be approximated by exclusion from taxable income of a fraction of realized gains or losses, as under present law or by a more elaborate system such as that in use in 1934–37 which scaled down the proportion of gain or loss taken into account for tax purposes according to the length of time the asset was held. The graduated exclusion method is as defective for relieving the effects of bunching as it is for correcting for inflation. Exclusion of a certain fraction of a gain from income gives a tax benefit that varies directly with the investor's marginal tax rate; the benefit from proration would be that attributable to a widening of the tax bracket for capital gains; the benefit from averaging would depend on the size of the gain relative to average income and the steepness of tax progressivity. To take an extreme example, partial exclusion would be most beneficial to those whose gains would fall entirely in the top rate bracket, whereas proration would not affect the liabilities of these persons and averaging would affect them only if their income had been lower during the base period.

A provision for constructive realization of capital gain or loss when assets are transferred by gift or at the death of the owner would be a desirable feature of any revision that increased tax rates on realized gains. Otherwise, the tax incentive for postponing the realization of gains would be unduly increased. (See the discussion of "locking-in" below.) In its capital gains tax which went into effect in 1972, Canada included constructive realization at the time of gift or death and also

22. U.S. Internal Revenue Service, *Statistics of Income—1970, Individual Income Tax Returns* (1972), pp. 7, 74–79. The 60 percent figure given in the text was obtained by doubling the amounts included in AGI, on the assumption that all net gains were long term, which is not true but which yields a figure that is accurate enough for present purposes. A useful estimate for those with net capital losses cannot be derived from *Statistics of Income* owing to the limitations on the deductibility of capital losses.

on the occasion of giving up residence in the country. The United Kingdom provides for constructive realization of transfers by gift, and from 1965 to 1971 realization was also deemed to occur at death.

Effects on Investment

However strong the equity argument for taxing capital gains at the same rates as other income, this will not be acceptable if there is reason to believe that the economic consequences would be highly detrimental. It has been stated that preferential taxation of capital gains is a necessary means of shielding investment from the effects of high tax rates, that the lure of lightly taxed capital gains is needed to entice investors into risky ventures.

Since the favorable treatment of capital gains applies to only one form of investment return, it does not offer general tax relief for investment. Indeed, on the assumption that total revenue is to be maintained, it requires that taxes be higher on other income, including investment income. A small general reduction in income tax rates or a substantial reduction in top-bracket rates would be possible without sacrificing revenue or overall progressivity if the differential in favor of capital gains were eliminated. Or consideration might be given to a more selective measure such as the further liberalization of depreciation allowances or operating loss offsets. On the other hand, the preferential taxation of capital gains may be supported on the grounds that the kinds of investment that benefit are especially likely to be discouraged by the income tax or have special social importance.

The lower tax rate on capital gains offers an inducement to seek out investments that promise a return in the form of capital appreciation in preference to those that offer dividends, interest, rent, or other annual yield. A Harvard Business School study, based on extensive interviews in 1949 with a sample of investors, confirmed that those with large incomes were greatly attracted by the comparatively low tax rate on capital gains and altered their investment choices to take advantage of it.[23] A 1964 interview survey of a sample of high-income persons found that the respondents who regarded capital gains as an

23. J. Keith Butters, Lawrence E. Thompson, and Lynn L. Bollinger, *Effects of Taxation: Investments by Individuals* (Harvard University, Graduate School of Business Administration, 1953), pp. 41–42.

important investment objective were considerably greater in number than those who stressed current yield.[24]

The limitation on the deductibility of capital losses must partly offset the attractions of the low tax rate on capital gains. The limitation, however, applies to the deduction of capital losses from ordinary income; capital losses may be deducted in full from capital gains in the current year and within an unlimited carry-forward period. For investors with diversified portfolios, the restriction on loss deductibility may not seem severe. Among the investors interviewed by the Harvard Business School group, a large proportion of whom had high incomes, many more were attracted by the favorable tax rate difference than were repelled by the restrictions on loss deductibility.[25]

Although investments promising capital gains are usually more risky than others, they are not always so. As already mentioned, a high-grade bond selling at a discount is virtually certain to produce a capital gain if held to maturity, but there is no economic difference between this security and another of the same quality and maturity that is selling at par because its coupon rate equals the market rate. Respondents to the 1964 survey of persons with high incomes apparently did not consider the pursuit of capital gains inconsistent with safety since the proportion of them who characterized the latter as an important investment objective exceeded the proportion who termed capital gains an important objective.[26]

On the whole, it seems likely that the tax difference in favor of capital gains causes individual investors to allocate a larger fraction of their resources to risky items than they would if capital gains and losses were taxed as ordinary income and losses. The difference almost certainly encourages the retention of corporate profits and thus favors investment that can be financed from this source.

Although risk-taking is commonly regarded as wholesome, it may waste capital when carried too far. A prudent policy, therefore, might

24. Sixty-two percent said that capital gains were "important" or "very important" while 40 percent characterized high current yield in the same way. See Robin Barlow, Harvey E. Brazer, and James N. Morgan, *Economic Behavior of the Affluent* (Brookings Institution, 1966), p. 200.

25. Butters, Thompson, and Bollinger, *Effects of Taxation*, p. 42. The capital loss provisions in 1949 were similar to the current ones but the carry-forward of losses was limited to five years.

26. Seventy percent said that safety was "important" or "very important" (Barlow, Brazer, and Morgan, *Economic Behavior of the Affluent*, p. 200).

aim at neutrality toward risk assumption rather than its stimulation or discouragement. According to this standard, a tax preference for capital gains could be supported to the extent that it counterbalanced discrimination against risk-taking arising from other provisions but would be undesirable if it did more. The standard is not very helpful because its application would require more precise knowledge about investors' reactions to taxation than is now available. A further difficulty is the lack of selectivity in capital gains tax treatment, which is extended to gains from land speculation and other activities that contribute little to innovation and growth as well as to gains from highly productive investments.

The consequences of a tax incentive for retaining corporate profits instead of paying dividends are debatable. Many economists argue that capital will be most efficiently allocated if profits are distributed and individual shareholders are allowed to decide whether they should be reinvested where earned or placed elsewhere. This attitude seems to be based on general confidence in the market mechanism rather than on a systematic comparison of the investment decisions of shareholders and the executives of profitable corporations. The dividend-payout ratio, moreover, may affect shareholders' consumption and thus the total amount of resources available to corporations as well as the allocation of capital among firms.

The conclusion about investment allocation must remain somewhat indefinite. On balance, the allocative effects of a tax difference in favor of capital gains may be economically desirable, but they are not unambiguously so. The capital gains potential of financial and real investments is not a reliable indicator of their social contribution, and there is much waste motion in turning investment income into capital gains.

"Locking-in"

A persistent criticism of the capital gains tax—which would become more powerful if the tax rate were raised—is that it "locks in" investors, making them reluctant to change their portfolios because by doing so they would incur a tax liability that could be postponed or avoided by not selling. Locking-in is said to accentuate fluctuations in security prices. At a time of rising security prices, when many investors have substantial unrealized gains, the discouragement of sales is alleged to cause the market to go still higher, ultimately provoking a greater corrective decline than would otherwise be necessary. The decline, in turn, may be accentuated if investors sell in order to take tax-deductible losses. Locking-in is also said to impair the efficiency of the capital market as a means of allocating resources. According to this view, efficiency is reduced because the capital gains tax discourages venturesome investors from selling appreciated shares and moving into unseasoned issues.[27]

Why Locking-in Occurs

Although its extent may often be exaggerated, some locking-in will occur so long as the income tax applies to capital gains only as realized. If the tax were assessed on accrued gains without waiting for realization, locking-in would disappear. Postponing the sale of appreciated assets is now encouraged, not only by the privilege of postponing tax, but also by the opportunity of escaping tax on assets held until death.[28]

The reason locking-in occurs may be shown by a simple illustration. Suppose an investor owns stock bought more than six months ago for $50 and now selling for $100. If he sells, he will pay a tax of $3.50 to $17.50 per share, depending on his marginal rate bracket and the size of the gain (this omits any possible liability for the minimum tax on preference items; see pages 242–43). It will be ad-

27. For effective presentations, see Harold M. Somers, "An Economic Analysis of the Capital Gains Tax," *National Tax Journal*, vol. 1 (September 1948), pp. 226–32; Somers, "Reconsideration of the Capital Gains Tax," *National Tax Journal*, vol. 13 (December 1960), pp. 292–99; and Somers, "Capital Gains Tax: Significance of Changes in Holding Period and Long Term Rate," *Vanderbilt Law Review*, vol. 16 (June 1963), pp. 509–33. A contrary view concedes that locking-in is destabilizing but holds that, on balance, the capital gains tax may have a stabilizing influence on security prices because the existence of the tax dampens the response of prices to changes in expectations. See Robert A. Haugen and Dean W. Wichern, "The Diametric Effects of the Capital Gains Tax on the Stability of Stock Prices," *Journal of Finance*, vol. 28 (September 1973), pp. 987–96.

28. Especially enlightening analyses of the considerations that are relevant for investors can be found in Charles C. Holt and John P. Shelton, "The Implications of the Capital Gains Tax for Investment Decisions," *Journal of Finance*, vol. 16 (December 1961), pp. 559–65; Holt and Shelton, "The Lock-in Effect of the Capital Gains Tax," *National Tax Journal*, vol. 15 (December 1962), pp. 337–52; and Beryl W. Sprinkel and B. Kenneth West, "Effects of Capital Gains Taxes on Investment Decisions," *Journal of Business*, vol. 35 (April 1962), pp. 122–34. I have drawn heavily on these papers.

vantageous to sell in order to switch investments only if the asset that can be bought with the remaining $96.50 to $82.50 promises a greater return, in the form of appreciation and dividends or other yield, than can be obtained from $100 worth of the old shares. For this to be true, the expected rate of return on the new asset, after any brokerage fees or other expenses of selling and buying have been allowed for, must be from 3.6 percent to 21.2 percent better than that on the old asset in this case.[29] Similar reasoning can be applied to a sale made in the expectation of a price decline and subsequent repurchase of the same asset. If the investor expects the value of an asset that he holds to decline by more than the amount of any tax liability that he avoids by not selling (plus selling expenses), he should certainly sell, because in this case a movement into cash will be advantageous. A smaller decline will justify a sale if there is an alternative investment with a positive yield.

The relationship that must be expected to exist between the rate of return on a new investment and that on an old one in order to justify a switch is shown for a wide range of situations in table 8-2. The additional rate of return that must be expected on the new asset increases with the size of the unrealized gain on the old asset in relation to its market value and the investor's marginal tax rate. Under present law the maximum marginal rate of tax on long-term capital gains is 25 percent on the first $50,000, and it rises to 35 percent on larger gains (not including any minimum tax on tax preference items that may be applicable). The higher rates are included in the table to indicate the

29. More generally, an investment switch will be advantageous if

$$r_2 [M - t_c (M-C)] > r_1 M,$$

where M is the current market value of the old asset; C is its cost or other basis; t_c is the marginal rate of tax on realized capital gains; and r_1 and r_2, respectively, are the ratios of the expected return to current value of the old asset and of the new asset. The expected return should include both dividends or other current yield and capital gain, both net of tax. It may be estimated in various ways. One method is to select a holding period and a discount rate and then to sum the present values of expected dividends over the period and the present value of the expected capital gain at the end of the period. Another method (which computes an annual rate of return) is to ascertain the rate of compound discount that would reduce the expected flow of dividends plus the expected value of the asset at the end of the holding period to an amount equal to the current value of the asset. Beazer showed that my formulation in the first edition lacked generality and was inexact in certain respects. William F. Beazer, "Expected Income Changes and the Lock-in Effect of the Capital Gains Tax," *National Tax Journal*, vol. 19 (September 1966), pp. 308–11.

Table 8-2. Return on New Investment Required for an Advantageous Switch, Selected Tax Rates and Gains on Old Investment[a]

Multiple of rate of return on old investment

Marginal tax rate on capital gains	*Gain on old asset as fraction of its market value*[b]				
	1/10	*3/10*	*5/10*	*7/10*	*9/10*
10	1.010	1.031	1.053	1.075	1.099
25	1.026	1.081	1.143	1.212	1.290
35	1.036	1.117	1.212	1.324	1.460
50	1.053	1.176	1.333	1.538	1.818
60	1.064	1.220	1.429	1.724	2.174
70	1.075	1.266	1.538	1.961	2.703

a. Returns computed in relation to current market values.
b. When the gain on the old asset is the indicated fraction of its market value, the ratio of the rate of return on the new asset to that on the old must exceed the figure given below. The ratio is

$$M/[M - t_c(M - C)],$$

where M is the current market value of the old asset, C is its cost or other basis, and t_c is the marginal rate of tax on realized capital gains.

situation that would exist if capital gains were fully taxed. The table shows, for example, that an investor subject to a 25 percent marginal tax rate who holds an asset that carries an unrealized gain equal to three-tenths of its current value (three-sevenths of its original cost) can gain by switching to a new asset that offers a rate of return more than 1.081 times that on the old asset; if the old asset yields 6.000 percent, the new one must yield more than 6.486 percent. With a marginal tax rate of 60 percent and conditions otherwise the same, the break-even point for the new investment is a yield of 7.320 percent.

Over most of the range covered by the table, the additional yield required under present law to justify an investment switch does not seem large in comparison to the short-run fluctuations that occur in the prices of stocks or the differences in dividend yields of stocks. Under full taxation of capital gains, however, the barriers to investment switches look more formidable toward the upper end of the rate scale.

Escape of Capital Gains Tax at Death

The possibility, which exists under present law, of escaping capital gains tax on assets held until death is an additional cause of locking-in. Certain switches that will increase the earning power of an investor's portfolio will nevertheless reduce the size of his estate. For example, a switch that is fully justified by rate-of-return calculations will reduce the estate if it involves the payment of a substantial capital gains tax and the investor dies shortly thereafter. If the deceased had held the old asset until his death, the switch could have been made by his executors or heirs without incurring a capital gains tax liability. It is difficult to decide what allowance to make for the possibility of escaping tax at death, not only because the date of death of any individual investor is unforeseeable, but also because the attitudes of investors toward the size of their estate and their heirs vary widely.

Holt and Shelton have made an illuminating analysis of the possibility of escaping capital gains tax at death.[30] They assume that an investor wishes to maximize his income and the value of his estate and that he will not consider an investment switch warranted unless he expects it to increase his income and also to leave his estate unimpaired (that is, to allow recovery of any capital gains tax that would have been avoided if the switch had not been made). This implies that the investor has a strong interest in the size of his estate—that he will not, in fact, deliberately sacrifice any part of his estate for additional income during his lifetime. On the basis of mortality tables, one can calculate the probability that capital gains tax will be avoided by reason of the investor's death during the period over which he would otherwise hold an asset. From such calculations it is possible to estimate the additional annual return required on a new investment to offset the actuarial value of the opportunity of tax avoidance at death.[31]

Table 8-3 shows the actuarial value of tax avoidance at death under present law, for investors at different ages and for different holding periods, as an annual percentage of the tax that would be paid on an immediate sale. These figures, of course, rise with the investor's age and the length of time that he would hold the old asset if he did not switch. To illustrate the use of table 8-3, consider again

30. In "Implications of the Capital Gains Tax for Investment Decisions," pp. 571–75, and, more elaborately, in "Lock-in Effect of the Capital Gains Tax," pp. 340–50.

31. An investor who follows the Holt-Shelton rule will consider an investment switch advantageous if

$$r_2 [M - t_c (M - C)] > r_1 M + p [t_c (M - C)],$$

where p is the weighted annual probability that the investor will die during the period in which he expects to continue holding the asset if he does not switch immediately, and the other symbols have the same meaning as in footnote 29 above.

Table 8-3. Expected Capital Gains Tax Saving at Death, Investors at Selected Ages and with Selected Holding Periods

Percent per year of potential tax liability on an immediate sale

	Extended holding period[a]		
Investor's age	*5 years*	*10 years*	*Life*
30	0.197	0.228	2.41
40	0.396	0.500	3.09
50	0.956	1.24	4.20
60	2.46	3.12	6.21
70	6.03	7.30	9.99
80	13.51	15.41	17.14

Source: Abstracted from Charles C. Holt and John P. Shelton, "The Implications of the Capital Gains Tax for Investment Decisions," *Journal of Finance*, vol. 16 (December 1961), p. 574.
a. Period over which the investor expects to continue to hold the asset if he does not sell immediately.

a stockholder whose shares have doubled in value and who is subject to a 25 percent tax on capital gains. If he sells $1,000 worth of shares he must pay a capital gains tax of $125, which his estate would escape if he held the shares until death. For an investor aged sixty, the table shows that the expected annual value of the tax saving at death is 6.21 percent of $125 or $7.76 if he assumes that the alternative to an immediate sale is to hold the shares the rest of his life. On the basis of his life expectancy, he can recoup the capital gains tax by earning an additional $7.76 a year, which equals 0.89 percent of the $875 that he will have left to invest in a new asset. If the old shares yield 6.00 percent, he must find another issue that he expects to yield 7.73 percent in order to maintain both his income and the probable value of his estate.[32] Of course, it will be hard for the investor to predict whether he will hold the old shares for the rest of his life, but even if he does not deliberately decide to do so, there is a calculable probability that he will die before he gets around to selling. Past experience, for example, may suggest that he would be likely to hold the shares for another five years; in that case, the table shows that the expected value of tax avoidance by death during the extended holding period is 2.46 percent of $125, or $3.08 a year (0.35 percent of the value of the new investment).

These calculations may exaggerate the importance of the oppor-

32. Calculations based on table 8-2 show that the new shares must offer a rate of return 1.14 times 6.00 percent, or 6.84 percent, in order to maintain income; adding 0.89 percentage point to cover the amortization of the capital gains tax brings this to 7.73 percent.

tunity of escaping capital gains tax at death because they imply that people are more interested in their estates and their heirs than they actually are. Furthermore, only an exceptional investor—or investment adviser—would make formal calculations along these lines. The actuarial approach nevertheless has the merit of posing the alternatives open to investors and of thus providing a common basis for discussion.

Extent and Consequences of Locking-in

Given preferential tax rates on long-term capital gains, the great uncertainty and differences of opinion about future investment yields that always prevail, and the wide short-run fluctuations in stock prices that often occur, Sprinkel and West seem justified in concluding that "investors frequently overestimate the extent of the 'lock-in' effect."[33] Whether because of misapprehension, careful calculation, or inertia, it is true that over considerable periods of time only small fractions of accrued capital gains have been realized. Bailey estimated that in the period 1926–60 individuals and fiduciaries in the United States realized only some 8 to 12 percent of their accrued gains on corporate shares.[34] According to Bhatia, realized gains on corporate stock, non-farm residential real estate, farm real estate, and livestock equaled 21.5 percent of total gains accrued on these assets in the years 1948–64.[35]

Investors' replies to questionnaires may be of some value in ascertaining the extent of locking-in but, like all such evidence, they have to be interpreted cautiously because the responses are likely to be self-serving unless the questions are adroitly posed. In 1949, a poor year in the stock market, the Harvard Business School survey found that only 6 percent of the investors who were interviewed alleged that the timing of their investment transactions was affected by the capital gains tax, except for the postponement of profit-taking for six months in order to qualify for the preferential rate on long-term gains.[36] In

33. "Effects of Capital Gains Tax on Investment Decisions," p. 133.

34. Martin J. Bailey, "Capital Gains and Income Taxation," in Arnold C. Harberger and Martin J. Bailey, eds., *The Taxation of Income from Capital* (Brookings Institution, 1969), p. 17.

35. Kul B. Bhatia, "Accrued Capital Gains, Personal Income and Saving in the United States, 1948–1964," *Review of Income and Wealth*, series 16 (December 1970), p. 374.

36. Butters, Thompson, and Bollinger, *Investments by Individuals*, p. 339.

1960, after a decade of generally rising stock prices, a survey of investors' attitudes conducted for the New York Stock Exchange indicated that the tax had great influence and that a reduction of its rates would unlock large amounts of securities.[37] The 1964 survey of high-income persons reported that three-fifths of those who held appreciated assets had neither sold them nor considered selling because they felt that no better investment opportunities were available, and about one-fifth had been deterred from selling by tax considerations.[38]

Locking-in would be increased if tax rates on capital gains were raised without making changes in realization rules. A provision that would lessen the advantage of postponing realization of gains and that could be supported on equity grounds would be an interest charge for the privilege of deferring tax on capital gains from the time they accrued until they were realized. This could be approximated by requiring the taxpayer to write up his realized gain by a factor varying directly with the length of time the asset was held, computed to reflect interest and tax at standard rates on the assumption that the gain accrued at a steady rate over the period.[39] This suggestion may appear strange, since it is the opposite of the common proposal that the proportion of gains included in taxable income should diminish as the holding period lengthens. The latter proposal presumably is intended as a means of adjusting for bunching or for inflation but, as shown above, is unsatisfactory for these purposes.

A less ambitious attack on locking-in would be to end the opportunity of avoiding tax on appreciated assets held until death by adopting a provision for constructive realization of gains on property held at death. Such a provision would be desirable under present capital gains tax rates and with higher rates would become more important for reasons of equity and economic policy.[40] Constructive realization,

37. New York Stock Exchange, "Revenue Effects of a Reduced Capital Gains Tax: Summary of a Detailed Study by Louis Harris and Associates, Inc." (New York Stock Exchange, Department of Research and Statistics, 1961; processed).

38. Barlow, Brazer, and Morgan, *Economic Behavior of the Affluent*, p. 119.

39. Brinner and Munnell, "Taxation of Capital Gains," pp. 15–17.

40. In 1963, President Kennedy recommended a tax on gains accrued at the time of death or gift, as part of a broad reform program. See *President's 1963 Tax Message Along with Principal Statement, Technical Explanation, and Supporting Exhibits and Documents Submitted by Secretary of the Treasury*, House Ways and Means Committee Print (1963), pp. 20, 49–51, 122–34. The recommendation was not accepted by Congress.

however, would not alleviate locking-in caused by income considerations.

The economic consequences of locking-in, as well as its extent, may be debated. Locking-in does not necessarily have any direct influence on the total volume of financial or real investment. If present holdings of appreciated securities were unlocked, funds would be transferred from the purchasers to the present holders, leaving the buyers less liquid and the sellers more liquid. In the simplest case, the sellers would use their receipts for the same purposes as the buyers would have, and the only result would be a reshuffling of the ownership of outstanding securities and new issues. Precisely this outcome does not seem likely, however, because seasoned securities and new issues are not perfect substitutes. Nevertheless, the principal effects of locking-in must be sought in the composition of portfolios and the allocation of real investment rather than in the amount of resources devoted to investment over a period of time.

Unlocking holdings of appreciated securities at a time when the stock market was rising would moderate the rise only if those who sold took part of the proceeds out of the market; to the extent that they merely switched holdings of stock, supply and demand would increase equally and prices would not be affected. Probably there would be some movement out of stocks into bonds and cash on the part of investors who felt that the general level of stock prices was too high, and hence some moderating influence, but the net outward movement would surely be much smaller than the total value of sales attributable to unlocking.

Although most commentators take it for granted that locking-in impairs the efficiency of real capital allocation, there have been skeptics. Keynes, for one, thought that excessive trading in the securities markets tended to destabilize real investment and suggested that there might be grounds for making "the purchase of an investment permanent and indissoluble, like marriage, except by reason of death or other grave cause."[41] He discarded this expedient—on the grounds that the liquidity, or the illusion of liquidity, offered by the stock market calmed the nerves of investors and made them more willing to take risks—but he did not seem at all disturbed by the impediments

41. John Maynard Keynes, *The General Theory of Employment, Interest and Money* (Harcourt, Brace, 1936), p. 160.

to trading in London in the form of high brokerage charges and transfer tax. Indeed, Keynes recommended that the United States consider a transfer tax as a means of mitigating "the predominance of speculation over enterprise."[42]

Since World War II, speculation does not appear to have affected real investment as badly as did the excesses of the 1920s and the subsequent crash, and Keynes' judgment on the stock market seems harsh today. Even if its social contribution is smaller than the financial press likes to believe, active trading does facilitate transactions that are convenient for individuals and, on the whole, useful for the community. Locking-in does not seem to be a great economic problem, but there is a legitimate presumption that it is an undesirable side effect of the taxation of realized capital gains.

"Roll-over" Proposals

A proposal for avoiding locking-in while raising taxes on capital gains is the so-called roll-over plan. This plan would defer tax on realized gains that were reinvested but collect tax when gains were withdrawn for consumption or at the time of death of the investor. The proposal calls for an extension of the present treatment of gains on the sale of a personal residence.

A specific roll-over proposal includes the following provisions.[43] The taxpayer would determine his realized net gain or loss each year without regard to the length of time he had held the assets disposed of during the year. Any net loss would be recognized immediately, and provisions for the deduction of capital losses against ordinary income would be liberalized. Tax on net gain would be deferred to the extent that it was reinvested in any capital asset, and the basis of the new asset would be reduced by the amount of untaxed gain on old assets. The adjustment of basis would be confined to assets acquired in the current year and would be apportioned among all such assets. If purchases were smaller than sales, it would be presumed that part of the gain had been withdrawn, and realized gain would be taxed dollar for dollar up to the amount of the excess of sales over pur-

42. Ibid., pp. 159–60. In this context, Keynes defined speculation as "the activity of forecasting the psychology of the market" and enterprise as "the activity of forecasting the prospective yield of assets over their whole life" (p. 158).

43. Reuben Clark, "The Paradox of Capital Gains: Taxable Income That Ought Not To Be Currently Taxed," in *Tax Revision Compendium,* vol. 2, pp. 1243–56.

chases (with perhaps a short grace period to allow for spillovers between years). No pairing of specific sales and purchases or detailed tracing of unrecognized gain would be required; all sales and purchases of any one year would be pooled. An essential part of the proposal would be that transfer of assets at death be considered a realization and tax be assessed at that time on previously unrecognized gains. The rate of tax applied to recognized gains might be the full rate for ordinary income, the full rate with provision for averaging or spreading gains over a period of years, or a preferential rate.

This plan appears to entail considerable, but not insuperable, problems of compliance or administration. Investors would be called on for more information and computations than are now required. Initially this would probably not arouse hostility since it would be part of a relief measure, but the requirements might seem more vexatious as the relief began to be taken for granted with the passage of time. The Internal Revenue Service would have more difficulty than it now does in verifying the taxpayer's representations concerning the basis of assets because of the adjustments, which would often introduce a big difference between the basis and purchase price. The basis of a listed security can now be verified from readily available publications if its purchase date is known. Under roll-over, both the government and the taxpayer would need a set of accounts showing the details of investment transactions for each year of the taxpayer's investment career.

The main objection to roll-over is that it would offer inequitable advantages to persons who realize capital gains. To illustrate, consider the unrealistic case of a person who receives all his income in the form of capital gains and reinvests all his savings in capital assets. During his lifetime, he would in effect be subject to a spendings tax rather than an income tax, since he would be taxed only on gains withdrawn for consumption. On the other hand, a person who received only ordinary income would be taxed on both his consumption and his saving. The arguments that can be advanced in favor of an expenditure tax do not support roll-over because it provides tax deferral for reinvested capital gains but not for other saving.

Roll-over would allow investors maximum opportunities for timing gains so that they would be assessed at relatively low rates. Thus gains might be withdrawn in years in which tax rates were temporarily reduced or in which the investor's other income was low or negative.

Most persons are subject to lower marginal tax rates after retirement, and deferral of gains until that time would be especially beneficial to them.

The outlines of a dilemma thus emerge. Roll-over seems unfair because it would broaden tax deferral opportunities for recipients of capital gains. But even without roll-over, investors can defer tax on capital gains by postponing realization. For this privilege they pay a price in the form of forgone freedom to switch investments, and the community may suffer a loss of efficiency in allocation of real capital owing to diminished fluidity of financial capital markets. Any social cost of this nature would be increased if higher tax rates were levied on all realized capital gains. The question for policymakers is whether the economic advantages of increased capital mobility would outweigh the inequities of roll-over. In my judgment, roll-over is unjustifiable so long as capital gains enjoy a substantial degree of rate preference but would be acceptable if its adoption were necessary to clear the way for full taxation of capital gains under a proration plan.

Improvements without Fundamental Revision

Worthwhile improvements in the taxation of capital gains and losses could be effected by measures less sweeping than those discussed so far in this chapter. If for any reason a fundamental revision is not acceptable, consideration should be given to the following actions.

1. Extension of the holding period for long-term gains and losses from six months to twelve months. A holding period shorter than one year is not needed to avoid bunching. The length of the holding period is not a satisfactory basis for distinguishing between speculation and ordinary investment; however, a twelve-month period seems slightly better in this respect than a six-month period inasmuch as investors who buy securities for income will usually plan to hold them for at least a year, if for no other reason than because profits and dividends are ordinarily related to annual accounting periods. A one-year holding period would cause a six-month delay of some sales of appreciated assets, but it is not evident that there would be a serious loss of market fluidity.

2. Withdrawal of long-term capital gains treatment from the special items such as coal and iron ore royalties, income from timber

cutting, executive compensation under stock-option plans, and lump-sum receipts from retirement plans and employment termination arrangements. In general, these items seem to be similar to other income that is subject to ordinary rates, and it is not clear why the treatment of capital gains should be considered the best means of offering their recipients any tax relief that may be warranted. General income averaging or special proration seems a more equitable way of avoiding hardship in the taxation of lump-sum payments and other irregular receipts. Present provisions that treat as ordinary income part of the gains on sales of depreciable property could justifiably be broadened to classify as ordinary income all such gains up to the full amount of depreciation deductions already taken, on the grounds that the gains are evidence that depreciation allowances have exceeded the value of the useful life of the property.

3. Elimination of the deferral of recognition and taxation of capital gains on owner-occupied dwellings and of the partial exclusion of such gains for persons over the age of sixty-five. The current taxation of all realized gains on dwellings would no doubt retard mobility to some degree, but little attention has been given to whether the economic effects would be objectionable enough to justify the special treatment. The present provision seems to have been supported mainly on grounds of equity, and by dubious logic. There is little merit in the common assertion that the sale of a dwelling in connection with a move from one neighborhood to another or from one city to another is an involuntary conversion or is not a true realization if another dwelling "must be bought." Except for condemnation proceedings, people must be presumed to decide whether to move and to buy a new house by balancing advantages and disadvantages—deliberately or impulsively, according to temperament. Decisions to sell and to replace houses seem to be essentially similar to other decisions to switch investments, even though noneconomic considerations play a bigger role in the former. The special exclusion for the elderly, which was added in 1964, is a highly discriminatory form of tax relief.

4. Adoption of the principle of constructive realization of gain or loss when capital assets are transferred by gift or at death. Existing provisions covering gifts allow appreciated assets to be transferred from owners in high tax brackets to persons in lower tax brackets without incurring an income tax liability and permit indefinite deferral of capital gains tax. Transfers at death wipe out potential capital

gains tax liability. The present provisions involve an arbitrary distinction between gratuitous transfers and other transfers, and they contribute to locking-in. Assessment of both capital gains tax and gift tax or estate tax at the time of gratuitous transfer would not be unfair double taxation. The fact that income tax was assessed in prior years on current income is not considered a reason for exempting the savings built up out of that income from gift tax or estate tax. The transfer of assets would be the occasion for the assessment of both income tax and estate or gift tax only if the holder had previously enjoyed income tax deferral, unlike a person who had taken his investment return in currently taxable form. The simultaneous assessment could more accurately be viewed as evidence of a prior tax advantage than as a hardship. The combined application of income tax and gift or estate tax would not be confiscatory since the income tax liability would be deductible from the value of the gift or estate subject to taxation.

Conclusion

Capital gains fall within a broad definition of income and are not clearly distinguishable from other kinds of income in contributing to taxpaying capacity or economic function. While special treatment of capital gains and losses is warranted because they often accrue over many years and are realized at irregular intervals, the present provisions go far beyond those required to avoid discrimination against capital gains. Realized capital gains, in fact, are taxed at much lower rates than other income. Taxpayers' attempts to convert ordinary income into capital gains and the government's efforts to prevent this are responsible for many complexities.

Realized net capital gains, though small relative to total income, are heavily concentrated in the hands of high-income investors. At very high income levels, the present capital gains provisions are the most important single factor accounting for the difference between nominal and effective tax rates and thus holding actual progressivity below apparent progressivity.

The present tax provisions offer investors an inducement to seek capital appreciation in preference to other returns. The investments that are fostered include risky commitments associated with innovations but also certain routine investments and various speculative activities. The preferential tax rates for long-term capital gains are less likely to inhibit changes of investment than would higher tax rates; however, prolonged holding of appreciated assets is encouraged by the opportunity for escaping income tax on accrued gains on property transferred by bequest.

Taking into account both equity and economic effects, I believe the best solution would be to tax capital gains fully and to allow capital losses to be fully deducted, under an averaging or proration plan, relying on reasonable rates and other provisions to avoid harmful economic consequences. If agreement cannot be reached on a fundamental reform, it would still be possible to make worthwhile improvements in the taxation of capital gains.

CHAPTER NINE

Rates and Personal Exemptions

AN OPINION that gained acceptance in the 1950s was that income tax rates were too high in the United States whereas the tax base was too narrowly defined. The Revenue Act of 1964 considerably reduced income tax rates, and this and subsequent legislation slightly curtailed some of the personal deductions. Meanwhile, growth, inflation, and other economic developments caused an appreciable increase in the proportion of total income subject to taxation. In the early 1970s, nevertheless, the view that the tax base should be broadened and tax rates simultaneously reduced continued to be influential.

Different combinations of tax rates and personal exemptions and income definitions that yield the same revenue are not equivalent in other respects. They result in different distributions of tax among income classes and among persons in the same income class. They may also produce different relations between average effective tax rates and marginal rates. An increase in personal exemptions, for example, will reduce the effective tax rate for all taxpayers, but for many persons, who remain in the same rate bracket, it will have no influence on the marginal tax rate payable on the last dollar of income.

This chapter examines several questions relating to personal exemptions and tax rates. Topics covered include the adequacy of the exemptions, the yield of various parts of the tax rate schedule, the significance of income splitting between husbands and wives, splitting of income among family members by trusts and similar devices, averaging of fluctuating incomes, and arguments for taxing earned income at lower rates than property income.

Personal Exemptions

Personal exemptions under the federal income tax were fixed at $600 each for the taxpayer, spouse, and each dependent during the period 1948 through 1969; thereafter they were increased in stages to $750 per person in 1972. In addition, a special exemption of $750 is allowed for a taxpayer or spouse who is sixty-five or older or who is blind. The exemptions are additive: a person who is both blind and sixty-five or older is entitled to three exemptions. The minimum standard deduction, adopted in 1964 and later liberalized, may be regarded as a supplement to the personal exemption at low income levels.

The regular personal exemptions for the whole population, including persons not covered on tax returns, amounted to $129 billion in 1970, or about 19 percent of total adjusted gross income (AGI).[1] In addition, almost 9 million exemptions for age and blindness were claimed on tax returns. Since there were more than 20 million persons sixty-five or older in 1970,[2] it is apparent that a large fraction of this group either did not file tax returns, because of low income or failure to observe the requirement to file, or did not claim the special exemption.

Since the modern income tax began in 1913, personal exemptions

---

1. Based on an estimated population (including armed forces abroad) at the end of 1970 of 206 million (derived by interpolation from midyear estimates in U.S. Bureau of the Census, *Statistical Abstract of the United States, 1973* [hereafter *Statistical Abstract,* followed by the year], p. 5), total AGI of $683 billion (table A-6), and the statutory exemption of $625 for 1970. The number of exemptions other than for age and blindness reported on tax returns was 195.1 million, or about 95 percent of the estimated total; U.S. Internal Revenue Service, *Statistics of Income—1970, Individual Income Tax Returns* (1972) (hereafter *Statistics of Income—1970*), p. 106.

2. *Statistical Abstract, 1973,* p. 31.

have been reduced sharply in dollar amounts, in purchasing power, and in relation to average income (table 9-1). In 1974 the exemptions were smaller in the latter terms than in 1944, when taxes were at their World War II peak. Exemptions for children and other dependents were not allowed until 1917, and until World War II they remained much lower than the exemption for a single taxpayer.

Functions and Adequacy

Personal exemptions have four major functions: (1) keeping the total number of returns within manageable proportions and particularly holding down the number with tax liability lower than the cost of collection; (2) freeing from tax the income needed to maintain a minimum standard of living; (3) helping achieve a smooth gradua-

Table 9-1. Personal Exemptions in Current and Constant Prices and as Multiples of Per Capita Personal Income, by Family Status, Selected Years, 1913–74
Dollars

Basis and family status	1913	1939	1944[a]	1948	1960	1970	1974
Current prices							
Single person	3,000	1,000	500	600	600	625	750
Married couple	4,000	2,500	1,000	1,200	1,200	1,250	1,500
Each dependent	0	400	500	600	600	625	750
Family of four	4,000	3,300	2,000	2,400	2,400	2,500	3,000
Constant prices[b]							
Single person	11,765	2,793	1,104	968	786	625	591
Married couple	15,686	6,983	2,208	1,935	1,573	1,250	1,181
Each dependent	0	1,117	1,104	968	786	625	591
Family of four	15,686	9,218	4,415	3,871	3,145	2,500	2,362
Multiple of per capita personal income[c]							
Single person	8.80	1.80	0.42	0.42	0.27	0.16	0.14
Married couple	11.73	4.50	0.84	0.84	0.54	0.32	0.28
Each dependent	...	0.72	0.42	0.42	0.27	0.16	0.14
Family of four	11.73	5.94	1.67	1.67	1.08	0.63	0.55

Sources: Exemptions, current prices, *The Federal Tax System: Facts and Problems, 1964*, Materials Assembled by the Committee Staff for the Joint Economic Committee, 88 Cong. 2 sess. (1964), p. 233, and public laws; other data, derived from U.S. Bureau of the Census, *Historical Statistics of the United States, Colonial Times to 1957* (1960), pp. 7, 125–26, 139, and *Economic Report of the President, February 1975*, pp. 268–69, 300.

a. The exemptions shown for 1944 were for surtax only. The normal tax exemption was $500 per tax return except for joint returns of husbands and wives, for which it was $500 plus the smaller of the two incomes but not more than $1,000.

b. Current-price figures deflated by the consumer price index (base shifted to 1970 = 100).

c. Exemptions in current prices divided by per capita personal income. The per capita personal income figure for 1913 is an average for 1912–16. The 1974 figure is a preliminary estimate.

tion of effective tax rates at the lower end of the scale; and (4) differentiating tax liability according to family size.

Although administrative considerations may have dictated exemption levels in the United States in the past and still may be decisive in less developed countries, they are unimportant in determining personal exemptions in the United States today. Experience with the income tax, the introduction of withholding, the growth of nonfarm employment, the spread of literacy, and the introduction of automatic data processing systems have lessened the administrative advantages of high exemptions. Indeed, for income that can be brought under withholding—salaries and wages, dividends, and interest—the simplest procedure would be to eliminate the exemptions. Their reduction to a low level would be less convenient but still possible.

The justification for freeing from direct taxation income for a minimum standard of living is that families below that level would feel excessive hardship in paying taxes or would suffer an impairment of health and working efficiency. Ideas about the minimum standard change over time and presumably are related to average levels attained. This is the reason for comparing income tax exemptions with average personal income. Such comparison, of course, does not imply that everyone below the average income should be free of personal income tax, but the figures on average income provide a rough indication of the probable trend of the socially acceptable minimum.

Many commentators reject the idea that people below a socially acceptable minimum standard of living should be exempt from income tax. They argue that government is a necessity and that everyone should pay his share of the cost just as he must pay for food and shelter. This argument, however, is not controlling. Although governmental costs are unavoidable for the community as a whole, their allocation among citizens is a matter of choice. Families with resources that are considered inadequate receive public assistance in paying for nongovernmental necessities, and there is a strong case for relieving them from part of the cost of government. Furthermore, those who pay no income tax make a contribution to government in the form of indirect tax payments.

As a means of freeing from tax the income needed for a minimum standard of living, the personal exemptions are supplemented by the standard deduction and in 1975 by a personal exemption tax credit. This function of the standard deduction became clearer with the adoption in 1964 of the minimum standard deduction of $300 for single persons and $400 for married couples. The minimum standard deduction was given the name "low-income allowance" in 1970 and was increased over a transitional period, becoming $1,300 for both single persons and couples in 1972. Despite the continuance of the uniform per capita personal exemption, the treatment of single persons relative to married couples, and of taxpayers relative to dependents, was thus made more favorable. This realignment, however, was partly reversed by the Tax Reduction Act of 1975 (Public Law 94-12), which restored a difference between the minimum standard deduction for single persons and married couples ($1,600 and $1,900, respectively) and added a tax credit of $30 per person. The resulting complex arrangement provides a tax-free minimum of $2,564 for a single person and $3,829 for a married couple, plus $964 for the couple's first dependent. (The tax-free minimum is the sum of the personal exemptions, the minimum standard deduction, and the amount of taxable income that would attract a tax liability of $30 per person computed at the applicable marginal rate.) The latest increase in the minimum standard deduction and the personal exemption tax credit were enacted for the year 1975 only, and it is not clear what provision will be made for later years.

One standard for judging the adequacy of the tax-free minimum is supplied by the official figures for the poverty or low income levels for families of various sizes. These figures, established by a federal interagency committee in 1969, are based on the cost of food as estimated in the Department of Agriculture's economy food plan. For nonfarm families, poverty-level income is about three times the cost of food, and the income figure is adjusted annually by reference to the consumer price index. For farm families, poverty levels are taken to be 85 percent of those for nonfarm families. The poverty level figures, though widely used, are somewhat higher than those adopted by Congress in the supplemental security income program, which established direct federal assistance to the aged, blind, and disabled effective in 1974 (Public Law 92-603).

When the low-income allowance (minimum standard deduction) was increased in 1969, the intention was to relieve single persons and families below the poverty level from federal income tax. This objective was not fully attained in 1970, a transitional year, or in 1973–74, when the poverty level had risen as a result of increases in the consumer price index. On the basis of the projected price index for 1975, which of course is subject to a considerable margin of error, the tax-free minimum will be above the poverty level for all except single persons under sixty-five (table 9-2).

The function of the personal exemptions, the minimum standard deduction, and the personal tax credit as instruments of progressivity is less obvious than their role in freeing from tax those below a minimum income level, but far more people are affected. This is because the great majority of these allowances are for persons who are subject to income tax.

Progressivity over the income range in which most taxpayers fall results mainly from the personal exemptions and the standard deduction rather than rate graduation. For example, rate graduation accounts for only a little more than one-fourth of the difference between the income tax payable by a four-person family at the top of the

Table 9-2. Average Poverty Income Levels of Nonfarm Families and Individuals Compared with Minimum Amounts Free of Federal Income Tax, 1970 and Estimated for 1975

Dollars

Family size and age	1970		1975	
	Poverty level	Tax-free minimum[a]	Poverty level[b]	Tax-free minimum[a]
Single person				
Under 65	2,010	1,725	2,842	2,564
Over 65	1,861	2,350	2,631	3,314
Couple				
Head under 65	2,604	2,350	3,682	3,829
Head over 65	2,348	2,975	3,320	4,579
Couple[c] with				
1 child	3,099	2,975	4,382	4,793
2 children	3,968	3,600	5,611	5,757
3 children	4,680	4,225	6,618	6,717
4 children	5,260	4,850	7,438	7,667

Sources: Derived from low-income-level figures for 1970 from *Statistical Abstract, 1974*, p. 390; consumer price index, 1970 and 1974, from *Economic Report of the President, February 1975*, p. 300; and projected consumer price index in 1975, from *The Budget of the United States Government, Fiscal Year 1976*, p. 41.

a. Includes the personal exemptions, the minimum standard deduction, and in 1975 the income equivalent of the $30 per person tax credit.

b. Estimated by increasing the 1970 amounts in proportion to the projected rise of the consumer price index—41.4 percent.

c. Husband and wife under sixty-five; children assumed to be dependents.

bottom fifth of family incomes and that payable at the lower limit of the highest fifth.[3]

Throughout the income scale, the personal exemptions cause the income tax to vary with the number in the family, but the amount of variation depends on the marginal tax rate. In the bottom bracket, the exemption for one child reduces a married couple's tax by $105. This sum rises with income and the marginal tax rate. It is about $240 for a married couple with a $25,000 income, and it reaches a maximum of $525 in the highest bracket.

Those who view personal exemptions primarily as a means of protecting a minimum standard of living often argue that exemptions are not needed in middle- and upper-income classes, since, in these classes, an income tax without exemptions would not infringe on the socially acceptable minimum. The suggestion has been made that the exemptions be gradually withdrawn as income increases. This arrangement, called a vanishing exemption, has been used by several countries in the British Commonwealth. For example, if the exemption for a family of three were $4,800 minus one-fourth of the amount by which net income exceeds $4,800, the exemption would fall to zero—vanish—at an income of $24,000. At that income the same tax would be paid by all taxpayers with no more than three exemptions.

The low-income allowance in the United States is similar to the addition of a vanishing exemption to the $750 per capita continuing exemption. The amount of income one can have before becoming subject to the income tax is raised, but the amount freed from tax by the low-income allowance diminishes as income increases and the regular standard deduction also increases. Under 1975 law, the regular standard deduction of 16 percent equals the low-income allowance for a single person at an AGI of $10,000 and for a married

3. In 1972 the two income levels were $5,612 and $17,760, respectively (*Statistical Abstract, 1974*, p. 384). On the assumption that these incomes increase at the same rate as per capita personal income, as implied in the projections for the 1976 budget (*The Budget of the United States Government, Fiscal Year 1976*, p. 41, and my projection of population), they would be roughly $7,160 and $22,660 in 1975. For a married couple with two dependents using the standard deduction the tax computed according to the 1975 law would be $212 on the lower income and $3,437 on the higher income, a difference of $3,225. With the same exemptions, standard deduction, and personal tax credit but with a maximum marginal rate of 16 percent (that applicable to the lower-income family), the amounts payable would be $212 and $2,580, respectively, a difference of $2,368.

couple at an AGI of $11,875, and the low-income allowance vanishes. An important difference between the low-income allowance and an ordinary vanishing exemption is that the former substitutes for other personal deductions and hence does not benefit a person whose itemized deductions exceed the low-income allowance.

Another view is that some differentiation of tax according to family size is justified above the socially acceptable minimum but that it is unfair to grant a tax reduction for an additional dependent that increases with the taxpayer's income and marginal tax rate, as is true with the continuing exemptions of the United States and many other countries. This approach leads to the proposal that fixed tax credits be substituted for personal exemptions. Tax credits are used in lieu of personal exemptions in several state income taxes. Interest in this technique is reflected in the Tax Reduction Act of 1975, but Congress merely added a personal tax credit for 1975 to the exemptions and the low-income allowance.

A quite different attitude is taken by critics who argue that uniform exemptions produce too small a difference between tax liabilities of large and small families in upper- and middle-income classes. They point out, for example, that the differences in amounts of taxes paid in these brackets by childless couples and by families with three or four children are small relative to the cost of rearing children. They suggest that personal exemptions be stated as a percentage of income, within limits, rather than as a fixed dollar amount.[4]

The choice between vanishing exemptions and increasing exemptions turns on the emphasis placed on the objective of varying the income tax with family size in middle- and high-income classes. Both forms of exemption can protect a minimum standard of living and facilitate progressivity at lower income levels, but the vanishing exemption deliberately omits differentiation by family size at upper income levels. While it seems clear that the principle of ability to pay requires differentiation of tax liability by family size at income levels close to the socially acceptable minimum, it is not obvious how far up the income scale this differentiation should be carried. In my opinion,

4. For discussions of the different kinds of personal exemptions and in-lieu credits, see Michael E. Levy, *Income Tax Exemptions: An Analysis of the Effects of Personal Exemptions on the Income Tax Structure* (Amsterdam: North-Holland, 1960); and Gerard M. Brannon and Elliott R. Morss, "The Tax Allowance for Dependents: Deductions versus Credits," *National Tax Journal,* vol. 26 (December 1973), pp. 599–609.

Table 9-3. Poverty Level and "Necessities Equivalent" Income Compared with Tax-Free Minimum Income under the Federal Income Tax, by Family Size
Relatives, four-person family = 100

Family size	Poverty level	Necessities equivalent income[a]	Tax-free minimum income, 1975
Single person[b]	51	...	45
Couple[b]	66	65	67
Couple[b] with			
1 child	78	82	83
2 children	100	100	100
3 children	118	113	117
4 children	133	127	133

Sources: Derived from table 9-2 and Joseph J. Seneca and Michael K. Taussig, "Family Equivalence Scales and Personal Income Tax Exemptions for Children," *Review of Economics and Statistics*, vol. 53 (August 1971), p. 257.

a. Arithmetic mean of estimates for $5,000 and $6,000 income levels in 1960.
b. Under sixty-five years of age.

the ability-to-pay principle does not require differentiation by family size at high income levels and vanishing exemptions are justifiable. (This is discussed further in the later section on income splitting.) Although the case for continuing exemptions or personal tax credits seems weaker in logic than that for either vanishing or increasing exemptions, the difference between the techniques may not be very important so long as the allowances are held to low or moderate levels.

Evidence on relative needs, as compared with the tax-free minimum for families of different sizes, is brought together in table 9-3. The table shows, in addition to previously mentioned poverty income levels, estimates of a "necessities equivalent" scale by Seneca and Taussig.[5] This latter scale defines incomes as equivalent when families spend the same proportion of income on necessities (food, housing, clothing, and transportation). Basing their estimates on the Bureau of Labor Statistics' 1960 Survey of Consumer Expenditures, Seneca and Taussig found that the equivalence scales differed considerably by income level and tended to converge as income increased. The relatives shown in table 9-3 are for incomes near the median.

5. Joseph J. Seneca and Michael K. Taussig, "Family Equivalence Scales and Personal Income Tax Exemptions for Children," *Review of Economics and Statistics*, vol. 53 (August 1971), pp. 253–62. This study covered urban families with two to seven members, excluding families with heads sixty-five and older.

The estimates of equivalent incomes given in table 9-3, being averages, conceal differences arising from the age of children and other family members. Budget studies indicate that the consumption requirements of children increase with age; hence the equivalent income for a family with young children will be less than that for a family with older children, other things being equal. Some countries take account of this by graduating the exemptions for children by age. In Canada the exemption for children sixteen and over is 83 percent greater than that for younger ones. The United Kingdom has three age brackets—up to eleven, eleven to sixteen, and over sixteen—but the allowance for the oldest is only 27 percent greater than that for the youngest.[6]

Possible Revisions

The relation between tax-free minimums for families of different sizes appears to be fairly satisfactory in the United States in 1975, though the amounts allowed may be comparatively low for single persons and comparatively high for large families. The low-income allowance decisively influences the pattern; equal per capita exemptions alone would be inequitable, on the basis of available information on living costs. The existing scheme, however, is unnecessarily complex, and the low-income allowance is arbitrary in that it benefits only taxpayers who do not itemize their personal deductions. An improvement could be made by increasing personal exemptions for taxpayers and eliminating the low-income allowance and the personal tax credit. If the personal tax credit is regarded as a temporary tax cut for 1975 only, the personal exemptions and the low-income allowance might be consolidated in personal exemptions of $2,350 for single persons, $3,400 for married couples, and $750 each for dependents. Other combinations that might be considered, if tax-free minimums closer to the 1975 levels are desired, are $3,000, $4,000, and $900 and $2,800, $3,800, and $1,000. The latter two combinations would produce roughly the 1975 tax-free minimum for the reference family of four but somewhat different general patterns.

Consolidation of the allowances would cost revenue and would be

6. For Canada the figures are those for 1974; for the United Kingdom, for the income year 1974–75.

beneficial to middle- and high-income taxpayers unless vanishing exemptions were adopted. If Congress wishes to develop the personal tax credit technique, it would be much simpler to substitute credits for the personal exemptions and the low-income allowance instead of adding the credits or offering them as elective alternatives.

Exemptions for Age and Blindness

The additional exemptions for age and blindness mean that the tax-free minimum for a family including an aged or blind person is $750 more than that for a family which is not entitled to either of the special exemptions. When both the husband and wife are over sixty-five, their tax-free minimum in 1975 will considerably exceed that of a younger family of three. Furthermore, many elderly people receive income that is excluded from AGI. In 1970, 61 percent of persons sixty-five and older were receiving tax-free social security retirement benefits,[7] and others were receiving railroad retirement or veterans' benefits, which are also excluded from AGI.

The special exemptions can justly be characterized as makeshift welfare legislation. It is true that the average income of the aged, and probably also of the blind, is low, but their income tax would be correspondingly low without special treatment. Presumably the special exemptions are based on the idea that the aged and the blind have special living expenses. For the aged, this is questionable. Although the elderly spend relatively much more for medical care than younger people, their outlays for other items are smaller. The poverty level incomes for persons over sixty-five are lower than those for persons under sixty-five (table 9-2). The budgets for urban families and retired couples prepared by the U.S. Bureau of Labor Statistics show a similar relationship. For example, the intermediate budget for a retired husband sixty-five or over and his wife in 1970 was 42 percent of the budget for a four-person family headed by a younger employed man.[8] Information on the budgets of the blind is not readily available. Although they are likely to incur some special expenses, it is not evident that these expenses are greater than those of other physically handicapped persons who receive no special tax concession.

The special exemptions are not related to need but are indiscriminately allowed to all. They do not benefit the most needy. Though

7. *Statistical Abstract, 1973,* pp. 292, 295.
8. Ibid., p. 356.

clumsy and inequitable, the special exemptions for the elderly and the blind are not quantitatively important. In 1970, they accounted for 4.4 percent of the number of exemptions on all returns, taxable and nontaxable.[9] Repeal of the special exemptions would be justified but is not a high-priority item.

Rates

Many comments on income tax rates exaggerate their severity because they neglect the influence of exclusions, personal deductions, preferential rates for long-term capital gains, and other special provisions. During the past decade, however, the difference between nominal and effective tax rates has been recognized much more frequently, and the "erosion of the tax base"—or the existence of "loopholes"—has become an important public issue.[10] Sometimes the emphasis on loopholes has gone too far, condemning desirable provisions and giving too unfavorable an impression of the income tax.

The influence on actual effective tax rates of personal exemptions, personal deductions, capital gains provisions, and income splitting are shown clearly in figure 9-1 and in appendix table A-11. Less clearly visible in the figure are the effects of certain preference items (as defined by the Tax Reform Act of 1969) and the maximum rate on earned income. In the figure, the highest curve, labeled "nominal rates," traces the effective rates that would have obtained had the statutory rates for married persons who file separate returns been applied to total income. The successively lower curves show the influence on the nominal rates of personal exemptions and the other provisions, leading finally to actual effective rates on total income.

Total income as defined for these estimates consists of AGI plus the excluded portion of realized capital gains, dividends, and sick pay; moving expenses; and the excluded portion of the narrow range

9. *Statistics of Income—1970*, p. 106.
10. Joseph A. Pechman deserves a large part of the credit for the better understanding of the difference between nominal and effective tax rates. See particularly Pechman, "What Would a Comprehensive Individual Income Tax Yield?" in *Tax Revision Compendium*, Papers Submitted to the House Committee on Ways and Means (1959), vol. 1, pp. 251–81; Pechman, *Federal Tax Policy* (Brookings Institution, 1966; rev. ed., 1971); and Pechman and Benjamin A. Okner, "Individual Income Tax Erosion by Income Classes," in *The Economics of Federal Subsidy Programs*, A Compendium of Papers Submitted to the Joint Economic Committee, 92 Cong. 2 sess. (1972), pt. 1, pp. 13–40.

**Figure 9-1. Influence of Various Provisions on Effective Rates of the Individual
Income Tax[a]**

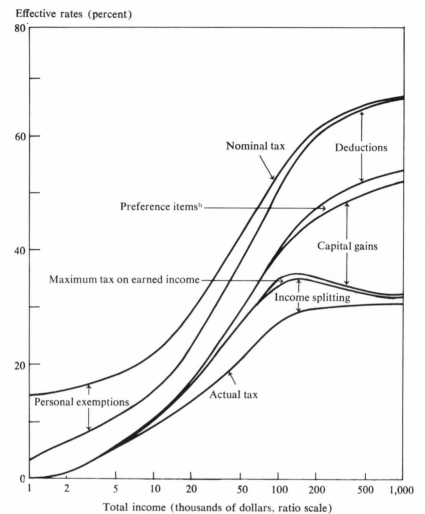

Effective rates (percent)

Total income (thousands of dollars, ratio scale)

Source: Appendix table A-11.
a. Income distribution of 1970; tax rates and other provisions in effect in 1973.
b. Preference items as defined by the Tax Reform Act of 1969, except excluded net long-term capital
gains.

of statutory preference items identified in the Tax Reform Act of
1969. It does not include other and much larger exclusions discussed
in chapter 6; deductions are not made for educational expenditures
and certain other costs of earning income, which were discussed in

chapter 5. No allowance is made for tax evasion. The estimates are for income and related items of 1970, but the rates and other provisions are those in effect in 1973 (thus avoiding the influence of certain transitional provisions of the 1969 act which were in effect in 1970).

The difference between the nominal and actual effective rates can be accounted for (in percent, rounded) as follows:

Nominal tax	26.9
Less allowance for	
Personal exemptions	6.4
Personal deductions	6.0
Capital gains provisions	0.8
Income splitting	2.3
Other provisions	0.1
Actual tax	11.4

In the aggregate, most of the difference between nominal and actual effective tax rates is due to the personal exemptions and deductions, but the influence of the various provisions differs greatly among income classes, as can be seen from figure 9-1 and appendix table A-11. For low incomes, personal exemptions are the main factor abating the potential tax; over a wide middle range the personal exemptions, deductions, and income splitting are most important; and at the highest income levels the influence of the capital gains provisions is notable. The significance of the personal deductions at low income levels is overstated because this item includes the low-income allowance, which could well be considered an additional personal exemption. A striking point is that the effective tax rate on total income exceeds 30 percent only above $150,000 and reaches a maximum of 31.4 percent in the income class over $1,000,000. These estimates, however, do not reveal any tendency for effective rates to decline over the highest income classes, such as appeared in similar tabulations for 1960.[11]

The estimates reveal that it would be possible to cut statutory income tax rates drastically without loss of revenue if offsetting structural revisions were adopted. For example, with the 1970 distribution

11. See the original edition of this book, p. 326. The difference between 1960 and 1970 appears to be due to the smaller effect of the capital gains provisions resulting from the decreased relative size of realized net gains in 1970 and the increase in rates on large gains resulting from the elimination of the maximum rate of 25 percent on long-term gains.

of income and related items and the 1973 statutory provisions, nominal rates could have been cut by 37 percent on the average, without revenue loss, if all personal deductions and the special provisions for capital gains had been eliminated.[12]

If this rate reduction were spread proportionately over all brackets, the statutory rates could be reduced from a range of 14 to 70 percent to a range of approximately 9 to 44 percent. This particular revision would considerably increase the overall progressivity of the income tax, since the provisions that would have been eliminated benefit high-income taxpayers relatively more than low-income taxpayers. A program that would preserve revenue yield without changing actual progressivity would allow deeper cuts in high bracket rates. Many intermediate distributions would be possible.

Despite many endorsements of the idea of combining base broadening and rate reduction, programs as drastic as that mentioned above draw little support in Congress. While I agree that the elimination of all personal deductions would go too far and that full taxation of realized capital gains would be too harsh unless averaging or prorating were allowed, the computations above omit other possibilities that would be worthy of serious attention, particularly the taxation of excluded items of income that are not taken into account here.

Even without structural revisions, top-bracket rates could be reduced with only minor revenue loss. Owing to the special provisions and the large aggregate amount of income received by those in the lower income classes, only a small part of the total income tax yield comes from the high-bracket rates. In 1970 all bracket rates above 50 percent could have been cut to 50 percent at a revenue loss of less than 1 percent of the total yield of the individual income tax. Fewer than one-half of 1 percent of taxpayers would have been affected.[13]

The small size of the yield of the top-bracket rates, however, is not a reliable indication of their importance. On the one hand, Congress and the executive branch, under both major political parties, have been unwilling to cut top rates without reducing other rates. The function of the top rates is primarily to establish a proper relation between taxes on large and small incomes; their revenue significance

12. The elimination of personal deductions and the capital gains provisions would have increased the average effective rate on total income, in percent, to $11.4 + 6.0 + 0.8 = 18.2$; $1 - (11.4/18.2) = 0.37$.

13. Derived from *Statistics of Income—1970*, p. 171.

is to be found mainly in their influence on lower-bracket rates. On the other hand, high rates accentuate the inequities caused by unjustifiable special provisions, and they stimulate efforts to take advantage of special provisions that entail waste and economic distortions.

Income Splitting

Husbands and wives who file joint returns use a rate schedule with brackets twice as wide as those for married persons who file separate returns. This arrangement is called income splitting because it originated as a provision defining the tax on a joint return as "twice the tax which would be imposed if the taxable income were cut in half." Single persons were formerly subject to the same schedule as married persons filing separate returns, but since 1971 they have used a schedule with lower rates. Single persons who qualify as "head of household" use a fourth rate schedule resulting in tax liabilities about halfway between those in the schedule for single persons and those in the schedule for married persons filing joint returns.[14]

Income splitting was adopted in 1948 to meet two kinds of inequity arising from the opportunities that some married persons had to divide their income for tax purposes. One inequity arose from the advantages enjoyed by residents of community property states, whose earned income and property income were considered as belonging equally to husbands and wives. The courts had upheld the right of married couples in these states to file separate federal income tax returns. The eight original community property states had inherited the arrangement from the civil law of Spain or France, but community property laws were being adopted in other states for the frank purpose of obtaining income tax advantages. The second inequity was attributable to opportunities for dividing property income between husbands and wives in common law states by transfers of property. Earned income could not be so divided.[15]

14. A head of household is a single person or a married person legally separated who maintains as his or her home a household that is the principal place of abode of a dependent relative. A widow or widower with dependent children or stepchildren, who has not remarried, may use the rates applicable to joint returns for the first two years after the spouse's death.

15. For a review of the background of the 1948 legislation, see Harold M. Groves, *Federal Tax Treatment of the Family* (Brookings Institution, 1963), pp. 57–65.

The 1948 legislation dealt effectively with these inequities, by extending to all married persons the benefits formerly enjoyed by residents of community property states, but at the same time it brought about a major income tax reduction and reallocation. Income splitting had little or no value for the great majority of couples whose income fell entirely in the first one or two brackets and had relatively little value for the few with extremely high incomes. In a wide intermediate range, the progressivity of the income tax was sharply reduced, and large differences were introduced between the amounts of tax paid by married and single persons with the same income.

Subsequent revisions of rates and the introduction of separate schedules for heads of households in 1952 and for single persons in 1971—together with rising prices and incomes—have considerably altered the initial results of income splitting. Relative to tax, the difference between the liability of a single person and that of a married couple filing a joint return is greatest at a taxable income of $24,000, where the single person pays 20 percent more (table 9-4). In absolute amount the difference rises to a maximum at a taxable income of $200,000. These comparisons do not take account of the ceiling rate on earned income or the difference arising from the larger personal exemption of the couple. The tax value of the latter, which ranges from $105 in the first bracket to $525 in the top bracket, is relatively large for low incomes but relatively small for high incomes.

Although this may sound paradoxical, income splitting provides for taxing a married couple as a unit. While aggregation of income of the two spouses on a joint return is optional, this ordinarily does not increase the aggregate tax liability, and if the incomes of the two parties are unequal, joint returns will often result in a smaller tax than would separate returns. Most married couples elect to file joint returns.[16] Aggregation and income splitting could be extended to minor children, as in France, thereby taxing the family as a unit.

---

16. In 1970, the number of separate returns of husbands and wives was 5.6 percent of the number of joint returns, and the amount of AGI and the amount of tax liability on separate returns were 2.3 percent and 2.1 percent, respectively, of the amounts on joint returns (*Statistics of Income—1970*, pp. 9–10). Husbands and wives may not file joint returns if they have different tax years or are legally separated under a decree of divorce or separate maintenance, or if one is a nonresident alien at any time during the year. They may find it worthwhile to file separate returns in certain capital gains situations or to allow one of the spouses to take advantage of the medical deduction.

Table 9-4. Federal Income Tax of Single Persons Compared with That of Married Couples, by Taxable Income, 1971 and Later[a]

Amounts in dollars

Taxable income	Tax liability		Difference	
	Single person	Married couple	Amount	As percent of married couple's tax
500	70	70	0	0
1,000	145	140	5	3.6
2,000	310	290	20	6.9
5,000	900	810	90	11.1
10,000	2,090	1,820	270	14.8
15,000	3,520	3,010	510	16.9
20,000	5,230	4,380	850	19.4
24,000	6,790	5,660	1,130	20.0
30,000	9,390	7,880	1,510	19.2
50,000	20,190	17,060	3,130	18.3
100,000	53,090	45,180	7,910	17.5
200,000	123,090	110,980	12,110	10.9
400,000	263,090	250,980	12,110	4.8
1,000,000	683,090	670,980	12,110	1.8

Source: Calculated from statutory tax rates.

a. Assumes that married couples file joint returns; the maximum rate of 50 percent on earned income (in effect beginning in 1972) and the personal exemption tax credit of $30 per person in 1975 are not reflected.

Acceptance of the principle of taxing husbands and wives or whole families as units does not necessarily imply any particular view on the appropriate relationship between the tax liabilities of married people and those of single people. This is demonstrated by the introduction of the separate rate schedule for single persons, which reduced their tax relative to that of married persons. (Under the current schedules, the rate for a single person is never more than 20 percent higher than that for a married couple with the same taxable income, whereas before 1971 the difference could be as much as 29.5 percent.) In my opinion, the change was in the right direction but did not go far enough.

The present rate schedules reflect a belief that a married couple with a given income has more than twice as much taxpaying ability as a single person with half that income. This appears to be based on an appraisal of the consumption opportunities and economic power of the two taxpaying units. At low and lower-middle income levels this generalization is supported by the budget studies cited above in the discussion of exemptions and by other studies. The advantage of married couples is attributable to economies of scale in consumption and the imputed value of housewives' services at home. In upper-middle income groups living standards depend to a great extent on customs and conventions that take the married couple as the norm. Veblen long ago recognized that, in these circles, a wife enhances her husband's status by carrying out vicarious consumption. At the highest income levels, the economic and political power conveyed by income is the primary consideration in rate graduation, and there seems no reason to suppose that the power of a couple with a given income is less than that of a single person with the same income.

An opposing view is that income can be meaningfully defined only on a per capita basis. Those with this view hold that any economies in consumption enjoyed by married couples are attributable to genuine efficiencies and should not be penalized by taxation. Some of them concede, however, that at very high income levels the per capita concept is inappropriate.[17]

A further movement in the direction of the recent change in the relation between the taxation of single persons and that of married couples could be made either by modification of the separate rate schedule for single persons or by applying the same rate schedule to single persons and married couples filing joint returns (with married persons who file separate returns required, as at present, to use a rate schedule with brackets half as wide as in the schedule for joint returns). Adoption of the latter measure would mean that the difference in taxation of single persons and couples with the same income would be due only to the difference in personal exemptions. The former approach would be more flexible. It would allow the marginal rates for single persons and married couples, which now come together at a taxable income of $200,000, to be brought together at a lower income level.

An unavoidable consequence of such a modification of tax rates would be to increase the frequency of the cases in which the marriage of a man and woman, both of whom have income, would raise their combined tax liability. To illustrate, if two single persons each have taxable income of $10,000 their combined tax is $4,180; if they

17. See the report of the debate at the experts' conference convened at the Brookings Institution in 1963 (Groves, *Federal Tax Treatment of the Family*, pp. 94–97).

marry and each continues to receive the same taxable income their combined liability will be $4,380, an increase of $200 (see table 9-4). If, however, single persons used the same rate schedule as married persons who file joint returns, marriage would increase the combined liability by $740 (from twice $1,820 to $4,380). For larger incomes the increases in tax resulting from marriage could be much greater. There are already complaints about the "tax penalty" on marriage under present law, and no doubt these would be intensified. Some critics have contended that marriage would be discouraged. The latter point has been debated in the United Kingdom, where joint returns without income splitting are the general rule. A royal commission concluded in 1954 that "very little weight" should be given to the argument that taxation discouraged marriage. The commission was "skeptical of the suggestion that men and women are in fact dissuaded from marriage by any such nice calculation of the financial odds," recording its view that "the reasons that impel men and women to prefer marriage to more casual associations are many and powerful."[18] An economic argument against a rate structure of the kind under discussion is that it might discourage the second spouse, usually the wife, from continuing to work after marriage or from taking a job. The United Kingdom has attempted to meet this problem by granting a special earned income allowance for working wives or, since 1972–73, by taxing their earnings separately.

Division of Income with Other Family Members

Income taxes may be reduced by dividing income with children or other family members. This cannot be accomplished merely by assigning the income itself, even by a legally enforceable contract. Income-producing property must be transferred.[19] This provision, al-

18. Royal Commission on the Taxation of Profits and Income, *Second Report,* Cmd. 9105 (London: Her Majesty's Stationery Office, 1954), p. 36.

19. However, the transferor need not always divest himself permanently of the property. He can escape tax on the income from property placed in trust that will revert to him after ten years or more or at the death of the beneficiary. For a summary of the complex provisions of law relating to the subject treated in this section, with brief comments on the adequacy of the provisions, see Harvard Law School, World Tax Series, *Taxation in the United States* (Commerce Clearing House, 1963), pp. 347–50, 434–41, 905–44. Summaries including later provisions appear in Commerce Clearing House, *1973 U.S. Master Tax Guide* (CCH, 1972), par. 401–97,

though a safeguard against tax avoidance, means that property owners have opportunities for tax minimization that are not open to those
who receive mainly earned income.

Intrafamily gifts will reduce the total taxes paid by the family if,
as is usually the case, the recipient has a smaller income than the
donor and is in a lower tax bracket. Minor children are taxable on the
income from the property given to them. (Minor children are each
entitled to the usual $750 personal exemption, and the parents may
also claim a $750 exemption for each of them if they provide more
than half the children's support; however, if a child is over nineteen
and is not a student, he qualifies as a dependent only if his gross income is less than $750.[20]) Under a uniform law for gifts to minors
(or similar legislation), which has been adopted by almost all states,
splitting property income with children is facilitated. A parent may
serve as custodian and manage the property but may not use the income for his or her own benefit. The parent may use the income to
support the child but remains taxable on it to the extent that this use
discharges the parent's legal obligation to provide support.

Trusts are an especially convenient vehicle for gifts because they
obviate the necessity for turning over immediate control to the beneficiary and allow flexibility in the final disposition of the property.[21]
A special income tax advantage of a trust is obtainable when income
is accumulated rather than distributed to the beneficiaries. The trust
is a legal entity and is separately taxable on its retained income (at the
rate schedule for married persons filing separate returns) but is not
taxed on income distributable to beneficiaries. The beneficiaries are
taxable only on the distributable income. When accumulated income
is distributed it is taxable, with some exceptions, to the beneficiary
under a "throwback" or averaging rule, with credit for the tax previously paid by the trust.[22] By establishing multiple trusts for the same

---

and Clarence F. McCarthy, *The Federal Income Tax: Its Sources and Applications*
(Prentice-Hall, 1974), pp. 719–33.

20. A child who files a separate return qualifies for the standard deduction, including the low-income allowance, but only for his earned income.

21. A trust is an arrangement under which a trustee (often a bank or trust company) holds legal title to property for the benefit of designated persons. Trusts may
be created by gifts during the life of the grantor or by will.

22. This allows tax postponement, but the present rule, adopted in 1969, represents a tightening of earlier provisions under which income retained by the trust
longer than five years was not taxable when distributed to the beneficiary.

beneficiary, it used to be possible to hold down the top tax rate payable during the accumulation period. Current regulations, however, provide that multiple trusts will be treated as one trust if they have the same grantor and substantially the same beneficiaries and have the avoidance or deferral of income tax as their principal purpose.[23]

Trusts are adaptable to the avoidance of estate taxes as well as income taxes. Despite their tax advantages, these entities do not appear to have grown disproportionately. From 1937 to 1965, the investment income of fiduciaries (trusts and estates) increased no more rapidly than that of persons, and there was no clear trend toward retention of a larger proportion of income by fiduciaries. Less reliable balance sheet data indicate that the assets of personal trusts grew somewhat faster than the assets of nonfarm households from 1912 to 1945 but more slowly than household assets from 1945 to 1958.[24]

For the income tax, the most equitable principle and the one that would be most conducive to the effectiveness of the tax in reducing the concentration of income and economic power would be to make the taxable unit identical with the economic family or consumer unit. Income would be aggregated for tax purposes to the extent that its control and use were pooled within the family. Ordinarily this would call for combining the income of minor children with that of the parents. In some cases, aggregation of income of older children and other family members would also be indicated.

It does not seem feasible, however, to work out an acceptable set of rules for aggregation of all family income. Property arrangements and family practices differ so greatly that attempts to carry out aggregation would be likely to be meddlesome and arbitrary. This

23. *Code of Federal Regulations,* Title 26, pt. 1 (1975), sec. 1.641(a)-0(c).

24. Investment income and retained income of fiduciaries, U.S. Internal Revenue Service, *Statistics of Income, Individual Income Tax Returns,* and *Statistics of Income, Fiduciary Income Tax Returns,* various issues; investment income of persons (dividends, rental income, and interest; imputed items excluded), derived from U.S. Department of Commerce, *The National Income and Product Accounts of the United States, 1929–1965: Statistical Tables* (1966), and Department of Commerce, *U.S. National Income and Product Accounts, 1964–67* (1971), tables 2.1, 7.2, 7.3 in each; balance sheet data, Raymond W. Goldsmith, Dorothy S. Brady, and Horst Mendershausen, *A Study of Saving in the United States* (Princeton University Press, 1956), vol. 3, pp. 44–45, 54–55; Raymond W. Goldsmith, Robert E. Lipsey, and Morris Mendelson, *Studies in the National Balance Sheet of the United States* (Princeton University Press for the National Bureau of Economic Research, 1963), vol. 2, pp. 118–21.

would be true even if aggregation were limited to parents and minor children. Parents sometimes lack effective control over the income of their minor children and in other cases have control over the income and property of adult children and other dependents.

Although income splitting through gifts of property cannot be stopped, efforts should be continued to ensure that it entails a genuine transfer of ownership of the income-producing property. The attractiveness of gifts can be reduced, moreover, by reform of the transfer taxes, a complex subject that cannot be reviewed here.[25]

While legislation and regulations have reduced the income tax advantages of trusts, they should be further limited to the extent possible without unduly interfering with property arrangements designed for purposes other than tax avoidance. One approach might be to further narrow opportunities for creators of inter vivos trusts to divest themselves of tax liability in cases where the income from trust property does not become currently taxable to a beneficiary or where the property may revert to the grantor.[26] A second possibility would be to continue to tax trusts as separate entities on their undistributed income but to determine the applicable tax rates by reference to the income of the beneficiaries or creators.[27]

Restriction of the tax advantages now available through trusts would not prevent their proper use for other purposes. Any lessening of the use of trusts owing to the decrease in their tax advantages would have the incidental economic result of freeing capital from the conservative control often exercised by trustees.

Averaging of Fluctuating Incomes

With progressive rates, the total tax payable on a given aggregate income over a period of years may be greater if the income is received in unequal installments than if it is obtained in equal annual installments. This is often considered inequitable and a discouragement to activities that are especially likely to result in fluctuating incomes.

25. From the large literature, see Carl S. Shoup, *Federal Estate and Gift Taxes* (Brookings Institution, 1966), and Gerald R. Jantscher, *Trusts and Estate Taxation* (Brookings Institution, 1967).

26. Dan Throop Smith, *Federal Tax Reform: The Issues and a Program* (McGraw-Hill, 1961), pp. 283–98.

27. Henry A. Fenn, "The Present Method of Taxing Trust Income: A Criticism and Proposed Revision," *Yale Law Journal*, vol. 51 (May 1942), pp. 1143–59.

The subject has received much attention, and several plans have been proposed for averaging income for tax purposes.

An averaging plan for persons experiencing a sharp increase in income was adopted in 1964 and liberalized in 1969. It has the effect of taxing part of the increased amount of income at the lower effective rate that would apply if it were averaged over five years. "Averageable income" is defined as the amount of "adjusted taxable income" of the current year in excess of 120 percent of the average of the four preceding years (the base period). In computing base-period income, years of net business losses do not give rise to negative income but are entered as zeros. If averageable income exceeds $3,000, the averaging rule applies; the tax on it is equal to that on one-fifth of averageable income multiplied by five. This is calculated by (1) computing the tax on the sum of 120 percent of the average base-period income plus one-fifth of averageable income; (2) subtracting the tax on 120 percent of average base-period income; and (3) multiplying the remainder by five. The final tax is the sum of the tentative tax on an amount equal to 120 percent of average base-period income plus the tax on the averageable income. The base period is a moving one, with the earliest year dropped and one year added annually.

Averaging applies to almost all kinds of income, including capital gains. (Exceptions are certain distributions from trusts and from pension plans of owner-employees.) A person who elects averaging may not apply the preferential maximum rate on earned income.

The approach followed is to abate the tax payable by a person who has realized the required increase in income either temporarily or as the result of a movement from a lower to a higher normal income level. Beneficiaries may include professional persons, writers, and businessmen who realize in one year rewards for work extending over several years. One who betters his income by changing his job or business activity may gain a little delay in the application of the full graduated rates. Tax relief could be obtained every year, if one's income grew fast enough.[28]

Persons experiencing a decline in income do not obtain any immediate tax relief under the averaging plan. To be sure, their current-year tax falls along with their income, but if averaging were available

28. A steady growth of 7.7 percent or more a year would satisfy the requirement that each year's income exceed average income of the preceding four years by at least one-fifth.

they might be entitled to a greater tax reduction or to the refund of prior taxes. Any averaging relief resulting from a temporary fall in income must wait for income to recover. Unless a severe drop in income is followed by prosperity, averaging will not apply. For example, a person who suffers unemployment or poor business which cuts his normally stable taxable income by two-thirds in one year will not be able to apply averaging when his income returns to normal.[29]

The timing of relief conflicts with the principle of taxing people most heavily "when their ship is in," which seems in accord with ability to pay and convenience. The plan, on the other hand, avoids giving tax refunds to persons who fully or partly retire, which would seem undesirable.

The present averaging plan will do nothing to relieve those whose income fluctuates just above and below the tax-free minimum. Such fluctuations result in wastage of personal exemptions and the low-income allowance and can have considerable influence on the effective tax rate. A person who would pay no income tax if his exemptions could be fully offset against his income over a period of years will be subject to tax in years in which his earnings temporarily rise above the exemption level. Most of those in this situation will be barred from averaging by the $3,000 limitation and by the plan's complexity. The $3,000 limitation was included in the 1964 legislation on the grounds that little benefit would be obtained from averaging when fluctuations were smaller.[30] This would not be true if wastage of personal exemptions were taken into account. The limitation does have the merit of helping keep down the number of cases and thus reducing the administrative burden. While this may be prudent, the denial of benefits to an especially needy group raises doubts about the plan.

---

29. This is because averaging is limited to income that exceeds the average of the base period by more than one-fifth. To illustrate, suppose a person's normal taxable income is $24,000 a year but that it drops to $8,000 in one year and then returns to $24,000 the next year. The average taxable income of the base period will be $20,000. Averageable income in year 5 will be

$$\$24{,}000 - 1.20(\$20{,}000) = 0.$$

30. *President's 1963 Tax Message, Along with Principal Statement, Technical Explanation, and Supporting Exhibits and Documents Submitted by Secretary of the Treasury,* House Ways and Means Committee Print (1963), p. 84; *Revenue Act of 1963,* H. Rept. 749, 88 Cong. 1 sess. (1963), p. 111; *Revenue Act of 1964,* S. Rept. 830, 88 Cong. 2 sess. (1964), p. 141.

In 1970, averaging was used on 1 million returns, and it reduced the liability of these taxpayers by $536 million (7.2 percent).[31] About half the reduction accrued to persons with income above $50,000, while those with income below $10,000 saved only a negligible proportion of the total.

A University of Wisconsin group examined the averaging plan in a study drawing on a simulation of income fluctuations based on Wisconsin state income tax returns. The study indicates that the requirement that averageable income exceed $3,000 is a stringent one, discriminating against low-income persons, and that the failure to allow relief for decline in income and for negative taxable incomes is also highly restrictive. The authors characterized the existing plan as "unnecessarily complex, excessively restrictive, and generally inadequate in conception and execution." They recommended a three-year averaging period, with the current year weighted one-half and the average of the prior two years one-half. Averaging would apply when income exceeded or fell short of the bracket in which the average lay by at least $1,000.[32]

The above proposal appears to be an improvement worthy of consideration. However, an attitude of mild skepticism concerning the desirability of any general averaging plan is justified. While strict annual accounting may result in inequities under a progressive income tax, not all kinds of income irregularity are equally deserving of tax relief. The case for relief is strongest for compensation received in one year for activities extending over several years and for cyclical fluctuations; it is weak for windfalls, movements from one normal income level to another, and sustained upward or downward trends in income. There is little information on income fluctuations and the actual severity of discrimination against irregular income. Many taxpayers can smooth out irregularities in taxable income by planning the timing of receipts, business expenditures, and personal deductions and by adopting plans for spreading income over long periods. From the economic standpoint, the most significant advantage of averaging

31. *Statistics of Income—1970*, p. 149. This represents 1.7 percent of all taxable returns.

32. Martin David and others, "Optimal Choices for an Averaging System—A Simulation Analysis of the Federal Averaging Formula of 1964," *National Tax Journal*, vol. 23 (September 1970), pp. 275–95.

may be attained by carry-backs and carry-forwards of business losses and capital losses, which do not require full averaging. Finally, averaging plans are unavoidably complex.[33]

Earned Income

Many hold that income from personal effort, commonly called earned income, should be taxed more lightly than property income. This could be accomplished by allowing part of earned income to be deducted or excluded from taxable income, by applying a lower rate schedule to earned income, or by imposing an additional tax on property income. In the United States, an earned income credit, in the form of a deduction, was allowed in 1924–31 and 1934–43. Certain minimum amounts of income ($3,000 in 1934–43) were treated as earned income, regardless of source, and above certain levels ($14,000 in 1934–43) all income was treated as unearned. The United Kingdom long had an earned income credit but replaced it in 1973–74 by a surcharge on investment income (although an allowance for working wives was continued). Schedular income taxes often differentiate in favor of earned income.

The U.S. Tax Reform Act of 1969, adopting a different approach from that previously accepted, established a maximum rate of 50 percent (for 1972 and later years) on earned income, contrasted with a maximum rate of 70 percent on other income. The Tax Reduction Act of 1975 provided, for that year only, a limited earned income credit with an unusual feature. The following discussion deals first with the general question of preferential treatment of earned income and then with the 1975 credit and the maximum rate.

One source of support for preferential taxation of earned income is closely allied to the belief that wealth, as well as income, should be taxed (chapter 2). A reduced rate for earned income, or an additional tax on property income, is regarded as a means of reaching

33. Many tax specialists take a more favorable view of averaging. See, for example, Henry C. Simons, *Personal Income Taxation: The Definition of Income as a Problem of Fiscal Policy* (University of Chicago Press, 1938), pp. 153–54; Harold M. Groves, *Postwar Taxation and Economic Progress,* Committee for Economic Development Research Study (McGraw-Hill, 1946), pp. 223–36; William Vickrey, *Agenda for Progressive Taxation* (Ronald Press, 1947), pp. 172–95; and Vickrey, "Tax Simplification Through Cumulative Averaging," *Law and Contemporary Problems,* vol. 34 (Autumn 1969), pp. 736–50.

the taxpaying capacity associated with wealth. This arrangement, however, is a poor substitute for a personal wealth tax since property income bears no uniform relation to wealth. Taxation of property income is not a satisfactory means of reaching holdings of idle or underemployed wealth.

A related consideration adduced in favor of an earned income credit is the "precarious" and terminable nature of income from personal effort, which depends on the health and working capacity of the individual. This attitude is embodied in Samuelson's remark: "A so-called 'personal income tax' that treats the perpetual earnings of securities the same as the earnings of a doctor or actor in the prime of life chooses to ignore a substantive difference."[34] Granted that differences exist between such incomes, it is not true that property income is always more secure and longer-lived than earned income. Differentiation between property income and earned income would not distinguish generally between precarious and secure incomes or between terminable and perpetual ones. An annual tax on income will apply only as long as income is received, whether the source is property or personal effort; it is not clear that differentiation of tax on the income when received is appropriate merely because of uncertain flow or limited duration. I have already argued in chapter 5 that an amortization allowance should be granted for the disappearance of personal earning capacity with the passage of time only to the extent that the capacity is attributable to past investment in education.

An additional argument for favoring earned income is that those who receive it incur real costs in the form of personal effort, sacrifice of leisure, and restricted choice of place of residence. Investors, to be sure, often spend time and effort in selecting and supervising their portfolios; however, they can hire someone else to do this for them if they choose and can deduct the fee from their taxable income. The fatal weakness of the real-costs argument is that the amount of earned income bears no ascertainable relation to presumed psychic costs. These costs depend on the nature of the employment, the hours of work, place of employment, and personal tastes. The best-paying

34. Paul A. Samuelson, "The Evaluation of 'Social Income': Capital Formation and Wealth," in F. A. Lutz and D. C. Hague, eds., *The Theory of Capital,* Proceedings of a Conference held by the International Economic Association (St. Martin's Press, 1961), p. 39, note. See also Royal Commission on the Taxation of Profits and Income, *Second Report,* pp. 66–69.

jobs usually have the greatest prestige and often seem the most interesting. Who can say how these attractions should be balanced against the long working hours and tensions of many executives and professional persons?

A weighty practical objection to an earned income credit is the difficulty of defining earned income of self-employed persons or that of stockholders who are active in the management of closely held corporations. In most cases, income from sole proprietorships and partnerships is a mixture of return from capital and reward for personal effort. In closely held corporations, the distinction between salaries and wages and profits is often tenuous. While it may be acceptable to separate mixed incomes according to arbitrary allocation rules when the amount of tax at stake is fairly small, as it would be, for example, in connection with the proposed plan for amortization of certain educational expenditures, this becomes questionable if large differences in tax liability are involved.

A substantial earned income credit, applicable over a wide range of income sizes, would not be a desirable addition to the U.S. income tax, in my opinion. However, it would be appropriate to grant a small allowance for certain monetary costs of earning income and for the opportunities of doing household chores that are given up when one takes an outside job. One possibility would be to allow employed persons to deduct, not only certain identified work-connected expenses, but also a small additional amount. Canada, for example, grants employees a general employment expense deduction of 3 percent of net employment income up to a maximum of $150. Since the costs under discussion are particularly noticeable in the case of housewives, consideration might be given to a special credit or allowance when both husband and wife report earned income on a joint return. Precedents for this approach can be found in the United Kingdom and Sweden. The British tax provides a deduction equal to the first £675 (approximately $1,486 as of mid-1975) of the earned income of a working wife. The Swedish tax grants a child-care allowance when both spouses have earned income and they have one or more children under sixteen. This deduction, available to the spouse with the lower income (and also to a single person with earned income who has a child under sixteen living at home), may be claimed regardless of whether child-care expenses are actually incurred. It is equal to 25 percent of net earned income up to a maximum of 2,000 kronor (approximately $508 as of mid-1975).[35]

The U.S. earned income credit of 1975, though superficially similar to the proposal discussed above, is actually a different kind of measure. This credit, effective for only one year, is equal to 10 percent of earned income but is subject to a maximum of $400. It is phased down to zero between an AGI of $4,000 and one of $8,000. To be eligible for the credit, an individual must maintain a household in the United States that includes a dependent child. Those whose income tax liability is lower than the credit will receive a cash payment from the Treasury for the excess. Congressional committee reports make clear that the purpose of the legislation is "to use the income tax system to offset the impact of the social security taxes on low-income persons in 1975" and thus "to assist in encouraging people to obtain employment, reducing the unemployment rate and reducing the welfare rolls."[36] Even for this purpose, the restriction of the credit to persons with children is hard to justify. Both this restriction and the cash payment for the unused portion of the credit would be anomalous if the credit were intended as an allowance for unitemized costs of earning income. In a limited way, the cash-payment provision introduces a feature of a negative income tax or guaranteed minimum income. It will be interesting to see whether this feature is continued and developed.

In contrast to the usual form of earned income credit or allowance, the maximum rate on earned income adopted by the United States in 1969 benefits only a small number of high-income persons. The marginal rate of income tax exceeds 50 percent on taxable income above $38,000 for a single person and above $52,000 for a married couple filing a joint return. If they have earned income, these persons can take advantage of the maximum rate. Earned income is defined as salaries and wages, professional fees, and other compensation for personal services, less trade or business deductions properly allocable to the earned income. If the taxpayer engages in a trade or business in which both personal services and capital are material income-

35. Martin Norr, Claes Sandels, and Nils G. Hornhammar, *The Tax System in Sweden* (Stockholm: Skandinaviska Enskilda Banken, 1972), p. 83.

36. *Tax Reduction Act of 1975*, Report of the Senate Committee on Finance, S. Rept. 94-36, 94 Cong. 1 sess. (1975), p. 33.

producing factors, a reasonable proportion of the income, but not more than 30 percent, is classified as earned income. Personal deductions and exemptions are prorated between earned income and other income.[37] At 1970 income levels, the estimated amount of tax reduction that would have resulted from the 50 percent maximum rate, had it been in effect, is about $250 million, nearly all of which would have accrued to persons with total income in excess of $50,000.[38]

The purpose of the maximum tax is to reduce the attraction of tax avoidance schemes intended to convert earned income into capital gains or to generate artificial accounting losses, and to lessen the deterrent effects of high tax rates.[39] As brought out in chapters 3 and 4, however, the effect of high tax rates on the amount and quality of work done by business executives and professional persons is uncertain. Tax avoidance schemes remain sufficiently attractive to them and to others to elicit much attention and ingenuity. The case for preferential taxation of earned income is no more persuasive for the few at top income levels than for the many below.

Minimum Tax on Preference Items

Dissatisfaction about the extent to which many persons with large gross incomes were able to escape income taxation came to a head in early 1969. Both the outgoing Johnson administration and the incoming Nixon administration recommended legislation to curb these opportunities. While the proposals differed substantially in content, both were intended to have the effect of applying the graduated income tax to a portion of so-called tax preference items consisting of certain exclusions and deductions.[40] Congress followed a different

37. For purposes of the maximum tax, earned income is subject to an offset for long-term capital gains and other tax preference items when these exceed $30,000. The effect is to subject part of earned income to rates above 50 percent. For a clear analysis of these complex interrelationships, see Emil M. Sunley, Jr., "The Maximum Tax on Earned Income," *National Tax Journal,* vol. 27 (December 1974), pp. 543–52.

38. Based on the Brookings 1970 Tax File. Although enacted in 1969, the 50 percent maximum rate did not take effect until 1972.

39. *Tax Reform Act of 1969,* H. Rept. 91-413, 91 Cong. 1 sess. (1969), pt. 1, pp. 208–09.

40. The Johnson administration proposed a minimum income tax at half the regular rates on certain items (*Tax Reform Studies and Proposals, U.S. Treasury*

approach and imposed an additional tax of 10 percent on a selected list of preference items to the extent that they exceed the sum of a $30,000 exemption and the regular income tax. The principal tax preference items are the one-half of net long-term capital gains that is excluded from ordinary taxable income, accelerated depreciation on real property, the excess of percentage depletion over the cost basis of mineral property, and income realized by an employee from the exercise of a stock option. Payments of regular income tax in excess of tax preference items may be carried forward for seven years.

In 1970, the additional tax was applicable on 18,942 returns and amounted to $122 million. It increased the tax liabilities of those to whom it applied by 10 percent on the average, but in one-fourth of the cases the provision at least doubled the tax otherwise payable. More than four-fifths of the reported preference items consisted of capital gains.[41]

The minimum tax is a weak measure because it does not apply to many of the questionable exclusions and deductions and because of the large exemption and the low ungraduated rate. In practice, it is mainly a minor additional tax, of an unnecessarily complex character, on capital gains. If the minimum tax is to be continued, it should be broadened and strengthened.

In my view, however, the minimum tax is a poor approach to the goal of broadening the tax base. It is illogical in concept and appears to lack the elements of a durable political compromise. The existence of the minimum tax may serve as an excuse for inaction on fundamental reform while the consideration of complicated proposals for its modification diverts attention from more basic questions.

Department, Joint Publication, House Committee on Ways and Means and Senate Committee on Finance, 91 Cong. 1 sess. [1969], pt. 2, pp. 132–42). The Nixon administration recommended, for a different list of items, that the exclusions and deductions not be allowed to reduce potential taxable income by more than one-half (*Tax Reform Proposals Contained in the Message from the President of April 21, 1969,* presented to the House Committee on Ways and Means, 91 Cong. 1 sess. [1969]). For comments on the legislative history, see the statements of Paul R. McDaniel and Martin D. Ginsburg in *General Tax Reform,* Panel Discussions before the House Committee on Ways and Means, 93 Cong. 1 sess. (1973), pp. 711–12, 882–84. A later Treasury Department proposal to establish a minimum taxable income is set out in the statement of the Secretary of the Treasury before the House Ways and Means Committee, April 30, 1973, in *Proposals for Tax Change* (Department of the Treasury, 1973), pp. 83–91.

41. *Statistics of Income—1970,* pp. 184, 185, 191.

Conclusion

The most important function of personal exemptions is to free from income tax the amount necessary for a minimum standard of living. For this purpose, equal per capita exemptions, effective in the United States since 1944, are too low for single persons relative to married couples and too high for children relative to adults. The addition of the low-income allowance (minimum standard deduction) resulted in a great improvement, but the change in this allowance for 1975 and the addition for that year of a per capita personal tax credit raise doubts about future relationships. The system is unnecessarily complex and is unfair in that the low-income allowance is not available to taxpayers who itemize their personal deductions. The substitution of a set of increased and restructured personal exemptions would be an improvement. The special exemptions for age and blindness are welfare measures of doubtful efficiency and fairness.

Owing to exclusions from the tax base, personal deductions, capital gains provisions, and income splitting, actual effective tax rates are much lower and less progressive than the statutory rate schedule. If the gap between nominal and effective tax rates were equally wide everywhere and this were generally known, the result might be a harmless illusion. In fact, the operation of the provisions that mitigate the nominal rates is neither uniform nor generally appreciated. These conditions create inequities, public confusion, and the risk of economic damage from marginal tax rates higher than would otherwise be required. The minimum tax on preference items is not a promising means of rectifying these ills.

Under the separate rate schedules now applicable to single persons and married couples, the former pay considerably more tax than the latter on a given amount of income except at very low and very high levels. While the difference is smaller than it was before 1971, I believe that it could justifiably be reduced still further. Tax avoidance by dividing income with children and other family members cannot be prevented but could be somewhat restricted.

The present provisions for averaging income for tax purposes are unsatisfactory in various respects and could be improved without introducing excessive complications. The subject of averaging, however, may be less important than is suggested by the amount of attention that it has received from experts.

The arguments that have been advanced for a substantial earned income credit or preferential rates for income from personal effort, and for the special limit on the maximum tax rate on earned income, seem to me unconvincing. A small concession to all employed persons or to married couples when both spouses are employed would be justified in recognition of certain nondeductible costs of working and forgone opportunities for doing household and personal tasks.

CHAPTER TEN

Effects on the Distribution of Income and Wealth

A BASIC SOURCE of support for a progressive income tax is the expectation that it will reduce economic inequality or check the growth of inequality. The influence of the income tax on the size distribution of income and wealth, therefore, is an important part of the evaluation of American experience with the tax.

Beliefs vary concerning the actual influence of the income tax in the United States. A common opinion is that steeply progressive income tax rates have greatly narrowed economic inequality. Although this view has been taken more often by journalists than by scholars, it has had adherents among well-informed economists. Schumpeter, for example, in discussing redistributive taxation in 1947, wrote, "To an extent which is not generally appreciated, the New Deal was able to expropriate the upper income brackets even before the war" and added that "irrespective of the war, a tremendous transfer of wealth has actually been effected, a transfer that quantitatively is comparable with that effected by Lenin."[1] Among specialists in income

1. Joseph A. Schumpeter, *Capitalism, Socialism and Democracy*, 3d ed. (Harper and Row, 1962), p. 381. The passage cited was introduced in the second edition, originally published in 1947.

distribution, on the other hand, the tendency has been to regard the income tax as a relatively unimportant influence. For example, Kravis refers to statistical support for the "impression that an increase in the progressivity of the tax structure has played little if any part in making the income distribution more equal" after 1929.[2]

In view of these differences and the unavoidable complexity of the subject, readers will not be surprised by a warning that the facts concerning the influence of the income tax on the distribution of income and wealth, like many other questions relating to the tax, are far from clear and that skeptics question the statistics that are available. The purpose of this chapter is to bring together some of the relevant information and attempt to interpret it. Emphasis is placed on the shares of groups with high incomes or large estates since this is the area in which the direct impact of a progressive income tax can be most clearly observed.

The first step is to consider the simplest aspect of the influence of the income tax on economic inequality; that is, its impact on a given distribution of income before taxes. For this purpose, the before-tax and after-tax distributions of 1966 are compared with each other and with the after-tax distribution that would have obtained in that year with a different income tax structure.

The second and more difficult step is to consider whether the income tax has caused an alteration of the before-tax distribution of income that either reinforces or counteracts the equalizing effects of progressive rates.

Third, limitations of the available statistics are examined to ascertain whether they understate or overstate changes in the concentration of income and the possible influence of the income tax.

Fourth, the distribution of wealth is briefly surveyed because it may be affected by the income tax through changes in saving and accumulation and by the division of property for the purpose of avoiding top income tax rates. Also, data on wealth holdings are helpful as a check on the completeness and reliability of income statistics.

Finally, some concluding remarks are offered concerning the objective of greater economic equality and the contribution that the income tax and other measures can reasonably be expected to make to its attainment.

2. Irving B. Kravis, *The Structure of Income* (University of Pennsylvania, 1962), p. 220.

To isolate the influence of the income tax, government expenditures will be taken as given and it will be assumed that the same public expenditures would be financed by other taxes if the income tax were not levied. Thus the discussion abstracts from the possibility that the direct distributional effects of the income tax are offset by government expenditures that are made possible or induced by the levy of the tax. Although this simplifying assumption does not seem so unrealistic as to be seriously misleading, it cannot be denied that a radical change in the tax system would be likely to have some influence on public expenditures. For example, the substitution of regressive taxes for the income tax might stimulate additional welfare expenditures which would mitigate the distributional effects of the change. If more reliance were placed on indirect taxes, it is possible—though, in my judgment, unlikely—that political opposition to government spending would diminish and the budget would grow more rapidly.

Impact on a Given Before-Tax Income Distribution

Ideally, the influence of the income tax on income concentration should be measured by reference to reliable statistics based on a comprehensive definition of accrued or realized income such as that described in chapter 2. The data available in the past have departed considerably from this ideal; however, the recent work of Pechman and Okner has produced estimates for the single year 1966 that approach the preferred definition much more closely.[3] By skillfully combining data from a large field survey, income tax returns, the national income and product accounts, and other sources, Pechman and Okner developed a distribution of "adjusted family income" by family units (consisting of single persons and units of two or more persons). Adjusted family income comprises net national product at market prices (that is, national income at factor costs plus indirect business taxes) plus transfer payments to persons and accrued capital gains, with certain adjustments. Capital gains on corporate stock are assumed to be equal to retained corporate profits. Gifts and bequests are not included because of the lack of a satisfactory basis for estimating them. Adjusted family income is a much broader concept

3. Joseph A. Pechman and Benjamin A. Okner, *Who Bears the Tax Burden?* (Brookings Institution, 1974).

than money income or family personal income, which have been employed in past estimates of income distribution. It includes important items of nonmoney income, accrued capital gains, and most taxes.[4]

While adjusted family income may be the best concept for the purpose of measuring the burden of all taxes, which was the objective of Pechman and Okner, I consider it advisable for my purposes to eliminate three items. These are (1) corporation income taxes; (2) employer payroll taxes and other employer contributions for social insurance; and (3) indirect business taxes in the form of sales and excise taxes, property taxes, and motor vehicle licenses. The remainder may be called—somewhat awkwardly—"net adjusted family income." The three items are eliminated because they do not accrue to families and would not be subject to the individual income tax even if the broad Haig-Simons definition were followed. Regardless of whether they are borne by the factors of production or are shifted to consumers, these taxes constitute a part of the market value of the net national product that does not go to persons.[5] In the aggregate, the three items represent 14.8 percent of adjusted family income in 1966.

The Pechman-Okner estimates for 1966, as modified, are summarized in table 10-1, which shows the distribution of net adjusted family income before and after federal individual income tax. The statistics indicate that the tax does reduce income concentration. The percentages of after-tax income accruing to the top 1 percent and to the remainder of the top quintile are smaller than their shares of before-tax income, whereas the reverse is true of all lower quintiles. However, the impact on income distribution is not impressive. The percentage share of the top 1 percent of units in after-tax income is only about one-tenth smaller than their share in before-tax income (8.3 percent compared with 9.2 percent), and the differences are smaller for other groups.

Two characteristics of the federal income tax explain why its impact on income distribution is less impressive than many readers

4. See appendix D.

5. This is merely a matter of social accounting identities. Corporate profit taxes and employer contributions for social insurance are part of factor income, as conventionally defined, but are not received by individuals. Indirect business taxes represent the difference between net national product at market prices and national income at factor costs.

Table 10-1. Distribution of Net Adjusted Family Income,ᵃ before and after Federal Individual Income Tax, and Effective Rates of Income Tax, by Population Percentiles and Quintiles, 1966

Before-tax income rank	Percent of income		Mean income (dollars)		Effective tax rate (percent)
	Before tax	*After tax*	*Before tax*	*After tax*	
Top 1 percent	9.2	8.3	92,245	75,685	18.0
Next 4 percent	11.7	11.5	29,340	26,227	10.6
Remainder of top quintile	25.8	25.6	17,257	15,573	9.8
4th quintile	23.2	23.4	11,638	10,675	8.3
3d quintile	16.1	16.4	8,076	7,482	7.2
2d quintile	10.0	10.5	5,016	4,790	5.1
Lowest quintile	4.0	4.3	2,006	1,962	2.5
All units	100.0	100.0	10,033	9,124	9.1

Source: Derived from Joseph A. Pechman and Benjamin A. Okner, *Who Bears the Tax Burden?* (Brookings Institution, 1974), and unpublished appendix.

a. Net adjusted family income is adjusted family income minus the sum of corporation income taxes, employer contributions for social insurance, and indirect business taxes under Variant 1c in the source.

might expect. When measured against a broad definition of income, the tax is both less heavy and less progressive than commonly believed. With a yield equal to only 9.1 percent of aggregate net adjusted family income, the tax would have to be confined to a narrow group of high-income recipients to cause a major difference between that group's before-tax and after-tax income shares. The federal income tax, in fact, extends far down the income scale. While effective rates rise with income, the slope of the curve is not steep.

The combined influence of the weight of taxation and its progressivity shows itself in the absolute differences in effective rates on high, middle, and low incomes. These differences determine the equalizing impact on percentage shares in disposable income. All groups whose effective tax rates are above the average for the whole population will have smaller percentage shares in after-tax income than in before-tax income, and the reverse will be true for groups whose effective rates are below the average; however, the differences between before-tax and after-tax percentage shares will be small unless the absolute differences in effective rates are considerable.[6]

6. The ratio of a group's after-tax share to its before-tax share is

$$(1 - r) / (1 - R),$$

where r is the effective tax rate of the group and R is the effective tax rate for the whole population. This can be readily seen by noting that the group's before-tax

This can be seen in table 10-1. The difference between the effective rates of the top 1 percent and the middle quintile is only 10.8 percentage points and between the middle quintile and the lowest quintile only 4.7 percentage points.

The effective rates of tax shown in table 10-1 are calculated, as mentioned above, on a broader income base than most previous estimates. These rates are lower, therefore, than rates relating to income concepts such as statutory adjusted gross income, money income, and family personal income. The effective rates for net adjusted family income may also be somewhat less progressive than effective rates relating to the other income concepts, but this is less clear. Appendix D contains a further discussion of the various concepts that have been used.

As mentioned above, a limitation on the equalizing power of the income tax is its rather small yield relative to total income. Even if all of the 1966 federal income tax had been assessed against the 5 percent of family units with the highest incomes, this group would have had 13.0 percent of total after-tax income, and its average after-tax income would have been 2.8 times as great as that of the remainder of family units. These computations make no allowance for the effects that a steep increase in income tax progressivity might have on the total amount and distribution of income before tax.

Changes in Before-Tax Income Distribution

Statistics of the kind examined in the preceding pages will understate or overstate the equalizing power of the income tax if its existence causes the before-tax distribution to be less concentrated or more concentrated than it would otherwise be. The income tax may lessen the inequality of before-tax income by reducing the saving, wealth accumulation, and property income of high-income families; by inducing high-income investors to shift toward assets with lower actual or nominal rates of yield; by encouraging the splitting of property and income among family members who are in separate income units or its dispersal through philanthropic contributions; and by deterring highly remunerated personal effort. On the other hand, the

---

share is y/Y, where y is the amount of its before-tax income and Y is total before-tax income, and that the group's after-tax share is

$$[(1 - r)y]/[(1 - R)Y].$$

inequality of before-tax income can be increased if the income tax causes compensating increases in profit rates, executive salaries and bonuses, and professional fees. The existence of the tax may stimulate the use of forms of compensation that do not enter into the income statistics and may thus impair their reliability as indicators of inequality. Of course, the income tax is only one of many factors affecting the before-tax distribution of income.

Historical Information

Information on income distribution is scanty for the period before the introduction of the mass income tax and the development of large-scale field surveys of consumer budgets. Expert opinion, based on conjecture and scattered evidence, holds that a period of growing concentration of income in the United States ended about 1890 and was followed by a phase of diminishing inequality lasting until about 1920.[7]

There appears to have been no marked trend in income concentration in the 1920s, while inequality declined markedly during the Great Depression of the 1930s and World War II. Thereafter, there seems to have been little change in income distribution but perhaps a slight decline in the share of top-income groups.

The best evidence on the 1920s is a study by Kuznets based on income tax returns.[8] Kuznets detected no increasing or decreasing trend in the income shares of the top 1 percent and top 5 percent of the population in this period.

Another series, showing the distribution of family personal income, is available for 1929, 1935–36, and 1941; for most years from 1944 to 1963; and for 1964, 1970, and 1971. For 1944 and later years, the statistics are official estimates of the Office of Business Economics (OBE), U.S. Department of Commerce (since 1972 called the Bureau of Economic Analysis); for the earlier years they are based on

7. Kravis, *Structure of Income*, pp. 208–15. On the basis of Kuznets' study (see footnote 8), Herman P. Miller assumes that there was no change in income distribution as measured by the Lorenz curve from 1913 to 1929 (*Income Distribution in the United States*, U.S. Bureau of the Census, 1960 Census Monograph [1966], p. 19).

8. Simon Kuznets, *Shares of Upper Income Groups in Income and Savings* (National Bureau of Economic Research, 1953). Kuznets also gives estimates for 1913–19.

Table 10-2. Distribution of Family Personal Income before Tax
among Consumer Units, by Income Level, Selected Periods, 1929–71

Percent

Income level	1929	1935–36	1944	1950–59[a]	1960–62[a]	1970–71[a]
Top 5 percent	30.0	26.5	20.7	20.4	19.6	19.2
Next 15 percent	24.4	25.2	25.1	24.9	25.9	25.6
4th quintile	19.3	20.9	22.2	22.4	22.7	23.3
3d quintile	13.8	14.1	16.2	16.4	16.3	16.4
2d quintile	⎱ 12.5	9.2	10.9	11.2	10.9	10.8
Lowest quintile	⎰	4.1	4.9	4.8	4.6	4.7

Sources: Derived from U.S. Bureau of the Census, *Historical Statistics of the United States, Colonial Times to 1957* (1960), p. 166; Jeannette M. Fitzwilliams, "Size Distribution of Income in 1963," *Survey of Current Business*, vol. 44 (April 1964), p. 8; Daniel B. Radner and John C. Hinrichs, "Size Distribution of Income in 1964, 1970, and 1971," *Survey of Current Business*, vol. 54 (October 1974), p. 27.

a. Averages (arithmetic means) of annual percentages.

other studies adjusted for comparability.[9] Family personal income is the portion of total personal income received by consumer units consisting of families and unattached individuals. Income received by members of the armed forces living on posts, persons in institutions, and nonprofit organizations is excluded. The series includes imputed income and transfer payments but does not include capital gains. The omission of capital gains is an important difference between it and net adjusted family income.[10]

The percentage share of family personal income received by the top 5 percent of consumer units was reduced by almost one-third between 1929 and 1944, while the share of the next 15 percent increased slightly and the share of lower income groups increased more (table 10-2). A further small decline in the share of the top 5 percent of units occurred after World War II. The year-to-year record of the share of the top 5 percent of consumer units from 1929 to 1971 is depicted in figure 10-1. The estimates for 1964 and 1970–71 are not fully comparable with those for earlier years.

9. U.S. Bureau of the Census, *Historical Statistics of the United States, Colonial Times to 1957* (1960), p. 166; Jeannette M. Fitzwilliams, "Size Distribution of Income in 1963," *Survey of Current Business*, vol. 44 (April 1964), pp. 3–11; Daniel B. Radner and John C. Hinrichs, "Size Distribution of Income in 1964, 1970, and 1971," *Survey of Current Business*, vol. 54 (October 1974), pp. 19–31.

10. Among other differences, family personal income includes, and net adjusted family income excludes, a substantial notional item of imputed interest from services of banks and financial intermediaries (Pechman and Okner, *Who Bears the Tax Burden?* pp. 89–91).

Figure 10-1. Percentage of Total Family Personal Income before Tax Received by the Top 5 Percent of Consumer Units, 1929–71

Percent

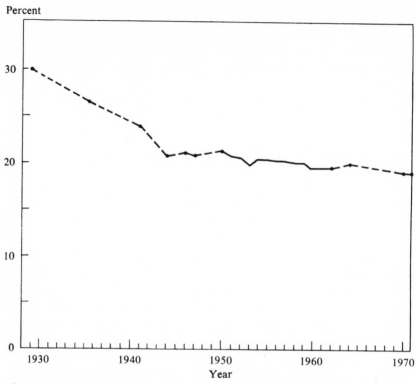

Sources: Same as table 10-2.

The use of 1929 as the beginning date for the historical record based on OBE estimates may somewhat exaggerate the decrease in inequality. Kuznets' estimates for 1929 show that the income share of the top group in that year, though not unprecedentedly large, was greater than the average for the preceding decade.[11]

Movements in the absolute size of income do not parallel changes in percentage shares. Between 1929 and 1944, when the percentage share of the top 5 percent of units was falling sharply, the average before-tax income of these families and individuals declined only slightly, measured in dollars of constant purchasing power. Between 1944 and 1962, the average income before taxes of the highest 5 per-

11. His "basic variant" estimates place the before-tax share of the top 5 percent of the population at 26.1 percent in 1929 and at 24.4 percent in 1919–28 (arithmetic mean of annual percentages); see *Shares of Upper Income Groups*, p. 599.

cent increased almost 15 percent in constant dollars.[12] The explanation for the diverse movements of percentage shares and dollar amounts is that total income grew faster than the population. These figures should be used cautiously, however, because of the usual statistical difficulties and because the price deflator may not adequately measure changes in prices of goods and services consumed by high-income groups.

Although the OBE estimates are the best available for any year before 1966, they may be biased toward stability in relative shares over time. This is probable because certain benchmark estimates of the relative distribution of income among single persons and farm families, as well as the pattern for combining income tax returns into nonfarm family units, were continued from 1950 through 1963 without change.[13] Indeed, the obsolescence of these benchmarks was a major reason for the decision of the OBE to discontinue the old series with the preliminary estimates for 1963.

Another series covering a long span of years is that of the Current Population Survey (CPS) of the Bureau of the Census. This is derived from an annual field survey and covers only money income. Property income, entrepreneurial income, and many forms of transfer payment are seriously underreported, and no statistical correction is made for this.[14] In addition, changes in interviewing, editing, and processing methods impair comparability over time.

Despite these limitations, it is interesting and perhaps significant that the CPS statistics on money income broadly corroborate the conclusion drawn from the OBE statistics on family personal income. Relative income shares changed little after 1944, but there appears to be a slight tendency for the shares of the highest income groups to decline.[15]

12. Deflated by the implicit price deflator for the personal consumption component of gross national product (*Economic Report of the President, February 1974*, p. 252). If the consumer price index is used as the deflator, the increase is 10.7 percent.

13. Edward C. Budd, "Postwar Changes in the Size Distribution of Income in the U.S.," in American Economic Association, *Papers and Proceedings of the Eighty-second Annual Meeting, 1969* (*American Economic Review*, vol. 60, May 1970), p. 258.

14. Ibid., p. 256.

15. The CPS statistics appear in U.S. Office of Management and Budget, *Social Indicators, 1973* (1973), p. 179; and U.S. Bureau of the Census, *Statistical Abstract of the United States, 1974*, p. 384. See also chapter 5 of the Annual Report of the

Salaries and Wages and Executive Compensation

During the first half of the twentieth century, the percentage differences between the wages of skilled and unskilled workers in the United States tended to narrow.[16] Evidently the introduction of the progressive income tax during this period and its extension to the majority of regularly employed persons did not cause wage adjustments that counteracted forces which were narrowing the spread between high-paid and low-paid workers. More recently, however, this trend seems to have stopped, and may have reversed.[17] It is still uncertain whether a lasting change in wage relationships has occurred and, if so, whether the income tax has been a contributory cause.

The compensation patterns of senior business executives are also pertinent to an appraisal of the equalizing power of the income tax. Sophisticated investigations have been made by two researchers. A study by Burgess covers the top three executives of each of the twenty-five largest manufacturing corporations in the United States for nine selected years from 1929 to 1958.[18] Studies by Lewellen relate to the five most highly compensated executives in fifty of the largest industrial corporations from 1940 to 1969.[19] Both obtained information on

Council of Economic Advisers, published with *Economic Report of the President, February 1974,* pp. 137–80; Herman P. Miller, *Rich Man, Poor Man,* rev. ed. (Crowell, 1971); and T. Paul Schultz, "Secular Trends and Cyclical Behavior of Income Distribution in the United States: 1944–1965," in Lee Soltow, ed., *Six Papers on the Size Distribution of Wealth and Income,* Studies in Income and Wealth, vol. 33 (Columbia University Press for the National Bureau of Economic Research, 1969), pp. 75–100.

16. Melvin W. Reder, "Wage Differentials: Theory and Measurement," in *Aspects of Labor Economics,* A Conference of the Universities–National Bureau Committee for Economic Research (Princeton University Press for the National Bureau of Economic Research, 1962), pp. 257–311; Paul G. Keat, "Long-Run Changes in Occupational Wage Structure, 1900–1956," *Journal of Political Economy,* vol. 68 (December 1960), pp. 584–600; Miller, *Income Distribution,* pp. 77–78.

17. Miller, *Income Distribution,* p. 84; Peter Henle, "Exploring the Distribution of Earned Income," *Monthly Labor Review,* vol. 95 (December 1972), pp. 16–27.

18. Leonard Randolph Burgess, *Top Executive Pay Package* (Graduate School of Business, Columbia University and Free Press of Glencoe, 1963). The twenty-five largest companies in each year were used.

19. Wilbur G. Lewellen, *Executive Compensation in Large Industrial Corporations* (Columbia University Press for the National Bureau of Economic Research, 1968), and Lewellen, "Managerial Pay and the Tax Changes of the 1960's," *National Tax Journal,* vol. 25 (June 1972), pp. 111–32.

salaries and bonuses and deferred compensation, including pensions, profit-sharing, and stock options. They were unable to include the value of life insurance coverage, liberal expense accounts, and compensation in kind. Both estimated the present value of deferred compensation by discounting, though they employed different valuation methods.

The salaries and bonuses of the senior executives increased considerably after 1940 (table 10-3), and with rising income tax rates there was a tendency to substitute pensions and other forms of deferred compensation for salaries and bonuses which were fully taxable on a current basis. After 1950, when favorable tax legislation became effective, stock options were widely used and rapidly became the most valuable form of deferred compensation. Whereas current salary and bonuses amounted to more than nine-tenths of the before-tax current income equivalent of the total compensation of senior executives in 1929 and four-fifths of the total in 1940, this fraction fell to less than one-fifth on the average in 1955–63. The significance of the change in form of remuneration is illustrated in table 10-3 by the dramatic rise in 1955–63 in the before-tax total compensation, which shows the amount of salary and bonuses that would have been necessary to leave as much after-tax income as the actual compensation arrangements provided. The cut in income tax rates effective in 1964 sharply reduced this current-income equivalent and increased the relative contribution of salary and bonuses (to 45 percent in 1964–69). As an element in after-tax compensation, the relative importance of salary and bonuses varied less, falling from 85 percent in 1940 to 52 percent in 1955–63 and 1964–69.[20]

Among the senior executives the relative size of the difference between the salary and bonuses of the top executive and of the top five executives as a group has narrowed. The growth of deferred compensation for the top executive, however, has largely offset this, and the relative size of total compensation has been remarkably stable (table 10-3).

From 1940 to the period 1964–69, the after-tax compensation of the senior executives included in Lewellen's sample increased only

20. Salary and bonuses constitute a greater fraction of the before-tax current income equivalent than of after-tax compensation because in estimating the former Lewellen, in effect, assumed that the various forms of deferred compensation were taxable at the marginal rates (*Executive Compensation*, pp. 145–48).

Table 10-3. Compensation of Senior Executives of Large Industrial Corporations, before and after Tax, 1940 and 1947–69

	Relative mean values[a] (1940 = 100)				Top 5 as percent of top executive
	Current prices		Constant prices[b]		
Period	Top executive	Top 5	Top executive	Top 5	
Before-tax salary and bonuses					
1940	100	100	100	100	59
1947–54	129	145	68	77	66
1955–63	150	176	68	80	70
1964–69	177	206	71	82	69
Before-tax total compensation[c]					
1940	100	100	100	100	49
1947–54	250	241	132	127	47
1955–63	782	741	354	335	47
1964–69	339	275	135	150	54
After-tax salary and bonuses[d]					
1940	100	100	100	100	66
1947–54	99	111	52	59	74
1955–63	112	131	50	59	78
1964–69	153	172	61	69	74
After-tax total compensation[d]					
1940	100	100	100	100	59
1947–54	111	126	59	67	66
1955–63	207	216	94	98	61
1964–69	266	282	106	112	62

Sources: Wilbur G. Lewellen, *Executive Compensation in Large Industrial Corporations* (Columbia University Press for the National Bureau of Economic Research, 1968), and Lewellen, "Managerial Pay and the Tax Changes of the 1960's," *National Tax Journal*, vol. 25 (June 1972), pp. 111–32; *Economic Report of the President, February 1974*, p. 252.

a. Based on arithmetic means.

b. Values in current prices deflated by the implicit price deflator for the personal consumption component of gross national product.

c. The current-income equivalent, which is the amount of before-tax salary and bonuses required to provide an after-tax income equal to the after-tax total compensation.

d. After deduction of estimated federal income and estate taxes; no allowance for social security taxes or state and local taxes.

moderately faster than the prices of consumer goods and much more slowly than the after-tax compensation of all employees in manufacturing or the per capita disposable income of the whole population. In constant prices, the after-tax compensation of the five top executives in the fifty large firms rose 12 percent, while the average after-tax compensation of all employees in manufacturing rose 90 percent and the per capita disposable income of the whole population rose 87 percent.[21] If these statistics are at all representative, they indicate some narrowing in relative terms of the wide gap between senior executives and others. But in the period 1964–69 the after-tax compensation of the executives was still twenty-three times that of other employees in manufacturing.

Composition of Income

A substantial part of the decline in the income shares of the top-income groups after 1929 seems to have been associated with changes in the composition of total income. Property income, which is a large proportion of the total income of the top groups, fell more rapidly than other income in the early 1930s and grew less rapidly than other income thereafter. On the other hand, government transfer payments to persons—including social insurance benefits, direct relief, and veterans' benefits—which are only a small part of the income of the top groups, increased faster than total personal income.

Statistical data are not available to allow precise estimates of the separate influences of changes in income composition and in the share of particular kinds of income received by the top groups. Some broad indications can be given, however. Between 1929 and 1960–62, when the income share of the top 5 percent of consumer units decreased by 10.4 percentage points (table 10-2), it would have declined by 4.3 percentage points because of the lag in the growth of property income even if this group had received the same fraction of total property income in 1960–62 as in 1929.[22] An independent estimate for 1962, though not exactly comparable with that for 1929,

---

21. Average before-tax compensation of full-time equivalent employees in manufacturing (including employer contributions for social insurance and private pension, health, and welfare plans) derived from U.S. Department of Commerce, *The National Income and Product Accounts of the United States, 1929–1965: Statistical Tables* (1966), and Department of Commerce, *U.S. National Income and Product Accounts, 1964–69* (1973), tables 6.1 and 6.4 in each. After-tax compensation, my estimates based on computed federal income tax liability for a married couple with two dependents and the standard deduction. Per capita disposable income from *Economic Report of the President, February 1974*, p. 269. All items are deflated by the implicit price deflator for the personal consumption component of GNP.

22. Property income is defined here as dividends, interest, and rent; no allowance is made for the property-income component of the net income from ownership of unincorporated enterprises. For details, see appendix D.

indicates that the fraction of total property income going to the top 5 percent of consumer units declined (appendix D); if so, this would explain part of the remaining decrease in this group's share of total income. Although estimates are not available on the participation of top-income groups in government transfer payments, it seems clear that the increase in these payments from 1.1 percent of total personal income in 1929 to 7.0 percent in 1960–62[23] was a factor in the deterioration of the relative position of high-income groups.

To what extent were the changes in income composition caused by the income tax? Some interpretations of political behavior indicate that the availability of large revenues from the progressive income tax stimulated the growth of government transfer payments. I do not find this convincing, especially since social insurance benefits, which constitute the bulk of these payments, are financed mainly by payroll taxes. The income tax may have been involved in the relative decline in the property-income component of total personal income. This decline reflects a decreasing capital–output ratio in the private sector and a decreasing average rate of return on private capital. From 1929 to 1960, the capital–output ratio fell from 4.3 to 3.8, while the computed average rate of return on private capital declined from 6.2 percent to 5.4 percent.[24] A decline in the capital–output ratio can be expected if, as is often alleged, the income tax retards saving and investment, and employment of labor is not equally depressed. Although this may have occurred, it is hard to reconcile with a stable or

23. Department of Commerce, *National Income and Product Accounts, 1929–1965*, table 3.9.

24. The capital–output ratio is the ratio of the value of private capital to that of private product, expressed in current prices. Private capital includes land, dwellings and other structures, and producers' equipment and inventories but does not include consumer durables or publicly owned assets. For 1929, the estimate is by Raymond W. Goldsmith, *The National Wealth of the United States in the Postwar Period* (Princeton University Press for the National Bureau of Economic Research, 1962), pp. 117–18; for 1960, the estimate is an extension of the Goldsmith series by the Securities and Exchange Commission (Bureau of the Census, *Statistical Abstract of the United States, 1973*, p. 343). Private product is national income minus income originating in government and government enterprises (Department of Commerce, *National Income and Product Accounts, 1929–1965*, table 1.11). The average rate of return on private capital is the ratio of the sum of rental income of persons, corporate profits before tax plus inventory valuation adjustment, and net interest (national income components, *National Income and Product Accounts*, table 1.10) to the value of private capital; it is understated because the numerator does not include the portion of proprietors' and partners' net income consisting of the return on capital.

declining before-tax rate of return on capital. Growing employment in the face of a retardation of investment would imply a capital shortage in the private sector and would lead one to expect a tendency toward rising rates of return.

A considerable part of the decline in property income and in the income share of top income recipients can be attributed to the behavior of dividends. According to the best available estimates, which are not exactly comparable, the amount of dividends received by the top 5 percent of consumer units was equal to 5.8 percent of total family personal income in 1929 but to only about 2 percent in 1962 (appendix D). Taxation no doubt was an important influence holding down dividends after 1929. The increase in the corporation income tax rate reduced funds at the disposal of corporations while the widening of the gap between shareholders' marginal tax rates on dividends and on capital gains offered an incentive for the retention of profits. Dividends might have been about 50 percent greater in 1962 if tax rates on corporate profits and on high-income shareholders had remained at their 1929 levels.[25] Other things being equal, the income share of the top 5 percent of units would have been about 1 percentage point greater.

The income tax no doubt causes some decline in the before-tax income share of high-income investors by inducing them to seek out tax-sheltered assets such as state and local government securities, owner-occupied residences, and property promising capital gains rather than current yield. These assets usually have a lower gross yield than fully taxable substitutes, although they may be attractive to high-income persons when their tax advantages are taken into account (see the discussion of tax-exempt securities in chapter 6).

The influence of this factor cannot be precisely measured because to do so would require knowledge about how people would act if the tax system were quite different. There are, however, reasons for doubting its importance. High-income persons probably obtain higher average yields on their financial assets than middle-income persons do. They generally hold a greater proportion of their assets in the form of corporate stock whereas the middle-income groups hold relatively more cash and savings deposits and have relatively

25. Estimated by applying Brittain's equation G-6, on the assumption that the tax shelter variable in 1962 was the same as in 1960. See John A. Brittain, *Corporate Dividend Policy* (Brookings Institution, 1966), p. 245 and passim.

larger equities in their houses.[26] In a study of financial asset holdings of individuals in Wisconsin in 1949, Atkinson found a pronounced tendency for average rates of yield to rise with size of income, owing mainly to differences in portfolio composition. However, average yields obtained on bonds declined as the investors' incomes rose. This was also true of traded stocks up to a high income level.[27] Estimates for 1960 and 1971 indicate that high-income investors obtained on the average smaller dividend yields on their holdings of corporate stock than low-income investors did, although in the later year the high-income investors enjoyed a greater total return, including accrued capital gains as well as dividends.[28] Since the Department of Commerce estimates do not include capital gains, they understate the contribution of stock ownership to inequality. Information is not available on rates of return on real estate and unincorporated business enterprises.

The most conspicuous item on which low yields are accepted to avoid taxation is tax-exempt state-local securities. The estimated difference in yield on the total of these securities owned by households in 1966, however, amounted to a sum equal to less than 0.1 percent of total net adjusted family income,[29] a small part of the income of high-income groups.

Evaluation

The timing of the changes in the distribution of before-tax income casts doubt on the importance of the income tax as a cause. While it

26. Dorothy S. Projector and Gertrude S. Weiss, *Survey of Financial Characteristics of Consumers* (Board of Governors of the Federal Reserve System, 1966), tables A-8 and A-10.

27. Thomas R. Atkinson, *The Pattern of Financial Asset Ownership: Wisconsin Individuals, 1949* (Princeton University Press for the National Bureau of Economic Research, 1956), pp. 79, 131, 141, 143.

28. Marshall E. Blume, Jean Crockett, and Irwin Friend, "Stockownership in the United States: Characteristics and Trends," *Survey of Current Business,* vol. 54 (November 1974), pp. 31, 40. Estimates of the total return on shares in 1960 are not given in this source.

29. The yield difference is roughly estimated at 1.3 percentage points, which is the difference between the market yields of Moody's Aaa corporate bonds and of Standard & Poor's high-grade municipal bonds (*Economic Report of the President, February 1974,* p. 317). The amount of state-local securities owned by households, including personal trusts and nonprofit organizations, is from Board of Governors of the Federal Reserve System, "Flow of Funds Accounts, 1945–1972" (1973; processed), p. 84. An estimate for 1960 of the relative size of the yield difference was of the same magnitude.

is true that the tax was increased sharply between 1929 and 1944, when the substantial reduction in concentration of before-tax income occurred, the usual analysis would stress delayed or cumulative effects on income distribution rather than immediate effects. Changes in compensation arrangements and investment patterns would be likely to take place slowly, and effects operating through wealth accumulation would be spread over a long period. It appears that other factors associated with the collapse of the boom in 1929, the Great Depression, and World War II were the major forces accounting for the reduction in income concentration between 1929 and 1944. The relative stability of income shares in the postwar period, despite continued high income tax rates, does not support the hypothesis that the tax had important cumulative effects on the distribution of before-tax income. It is possible, however, that long-run cumulative effects were operating but were offset by other forces.

In the light of admittedly incomplete and unsatisfactory evidence, it may be concluded that the individual income tax probably contributed to the reduction in the before-tax share of income received by top-income groups between 1929 and the end of World War II and to the prevention of a reversal of this change after the war. Among the consequences of the income tax that may have worked in this direction are a reduction in the amount of wealth accumulated by high-income people, increased attractiveness of tax-sheltered investments yielding comparatively low rates of return before tax, lower corporate dividend-payout ratios, and willingness of business executives to accept deferred compensation and other perquisities in lieu of part of current salaries. Although the influence of these factors cannot be reliably measured, there is no evidence that it was great in the aggregate.

Without an allowance for its influence on before-tax income, the individual income tax can be credited with only about one-eighth of the decline in the share of disposable family personal income of the top 5 percent of consumer units between 1929 and 1960–62.[30] While the net contribution of the tax probably was greater than this, it still

---

30. The share of the top 5 percent in after-tax income dropped from about 29.5 percent in 1929 (my estimate) to 17.7 percent in 1960–62 (OBE estimate), or by 11.8 percentage points. Since the share of the top 5 percent in before-tax income was 30.0 percent in 1929 and 19.6 percent in 1960–62, the drop in their disposable income in the absence of the individual income tax would have been 10.4 percentage points, which is about seven-eighths of 11.8 percentage points.

seems to have been only a minor factor in the reduction in inequality of measured disposable income.

Limitations of Statistics

The available statistics on income distribution are subject to important limitations. Comparability over time is impaired because of economic and demographic changes such as the increasing participation of women in the labor market, changes in the size of families, and the growing importance of various forms of fringe benefits that are either omitted or inadequately measured in income statistics. Another shortcoming is the omission of capital gains and losses from most of the statistics. These problems are discussed in appendix D. My evaluation is that the statistics probably overstate the reduction in income inequality after 1929 but that their deficiencies are not great enough to cast serious doubt on the conclusion that a genuine reduction in income concentration has occurred.

A basic question is whether statistics on income distribution in any one year or separate statistics on each of a series of years, however well constructed, correctly measure economic welfare or power. One line of criticism, deriving from the permanent income and life cycle theories that have gained much acceptance, stresses that transitory elements will cause the distribution of income in any one year to be more unequal than the distribution for identical persons or families over a period of years. While logically the direction of the bias is clear, the available evidence suggests that it may not be large. In the absence of direct information on lifetime income, attention is often directed to statistics on consumption. As one careful writer summarizes the approach: "Welfare is essentially a measure of the adequacy of economic means to satisfy specified wants. . . . lifetime average annual income is a superior measure of economic means, and . . . current consumption is a useful proxy for this more complex estimate of lifetime expected means."[31] My view is that this approach has merit but that it goes too far in downgrading the significance of cross-section income statistics and, particularly, that the assertion that cross-section consumption statistics are a superior measure of

31. T. Paul Schultz, *The Distribution of Personal Income: A Study of Statistics on the Size Distribution of Personal Income in the United States,* prepared for the Joint Economic Committee, 88 Cong. 2 sess. (1965), p. 25.

welfare relies too much on special deductive arguments assuming foresight and rationality and too little on empirical evidence.

Another criticism is based on the argument that, to measure economic position or welfare, income data should be supplemented by wealth data and that some combination of the two is better than either alone. Weisbrod and Hansen propose as a measure the unweighted sum of current income and the amount of a life annuity purchasable with the individual's wealth or net worth.[32] Unlike current consumption, this measure is more unequally distributed than current income. Although a combination of income and wealth may be conceptually superior to either alone as a measure of welfare, the choice of a particular formula is debatable, and wealth statistics are less good than income statistics.

Distribution of Wealth

Statistics on wealth, like those on income, show less concentration in recent years than in the 1920s. Lampman's study, based on estate tax data, finds that the share of top wealth-holders in total personal wealth fell sharply from 1929 to 1949.[33] Smith and Franklin, who carried forward the estimates for later years, conclude that there were no further significant changes up to 1969.[34] The estimates are summarized in table 10-4.

Lampman infers that the most important proximate cause of the change in the position of the richest group was that its share of personal saving was well below its share of personal wealth, particularly between 1939 and 1949. The progressive income tax must have been partly responsible, but a reliable quantitative estimate of its influence is not feasible. Some appreciation of the relevant orders of magnitude, nevertheless, may be gained from statistics relating to the top-income

32. Burton A. Weisbrod and W. Lee Hansen, "An Income–Net Worth Approach to Measuring Economic Welfare," *American Economic Review*, vol. 58 (December 1968), pp. 1315–29.

33. Robert J. Lampman, *The Share of Top Wealth-Holders in National Wealth, 1922–56* (Princeton University Press for the National Bureau of Economic Research, 1962).

34. James D. Smith and Stephen D. Franklin, "The Concentration of Personal Wealth, 1922–1969," in American Economic Association, *Papers and Proceedings of the Eighty-sixth Annual Meeting, 1973* (*American Economic Review*, vol. 64, May 1974), pp. 162–67.

Table 10-4. Share of Total Personal Wealth Held by Top Wealth-Holders, Selected Years, 1922–69

Percent of personal equity (1922–49) or net worth (1953–69)

Year	Top 0.5 percent of all persons	Top 1 percent of all persons	Top 1 percent of adults
1922	29.8	...	31.6
1929	32.4	...	36.3
1933	25.2	...	28.3
1939	28.0	...	30.6
1945	20.9	...	23.3
1949	19.3	...	20.8
1953	22.0	27.5	...
1958	21.7	26.9	...
1962	21.6	27.4	...
1965	23.7	29.2	...
1969	19.9	24.9	...

Sources: For 1922–49, Robert J. Lampman, *The Share of Top Wealth-Holders in National Wealth, 1922–56* (Princeton University Press for the National Bureau of Economic Research, 1962), p. 24. The estimates relate to the basic variant, which does not include interests in personal trust funds, annuities, and private and governmental pensions, but which does include estimated equity in life insurance. For 1953–69, James D. Smith and Stephen D. Franklin, "The Concentration of Personal Wealth, 1922–1969," in American Economic Association, *Papers and Proceedings of the Eighty-sixth Annual Meeting, 1973* (*American Economic Review*, vol. 64, May 1974), p. 166.

1 percent of the population, who are not of course identical with the top wealth-holders though there is no doubt much overlapping between the two groups. The total federal income tax paid by the top-income group over the period 1922–48, accumulated at compound interest, amounted to about $70 billion.[35] If all of this amount had come out of saving and wealth accumulation, personal wealth in 1949 would have been reduced by about 8 percent.[36] Clearly this is an extreme assumption. Kuznets cautiously suggests an average savings–income ratio of 0.4 for the highest-income 1 percent of the population over the period 1919–45.[37] His assumption implies that the income tax paid by the top 1 percent in 1922–48 reduced personal wealth in 1949 by about 3.5 percent. Even if all of this were

35. Derived from Kuznets, *Shares of Upper Income Groups*, pp. 571, 578–79, 596. Accumulated at a compound interest rate of 3.3 percent a year, which is approximately equal to the average yield of high-grade tax-exempt municipal bonds over the period (Bureau of the Census, *Historical Statistics, Colonial Times to 1957*, p. 656).

36. The denominator for the computation is total personal wealth, prime wealth variant, in 1949 (Lampman, *Share of Top Wealth-Holders*, p. 200), increased by $70 billion.

37. *Shares of Upper Income Groups*, p. 176.

assigned to the richest 1 percent—again an extreme assumption—only about one-third of the decline in their share of wealth between 1922 and 1949 would be explained.

A factor in the decline of wealth concentration is the increased importance of consumer durables and pension and retirement funds, which are more widely held than are securities and equities in unincorporated businesses.[38] Investment in durables and pension funds may have been encouraged by their favorable income tax treatment, but other social and economic forces probably were more important.

A second cause of decreased concentration of wealth, at least in the statistical sense, is changes in property-transfer practices, which placed a larger fraction of wealth in the hands of women and young persons after 1922.[39] Income tax considerations, as well as the desire to minimize estate taxes, may have encouraged the splitting up of fortunes. Income tax incentives for splitting between husbands and wives disappeared after the universalization of splitting privileges between spouses in 1948 but continued for splits with children and other relatives.

Changes in the relative prices of assets have had considerable cyclical influence on the position of top wealth-holders but do not appear to have been an important cause of the longer-run decline in their share of total wealth. It is true that the decline in the wealth share of the richest after 1929 coincided with a sharp fall in the prices of corporate stock, which is their most important asset. However, the change in wealth distribution was not reversed when stock prices recovered, surpassing their 1929 level in 1954 and continuing to rise. Between 1953 and 1969, when the average price of common stocks almost quadrupled, the value of the stockholdings of the richest 1 percent of the population increased somewhat more than the value of their other assets, but the fraction of the value of all stocks owned by them declined considerably.[40]

The statistics contradict the popular belief that the high income tax rates of the period after World War II prevented the creation of new

38. See Raymond W. Goldsmith, *A Study of Saving in the United States* (Princeton University Press, 1955), vol. 1, p. 162.

39. Lampman, *Share of Top Wealth-Holders*, pp. 237–43.

40. The average price of corporate stock is assumed to be represented by Standard & Poor's index of common stocks, annual averages from Bureau of the Census, *Historical Statistics, Colonial Times to 1957*, p. 657, and *Economic Report of the President, February 1974*, p. 342.

private fortunes. The estimated number of millionaires—that is, persons with a gross estate of $1 million or more—increased from 13,000 in 1944 to 148,000 in 1969.[41] Even with allowance for the fall in the purchasing power of the dollar and the growth of population, this increase is remarkable.

Concluding Remarks

This extended review neither corroborates the opinion that the income tax is a Draconian measure for redistribution nor justifies writing off its equalizing effects as inconsequential. Although the difference between the before-tax and after-tax distribution of income is not striking, neither is it trivial.

There is no evidence that the redistributive impact of the income tax has been offset by changes in before-tax income shares. Income before tax has become more nearly equal, and there is reason to believe that the tax has contributed to a minor extent to this change. Part of the apparent decline in the before-tax share of the highest income classes after 1929 probably is spurious, reflecting efforts to avoid taxes and other factors that changed measured personal income more than true income; however, it seems unlikely that the major part of the apparent change can be explained in this way. It appears, therefore, that although the individual income tax has contributed significantly to greater equality of disposable income, it has been considerably less important in this respect than other government actions and developments in the private economy.

If Congress were determined to bring about a drastic reduction in economic inequality, it could do much more by means of the income tax. But extreme equalization has not been accepted even as an ultimate goal. The primary popular and legislative support of progressive taxation seems to derive from ideas about ability to pay or sacrifice rather than from an intention to equalize incomes (chapter 2). Among those who explicitly advocate taxation to reduce inequality,

41. The 1944 estimate is from Lampman, *Share of Top Wealth-Holders*, p. 276; the 1969 estimate, which is not strictly comparable, is by the Internal Revenue Service (*Statistics of Income—1969, Personal Wealth* [1973], p. 54). The estimated number of persons with net worth of $1 million or more in 1969 is 121,000 (ibid., p. 19).

most would concede that substantial differences in income are justifiable on the basis of needs as indicated by family size, age, and other
personal circumstances and on the basis of contributions to production and the public good.[42] Another source of differences between
after-tax earned incomes that seem fully justifiable on egalitarian
premises is the amount of time invested in preparing for occupations.
A person in a profession requiring many years of education should
have a higher annual income than a clerk, if for no other reason than
because his earnings begin later and are received over a shorter period
of time. Relatively noncontroversial differences of these kinds can
account for a considerable amount of inequality.

Progressive taxation, moreover, is not the only means of reducing
economic inequality. It does not, for example, directly attack the
problem of poverty. The wider dissemination of education, improved
programs for health and medical care, and the breaking down of racial
discrimination are desirable in themselves and may make a lasting
contribution to the reduction of economic inequality by raising the
incomes of the poor. Transfer payments, though directed to the satisfaction of particular needs, also have a significant influence on the
distribution of personal income. Further improvements in these programs can be expected to reduce inequality unless the expenditures
are financed by regressive taxes.[43]

Progressive taxation and government expenditures cannot deal
with all kinds of inequality since differences in measured wealth and
income are not the only sources of privilege and power. Extreme efforts to reduce economic inequality would be subject to the risk that
they would merely transfer to government and corporate bureaucrats
powers that were formerly exercised by property owners.

The best approach to income distribution—both as a subject of

42. On the implications of such factors, see George Garvy, "Comment," in
Studies in Income and Wealth, Conference on Research in Income and Wealth, vol.
13 (National Bureau of Economic Research, 1951), pp. 217–18. Garvy remarks that
the standard of full equalization and departures from it, as measured by the Lorenz
curve (and Gini coefficient), have "a mathematical rather than economic meaning."

43. Allan G. B. Fisher, "Alternative Techniques for Promoting Equality in a
Capitalist Society," in American Economic Association, *Papers and Proceedings of
the Sixty-second Annual Meeting, 1949* (*American Economic Review,* vol. 40, May
1950), pp. 356–68; Robert J. Lampman, *Ends and Means of Reducing Income
Poverty,* Institute for Research on Poverty Monograph Series (Markham, 1971).

analysis and a field of social action—is to adopt what Dahl and Lindblom call an "incremental attitude."[44] This attitude directs attention toward small changes rather than drastic redistributions. It supports the belief that inequality can be moderately reduced or increased by changes in the effective progressivity of the income tax without radically altering the economic and political system.

44. Robert A. Dahl and Charles E. Lindblom, *Politics, Economics, and Welfare* (Harper, 1953), p. 148.

CHAPTER ELEVEN

Stabilization Aspects

THE YIELD of the individual income tax responds to cyclical fluctuations in the economy and increases over time with economic growth and inflation. Provided the cyclical movements of tax revenue do not induce equal changes in government expenditures, they cause variations in the budget surplus or deficit and moderate fluctuations in economic activity. Thus the tax acts as an automatic stabilizer. The long-run increase in individual income tax yield attending economic growth offers opportunities for financing larger government expenditures or reducing tax rates. If these opportunities are not seized, the tax will impose a "fiscal drag" on the economy. In inflationary periods tax liabilities increase faster than real income, which exacerbates discontent.

Variations of tax liabilities that occur automatically in response to cyclical or long-run changes in economic activity are called "built-in flexibility." In the next section this concept is explained more fully and quantitative estimates of the built-in flexibility of the federal individual income tax are presented. In later sections comparisons are drawn with the built-in flexibility of other major taxes, the effectiveness of taxation as an economic stabilizer is examined, and the special problems of inflation are briefly considered.

Built-in Flexibility and Elasticity

The built-in flexibility of a tax is measured by the ratio of change in tax liability (or tax collections) to change in aggregate income. Income may be represented by statistics of gross national product (GNP), personal income, or another broad aggregate. The change in tax liability reflects the change in the tax base and the marginal tax rate. Built-in flexibility therefore depends both on the extent of fluctuations in the tax base relative to fluctuations in aggregate income and on the marginal tax rate.

Relation of Built-in Flexibility to Elasticity

Built-in flexibility should be distinguished from income elasticity of yield. Elasticity is the ratio of the percentage change in tax yield to the percentage change in income.[1] A tax with a yield that is small relative to income and the change in income can have high elasticity but cannot have great built-in flexibility. Two taxes with the same built-in flexibility can have very different elasticities. The difference between the two concepts may be illustrated by comparing the behavior of three hypothetical taxes—T_1, T_2, and T_3—in two time periods, on the assumption that income increases from 100 in period 1 to 110 in period 2:

	T_1	T_2	T_3
Yield, period 1	20	1	10
Yield, period 2	21	1.20	11
Built-in flexibility	0.10	0.02	0.10
Elasticity	0.50	2	1

Built-in flexibility is more directly relevant to economic stabilization than is elasticity. Variations in tax liabilities act as stabilizers only to the extent that they offset the effects on income and output that would otherwise be associated with autonomous fluctuations in demand. The larger the offsets, the smaller will be the change in aggregate income resulting from any primary change in demand. Al-

1. Built-in flexibility equals $\Delta T/\Delta Y$, whereas income elasticity of yield equals $\Delta T/T{\cdot}Y/\Delta Y$, where T is tax liability and Y is income. An elasticity measure can be converted into a built-in flexibility measure by multiplying by a factor relating the tax yield to aggregate income: $\Delta T/T{\cdot}Y/\Delta Y{\cdot}T/Y = \Delta T/\Delta Y$.

though the size of the offsets attributable to different taxes should not be assumed to be proportional to their built-in flexibility, it is much more closely related to built-in flexibility than to elasticity.[2]

Elasticity measures, nevertheless, are useful in analyzing the effect of substituting one tax for another or of revising tax rates. If a tax has high elasticity but small built-in flexibility because its rates are low, its built-in flexibility might be increased by raising the rates. In the foregoing illustration, if the rate of T_3 could be doubled without affecting its elasticity, its yield in period 1 would equal that of T_1 and its built-in flexibility would then be twice that of T_1. In the following discussion, emphasis will be placed on built-in flexibility, but reference will be made also to elasticity, especially in comparisons of the individual income tax with other taxes.

Sources of Built-in Flexibility

The characteristics of the individual income tax that ensure great built-in flexibility are the broad base, the responsiveness of the base to changes in economic activity, and the rather high marginal rate. Progressivity resulting from personal exemptions and rate graduation may enhance built-in flexibility by raising the average marginal tax rate, but progressivity is not an essential condition for the existence of built-in flexibility. Given the tax base, the degree of built-in flexibility depends on the average marginal tax rate rather than the relation between the average marginal rate and the average effective rate.[3] A flat-rate tax or, indeed, a regressive tax can have an important degree of built-in flexibility. Built-in flexibility, moreover, does not require that the tax base fluctuate proportionately more than aggre-

2. Richard A. Musgrave and Merton H. Miller, "Built-in Flexibility," *American Economic Review,* vol. 38 (March 1948), pp. 122–28; E. Cary Brown, "The Static Theory of Automatic Fiscal Stabilization," *Journal of Political Economy,* vol. 63 (October 1955), pp. 427–30. According to these authors, and the approach adopted in the text, a tax is an automatic stabilizer if the absolute size of the change in income, in response to a fluctuation in autonomous demand, is smaller when the tax is in existence than it would be in the absence of the tax. Other definitions have been proposed.

3. As used here, the average marginal rate is the ratio of the change in tax to the change in the base, and the average effective rate is the ratio of the total tax to the total base. Sometimes the marginal and average rates are calculated with respect to aggregates broader than the tax base. For example, calculations for the income tax might relate tax liability or payments to GNP or personal income rather than taxable income.

gate income; the essential condition is that the base vary in the same direction as income.

Estimates of Built-in Flexibility and Elasticity

Historical data allow the change in income tax liabilities to be related to the change in aggregate income. For example, from 1950 to 1970 the increase in federal individual income tax liabilities equaled 9.4 percent of the increase in GNP or 11.3 percent of the increase in personal income. These computations, however, make no allowance for the changes in the tax law that occurred and hence do not measure built-in flexibility. In order to do this, it is necessary to establish the relationship between the chosen aggregate income series and the tax base and to ascertain the marginal tax rate, both under the same income tax structure (comprising personal exemptions, rates, and other relevant provisions). Various intermediate relationships between the income aggregate, such as GNP, and the tax base may be investigated with a view to explaining more fully the behavior of the tax base and laying a foundation for predicting built-in flexibility in the future. For example, the following series of functional relationships might be investigated:

$$PI = f_1(GNP)$$
$$API = f_2(PI)$$
$$AGI = f_3(API)$$
$$TI = f_4(AGI)$$
$$T = f_5(TI).$$

Here *PI* is personal income, *GNP* is gross national product, *API* is adjusted personal income (adjusted, for example, to exclude transfer payments and to include personal contributions for social insurance), *AGI* is adjusted gross income as defined in the tax law, *TI* is taxable income (the tax base), and *T* is individual income tax liabilities. Often these items are stated in per capita terms. Capital gains and losses and the tax associated with them may be excluded. Substitution of the appropriate values yields an estimate of the marginal relationship between income and tax liabilities and hence of built-in flexibility. Measured with respect to GNP, this is $\Delta T/\Delta GNP$.

The relationship between the income aggregates such as GNP and personal income can be statistically estimated from economic data. AGI, taxable income, and tax liabilities depend partly on the composition and distribution of income and partly on provisions of the tax law concerning exclusions and deductions, personal exemptions, and tax rates. Basically, there are three methods of estimating the tax functions under an unchanged tax system. One is to study a period during which the tax law did not change. The application of this method is severely limited by frequent changes in the tax law. A second method is to adjust historical data on the tax variables to convert them to estimated values under a common system of tax rates and other provisions. The third method seeks to avoid these complications by deriving the tax functions from cross-section data for one year.

The first edition of this book presented estimates for the period 1949–60 derived by a combination of the first two methods. These estimates indicated that under the 1954–60 tax law the built-in flexibility of the federal individual income tax was 0.087 with respect to GNP. The elasticity of tax liability with respect to GNP was 1.1 at the 1960 income level and about 1.2 at the average income level of the period 1949–60 (for details see appendix E). A surprising finding was that the marginal tax rate with respect to taxable income was approximately equal to the average tax rate, implying that rate graduation made no contribution to built-in flexibility and elasticity in this period.

Changes in the income tax structure, together with rapidly rising income, have made these estimates obsolete. Studies by Waldorf and Pechman[4] applying the second method yield revised results for the 1950s and estimates for recent years. These estimates cannot be directly compared with mine because of differences in concepts and data. Converted to a GNP base, however, Pechman's estimates of built-in flexibility for the years 1954–60 are considerably higher than my earlier estimates—about 0.100 rather than 0.087. Pechman corroborates my finding that in this period rate graduation did not contribute to built-in flexibility or elasticity; nevertheless, his estimate of the elasticity of tax liabilities with respect to total income is considerably higher than mine—about 1.3 with respect to GNP as compared with my 1.1 to 1.2. Despite reductions in tax rates and increases in exemptions (including the institution of the low-income

4. William H. Waldorf, "The Responsiveness of Federal Personal Income Taxes to Income Change," *Survey of Current Business*, vol. 47 (December 1967), pp. 32–45; and Joseph A. Pechman, "Responsiveness of the Federal Individual Income Tax to Changes in Income," *Brookings Papers on Economic Activity, 2:1973*, pp. 385–421.

allowance), Pechman finds that built-in flexibility has increased over time; his estimate implies that by 1970 it was approximately 0.113 with respect to GNP. Further details are given in appendix E.

The third method of deriving tax functions mentioned above relies on cross-section data for various income classes or regional data for a single year. Pechman applied this method by using a sample file of income tax returns to simulate tax variables under conditions of growing income and population. He found that estimates of built-in flexibility and elasticity obtained in this way and those that he derived from time series relationships were similar for short projections (or extrapolations only moderately beyond the observed range) but that the estimates diverged more as the projections were extended.

Tanzi's cross-section studies for the United States use data on income and federal income tax liabilities for each of the fifty states.[5] The assumption is that the relationship between per capita tax and per capita income for the states in a given year is equivalent to what would prevail for the country as a whole if national per capita income fluctuated over the range of state per capita incomes while the income tax structure remained unchanged. Since per capita income in the richest state has been about twice that in the poorest state in recent years and the range was even wider in earlier years, this method yields as wide a range of observations as does a historical series extending over a considerable number of years, without the complications of adjusting for changes in tax structure. Tanzi's estimate of built-in flexibility for 1971 is equivalent to approximately 0.109 with respect to GNP. His estimates of elasticity with respect to AGI for selected

5. See Vito Tanzi, "Measuring the Sensitivity of the Federal Income Tax from Cross-Section Data: A New Approach," *Review of Economics and Statistics,* vol. 51 (May 1969), pp. 206–09; Vito Tanzi and Thomas P. Hart, "The Effect of the 1964 Revenue Act on the Sensitivity of the Federal Income Tax," *Review of Economics and Statistics,* vol. 54 (August 1972), pp. 326–28. I am indebted to Tanzi for making available to me his unpublished estimates for 1969, 1970, and 1971, prepared with the assistance of Anita Basak in the same way as the estimates included in the two published papers. For another study using cross-section data of a regional nature, see Palle Schelde Andersen, "Built-in Flexibility and Sensitivity of the Personal Income Tax in Denmark," *Swedish Journal of Economics,* vol. 75 (March 1973), pp. 1–18. Two British studies that combine cross-section data for income classes with time-series analysis are A. R. Prest, "The Sensitivity of the Yield of Personal Income Tax in the United Kingdom," *Economic Journal,* vol. 72 (September 1962), pp. 576–96; and J. C. Dorrington, "A Structural Approach to Estimating the Built-in Flexibility of United Kingdom T. es on Personal Income," *Economic Journal,* vol. 84 (September 1974), pp. 576–94.

years between 1963 and 1971 (under the varying tax structures of that period) all round to 1.4, which is close to Pechman's estimates made from time series relationships. Estimates of the marginal tax rate derived by the cross-section method differ somewhat, however, from those obtained from historical data (see appendix E for details).

Comparison with Other Taxes

To put the estimates of built-in flexibility of the individual income tax in perspective, the behavior of this tax may be compared with that of other taxes. Corporate profits and profits tax accruals fluctuate widely in response to business conditions. They have declined during postwar recessions and have risen during subsequent expansions. Declines have also occurred in some periods that are not generally classified as recessions. The relationship between profits and GNP appears to have been a variable one and to have been characterized by a downward trend in the ratio of profits to GNP.[6] Precise measurements, however, are greatly complicated by revisions of depreciation methods, the effects of inflation, changes in debt–equity ratios and interest rates, and other factors. At the present time it does not seem feasible to make useful estimates of the built-in flexibility and elasticity of the corporation income tax.

Social insurance payroll taxes and contributions have become the second largest source of federal revenue. In fiscal years 1970–75 they accounted for about one-fourth of total federal receipts and equaled about 5 percent of GNP. These taxes apply at flat rates to covered wages and salaries but only up to a ceiling amount. In the past the ceiling was fixed by statute, and the elasticity of the taxes with respect to wages and salaries and GNP was considerably less than 1. The ceiling is now subject to periodic automatic adjustment in proportion to the rise in average taxable wages;[7] hence the elasticity of the taxes should be approximately 1 and their built-in flexibility with respect to GNP on the order of 0.05.

6. Annual Report of the Council of Economic Advisers, published with *Economic Report of the President, January 1973*, pp. 37–39; William D. Nordhaus, "The Falling Share of Profits," *Brookings Papers on Economic Activity, 1:1974*, pp. 169–208.

7. Beginning in 1975, the taxable wage ceiling is adjusted when there has been a cost-of-living benefit increase. The latter increases are made automatically at yearly intervals when the consumer price index has risen by at least 3 percent since the last benefit increase (Social Security Act, secs. 230(a), 215(i), respectively).

Since consumption is more stable than income, the short-run elasticity of yield of a personal tax on consumption expenditures would be lower than that of the individual income tax, given comparable personal exemptions and rate graduation. This means that the substitution of an expenditure tax for the income tax would reduce the built-in flexibility of the revenue system. I have not attempted to quantify the difference between the two taxes in this respect.

A uniform indirect tax on all consumption expenditures would have lower elasticity and smaller built-in flexibility than a direct tax on consumption because of the lack of personal exemptions in the former. In practice, however, indirect taxes do not cover all consumption items. Even a value-added tax or a broad-based retail sales tax would omit many goods and services that are included in consumption in the national accounts. Whether the yield of such a tax would be more or less elastic than that of a hypothetical tax on all consumption expenditures is not clear. It seems safe to surmise, nevertheless, that the short-run yield elasticity of a value-added tax or a retail sales tax would be considerably less than that of the individual income tax and that the substitution of either of these taxes for the income tax would appreciably reduce built-in flexibility.[8]

A wealth tax would be likely to have the minimum short-run elasticity. Personal wealth includes a large amount of fixed claims, which maintain a fairly stable value in money terms. The values of personal equities in dwellings, corporate stock, and unincorporated businesses are more variable. The value of corporate stock, in particular, is highly variable; however, movements of stock prices do not coincide closely with general business cycles. Information on short-run changes in the values of personal equities in dwellings and unincorporated businesses is not reliable enough to indicate their sensitivity to the business cycle. In practice, wealth tax assessments probably would be more stable than "true" market values and hence would lag behind changes in market values, except for marketable securities on which current quotations could easily be obtained.

Economic Significance of Built-in Flexibility

Built-in flexibility acts as an automatic economic stabilizer if variations in tax liabilities cause a reduction in fluctuations in private con-

8. See appendix E.

sumption and investment and the government does not alter its own expenditures because of the revenue variations. Built-in flexibility can moderate the secondary or cumulative effects on income of an autonomous change in investment or an external shock to the economy, but it cannot prevent fluctuations and cannot itself reverse upward or downward movements. The limitation of a recession or an expansion, however, may advance the date at which other forces operate to bring about a reversal of direction.

The principal stabilizing effect of built-in flexibility has usually been attributed to its influence on consumption. Built-in flexibility of direct taxes reduces the change in disposable personal income that would otherwise be associated with any initial fluctuation in GNP. To the extent that consumption expenditures depend on current disposable income, built-in flexibility of direct tax yield will help stabilize this important segment of aggregate outlay.

Some quantitative estimates may bring out the significance of these generalizations. As noted above, Pechman's estimates indicate that the built-in flexibility of the federal individual income tax with respect to GNP was 0.113 in 1970. This means that the tax diverted this fraction of any change in GNP from the disposable income of consumers. It appears that on the average the ratio of the change in personal consumption to the change in disposable personal income from one year to the next—the marginal propensity to consume—is about 0.760 (see the last section of appendix E). Combining these two estimates implies that the income tax reduces the change in potential consumption by an amount equal to 0.086 of any change in GNP. More significant, the estimates also imply that the total change in GNP associated with any autonomous or primary change in demand is smaller than it would be if the income tax were replaced by a tax with less built-in flexibility. At the extreme, the fluctuation in income is about 15 percent smaller than it would be if the substitute tax had zero built-in flexibility, that is, if its yield were invariant to changes in GNP.[9]

The foregoing is based on a highly simplified explanation of consumption behavior. The statistical relationship between changes in aggregate disposable income and consumption takes no explicit

9. The ratio of the total change in income to a primary change may be summarized by the income multiplier, which is reduced by the imposition of a tax with positive built-in flexibility. For further details, see appendix E.

account of other factors that may influence consumption, including the composition of income, wealth, liquidity, previous and expected future levels of income and consumption, and demographic variables. Adherents to the permanent-income or life-cycle hypotheses, which have been mentioned several times in preceding chapters, argue that short-run fluctuations of disposable income will be reflected mainly in saving rather than in consumption. Others reach similar conclusions by stressing the influence of habit and fixed commitments. Econometric studies usually include among variables explaining consumption not only current disposable income but wealth or past income or consumption. Theoretical considerations and statistical evidence point to a lag between changes in tax liabilities and disposable income and changes in consumption outlays. Under certain assumptions about the length of the lag and the rapidity of income fluctuations, built-in flexibility of the income tax would accentuate fluctuations rather than reduce them, but there is no convincing evidence that these assumptions approximate real-world conditions. Recognition of the additional factors that influence consumption and of lags in response to changes in tax liabilities detracts from the stabilizing value attributed to built-in flexibility but does not support the conclusion that its influence is unimportant or perverse. Although simple calculations such as those presented above should be treated cautiously, they illustrate the significance of built-in flexibility and appear to offer a useful basis for comparing taxes. The question of lags and certain other issues related to the effects of built-in flexibility are discussed below in connection with discretionary changes in tax rates.

The effect on consumption of the built-in flexibility of the corporation income tax is the indirect result of its influence on dividend distributions and disposable income of stockholders. (There may also be some relation through influences on stock prices and capital gains, but its nature is obscure.) Although a change in the statutory rate of the corporate tax would doubtless affect dividend payments, it is not clear how the changes in corporate tax liabilities that accompany cyclical fluctuations of profits influence the amount and timing of distributions. In many corporations, management seems reluctant to alter dividend payments abruptly in response to an increase or decrease in profits after taxes. Statistical studies covering long spans of time indicate that dividend payments may change by only about 15 percent to 20 percent of the year-to-year change in profits after taxes or cash flow, although in the long run corporations seem to aim at distributing larger fractions.[10] Disposable income of stockholders does not change by the full amount of dividend payments since dividends received by stockholders are subject to the individual income tax.

The cushioning effect of corporate saving and the individual income tax reduce the influence on disposable income of the built-in flexibility of the corporate tax to a small fraction of the automatic change in corporate tax liabilities. If, for example, dividend distributions change from one period to the next by 15 percent of the change in profits after tax or in cash flow and the marginal rate of individual income tax of stockholders is 25 percent, the change in disposable income of stockholders is about 11 percent of the change in corporate profits tax liabilities ($0.15 \times 0.75 = 0.11$).

The built-in flexibility of the corporation income tax operates mainly through its influence on internal funds of corporations. Although profits after taxes decline less than profits before taxes, any profits realized from current operations or new investment will be subject to the tax. For large firms, which account for most of the production in the corporate sector, the marginal tax rate is constant over the relevant range. Hence, the incentive effects of the corporate tax should be essentially the same during a recession as in a prosperous period.

The built-in flexibility of sales taxes and excises also lessens the impact on business receipts of changes in final demand but does not directly affect disposable income of consumers. To illustrate, suppose consumer expenditures on a commodity subject to a 20 percent ad valorem tax drop from 100 to 70. Tax payments will fall by 6 and sellers' receipts net of tax by 24. Business firms are likely to cut their production and inventories less than they would if they had suffered a decline of 30 in receipts, as they would have in the absence of the excise tax; if so, the built-in flexibility of the excise tax will help

10. John Lintner, "Distribution of Incomes of Corporations among Dividends, Retained Earnings, and Taxes," in American Economic Association, *Papers and Proceedings of the Sixty-eighth Annual Meeting, 1955 (American Economic Review,* vol. 46, May 1956), pp. 97–113; John A. Brittain, "The Tax Structure and Corporate Dividend Policy," in American Economic Association, *Papers and Proceedings of the Seventy-sixth Annual Meeting, 1963 (American Economic Review,* vol. 54, May 1964), pp. 272–87; and Brittain, *Corporate Dividend Policy* (Brookings Institution, 1966), p. 56.

maintain employment and consumer income. The fall in excise tax payments does not warrant a price cut since tax rates (taxes per dollar of sales) remain unchanged.[11] In the United States the major federal excises—those on alcohol, tobacco, and gasoline—are specific taxes, which must have somewhat less built-in flexibility than would ad valorem taxes on the same commodities.

A large volume of internal funds is favorable to current operations and to new investment since many companies lack ready access to external capital and managers often seem to be more willing to invest internal funds than to seek outside capital. The built-in flexibility of the corporation tax and of indirect taxes, therefore, should have some stabilizing influence because it reduces fluctuations in internal funds. Whether this influence is important is not clear. Internal funds (retained profits plus depreciation and depletion accruals) of corporations are usually larger relative to the increase in plant and equipment, inventories, and receivables in recession years than in other years, but internal funds were insufficient to cover the nonfinancial investment of corporations in the 1957–58 and 1960–61 recessions.[12] Substantial amounts of external finance have been obtained by corporations at cyclical peaks. Although firm quantitative estimates are not available, it seems unlikely that the built-in flexibility of the corporation tax and the excises has much power as a stabilizer of investment. This does not imply that investment is unresponsive to permanent changes in tax rates.[13]

Policies that stabilize consumption and investment are mutually reinforcing. If consumption demand is cushioned by built-in flexibility, manufacturers and distributors are likely to vary their inven-

11. Lewis classifies excises as "indirect stabilizers" and cautions against "the temptation . . . to apply ordinary incidence theory—according to which excise taxes are for the most part paid by consumers—in assessing their effects as built-in stabilizers." Wilfred Lewis, Jr., *Federal Fiscal Policy in the Postwar Recessions* (Brookings Institution, 1962), p. 66.

12. *Variability of Private Investment in Plant and Equipment,* Materials submitted to the Joint Economic Committee, 87 Cong. 1 sess. (1962), pt. 1, "Investment and Its Financing" (report prepared by the U.S. Department of Commerce), p. 43; Board of Governors of the Federal Reserve System, "Flow of Funds Accounts, 1945–1972" (1973; processed), p. 17.

13. For a fuller statement of reasons for skepticism concerning the countercyclical effectiveness of the corporate tax, see my paper "The Corporate Income Tax in a Depression," in *Policies to Combat Depression,* A Conference of the Universities–National Bureau Committee for Economic Research (Princeton University Press for the National Bureau of Economic Research, 1956), pp. 149–70.

tories less than they would if consumption fluctuated more widely over the business cycle, and plant and equipment outlays may be similarly affected. Reduction of fluctuations in investment outlays, in turn, helps stabilize disposable income and consumption. A full quantitative analysis of built-in flexibility would have to try to incorporate these interrelations in an econometric model.

Flexible Tax Rates

Since the automatic stabilization obtained through built-in flexibility cannot prevent fluctuations, but only moderate them, the question arises whether economic stability can be enhanced by changes in tax rates and government expenditures. This deceptively simple question touches many issues that cannot be examined here. Some consideration will be given, however, to the possible contribution of flexible income tax rates.

Given accurate forecasting, it would be possible to vary tax rates so as to relate liabilities and payments to economic conditions in the same way that built-in flexibility does. In practice, however, forecasting is subject to major errors, and delays will be inevitable until statistics become available, experts agree on their interpretation, policymakers decide that tax rates should be altered, and legislation is enacted. As a means of reducing these delays, suggestions have been made for "formula flexibility," which would provide for increases or decreases in tax rates in response to movements in selected economic indicators. Another approach would be to give the President discretionary authority to vary tax rates within limits.[14] Neither of these approaches has attracted much support in recent years.

Owing to the probable delays in making changes in tax rates, the lags in taxpayer response to the changes become particularly significant. Although econometric models differ considerably in their estimates of the magnitude of the response of GNP to a change in individual income tax rates, they tend to agree that a large part of the

14. Proposed by the Commission on Money and Credit in its 1961 report, *Money and Credit: Their Influence on Jobs, Prices, and Growth* (Prentice-Hall, 1961), pp. 129–37; and by President Kennedy in the three annual presidential messages at the beginning of 1962 (State of the Union Message of January 11, 1962, Budget Message of January 18, 1962, and *Economic Report of the President, January 1962*, pp. 18–19); and advocated by the Council of Economic Advisers, in the *Economic Report of the President, January 1964*, pp. 39, 41.

ultimate response will occur rather quickly, within about four calendar quarters.[15] Long-range forecasting does not seem to be required to detect when discretionary tax changes would be desirable for stabilization purposes, but the ability to forecast fairly well for a few quarters is essential. The risk of perverse economic effects is much greater for discretionary changes than for built-in flexibility.

Variation of tax rates for stabilization purposes is likely to involve temporary increases or decreases to compensate for departures of the economy from a desired path. But temporary changes in individual income tax rates will have less effect on consumption outlays than permanent changes if, as is plausible, families base their spending at least partly on estimates of their normal or lifetime income or their wealth. Some economists argue that the effect of temporary changes in the income tax will be small or even negligible. On the other hand, temporary changes in indirect taxes, if reflected promptly in prices, will offer inducements to accelerate or defer spending and may therefore be especially potent stabilizers when well timed. Granted that the impact of temporary changes in tax rates must be discounted in the case of the income tax and written up in the case of indirect taxes, the question remains—how large should the allowances be? The extreme version of the permanent-income or life-cycle hypothesis, which would assign a very low value to the effect of a temporary change in income tax rates, seems to be based on the assumption that consumers have a great degree of foresight and discipline in planning their expenditures and are ready to believe that a tax change announced as temporary will actually prove to be so. The quite different judgment, that temporary changes in income tax rates are almost as effective as permanent changes, derives some support from statistical studies on consumers' use of nonrecurrent receipts.[16] In the existing

15. A comparative simulation of six econometric models of the United States found that they indicated that the timing of the ultimate maximum effect on real GNP of a cut in personal income tax rates would be as follows: 38 percent after one quarter, 61 percent after two quarters, 75 percent after three quarters, and 87 percent after four quarters. These are unweighted averages of the results of the six models. See Gary Fromm and Lawrence R. Klein, "A Comparison of Eleven Econometric Models of the United States," in American Economic Association, *Papers and Proceedings of the Eighty-fifth Annual Meeting, 1972* (*American Economic Review*, vol. 63, May 1973), p. 392.

16. Ronald Bodkin, "Windfall Income and Consumption," *American Economic Review*, vol. 49 (September 1959), pp. 602–14; Arthur M. Okun, "The Personal Tax Surcharge and Consumer Demand, 1968–70," *Brookings Papers on Economic*

state of uncertainty the "reasonable guess" of Blinder and Solow that a temporary change in income tax rates is half as effective as a permanent one[17] has the appeal that middle-of-the-road positions often have but is exposed to attack from two sides.

Two important changes in individual income tax rates were made in the United States in the 1960s for stabilization purposes—the 1964 permanent reduction and the temporary surcharge applicable in 1968–70.[18] The 1964 tax cut appears to have stimulated consumer spending quickly[19] and was acclaimed as a successful application of the "new economics." The 1968 surcharge, in contrast, is widely regarded as a failure. Certainly, inflation was not checked. Although the issue is still subject to debate, there is evidence that the surcharge curbed real consumption by about as much as should have been expected,[20] but that it was inadequate for the intended purpose because the expansionary forces had been underestimated. The episode nourished doubts about the effectiveness of fiscal policy in controlling inflation.[21]

Once a change in individual income tax rates has been decided on, it can be put into effect quickly. About four-fifths of gross collections is in the form of withholding from salaries and wages. Withheld tax is deducted in each payroll period and remitted four times a month

---

Activity, 1:1971, pp. 176–78; Robert Ferber, "Consumer Economics: A Survey," *Journal of Economic Literature*, vol. 11 (December 1973), pp. 1306–09.

17. Alan S. Blinder and Robert M. Solow, "Analytical Foundations of Fiscal Policy," in *The Economics of Public Finance* (Brookings Institution, 1974), p. 109.

18. The 1964 act cut the individual income tax by about 13 percent in 1964 and 20 percent in 1965. The surcharge increased individual income tax liabilities by 7.5 percent in 1968, 10 percent in 1969, and 2.5 percent in 1970, but certain low-income taxpayers were exempted.

19. Albert Ando and E. Cary Brown, "Personal Income Taxes and Consumption Following the 1964 Tax Reduction," in Ando, Brown, and Ann F. Friedlaender, eds., *Studies in Economic Stabilization* (Brookings Institution, 1968), pp. 117–37; Arthur M. Okun, "Measuring the Impact of the 1964 Tax Reduction," in Walter W. Heller, ed., *Perspectives on Economic Growth* (Random House, 1968), pp. 25–49.

20. Okun, "Personal Tax Surcharge and Consumer Demand."

21. For vigorous statements of the thesis that the surcharge "should never, on basic theoretical grounds, have been considered an effective anti-inflationary device" —mainly because of permanent-income and monetary considerations—see Robert Eisner, "Fiscal and Monetary Policy Reconsidered," *American Economic Review*, vol. 59 (December 1969), pp. 897–905, and Eisner, "What Went Wrong?" *Journal of Political Economy*, vol. 79 (May–June 1971), pp. 629–41. A more favorable, though cautious, evaluation is given by Blinder and Solow in "Analytical Foundations of Fiscal Policy," pp. 102–15.

by large employers, monthly by others, and quarterly by the smallest firms. When a special effort is made, new withholding rates can be put into effect one or two weeks after Congress approves them.

For the nonwithheld tax, the adjustment will be slower. This part of the tax is payable in quarterly installments on the basis of annual estimates of current-year liabilities. For taxpayers who report on a calendar-year basis, as most individuals do, the estimate and the first installment are due April 15, and the subsequent installments are payable June 15, September 15, and January 15. The fourth installment is usually substantially larger than the first three. The final settlement is not made until the definitive return is filed by April 15 of the next year. When a change in tax rates is made during the year, taxpayers can be instructed to adjust their subsequent installments, but there is no easy way of ensuring full compliance. Under present law, taxpayers have great freedom in revising their estimates of current-year liability and could usually avoid paying an increase in tax until after the end of the year. Some inequity in the treatment of wage and salary earners and other taxpayers would occur, but this may not be considered any more serious than the differences between the treatment of these groups even when tax rates do not change.

Long-Run Implications of Revenue Elasticity

With unchanged personal exemptions and rates, the yield of the individual income tax will increase faster than total income in a growing economy. Projected over long periods, impressive increases in the tax ratio can be computed. Thus, on the assumption that the income elasticity of individual income tax yield is 1.4 and income grows by 5 percent a year, the ratio of individual income tax liability to GNP would rise over twenty years from the 1970 level of 8.6 percent to 10.7 percent in 1990.

Projections of this kind have stimulated two kinds of concern. Some observers, assuming that government expenditure will not grow as rapidly as tax yield, have pointed to the danger of a "fiscal drag" on purchasing power which will tend to cause the economy to operate below its full potential. Others, fearing that the growth of revenue will induce additional government spending, have warned that the public sector will become too large.

The weight of either of these two inconsistent worries is reduced by the fact that the revenue system includes taxes with elasticities much lower than the individual income tax. Social insurance taxes and contributions and excises and customs duties, whose combined elasticity may be somewhat less than 1, account for more than one-third of total federal receipts (appendix table A-2).

More important, it is unrealistic to project unchanged tax rates over a long period of time. Although the revision of tax rates is cumbersome in the American political system, income tax rates and exemptions have in fact been altered frequently. Government expenditures have tended to grow more rapidly than GNP, though with interruptions of the trend. Since tax cuts and increases in public expenditure usually are more popular than tax increases and budget cuts, one does not have to be a cynic to conclude that the high income elasticity of yield of the individual income tax is a desirable safeguard against excessive budget deficits. Considerations of this kind may have been in the minds of members of the House Ways and Means Committee in 1913 when they recommended the new income tax as an elastic revenue source. This feature of the tax has been attractive in many other countries.

Inflation and the Income Tax

The preceding pages relate mostly to fluctuations of real output and its long-run growth and to the interaction between taxation and real output (or income measured in constant prices). Earlier discussions generally assumed that if built-in flexibility or changes in tax rates helped stabilize output they would also help stabilize the price level. Inflation was seen as the result of excessive demand when activity expanded too fast and particularly when the economy approached full utilization of labor and other resources. An increase in income tax liabilities or payments was expected to curtail spending and thus retard the price rise. In a paper published in 1955, E. Cary Brown drew a distinction between stabilization of prices and of output. He argued that, whereas positive built-in flexibility will always act as an automatic stabilizer of output, a tax will serve as a price stabilizer only if its elasticity with respect to money income and expenditure exceeds unity. When the latter condition is met, the real yield of the tax will rise during inflation and ultimately will eliminate excess demand. Brown concluded: "Almost any tax, other than lump-sum levies, can meet the test of output stabilization in greater or less degree. But only corporate income and personal income taxes, when their structure is defined in money terms, can act as price stabilizers."[22] Brown's distinction is valid, though a less exacting definition might classify as a price stabilizer a measure that retarded the rate of inflation even if not strong enough ever to halt it. This would expand the category to include taxes whose nominal yield rises during inflation regardless of whether their real yield also increases.

With personal exemptions, bracket limits, and certain deductions fixed in money terms and with graduated rates, the average effective rate of income tax will rise during inflation. The relative increase (that is, the elasticity, defined as the percentage increase in tax divided by the percentage increase in income) will be greatest for taxpayers whose income is near the exemption limits; under most rate schedules the relative increase will taper off fairly rapidly over higher income ranges. The rise in the average tax ratio and the change in the relative positions of taxpayers may be regarded as inconsistent with the original intentions of legislators and as unfair. In an inflationary period, moreover, the irritation that consumers feel because their incomes do not go as far as expected may come to be directed to a disproportionate degree against direct taxes, which are recognized as under government control. These reactions appear to have influenced decisions in a number of countries to make ad hoc reductions in income tax rates and increases in personal exemptions.

Several countries have adopted measures tying income tax exemptions and rate brackets in some way to a price index or to a minimum wage that is related to the price level. These include countries with a history of high inflation rates such as Chile, Brazil, Argentina, Uruguay, Iceland, and Israel and also Denmark, the Netherlands, some of the Swiss cantons, and Canada. The Canadian plan, introduced in 1973 to take effect in 1974, is an automatic indexing plan. Bracket limits and personal exemptions are increased at the beginning of each calendar year by applying a factor equal to the ratio of the average consumer price index for the twelve-month period ended the preceding September 30 to the corresponding average for a twelve-month period ended one year earlier. No provision is made for downward adjustments if the price level falls, and no price-level corrections are

22. "Static Theory of Automatic Fiscal Stabilization," p. 440.

provided for determining gross income or capital gains. Most other plans call for only partial adjustments or allow the government some discretion in their application.

These inflation-adjustment plans reduce built-in flexibility and elasticity with respect to money income but presumably are not intended to alter the response of the income tax to fluctuations of real income or its long-term growth. According to the theory that dominated thinking about fiscal policy until recently, application of indexing at a time when the price level is rising will accelerate inflation. Any gain in tax equity will have to be balanced against the cost of more inflation, and the expected gain in political tranquillity is likely to be of brief duration or illusory.

Lately, however, this analysis has been questioned by economists who argue that in industrial countries a close direct connection does not exist between the degree of utilization of productive capacity and the rate of inflation. They stress cost-push factors such as wage increases and administered prices as the cause of inflation. They contend that rising income tax liabilities will not cure inflation but will lead either to demands for still higher wages or to stagnation and further increases in unit costs and prices in many industries. In these circumstances, the argument continues, indexing the income tax for inflation may actually slow down the increase in prices by moderating wage demands. Another line of argument is that in modern economies price movements tend to lag behind output movements so that the price level reaches its peak after output has stopped increasing and begun to decline. At the upper turning point, indexing could prevent tax liabilities from continuing to increase in real terms after output has peaked.[23]

The debate about the desirability of indexing the income tax for inflation touches on a number of unsettled questions. I am skeptical about the advisability of automatic indexing in a country that can be expected to experience moderate inflation on the average. Inequities arising from unintended changes in relative income tax liabilities

23. In Canada simulations carried out with an econometric model have indicated that the lag structure of that economy is such that the indexing of the income tax does not significantly affect the response of prices to a nonrecurrent increase in autonomous demand such as a balance-of-trade surplus. See John Bossons and Thomas A. Wilson, "Adjusting Tax Rates for Inflation," *Canadian Tax Journal,* vol. 21 (May–June 1973), pp. 185–99.

seem minor in comparison with the many injustices resulting from arbitrary redistributions of income and wealth caused by inflation. It is not obvious that a partial adjustment plan, confined to a few features of the income tax, would bring about a net improvement in equity.

As regards economic effects, the contention that indexing would improve output stability without worsening inflation is based on tenuous evidence. The lag structure of modern economies is not well understood, and lags appear to be variable. Without denying the existence of cost-push forces in inflation, I emphasize the role of demand in validating them and would be reluctant to give up the contribution of built-in flexibility to checking the rise of disposable income in boom periods and in keeping down the budget deficit and the money creation likely to be associated with it. In the longer run, indexing the income tax may help win acceptance of a policy of income and price restraint, but it can form only a small part of a program for that purpose. As the price level rises over time, tax adjustments, particularly increases in personal exemptions, may become expedient, but it seems safer to make these on an ad hoc basis than to predetermine them by automatic indexing. An important consideration in the long run is that the prices paid by government, including salaries and wages, are likely to rise more rapidly than other prices because there is less scope for productivity improvements in government activities than in manufacturing, agriculture, and several other sectors. In the United States the average price of goods and services purchased by the federal government rose half again as much as all prices in the two decades 1950–70.[24]

Under conditions of rapid inflation, on the other hand, it seems unrealistic to expect that income tax exemptions and rate brackets will be left constant in money terms long enough to allow tax liabilities to increase drastically relative to income. Delinquencies and defaults would be likely to prevent a corresponding increase in tax collections even if legal liabilities were not adjusted. Indexing of exemptions and rate brackets and application of a monetary correction to

24. The implicit price deflator for federal government purchases rose 105 percent while the implicit price deflator for GNP increased 69 percent. U.S. Department of Commerce, *The National Income and Product Accounts of the United States, 1929–1965: Statistical Tables* (1966), and *Survey of Current Business,* vol. 54 (July 1974), table 8.1 in each.

income measurement may become expedient. The point at which moderate inflation turns into rapid inflation cannot be precisely specified in advance because this depends on public attitudes toward rising prices.

Conclusion

The built-in flexibility of the tax system would be somewhat reduced and instability of output increased if the individual income tax were replaced by a broad direct or indirect tax on consumption or by a wealth tax. This would also be a result of enlarging the role of social insurance payroll taxes and contributions relative to that of the individual income tax. The consequences of substitution between the individual income tax and the corporation income tax are unclear because an acceptable measure of the elasticity of the latter with respect to GNP is not available.

Discretionary changes in income tax rates can also help stabilize output, but their successful use requires the ability to forecast the course of the economy for at least a short period. Temporary changes in income tax rates are likely to be less potent in influencing spending than permanent changes, whereas temporary changes in consumption tax rates will have a greater immediate effect than permanent changes.

The elastic response of individual income tax revenue to long-run growth is advantageous, although poor economic management could cause this feature of the tax to contribute to stagnation or excessive government spending.

Earlier confidence in our ability to control inflation by taxation has been weakened by increased recognition both of the importance of cost-push factors as a cause of inflation and of the complexity of the inflation process. In an economy characterized by a moderate inflationary trend, with cyclical movements above and below the trend, increases of personal exemptions and rate bracket limits to reflect the declining real value of fixed amounts may become advisable, but it seems more prudent to make these by ad hoc changes than by adoption of automatic indexing. In rapid inflation, comprehensive indexing, including corrections of taxable income measurement, may be expedient.

CHAPTER TWELVE

The Future of the Income Tax

TWO GENERATIONS later, the judgment, stated by the Ways and Means Committee in 1913, that an individual income tax is the fairest of all taxes still commands assent. No other tax accords as well with ability to pay or serves better to moderate economic inequality.

A well-designed income tax also has economic advantages. For the broad range of activities that call for neither special promotion nor restraint, the income tax, though not completely neutral, is more impartial than other widely used taxes. Where special encouragement or discouragement is desired, preferential or penalty income tax provisions are convenient and sometimes effective. The built-in flexibility of individual income tax yield helps reduce fluctuations in employment and production. These characteristics, together with a large and elastic yield potential, have won for the individual income tax a prominent place in the revenue systems of the United States and many other countries.

While proposals to repeal the income tax are occasionally heard, they now seem outside the range of realistic alternatives. The significant questions are how big a role the income tax should play and what modifications in it are desirable.

No one contends that the U.S. income tax is a model tax, that it attains, in the highest degree possible, equity and economic efficiency.

Opinions differ greatly, however, on the seriousness of its defects and the feasibility of remedying them.

Remediable Defects

Many of the present defects of the income tax are due to unjustifiable exclusions and deductions from taxable income rather than to inherent characteristics of income taxation. The clearest objection to these provisions is their inconsistency with the high standards of equity and reasonable progressivity that are rightly applied to the income tax. But such provisions also have economic disadvantages. Their existence causes rates on fully taxable income to be higher than would otherwise be required and induces behavior that would not occur under a more uniform tax. Economic efficiency is likely to be impaired and the growth of national product retarded. More subtly and perhaps more seriously, tax-induced changes in production may lessen the satisfaction obtained from measured income and output.

The origin of some of the exclusions and deductions is obscure; they were adopted without wide public discussion or appreciation of their consequences. Others were enacted after successful campaigns by interested groups. Some exclusions and deductions were intended to serve widely approved purposes but were adopted without enough consideration of their efficiency and likely side effects. Regardless of origin, special provisions are difficult to eliminate both because of inertia and because beneficiaries are often alert in their defense whereas most other citizens give little thought to the advantages of uniform taxation. The subject of income tax reform, however, has attracted much wider attention in the United States during the past decade than previously. Although legislative progress has been limited, many special provisions are being attacked, not only by tax specialists, but also by politicians, labor leaders, journalists, and others.

One reaction to the deficiencies of the income tax is to recommend that their importance be lessened by reducing income tax rates and relying more on other taxes. Direct taxes on personal consumption and wealth have been advocated partly as a means of circumventing the special provisions that have grown up in the income tax over the years. However, the introduction of the new taxes would be more difficult, technically and politically, than the revision of the income tax. It would be easier to expand excises or to introduce a federal sales tax or value-added tax, but this would not minimize nonfunctional inequalities of taxation. The burden of the indirect taxes always varies greatly with personal tastes and needs. Where income tax administration and compliance are as good as in the United States, the substitution of indirect taxes for part of the income tax would aggravate inequalities in taxation of people with similar means.

The Issue of Progressivity

Greater reliance on indirect taxation has been recommended by those who believe that the income tax lends itself too readily to excessive rate graduation. They favor not only overt substitution of federal excises or sales taxes for part of the income tax, but also a policy of concentrating tax reductions on the income tax and of increasing the fraction of total revenue raised by state and local governments. Since state and local governments use the income tax far less than the federal government does, an enlargement of their share in total taxation is expected to reduce overall progressivity.

Uncommitted citizens may find it easier to pass judgment on tax programs if the question of progressivity is more sharply separated from the choice of tax form and the relative size of federal and state-local revenues. The income tax, though historically an instrument of progressivity, allows an infinite choice of rate schedules. Any agreed reduction of tax progressivity could be achieved by modifying income tax rates and exemptions. It would even be possible to discard progressivity by eliminating rate graduation and personal exemptions. The adaptability of the income tax to the desired degree of progressivity is one of its great strengths. Advocates of indirect taxation as a means of reducing progressivity seem to concede that their objective would not win public support if explicitly presented in the form of a revision of income tax rates.

The division of fiscal resources between levels of government is less easily separated from the question of progressivity, given the practical limitations on state-local income taxes, but flexibility can be attained through grants-in-aid and tax credits. Federal grants to support particular programs have grown rapidly and a general revenue sharing program was adopted in 1972. It is too early to say whether general revenue sharing will check the increase of state-local taxation, which in the 1960s expanded at a much faster rate than federal tax revenue. The tax-credit idea contemplates allowing persons who pay state income taxes to deduct them from their federal income tax liability, within limits, rather than treating them as personal deductions from adjusted gross income, as at present. The purpose would be to overcome interstate tax competition and to offer a special inducement to state income taxation together with a conditional decrease in the federal income tax. Interest in this approach has subsided since the early 1960s, when it attracted much attention, but the idea continues to draw some support both from those who wish to decentralize fiscal authority and responsibility and from those who desire to encourage the states to make greater use of income taxes.

The proportion of federal revenue obtained from the individual income tax has increased moderately since World War II and would have increased much more had not income tax rates been cut and exemptions increased on several occasions. The rate reductions, including the establishment of the 50 percent ceiling for the rate on earned income, weakened support for a drastic realignment of revenue sources but did not go far enough to satisfy critics who believed that the United States was relying much too heavily on progressive taxation.

Those who wish to lessen or eliminate tax progressivity argue that graduated income taxation impedes economic growth and efficiency. The extent to which fear of economic harm is well founded is debatable, partly because of analytical difficulties and partly because the U.S. income tax is actually much less progressive than the nominal rates suggest. Empirical evidence is lacking, but deductive reasoning confirms the apprehension that tax progressivity may have an economic cost. It shows that a person who has to pay a given amount of tax would be more likely to be discouraged from working and investing when faced by graduated rates than when taxes are proportional or regressive. This generalization, though significant, is of uncertain value for policymaking because it does not allow for possible differences in attitudes of high-income groups and low-income groups, who are differently affected by progressive and regressive taxes, and because it does not tell whether the effects of progressivity are great or small.

Any reduction in tax progressivity, especially the substitution of indirect consumption taxes for the income tax, would tend to increase to some degree the amount of personal saving out of any given total personal income. The available evidence suggests that the effect on saving of a reduction in tax progressivity would be small; the influence of a switch from income taxation to consumption taxes is conjectural.

An increased propensity to save permits more rapid economic growth because it allows greater capital formation, but it does not ensure faster growth. An attempt to save more may depress economic activity when output is being limited by inadequate demand rather than scarcity of capital. Although it would always be possible to overcome demand deficiencies, and thus prevent abortive saving, by sufficiently vigorous fiscal and monetary policy, this kind of policy remains an aspiration rather than a firm basis for planning. Statistical studies, moreover, indicate that even large increases in net saving may bring rather small increases in economic growth. Probable effects on personal saving are not, in my view, a convincing reason for partially replacing the income tax with indirect consumption taxes or for experimenting with a personal expenditure tax.

Goals and Reforms

In appraising the income tax or any other tax, it is well to recognize that the desirable features are to some extent competing. Equity and progressivity have a cost in complexity and administrative difficulty and also may have an economic cost. While it is my judgment that these conflicts are less acute than has often been implied, as long as no one objective is pursued to extreme lengths, their existence should not be denied. Policy differences often reflect unstated opinions concerning priorities of objectives and the terms of exchange between them.

The individual income tax compares favorably with other taxes but should not be regarded as a modern single tax. The corporation income tax, estate and gift taxes, and special-benefit excises have well-established and well-deserved places in the federal revenue system. Sole reliance on the individual income tax would magnify its shortcomings, which even now are serious enough to call for remedial action.

An income tax reform that would contribute greatly to equity is more effective taxation of capital gains, accompanied by more liberal treatment of capital losses. Since capital gains are not clearly distinguishable from other income, their preferential taxation conflicts with the ability-to-pay principle and invites taxpayers to rearrange their affairs to take advantage of the low rates. The economic effects of the present provisions are partly desirable and partly undesirable and, on balance, ambiguous. The goal, in my opinion, should be full taxation of gains and full deduction of losses, with averaging or proration to avoid discrimination against investors whose gains or losses accrue over several years and with constructive realization of gains on assets transferred by gift or at death. Short of sweeping reforms, worthwhile revisions could be made by narrowing the applicability of preferential rates for capital gains. Although, in my judgment, a correction for inflation in measuring capital gains would not be appropriate at present, it would become advisable at some point if the rapid increase in the price level experienced in 1973–74 should persist.

The definition of taxable income should be rationalized by the elimination of unjustifiable exclusions and personal deductions and the addition of one or two new deductions. A little progress has been made in this direction, beginning with the Revenue Act of 1964, but much more is needed.

Several items now omitted from adjusted gross income might justifiably be included. In declining order based on both importance and feasibility of assessment, they are as follows: (1) capital gains constructively realized by transfer of property by gift or at death; (2) interest on state and local government securities; (3) one-half of old-age and disability benefits under social security and railroad retirement programs; (4) unemployment insurance benefits; (5) imputed net rent of owner-occupied dwellings; (6) employer contributions to the cost of all life, accident, health, and medical insurance for employees; (7) the part of sick pay that is excluded; and (8) policy-holders' interest income from life insurance reserves.

To define net income more accurately, the following seem desirable: (1) current deductions or amortization allowances for students —but not for their parents—for certain out-of-pocket costs of college, university, vocational, and technical education; (2) a small special deduction or earned income credit for all employed persons or for working couples only; and (3) stricter limits on the deductibility of travel and entertainment expenses by self-employed persons, together with the inclusion in taxable income of reimbursements to employees for expenses similar to those that would not be deductible by self-employed taxpayers.

Deductions for interest paid, casualty losses, property taxes, and most other taxes should, in my opinion, be restricted to items connected with the production of taxable income. However, in the interest of harmonious intergovernmental relations and the fiscal strength of the states, the personal deductions should be continued for state-local income taxes and broad sales taxes. If these revisions were made, homeowners would be allowed to deduct mortgage interest and property taxes only if imputed net rent were included in gross income for tax purposes.

Personal deductions for medical expenses and philanthropic contributions are justifiable; however, consideration should be given to restricting the deductions to expenditures or gifts exceeding routine amounts. This would involve restoring the floor for medical expenditures to a level nearer to average outlays and adopting a floor for philanthropic contributions that would make contributions deductible only to the extent that they exceeded a certain percentage of income. The ceiling on the deduction for contributions could appropriately be removed, provided the treatment of gifts of appreciated property and other gifts were equalized.

These revisions would broaden the tax base, but they do not go as far as proposals by several tax specialists. Experts have rightly sounded the alarm about the erosion of the tax base and have stimulated discussion and a little legislative action to restore items to the base. Continued attention to these problems is desirable. While exclusions and personal deductions should always be viewed skeptically, a number of them, in my judgment, satisfactorily serve valid social purposes. Certain exclusions, though questionable, should be left undisturbed because it would be too costly or inconvenient to end them. New deductions should be introduced where needed to cover costs of earning income.

Reform of exclusions and deductions and full taxation of capital gains would be superior to reliance on strengthening the minimum tax on tax preference items. The latter measure lacks a clear rationale, and tinkering with it will only divert energy from tedious but more promising work on fundamentals. Broadening the tax base would greatly increase the yield of present income tax rates and would allow substantial reductions in the rates of this tax or other taxes without loss of revenue. The tax cuts could be allocated in many ways, depending on how they were divided between the individual income tax and the corporation income tax and excises and how the individual income tax reductions were distributed among brackets. If structural reforms were combined with a compensating change in individual income tax rates equal to the same fraction in all brackets, progressivity would be increased; if the objective were to preserve the existing degree of progressivity, statutory rates would have to be cut much more deeply in the upper brackets than in the lower brackets. This is true because the exclusions, deductions, and capital gains provisions diminish effective rates more in upper brackets than in lower brackets. The revisions would narrow the gap between nominal and effective rates and between marginal and average rates, with beneficial effects on public understanding and economic incentives. In my opinion, the same income tax rate schedule should apply to married couples and single persons, thus further narrowing the differences between nominal and effective rates and reducing the relative tax load of single people.

The combination of personal exemptions, the low-income allowance, and, in 1975, the personal tax credit constitutes an unnecessarily elaborate system of personal allowances. It is also unfair in that the low-income allowance can be used only by those who do not itemize their personal deductions. The three provisions could be replaced by a set of restructured personal exemptions or tax credits that would be simpler and more equitable.

Experience has repeatedly shown that it is hard to muster decisive support for tax reforms that withdraw preferential treatment from even a small minority of taxpayers. A fight must be waged merely to prevent the introduction of new preferences whenever tax legislation is before Congress. A great part of the difficulty is due to the complex nature of tax problems and the lack of understanding of them. Legislators and the public need to be better informed about taxation if reform proposals are to be more favorably received. Leadership can best come from the executive branch, which, because of its technical resources and the President's national constituency, can take a broad view of the public interest. It would be overoptimistic to expect a sweeping reform that would resolve all outstanding issues at once. But gradually, with patience and energy in the study of taxation, in the dissemination of research results, and in persuasion, income tax reforms can be achieved and a good tax made better.

APPENDIX A

Statistical Tables

Table A-1. Federal Receipts by Source, Fiscal Years 1914–75[a]

Averages for fiscal years ended June 30, in millions of dollars

Period	Total receipts	Individual income tax	Corporate income and excess profits taxes	Excises and customs[b]	Social insurance taxes[c]	Estate and gift taxes	Other receipts[d]
1914–16	738	46[e]	46[e]	582	...	...	64
1917–20	4,159	764[e]	1,645[e]	1,188	...	60	502
1921–29	4,189	953	1,187	1,299	...	108	641
1930–40	4,425	789	881	1,747	231	211	566
1941–45	29,477	9,842	9,242	4,574	1,431	482	3,905
1946–49	43,500	17,211	10,319	7,684	2,150	777	5,359
1950–59	68,244	29,306	18,541	10,207	7,371	1,022	1,798
1960–69	124,448	54,567	26,289	14,880	24,570	2,538	1,603
1970–75	228,144	102,650	34,530	19,323	62,590	4,559	4,492

Sources: 1914–33, U.S. Bureau of the Census, *Historical Statistics of the United States, 1789–1945* (1949), pp. 295–96, 304, 307–08; 1934–47, unpublished statistics compiled by the U.S. Bureau of the Budget from its records, and various issues of U.S. Department of the Treasury, *Treasury Bulletin*, and *Annual Report of the Secretary of the Treasury;* 1948–53, *The Budget of the United States Government for the Fiscal Year Ending June 30, 1959*, p. 879; 1954–63, *Statistical Appendix to Annual Report of the Secretary of the Treasury for the Fiscal Year Ended June 30, 1972*, pp. 14, 17, and *Budget . . . 1965*, p. 456; 1964–65, *Budget . . . 1974*, pp. 362–63; 1966–74, *Budget . . . 1976*, pp. 358–59; 1975 (preliminary), *Treasury Bulletin* (August 1975), pp. 3–4.

a. Total Treasury receipts, 1914–33, excluding trust account receipts for 1931–33; the data for 1934–53 are cash receipts from the public; the 1954–75 data are budget receipts. For 1934–47, the figures may not be precise because adjustments were made for major intragovernmental transactions only; additional adjustments might be appropriate for some of the items included in "other receipts."

b. Includes capital stock tax.

c. For years before 1954, employment taxes; for 1954 and later years, employment taxes and contributions, unemployment insurance, and contributions for other insurance and retirement.

d. For years before 1954, includes unemployment insurance deposits by states.

e. For fiscal years 1914–15 and 1917–24, total income and profits taxes were allocated between individuals and corporations on the basis of liabilities of the preceding calendar years (*Historical Statistics, 1789–1945*, pp. 307–08).

Table A-2. Composition of Federal Receipts, Fiscal Years 1914–75

Averages for fiscal years ended June 30, in percent

Period	Total receipts	Individual income tax	Corporate income and excess profits taxes	Excises and customs	Social insurance taxes	Estate and gift taxes	Other receipts
1914–16	100.0	6.2	6.2	78.9	...	...	8.7
1917–20	100.0	18.4	39.6	28.6	...	1.4	12.1
1921–29	100.0	22.8	28.3	31.0	...	2.6	15.3
1930–40	100.0	17.8	19.9	39.5	5.2	4.8	12.8
1941–45	100.0	33.4	31.4	15.5	4.9	1.6	13.2
1946–49	100.0	39.6	23.7	17.7	4.9	1.8	12.3
1950–59	100.0	42.9	27.2	15.0	10.8	1.5	2.6
1960–69	100.0	43.8	21.1	12.0	19.7	2.0	1.3
1970–75	100.0	45.0	15.1	8.5	27.4	2.0	2.0

Source: Derived from table A-1. Notes for that table also apply here. Figures are rounded.

Table A-3. Taxable Individual Income Tax Returns and Population Covered, 1918–70

Averages for calendar years, in thousands

Period	Number of taxable returns[a]	Number of taxpayers and dependents covered[b]	Total population[c]	Percent of total population covered
1918–20	4,381	9,983	104,727	9.5
1921–29	3,158	5,996	115,467	5.2
1930–40	2,879	5,111	127,394	4.0
1941–45	34,073	78,279	137,178	57.1
1946–49	37,884	82,969	145,902	56.9
1950–59	44,353	112,728	164,744	68.4
1960–69	54,346	148,519	192,499	77.2
1970	59,317	165,595	204,879	80.8

a. Figures for 1918–36 include taxable fiduciary returns. From U.S. Internal Revenue Service, *Statistics of Income—1970, Individual Income Tax Returns* (1972), and selected preceding volumes.

b. 1918–65, from Lawrence H. Seltzer, *The Personal Exemptions in the Income Tax* (Columbia University Press for the National Bureau of Economic Research, 1968), p. 62; 1966–70, from *Statistics of Income*, annual volumes, with allocation between taxable and nontaxable returns for 1967–69 made on basis of dollar amounts of exemptions claimed on the two categories.

c. Beginning with 1940, includes armed forces abroad and population of Alaska and Hawaii. From U.S. Bureau of the Census, *Statistical Abstract of the United States, 1973*, p. 5.

Table A-4. Personal Income Taxes as Percentages of Total Tax Revenue and Gross National Product, Selected OECD Countries, 1965, 1970, and 1972[a]

Country	Percent of total tax revenue			Percent of gross national product[b]		
	1965	*1970*	*1972*	*1965*	*1970*	*1972*
Austria	20.5	21.6	22.6	7.0	7.8	8.4
Belgium	20.8	24.7	27.4	6.3	8.5	9.6
Canada	23.0	32.4	34.5	6.3	10.8	11.6
Denmark	38.3	46.3	48.0	11.8	19.8	21.5
France	10.1	10.7	11.1	3.6	3.8	4.0
Germany	25.0	25.6	28.1	8.2	8.6	10.1
Italy	11.1	11.0	12.7	3.2	3.3	4.0
Japan	22.0	21.9	25.5	4.1	4.4	5.4
Netherlands	27.9	26.6	27.9	9.6	10.4	11.7
Norway	31.6	27.9	27.4	10.7	11.0	12.5
Sweden	44.7	45.8	42.1	16.1	18.7	18.5
Switzerland	31.2	33.2	33.5	6.6	8.1	8.1
United Kingdom	31.1	31.8	32.1	9.5	12.1	11.1
United States	30.5	35.2	33.6	7.6	10.2	9.4
Median	26.4	27.2	28.0	7.3	9.4	9.8

Source: Organisation for Economic Co-operation and Development, *Revenue Statistics of OECD Member Countries, 1965–1972* (Paris: OECD, 1975), p. 79.

a. Includes all levels of government.

b. Gross national product at market prices.

Table A-5. Personal Income, Adjusted Gross Income, and Taxable Income, Selected Years, 1918–72

Billions of dollars

Year	Personal income[a]	Adjusted gross income[b]		Taxable income[b]	
		Amount	Percent of personal income	Amount	Percent of personal income
1918	62.5[c]	50.3	80.5	8.1	13.0
1926	79.5	69.4	87.3	11.2	14.1
1939	72.8	64.7	88.9	7.2	9.9
1945	171.1	140.2	81.9	57.1	33.4
1950	227.6	202.7	89.1	84.3	37.0
1960	401.0	349.1	87.1	171.5	42.8
1970	808.3	682.8	84.5	400.7	49.6
1972	944.9	798.4	84.5	446.6	47.3

a. 1918 and 1926, Raymond W. Goldsmith's estimates, from U.S. Bureau of the Census, *Historical Statistics of the United States, Colonial Times to 1957* (1960), p. 139; 1939 and later, estimates of U.S. Department of Commerce, from *The National Income and Product Accounts of the United States, 1929–1965: Statistical Tables* (1966), table 2.1, and *Survey of Current Business*, vol. 54 (July 1974), table 2.1.

b. AGI includes estimated amounts not reported on tax returns. 1918 and 1926, from C. Harry Kahn, *Personal Deductions in the Federal Income Tax* (Princeton University Press for the National Bureau of Economic Research, 1960), p. 18; AGI, 1939 and 1945, is also from Kahn (pp. 18, 194), but taxable income for these years is from Joseph A. Pechman, *Federal Tax Policy*, rev. ed. (Brookings Institution, 1971), p. 276; 1950 and later, estimates of the Department of Commerce, from John C. Hinrichs, "The Relationship Between Personal Income and Taxable Income," *Survey of Current Business*, vol. 55 (February 1975), p. 34. The income of taxable fiduciaries is included for 1918 and 1926.

c. Average of 1917–21.

Table A-6. **Derivation of Adjusted Gross Income from Personal Income, 1970**[a]

Billions of dollars

Item	Amount
Personal income	**808.3**
Deduct items included in personal income but not in AGI	**173.2**
Transfer payments	71.4[b]
Selected government programs[c]	57.4
Other, net	14.0[d]
Other labor income	29.9[e]
Employer contributions to private retirement plans[f]	12.6
Employer contributions to life, accident, and health insurance plans	12.3
Other, net	5.0[d]
Imputed income	44.9
Net rent, owner-occupied nonfarm dwellings	13.9
Interest on life insurance policy reserves	5.1
Other imputed interest	21.9
Farm produced and consumed food and fuel	0.7
Food, lodging, and clothing furnished to employees	3.0
Adjustment for discrepancy	0.3
Miscellaneous items	21.0
Excludable sick pay	0.8
Excluded dividends	1.2
Tax-exempt interest, state-local debt	1.7[g]
Tax-exempt military pay and allowances	4.5
Excluded business expenses	5.3
Property income of nonprofit institutions and property income retained by fiduciaries	6.5
Other, net	1.0[d]
Differences in accounting treatment	6.0[h]
Add items included in AGI but not in personal income	**47.7**
Personal contributions for social insurance	28.0
Net capital gains	9.0
Other	10.7[d]
Equals adjusted gross income	**682.8**

Sources: Derived from worksheets, Bureau of Economic Analysis (BEA), U.S. Department of Commerce; *Survey of Current Business*, vol. 53 (July 1973); and text and tables, chapter 6 above. See also Hinrichs, "Relationship Between Personal Income and Taxable Income."

a. Compared with the basic source—the BEA worksheets—this table gives more detail for items under transfer payments, other labor income, and imputed income, but less detail for miscellaneous items and differences in accounting treatment.

b. Does not include military retirement pay.

c. Total of government transfer payments from table 6-1 above for benefits under (1) public assistance, (2) old-age, survivors, disability, and health insurance, (3) railroad retirement, (4) veterans' retirement, disability, and survivor programs, and (5) unemployment insurance.

d. Residual.

e. Does not include fees and military reserve pay.

f. See table 6-3 above.

g. My estimate from table 6-7 above; differs considerably from BEA figure; may include some income covered in property income of nonprofit institutions and fiduciaries.

h. The major items are the excess of tax depreciation over BEA depreciation; gain on sale of livestock, timber, and real estate; excess of interest accrued over interest paid on U.S. savings bonds; and the inventory valuation adjustment for nonfarm noncorporate business (a negative item).

Table A-7. Difference between Adjusted Gross Income and Taxable Income, 1939, 1960, and 1970

Billions of dollars

Item	1939	1960	1970
Adjusted gross income (AGI)	64.7	349.1	682.8
Deduct: AGI not reported on returns	⎫ 47.2	33.6	51.1
AGI on nontaxable returns	⎭	18.3	21.4
Equals: AGI on taxable returns	17.5	297.2	610.3
Deduct: Personal deductions[a]	1.7	44.5	102.6
Personal exemptions[a]	6.6	81.2	107.0
Earned income credit[a]	0.9	. . .	. . .
Equals: Taxable income[a]	8.3[b]	171.5	400.7

Sources: For 1939, Kahn, *Personal Deductions in the Federal Income Tax*, p. 18; includes taxable fiduciaries. For 1960 and 1970, Hinrichs, "Relationship Between Personal Income and Taxable Income," p. 34.
a. On taxable returns.
b. Pechman's estimate, which is used in table A-5, is $7.2 billion. See *Federal Tax Policy*, p. 276.

Table A-8. Percentage of Individual Income Tax Returns with Selected Deductions, by Adjusted Gross Income Class, Taxable Returns with Itemized Deductions, 1970

AGI class (thousands of dollars)	Interest paid	Medical expenses	Contributions	Taxes paid
Under 2[a]	28.3	79.7	83.5	90.5
2–3	50.9	79.7	87.6	97.1
3–5	60.4	82.3	90.3	98.7
5–10	81.9	79.2	93.8	99.3
10–25	89.5	75.5	97.2	99.8
25–50	81.9	73.6	98.3	99.9
50–100	78.1	68.4	98.5	99.8
100–500	75.4	64.7	98.4	99.8
500 and over	77.8	56.5	98.8	99.9
All classes	83.4	77.2	95.4	99.5

Source: Derived from *Statistics of Income—1970, Individual Income Tax Returns*, p. 120.
a. Statistics shown relate to returns with AGI above $1,000; returns with AGI under $1,000 are omitted here because of high sampling variability but are included in the totals.

Table A-9. Selected Deductions as Percent of Adjusted Gross Income, by Adjusted Gross Income Class, Taxable Individual Income Tax Returns with Itemized Deductions, 1970

AGI class (thousands of dollars)	Total itemized deductions	Interest paid	Medical expenses	Contributions	Taxes paid	Other itemized deductions
Under 2[a]	37.1	1.5	15.2	6.1	11.1	2.7
2–3	34.1	4.8	9.6	5.4	10.7	3.5
3–5	26.8	4.1	7.1	4.3	8.2	3.0
5–10	22.1	5.8	3.8	3.0	7.1	2.4
10–25	18.0	5.3	1.7	2.4	6.9	1.6
25–50	16.5	4.2	1.0	2.6	7.1	1.5
50–100	16.6	4.0	0.7	3.3	7.0	1.7
100–500	20.9	4.9	0.5	5.7	7.3	2.5
500 and over	27.1	5.1	0.1	13.3	5.9	2.7
All classes	19.0	5.2	2.1	2.8	7.0	1.8

Source: Same as table A-8.

a. Statistics shown relate to returns with AGI above $1,000; returns with AGI under $1,000 are omitted here because of high sampling variability but are included in the totals.

Table A-10. Individual Income Tax Rate Schedules, Selected Calendar Years, 1944–74
Percent

Taxable income[a] (thousands of dollars)	1944–45	1946–47[b]	1948–49[b]	1952–53	1954–63	1965–74[c]
Under 0.5						14
0.5–1.0	23	19.0	16.6	22.2	20	15
1.0–1.5						16
1.5–2.0						17
2.0–4.0	25	20.9	19.4	24.6	22	19
4.0–6.0	29	24.7	22.9	29.0	26	22
6.0–8.0	33	28.5	26.4	34.0	30	25
8.0–10.0	37	32.3	29.9	38.0	34	28
10.0–12.0	41	36.1	33.4	42.0	38	32
12.0–14.0	46	40.8	37.8	48.0	43	36
14.0–16.0	50	44.6	41.4	53.0	47	39
16.0–18.0	53	47.5	44.0	56.0	50	42
18.0–20.0	56	50.4	46.6	59.0	53	45
20.0–22.0	59	53.2	49.3	62.0	56	48
22.0–26.0	62	56.0	51.9	66.0	59	50
26.0–32.0	65	58.9	54.6	67.0	62	53
32.0–38.0	68	61.8	57.2	68.0	65	55
38.0–44.0	72	65.6	60.7	72.0	69	58
44.0–50.0	75	68.4	63.4	75.0	72	60
50.0–60.0	78	71.2	66.0	77.0	75	62
60.0–70.0	81	74.1	68.6	80.0	78	64
70.0–80.0	84	77.0	71.3	83.0	81	66
80.0–90.0	87	79.8	73.9	85.0	84	68
90.0–100.0	90	82.6	76.6	88.0	87	69
100.0–136.7	92	84.6	78.3	90.0	89	70
136.7–150.0			80.3			
150.0–200.0	93	85.5	81.2	91.0	90	70
200.0 and over[d]	94	86.4	82.1	92.0	91	70

Sources: Compiled from *The Federal Tax System: Facts and Problems, 1964*, Materials Assembled by the Committee Staff for the Joint Economic Committee, 88 Cong. 2 sess. (1964), p. 234; public laws; and instructions accompanying tax return forms.

a. Before 1954, net income subject to surtax. For 1948 and later years, the rate brackets for husbands and wives filing joint returns have been twice as wide as those shown, which apply to separate returns of husbands and wives and, until 1971, to single persons. For 1952 and later years, a separate schedule applies to unmarried heads of households, providing approximately one-half the benefits of income splitting by husbands and wives. For 1971 and later years, a separate schedule applies to single persons, in order to limit their tax to an amount not more than 20 percent above the tax of married couples with the same taxable income.

b. After reductions from tentative tax.

c. In addition, a surcharge was applied to tax liability as follows: 7.5 percent in 1968, 10.0 percent in 1969, and 2.5 percent in 1970; brackets below $2,000 were partially exempt. Earned income was subject to a maximum marginal rate of 60 percent in 1971 and 50 percent thereafter. For 1974, a rebate of 10 percent of the tax was allowed, subject to (1) a minimum of the full tax or $100 and (2) a maximum of $200, phased down to $100 for returns with adjusted gross income between $20,000 and $30,000. For married persons filing separate returns, the minimum and maximum rebates were $50 and $100, respectively.

d. Subject to maximum effective rate limitations as follows: 1944–45, 90 percent; 1946–47, 85.5 percent; 1948–49, 77 percent; 1952–53, 88 percent; 1954–63, 87 percent.

Table A-11. Influence of Various Provisions on Effective Rates of the Individual Income Tax, by Total Income Class[a]

Percent of total income

Total income class (thousands of dollars)	Nominal tax[b]	Reduction resulting from						Actual tax[h]
		Personal exemptions	Deductions[c]	Preference items[d]	Capital gains[e]	Maximum tax[f]	Income splitting[g]	
Under 1	14.2	13.4	0.8	*	*	*	*	*
1–2	15.1	9.9	5.1	*	*	*	*	*
2–3	16.2	9.0	5.8	*	*	*	*	1.4
3–4	17.0	8.2	5.3	*	*	*	0.1	3.4
4–5	17.8	7.5	5.0	*	0.1	*	0.2	5.0
5–6	18.6	7.1	4.9	*	0.1	*	0.2	6.3
6–7	19.3	7.0	4.6	*	0.1	*	0.4	7.2
7–8	20.0	7.0	4.4	*	0.1	*	0.6	7.9
8–9	20.8	7.0	4.4	*	0.1	*	0.7	8.6
9–10	21.6	6.8	4.4	*	0.1	*	0.9	9.3
10–15	23.9	6.8	5.1	*	0.1	*	1.6	10.3
15–20	28.0	6.4	6.1	*	0.2	*	2.9	12.4
20–25	32.0	5.9	7.1	*	0.5	*	4.4	14.2
25–50	38.4	4.7	8.3	*	1.3	*	6.6	17.4
50–100	49.0	2.9	9.8	0.2	3.3	0.4	7.2	25.2
100–150	57.0	1.7	12.0	0.7	6.4	0.8	5.9	29.6
150–200	60.6	1.1	12.6	1.5	9.5	0.8	4.9	30.2
200–500	63.8	0.7	13.4	1.7	13.9	0.6	3.2	30.4
500–1,000	66.9	0.3	13.0	2.0	19.1	0.4	1.4	30.7
1,000 and over	67.5	0.1	11.4	1.2	23.0	0.1	0.4	31.4
All classes	26.9	6.4	6.0	0.1	0.8	*	2.3	11.4

Source: Derived from the Brookings 1970 Tax File (sample of about 95,000 returns). Rates and other provisions are those in effect in 1973.

* Less than 0.05.

a. Total income is the sum of adjusted gross income, the excluded portion of net realized capital gains and other preference items as defined by the Tax Reform Act of 1969, excludable sick pay, excludable dividends, and moving expenses.

b. Rate schedule for married persons filing separate returns applied to total income.

c. Standard deduction (including low-income allowance), itemized deductions, plus excluded dividends, sick pay, and moving expenses.

d. Preference items other than excluded net long-term capital gains, as estimated by Joseph A. Pechman and Benjamin A. Okner. Calculations show the difference between the minimum tax on these items and the tax at the regular rates that would accrue if they were fully included in income.

e. Combined effect of the exclusion and the alternative tax.

f. Maximum marginal rate of 50 percent on earned taxable income.

g. Includes effects of income splitting between husbands and wives and the special rate schedules for single persons and heads of households.

h. Actual tax after foreign tax credit and retirement income credit, not shown separately.

Table A-12. Increase in Federal Individual Income Tax Liabilities If Certain Exclusions and Deductions Were Ended, Official Estimates, 1970, 1971, and 1974[a]

Millions of dollars

Exclusion or deduction	1970	1971	1974
Exclusions			
Public assistance benefits	50	65	75
Veterans' benefits	650	700	800
Unemployment insurance benefits	400	800	1,050
Old-age retirement benefits	2,225[b]	...	2,690[c]
Disability insurance benefits	130	155	235
Workmen's compensation	210	320	520
Excludable sick pay	105	120	255
Pension contributions and earnings			
Plans for employees	3,075	3,650	4,790
Plans for self-employed	175	250	230
Premiums on group term life insurance for employees	440	500	680
Premiums and benefits, medical insurance for employees	1,450	2,000	2,940
Meals and lodging for employees	170	170	175
Benefits and allowances to armed forces personnel	500	650	650
Scholarships and fellowships	60	110	195
Interest on life insurance policy reserves	1,050	1,100	1,420
Interest on state and local bonds	...	800	1,060
Excludable dividends	280	300	320
Deductions			
Interest paid			
Mortgages on owner-occupied dwellings	2,800	2,400	4,870
Consumer debt	1,700	1,800	2,435
Medical expenses	1,700	1,900	2,125
Child and dependent care expenses	25	30	230
Casualty losses	80	165	255
Charitable contributions	3,750	3,475	4,175
Nonbusiness taxes			
Property taxes on owner-occupied dwellings	2,900	2,700	4,060
Other	5,600	5,600	7,820

Sources: 1970–71, Treasury Department estimates, from *General Tax Reform*, Panel Discussions before the House Committee on Ways and Means, 93 Cong. 1 sess. (1973), pt. 1, pp. 29–30; 1974, *Special Analyses, Budget of the United States Government, Fiscal Year 1976*, pp. 108–09.

a. Estimates are made on an individual basis for each item on the assumption that the exclusion or deduction of this item alone would be ended, without change in other provisions of the tax law. If two or more changes were made simultaneously, the aggregate revenue effect would frequently not equal the sum of the revenue effects of the separate items. Hence the items are not additive.

b. Old-age and survivors insurance (OASI) benefits, my estimate derived from the source.

c. OASI benefits for the aged and railroad retirement benefits.

Table A-13. Distribution of Increase in Federal Individual Income Tax Liabilities If Certain Exclusions and Deductions Were Ended, by Adjusted Gross Income Class, 1971[a]

Percent

Exclusion or deduction	AGI class (thousands of dollars)		
	0–7	7–15	15 and over
Exclusions			
Public assistance benefits	92	8	*
Veterans' benefits	34	50	16
Unemployment insurance benefits	36	52	12
Old-age retirement benefits[b]	61	26	14
Disability insurance benefits	64	26	10
Workmen's compensation	26	48	26
Excludable sick pay	26	42	32
Pension contributions and earnings			
Plans for employees	12	42	47
Plans for self-employed	7	14	79
Premiums on group term life insurance for employees	11	42	47
Premiums and benefits, medical insurance for employees	12	42	46
Meals and lodging for employees	22	41	36
Benefits and allowances to armed forces personnel	48	45	7
Scholarships and fellowships	54	34	12
Interest on life insurance policy reserves	6	26	68
Interest on state and local bonds	1	2	98
Excludable dividends	12	28	60
Deductions			
Interest paid			
Mortgages on owner-occupied dwellings	4	42	54
Consumer debt	6	34	60
Medical expenses	16	42	42
Child and dependent care expenses	67	27	7
Casualty losses	9	42	48
Charitable contributions	4	22	74
Nonbusiness taxes			
Property taxes on owner-occupied dwellings	5	34	62
Other	3	20	77

Source: Derived from *General Tax Reform*, Panel Discussions, pt. 1, pp. 31–34.

* Negligible.

a. U.S. Department of the Treasury estimates. The estimates are made on an individual basis for each item on the assumption that the exclusion or deduction of this item alone would be ended, without change in other provisions of the tax law.

b. Distribution of the combined effect of the additional exemption for the aged, the retirement income credit, and the exclusion of old-age, survivors, and disability insurance benefits for the aged.

Notes on Effects of Taxes on Income, Consumption, and Wealth

THIS APPENDIX supplements chapter 3 with notes on a few major points that are relevant to a comparison of the economic effects of taxes on income, consumption, and wealth.

Equal-Yield Rates of Income and Expenditure Tax

For equal-yield taxes,

$$t_e C = t_y Y,$$

where t_e is the expenditure tax rate, C is personal consumption when the expenditure tax is employed, t_y is the income tax rate, and Y is personal income. C may be stated as

$$C = c(Y - t_e C),$$

where c is the fraction of income, net of tax, which is consumed with the expenditure tax in effect. Since equal yields are assumed, $t_y Y$ may be substituted for $t_e C$ in the consumption equation:

$$C = c(Y - t_y Y) = c(1 - t_y)Y.$$

When the last expression is substituted for C in the first equation, the requirement for equal yields becomes

$$t_e[c(1 - t_y)Y] = t_y Y,$$

which reduces to

$$t_e = t_y/[c(1 - t_y)].$$

When there is zero saving, $c = 1$ and equal-yield tax rates are

$$t_e = t_y/(1 - t_y).^1$$

Reward for Saving-and-Investing under Income Tax and Expenditure Tax

Under the income tax, when one saves an amount, S, he gives up current consumption of that amount and by investing at the market rate of interest, r, can obtain a gross yield of rS, which is reduced by the tax to $(1 - t_y)rS$. In relation to the amount of consumption forgone, the rate of net yield is $(1 - t_y)r$.

Under the expenditure tax, when one saves S he also avoids (or postpones) tax; $S = C' + t_eC' = C'(1 + t_e)$, where C' is the current consumption forgone and t_eC' the tax avoided or postponed. $C' = S/(1 + t_e)$. The saver can obtain an annual yield of rS, from which he can consume $rS/(1 + t_e)$. In relation to the amount of consumption earlier forgone, the additional annual consumption is

$$\frac{rS/(1 + t_e)}{S/(1 + t_e)} = r.$$

Thus the reward for saving-and-investing, in relation to the amount of consumption forgone, is equal to the market rate of interest under the expenditure tax as it would be in the absence of taxation.[2]

Response of Saving to Changes in the Rate of Return

The response of saving to tax-caused changes in the rate of return obtained from real or financial investment is usually considered to be a matter of the interest elasticity of saving. Economists have long recognized that an increase in the market rate of interest may cause some individuals to save more in order to take advantage of the higher yield and others to save less because a smaller capital sum will satisfy their demands for retirement income and family security. The earlier tendency was to argue that an increase in saving was the usual response and that saving had positive interest elasticity, but there followed a period during which lead-

1. The foregoing is based on a paper by A. R. Prest, "The Expenditure Tax and Saving," *Economic Journal,* vol. 69 (September 1959), pp. 483–89. See also Prest's book, *Public Finance in Theory and Practice,* 5th ed. (London: Weidenfeld and Nicolson, and English Language Society, 1974), pp. 48, 83–89.

2. This is the conclusion reached by Nicholas Kaldor, *An Expenditure Tax* (London: Allen and Unwin, 1955), pp. 81–87, and Prest, "Expenditure Tax and Saving," pp. 483–84.

ing theorists took an agnostic position on the subject.[3] Later, attempts
were made to reestablish the presumption that the interest elasticity of
saving is positive.[4] Although I do not find the arguments wholly persuasive
with respect to changes in the market rate of interest, I now think that
when applied to the tax question they establish a reasonable presumption
that the propensity to save will be greater under an expenditure tax than
under an equal-yield income tax.

Hicks analyzes the effect of a change in the market rate of interest in
the same way as a change in a commodity price, showing that it produces
a substitution effect and an income effect (*Value and Capital,* pp. 232–35).
The substitution effect of an increase in the interest rate is to lower the
prices of future purchases relative to current purchases and hence is in the
direction of increased saving. The income effect makes persons who plan
to be lenders in the present and near future better off and will tend to
induce them to spend more and save less. For lenders as a group, it is uncertain whether the substitution effect or the income effect will dominate.
For borrowers, the income effect is the opposite of that for lenders. Hicks
believes that, in general, the positive and negative income effects will
cancel out and that the substitution effect will dominate. Bailey's analysis
of an arbitrary change in the interest rate with constant real resources is
similar ("Saving and the Rate of Interest," p. 280). My principal reserva-
tion about these analyses is that I do not think positive and negative income effects can be expected to cancel out in any period in which the
government and the central bank are significant net borrowers or lenders
because, in my judgment, these institutions do not respond to the income
effect in the same way as households.

Hicks' analysis does not indicate the effect on the average propensity to
save of an increase or decrease in total taxation because, if taxpayers
ignore the benefits from government expenditures, they will all experience
a negative income effect when taxes rise and a positive income effect
when taxes fall. But the analysis can be applied to the replacement of one
tax by another. When an income tax is replaced by an equal-yield expenditure tax, there is a redistribution of current and expected after-tax

3. For selected citations, see my paper "Taxation of Saving and Consumption
in Underdeveloped Countries," *National Tax Journal,* vol. 14 (December 1961),
p. 307.

4. J. R. Hicks, *Value and Capital: An Inquiry into Some Fundamental Principles
of Economic Theory* (Oxford: Clarendon Press, 1939), pp. 232–35; Martin J. Bailey,
"Saving and the Rate of Interest," *Journal of Political Economy,* vol. 65 (August
1957), pp. 279–305; and D. V. T. Bear, "The Relationship of Saving to the Rate of
Interest, Real Income, and Expected Future Prices," *Review of Economics and
Statistics,* vol. 43 (February 1961), pp. 27–35. For a critical comment on Bailey's
paper by James M. Buchanan and Bailey's reply, see *Journal of Political Economy,*
vol. 67 (February 1959), pp. 79–86.

income within the household sector, households with below-average ratios of consumption to income becoming better off and those with above-average ratios becoming worse off. For the first group the income and substitution effects work in opposite directions, just as they do for an increase in the market rate of interest, but the second group suffers a loss of after-tax income equal to the gain of the first group and the income effects will cancel out if the two groups have similar psychologies. Allowance for possible differences between the attitudes of the two groups seems more likely to reinforce than to weaken the presumption that the substitution effects will dominate.

The conclusion is not vitiated by provisions for the deduction of interest paid from taxable income under the income tax and the exclusion of interest payments on consumer debt from taxable consumption under the expenditure tax. An income tax that allows the deduction is more favorable to dissaving through consumer borrowing than a tax that does not allow it; in this sense the deduction accentuates the substitution effect without eliminating the income effect. Under the expenditure tax, the exclusion of interest paid somewhat reduces the negative income effect on borrowers but does not eliminate it. The income effect would persist even if consumer debt could be contracted without payment of interest; fundamentally the negative income effect arises out of a redistribution of taxation between persons with different propensities to consume.[5]

Rate of Return on Personal Wealth

On their net worth, exclusive of consumer durables, nonfarm households obtained the following estimated rates of return (in percent):

1929	5.0
1946–58 (average)	3.6

For purposes of these calculations, property income is represented by the sum of rental income of persons, dividends, and personal interest.[6] The net worth estimates are from a study by Raymond W. Goldsmith, Robert E. Lipsey, and Morris Mendelson.[7] Both the income and asset statistics

5. Michael A. Willemsen's argument on this point seems to me incorrect ("The Effect Upon the Rate of Private Savings of a Change from a Personal Income Tax to a Personal Expenditure Tax," *National Tax Journal*, vol. 14 [March 1961], pp. 101–02), although his paper is a good treatment of the general subject.

6. Personal income components as estimated by the Bureau of Economic Analysis, U.S. Department of Commerce, from *Economic Report of the President, February 1975*, p. 271.

7. *Studies in the National Balance Sheet of the United States* (Princeton University Press for the National Bureau of Economic Research, 1963), vol. 2, pp. 78, 118–19.

include owner-occupied houses and exclude unincorporated business enterprises.

On net financial assets, the estimated average rate of return (in percent) was:

1950–59	4.0
1960–69	4.5
1970	5.4

The asset statistics are estimates for households, personal trust funds, and nonprofit institutions. Net financial assets are total financial assets minus liabilities other than home mortgages. The estimates are derived from the flow of funds accounts.[8] The return on net financial assets consists of dividends and personal interest (personal income components).

While the sectors covered in the two sets of estimates cited above are not identical, a comparison of net financial assets shows that the average amount of these assets in 1946–58 derived from the flow of funds accounts exceeds that derived from Goldsmith, Lipsey, and Mendelson by less than 2 percent.

8. Board of Governors of the Federal Reserve System, "Flow of Funds Accounts, 1945–1972" (1973; processed), pp. 83–84.

Distribution of Taxes by Income Groups and Impact of Taxation on Saving

THE ESTIMATES of tax distribution and of the impact of taxation on saving presented in chapter 4 are based on data for 1960–62 from three sources. The statistics and the estimation methods are described in this appendix, and these are briefly compared with those used in the first edition of this book.

Basic Statistics

The basic data on money income, consumption, and saving are from the Survey of Consumer Expenditures, 1960–61 (SCE). They cover a sample of consumers living in urban and rural areas throughout the United States and were collected jointly by the U.S. Departments of Labor and Agriculture. The statistics were published by the Bureau of Labor Statistics (BLS) in February 1965 in its Report 237-93, *Consumer Expenditures and Income, Total United States, Urban and Rural, 1960–61.*

The SCE data relate to families and single consumers—here called "consumer units"—which consist of groups of people "usually living together who pooled their income and drew from a common fund for their major items of expense" and of persons "living alone or in a household with others" who were financially independent and whose income and expenditures were not pooled (*Consumer Expenditures*, page 5). Money income includes earnings from employment and self-employment; investment income; social security benefits, pensions, and miscellaneous government payments; small gifts of cash; regular contributions for support; and public assistance. The value of home-produced food is not included in income or expenditures. Consumption includes durable goods except purchases of houses. The definition of saving is discussed below.

The data on net worth, which are for December 31, 1962, are from the Survey of Financial Characteristics of Consumers (SFCC) conducted by the Board of Governors of the Federal Reserve System in collaboration with the U.S. Bureau of the Census. The sample differed from that for other consumer surveys in being designed to include a much higher proportion of wealthy persons than are found in the total population. Great detail was obtained on assets and debts. The statistics used here were published by the Board of Governors in August 1966 in *Survey of Financial Characteristics of Consumers* by Dorothy S. Projector and Gertrude S. Weiss.

Net worth in the SFCC consists of the assets covered by the survey less all debts. The assets comprise dwellings, automobiles, farm and nonfarm business, checking and savings accounts, U.S. savings bonds, other securities, investment real estate, mortgage assets, and property held in trust. Items not included comprise equity in life insurance, annuities, and retirement funds; household furnishings and equipment; and works of art. In my usage, net worth is equivalent to net wealth (or simply wealth). In the SFCC, wealth is defined as the value of assets covered less debts secured by these assets; it exceeds net worth by the amount of unsecured debts and debts secured by life insurance and other assets not covered by the survey. The net worth statistics used here are the SFCC data for December 31, 1962, classified by money income in 1962.

The statistics of federal individual income tax liability are averages of estimates for 1960 and 1961 made by the Office of Business Economics, U.S. Department of Commerce, and published in *Survey of Current Business,* April 1964. The estimated tax liability on capital gains is excluded. The OBE estimates are for consumer units classified by family personal income before taxes. This income concept is broader than money income in that it includes the imputed rental value of owner-occupied dwellings, the value of farm-produced-and-consumed food and fuel, and other imputed income.

Distribution and Effective Tax Rates

The estimated distribution of money income, consumption expenditures, net worth, and federal individual income tax liability, for all consumer units classified by money income deciles, is shown in table C-1. In drawing up the estimates underlying the table, statistics for income classes were converted to deciles by interpolations which were linear in the logarithms of cumulative distributions of money amounts and numbers of units. Aggregates of money income, consumption, and net worth were computed by multiplying average amounts by numbers of units.

Elements of inaccuracy and noncomparability result from bringing together statistics from different sources. While the money income concepts of the SCE and the SFCC appear to be the same, the SCE statistics are reported for classes representing income after personal taxes and the SFCC statistics are classified by income before taxes. The OBE estimates are also reported by income before taxes but for a broader income concept. The combination of estimates given in table C-1 is based on the assumption that the rank order of consumer units is the same for money income before taxes, money income after taxes, and family personal income before taxes. This means that the same units would make up each decile regardless of which of the three income measures was used as the basis of classification. The method, however, does not require the conversion of income class limits from one basis to another. As noted above, the statistics of net worth are for the end of 1962 and are classified by income in 1962, whereas the other items are averages for 1960–61.

Table C-1. Distribution of Money Income, Consumption, and Federal Individual Income Tax, 1960–61, and Net Worth, 1962, by Money Income Decile[a]

Percent

Income decile	*Money income*	*Consumption*	*Net worth*	*Federal individual income tax*
Lowest	1.6	3.0	⎫	⎫
2d	3.6	4.6	⎬ 10.9	⎬ 1.5
3d	5.1	6.2	⎭	2.6
4th	6.6	7.7	4.6	3.7
5th	8.1	8.9	5.1	5.2
6th	9.5	10.1	6.0	6.9
7th	11.1	11.4	6.6	8.7
8th	12.9	12.8	8.8	10.6
9th	15.6	14.8	11.3	14.7
Highest	25.9	20.5	46.7	46.0
Total	100.0	100.0	100.0	100.0

Sources: For sources and derivation, see text. Figures are rounded.

a. Money income and consumption data are from surveys of rural nonfarm and farm families in 1961 and surveys of urban families in both 1960 and 1961. The data were combined with a system of weights to obtain national averages for 1960–61. Net worth is as of December 31, 1962. Tax liabilities (tax on capital gains is excluded) are averages of 1960 and 1961 data.

The effective tax rates shown in table C-2 were computed from the money amounts underlying table C-1. The total amounts of the consumption tax and the wealth tax are equal to the average of the estimated aggregate federal individual income tax liabilities (excluding the tax on capital gains) of 1960 and 1961—$39.5 billion.

Saving Ratios

Two estimates of the marginal propensity to save, by money income deciles, are given in table C-3. Both are derived from the SCE. To clarify their meaning and derivation, it is helpful to set down some definitions and relationships.

Let

Y = money income;

T = personal taxes, composed of federal, state, and local income taxes, poll taxes, and personal property taxes;

OR = other receipts, composed of inheritances and occasional large gifts of money less taxes, legal fees, and other expenses required to obtain the receipts, and net receipts from the lump-sum settlement of fire and accident insurance policies; gifts and inheritances in the form of real estate, securities, and property other than money are not included unless sold during the year;

Table C-2. Effective Rates of Alternative Taxes on Consumption and Wealth and of the Federal Individual Income Tax, by Money Income Decile, 1960–62

Percent of money income

Income decile	Flat-rate consumption tax	Proportional wealth tax	Federal individual income tax
Lowest	21.4	⎫	⎫
2d	14.6	⎬ 12.1	⎬ 3.4
3d	13.9	⎭	5.7
4th	13.3	8.0	6.5
5th	12.5	7.2	7.3
6th	12.1	7.2	8.3
7th	11.7	6.8	8.9
8th	11.3	7.8	9.4
9th	10.8	8.3	10.8
Highest	9.0	20.6	20.3
Total	11.4	11.4	11.4

Source: Derived from data underlying the distributions shown in table C-1.

Table C-3. Two Estimates of Marginal Propensity to Save, by Money Income Decile, All Consumer Units, 1960–61

Fraction of disposable receipts

Income decile	Estimate 1[a]			Estimate 2[a]
	MPC	*MRG$_c$*	*MPS$_1$*	*MPS$_2$*
Lowest	.836	.053	.120	.134
2d	.813	.053	.144	.134
3d	.796	.053	.162	.134
4th	.779	.053	.180	.143
5th	.762	.053	.198	.143
6th	.746	.053	.214	.166
7th	.728	.053	.233	.184
8th	.708	.074	.240	.240
9th	.678	.097	.256	.277
Highest	.561	.181	.337	.445

Sources: Both estimates are based on U.S. Bureau of Labor Statistics, *Consumer Expenditures and Income, Total United States, Urban and Rural, 1960–61*, Report 237-93 (1965); for details, see the text.

a. Symbols: *MPC*, marginal propensity to consume with respect to disposable receipts; *MRG$_c$*, marginal ratio of *gifts* and contributions to consumption; *MPS*, marginal propensity to save with respect to disposable receipts; the subscripts 1 and 2 identify the two estimates.

DR = disposable receipts, defined as $Y - T + OR;$

C = consumption expenditures;

G = gifts and contributions, made up of gifts to persons outside the family and contributions to welfare, religious, educational, and other organizations;

PI = personal insurance, composed of payments or deductions from pay for life, endowment, and annuity insurance, social security, and retirement plans; employers' contributions are not included;

NA = increase in assets minus liabilities;

B = account balancing difference; that is, reported total receipts minus reported total disbursements.

By definition,

$$Y - T + OR = DR = C + G + PI + NA + B.$$

I have chosen to define saving (S) as

$$S = DR - C - G = PI + NA + B.$$

The inclusion of the whole of *PI* in *S* results in some overstatement, since insurance premiums include elements for loading costs and current insurance protection as well as saving. Also, the inclusion of social security contributions in personal saving is debatable. The proper treatment of *B* is not obvious. This item is negative, indicating an excess of reported disbursements over reported receipts, in each of the ten income classes shown in the BLS report. For the whole sample, B equals only 3 percent of DR, but it amounts to 60 percent of S. An alternative approach would have been to allocate B among the "uses" of DR; that is, among C, G, PI, and NA. It seems plausible to suppose, however, that NA is less accurately reported than the other items. If this is so, my treatment, which combines NA and B, is preferable.

The marginal propensity to save (MPS) is measured with respect to DR, rather than disposable income ($Y - T$). An alternative procedure would have been to subtract OR from both receipts and disbursements. For the whole sample, OR equals only 1 percent of DR but 26 percent of S.

The first estimate of the marginal propensity to save (MPS_1) is based on an estimate of the long-run consumption function made by Husby.[1] Husby's equation (stated with my symbols) is

$$C = 599 + 0.8538 \, DR - 0.000009033 \, DR^2.$$

From this equation MPC was computed for the mean DR of each income decile; the results are reported in table C-3. The marginal ratio of gifts and contributions to consumption (MRG_c) was estimated by a graphic method from charts based on data from the SCE; the fit was judged to be linear in the lower deciles and approximately semilogarithmic for the upper deciles. The results appear in table C-3. The first estimate of the marginal propensity to save was then derived from the following relationship:

$$MPS_1 = (1 - MPC) - (MPC \times MRG_c).$$

The second estimate of the marginal propensity to save was derived graphically from figure C-1 showing the relationship between S and DR. The curve was smoothed over the lower range of DR, implying a constant MPS over the first three deciles.

Two sets of estimates of the impact of alternative taxes on personal saving were derived by applying MPS_1 and MPS_2 to the data underlying the distributions in table C-1. The estimated percentages of the yield coming from potential personal saving are as follows:

	Estimate 1	Estimate 2
Federal individual income tax	27.7	31.7
Proportional income tax	24.8	26.0
Flat-rate consumption tax	23.8	24.3
Flat-rate wealth tax	27.0	31.1

Owing to the definition of S, personal saving includes not only private

1. Ralph D. Husby, "A Nonlinear Consumption Function Estimated from Time-Series and Cross-Section Data," *Review of Economics and Statistics*, vol. 53 (February 1971), pp. 76–79.

Figure C-1. Disposable Receipts and Saving, All Consumer Units, 1960–61

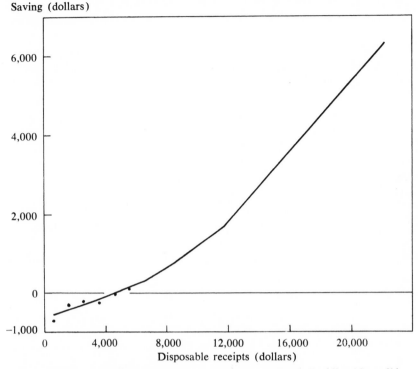

Saving (dollars)

Disposable receipts (dollars)

Source: U.S. Bureau of Labor Statistics, *Consumer Expenditures and Income, Total United States, Urban and Rural, 1960–61*, Report 237-93 (1965).

saving but employee contributions to social security. Since these contributions are fixed by law, the reduction in saving must be concentrated on the remaining parts of saving, including private insurance and retirement systems.

The estimates take account only of differences resulting from the distribution of the alternative taxes among income deciles and not of any difference as a consequence of reactions to the form of taxation or of characteristics of taxpayers other than their income (or disposable receipts). The procedure makes no distinction between a direct tax on consumption and an indirect tax on the assumption that both forms of tax would reduce real disposable receipts by the same amount, regardless of whether the tax was paid directly to the government or indirectly in the form of higher prices.

An alternative approach would be to look on a permanent tax on consumption (either a fully shifted sales tax or a direct tax on personal expenditures) as a measure that reduces the purchasing power of all money income, including both the part of income that is spent immediately and the part that is saved for future consumption. This would suggest that the levying of a consumption tax would reduce a nominal income of Y to $Y/(1 + t_c)$, where t_c is the consumption tax rate. When saving is positive, this approach will indicate a smaller real disposable income under a consumption tax than under an equal-yield income tax. Furthermore, if aggregate real consumption is an increasing function of aggregate real disposable income and saving is positive, this procedure will indicate that a consumption tax will reduce real consumption more (and saving less) than an equal-yield income tax,[2] whereas my procedure will indicate that the two forms of tax will have the same effects if they are distributed among income classes in the same proportions.

The choice between the two approaches involves theoretical issues and broader implications into which I do not wish to enter; however, it does not greatly affect estimates of the kind described here. If disposable income under the consumption tax had been measured by the alternative method (by deflating total income by an index of the price of consumer goods and services), the estimates of the impact on potential saving would have been the same for the flat-rate consumption tax and the proportional income tax.

Estimates in the First Edition

The estimates of tax distribution and impact on saving published in the first edition of this book were based on data for 1950 on money income, federal individual income tax liability, consumption expenditures, and saving from the Survey of Consumer Finances (SCF) sponsored by the Board of Governors of the Federal Reserve System and conducted by the Survey Research Center of the University of Michigan. Findings were published in the *Federal Reserve Bulletin,* August 1951 and September 1951. Additional details regarding disposable income and net saving appear in a paper by John B. Lansing and Harold Lydall.[3]

The data on net worth came indirectly from the SCF via estimates by Goldsmith.[4] The coverage of the 1949 net worth data is narrower than

2. See E. Cary Brown, "Analysis of Consumption Taxes in Terms of the Theory of Income Determination," *American Economic Review,* vol. 40 (March 1950), pp. 74–89; Challis A. Hall, Jr., *Fiscal Policy for Stable Growth: A Study in Dynamic Macroeconomics* (Holt, Rinehart and Winston, 1960), pp. 184–85.

3. "An Anglo-American Comparison of Personal Saving," *Bulletin of the Oxford University Institute of Statistics,* vol. 22 (August 1960), p. 242.

4. Raymond W. Goldsmith, Dorothy S. Brady, and Horst Mendershausen, *A Study of Saving in the United States,* vol. 3 (Princeton University Press, 1956).

that of the 1962 SFCC in that the former do not include bonds other than U.S. government issues, privately held mortgages, or personal trust funds.

The method of estimating the impact on saving in 1950 was more comparable to the graphic method that yielded MPS_2 above than to the estimates based on Husby's long-run consumption function (which yielded MPS_1). For the 1950 estimates it was necessary to extrapolate the saving curve well above the mean of the highest income class reported in the SCF—an expedient that was not required for the 1960–61 estimates.

Contribution of Additional Saving to Growth

The illustrative estimate of the contribution to the growth of potential national income of the increase in potential saving that would have resulted from applying a less progressive tax system, which is given on pages 72–73, was derived as follows. Total federal individual income tax liabilities, including the tax on capital gains but net of credits, were $880 billion in 1948–69.[5] According to my estimates, if the income tax had been replaced by a flat-rate consumption tax, potential saving would have increased (under both 1950 and 1960–61 conditions) by 6 percent of the yield, or $53 billion. Total net saving, defined as gross saving minus capital consumption allowances, was $814 billion in 1948–69.[6] The tax change, therefore, would have increased potential net saving by $53/814 = 6.5$ percent. Denison estimates that in 1948–69 net investment (conceptually equal to net saving) contributed 0.80 percentage point a year to the growth of potential national income.[7] The computed value of the contribution to the growth rate of the additional potential saving is $0.065 \times 0.80 = 0.05$ percentage point.

This estimate makes no allowance for economies of scale or the declining marginal productivity of capital. It is implicitly assumed that the tax change would not have affected corporate saving or government saving (the net surplus or deficit) and that the additional potential saving of individuals would have been immediately invested in the principal forms of capital in the same proportions as the additional capital inputs in 1948–69.

5. U.S. Bureau of the Census, *Historical Statistics of the United States, Colonial Times to 1957* (1960), p. 714; U.S. Internal Revenue Service, *Statistics of Income— 1960, Individual Income Tax Returns* (1962), p. 98, and ibid., *1970* (1972), p. 309.

6. Derived from Department of Commerce estimates, in *Economic Report of the President, February 1975*, pp. 265, 272.

7. Edward F. Denison, *Accounting for United States Economic Growth, 1929– 1969* (Brookings Institution, 1974), p. 127.

Statistics on the Size Distribution of Income

THIS APPENDIX discusses alternative concepts for the estimation of the impact of the individual income tax on the size distribution of income in 1966, historical data on the distribution of income, and limitations of income distribution statistics.

Income Concepts for 1966

As stated in the text I have used the Pechman-Okner estimates of the distribution of income and federal individual income tax liability in 1966 but have modified their income concept.[1] The basic income concept used by Pechman and Okner is "adjusted family income." This comprises (1) national income at factor costs, including employees' compensation, proprietors' income, net interest, net rental income of individuals, and corporate profits before taxes; (2) transfer payments; (3) accrued capital gains, whether realized or not; and (4) indirect business taxes that are included in net national product at market prices but not in national income at factor costs. Income received by persons who are not members of households (the institutional population and members of the armed forces living on posts) and by pension funds and nonprofit organizations is excluded.

1. Joseph A. Pechman and Benjamin A. Okner, *Who Bears the Tax Burden?* (Brookings Institution, 1974).

For my purposes I narrowed this broad income concept somewhat by excluding from adjusted family income (1) corporation income taxes; (2) employer payroll taxes and other employer contributions for social insurance; and (3) indirect business taxes in the form of sales and excise taxes, property taxes, and motor vehicle licenses. My reason for excluding these three items is given in the text.

The question may be raised whether "other labor income" should not also be excluded from net adjusted family income. This item amounted to $21.3 billion in 1966. It constitutes mainly employer contributions to private pension and welfare funds. These contributions, like employer contributions for social insurance, are a supplement to wages and salaries which is not paid directly to employees. Employer contributions to private pension and welfare funds, however, may be distinguished from contributions for social insurance on two grounds. First, the contributions to the private funds are subject to negotiation and collective bargaining and are therefore a closer substitute for wage and salary payments than are contributions for social insurance, which are fixed by law under the taxing power. Second, employees often have vested rights in private pension plans, whereas there is no comparable vesting of their rights to social insurance contributions of their employers.

The treatment of capital gains is subject to debate. Size distribution statistics derived from national income and product accounts usually have not included capital gains. I think capital gains should be taken into account in appraising income distribution and consider their inclusion in adjusted family income a desirable feature of this concept. I agree also with Pechman and Okner that including accrued gains is preferable for measurement purposes to including only realized gains, though I do not support proposals to attempt to tax capital gains on an accrual basis. Their decision to assume that accrued capital gains on corporate stock are equal to undistributed profits[2] is more questionable, in my opinion. It is true that Bailey has concluded that over long periods of time accrued capital gains on corporate stock are roughly equal to "true" retained profits.[3] This conclusion is based partly on the deductive proposition that if management invests retained profits wisely (and earns a return equal to the discount rate applied by shareholders) a dollar of retained earnings will add a dollar to the value of shares. In testing this hypothesis Bailey adjusted reported retained profits to correct for an alleged understatement of depreciation allowances and corrected accrued capital gains for

2. Ibid., p. 13.
3. Martin J. Bailey, "Capital Gains and Income Taxation," in Arnold C. Harberger and Martin J. Bailey, eds., *The Taxation of Income from Capital* (Brookings Institution, 1969), pp. 40–45.

inflation. I am skeptical of the merits of these adjustments. Even if they are accepted, there are wide year-to-year differences between retained profits and accrued gains. This is notably true in 1966, when stock prices declined despite large retained profits. At best, equating the two implies that fluctuations in accrued gains on corporate stock should be averaged out but that fluctuations in other income items need not be similarly treated.

Table D-1 gives several broad measures of income in 1966. It can be seen that adjusted family income or net adjusted family income is larger

Table D-1. Income Concepts, 1966
Billions of dollars

Concept	Amount
Gross national product[a]	749.9
Net national product at market prices[a]	685.9
National income at factor costs[a]	620.6
Personal income[a]	587.2
Family personal income[b]	548.7
Family money income[c]	536.2
Adjusted gross income[d]	514.0
Adjusted family income[e]	720.1
Net adjusted family income[f]	613.8
Net adjusted family income with capital gains on corporate stock estimated on current basis[g]	546.2
Net adjusted family income with capital gains on realization basis[h]	576.2

a. National income and product account estimate, from Bureau of Economic Analysis, U.S. Department of Commerce, *U.S. National Income and Product Accounts, 1964–69* (1973), p. 3.

b. Personal income minus estimated amount not received by the household population, which is composed of income of persons in the military and institutional population and property income received by fiduciaries, pension funds, and nonprofit organizations. The amount not received by the household population is from Joseph A. Pechman and Benjamin A. Okner, *Who Bears the Tax Burden?* (Brookings Institution, 1974), p. 15.

c. Money factor income plus transfer payments; from ibid., p. 45.

d. Includes taxable and nontaxable individuals; estimate of Bureau of Economic Analysis, Department of Commerce, *Survey of Current Business*, vol. 55 (February 1975), p. 34.

e. Pechman and Okner, *Who Bears the Tax Burden?* p. 92, incidence variant 1c.

f. Adjusted family income minus the sum of: (1) corporation income tax ($28.1 billion); (2) employer contributions to social insurance ($19.9 billion); and (3) indirect business taxes ($58.3 billion). The items deducted are from Pechman and Okner, *Who Bears the Tax Burden?* pp. 90, 92, incidence variant 1c.

g. Net adjusted family income minus the sum of: (1) undistributed corporate profits included in family income ($22.2 billion); (2) the estimated decrease in the value of corporate stock held by households from the end of 1965 to the end of 1966 ($46.2 billion); and (3) estimated net acquisitions of corporate stock by households in 1966 (−$0.8 billion). The first item deducted is from Pechman and Okner, ibid., p. 90. The estimated values of corporate stock holdings of households are $483.9 billion at the end of 1965 and $437.7 billion at the end of 1966. These figures and the estimate of net acquisitions by households in 1966 are 76 percent of the amounts for households, personal trusts, and nonprofit organizations (Board of Governors of the Federal Reserve System, "Flow of Funds Accounts, 1945–1972" [1973; processed], pp. 12, 84). The 76 percent ratio is derived from the estimate by Pechman and Okner of the amount of dividends included in family income and of the amount included in national income (*Who Bears the Tax Burden?* p. 90).

h. Net adjusted family income minus accrued capital gains included in it ($57.4 billion; Pechman and Okner, *Who Bears the Tax Burden?* p. 90) plus net realized capital gains reported on individual income tax returns ($19.8 billion; U.S. Internal Revenue Service, *Statistics of Income—1966, Individual Income Tax Returns* [1968], pp. 41–42).

Table D-2. Distribution of Money Income before Tax among Families, 1947–71[a]

Arithmetic mean of annual percentages

Before-tax income	1947–49	1950–59	1960–62	1963–69	1970–71
Top 5 percent	17.2	16.5	16.7	15.2	15.3
Highest quintile	42.9	41.6	42.1	41.1	41.6
4th quintile	23.3	23.7	23.7	23.7	23.5
3d quintile	17.2	17.7	17.5	17.6	17.4
2d quintile	11.9	12.2	11.9	12.3	11.9
Lowest quintile	4.9	4.8	4.9	5.4	5.6

Source: Derived from U.S. Bureau of the Census, Current Population Survey data, published in U.S. Office of Management and Budget, *Social Indicators, 1973* (1973), p. 179.

a. A family is defined as a group of two or more persons related by blood, marriage, or adoption and residing together in a household. Unrelated individuals are not included.

than other income measures that have been used as the basis of income distribution and tax incidence statistics, including family personal income, family money income, and adjusted gross income.

Historical Data

The Current Population Survey data on the size distribution of money income to which reference was made in the text are summarized in table D-2. Descriptions, comparisons, and criticisms of this series and of other series on the distribution of income in the United States may be found in a monograph by Schultz and a paper by Budd.[4]

The estimates of the influence of the relative decline of the property income component of total family personal income on the share of the top 5 percent of consumer units mentioned in chapter 10 were derived as follows. (1) The amounts of dividends, interest, and rent received in 1929 by the 5 percent of individuals with the highest incomes were derived from estimates by Kuznets.[5] (2) Ratios were computed of these amounts to the corresponding components of total personal income as estimated by the U.S. Department of Commerce, Office of Business Economics (OBE).[6] (3) The amounts of dividends and interest received by all individuals for the years 1960, 1961, and 1962 were estimated by deducting from the

4. T. Paul Schultz, *The Distribution of Personal Income: A Study of Statistics on the Size Distribution of Personal Income in the United States,* prepared for the Joint Economic Committee, 88 Cong. 2 sess. (1965); Edward C. Budd, "Postwar Changes in the Size Distribution of Income in the U.S.," in American Economic Association, *Papers and Proceedings of the Eighty-second Annual Meeting, 1969* (*American Economic Review,* vol. 60, May 1970), pp. 247–60.

5. Simon Kuznets, *Shares of Upper Income Groups in Income and Savings* (National Bureau of Economic Research, 1953), pp. 571, 649.

6. *The National Income and Product Accounts of the United States, 1929–1965: Statistical Tables* (1966), table 2.1.

personal income components of these years the estimated amounts of these items received by nonprofit organizations or retained by fiduciaries (from OBE worksheets). In making the estimates, the deductions were allocated between dividends and interest in proportion to their respective amounts; no deduction from rental income of persons was made for receipts by nonindividuals. No comparable adjustment for receipts of property income by nonindividuals was made for 1929, owing to lack of information. There is, however, reason to believe that the percentage of such income received by nonprofit organizations was smaller in 1929 than in 1960–62. (4) The hypothetical amounts of property income that would have been received by the top 5 percent of consumer units in 1960–62 if they had maintained their 1929 shares of the three components were computed by applying the ratios derived in step 2 to the amounts obtained in step 3. (5) The amounts obtained in step 4 were related to total family personal income as estimated for 1960, 1961, and 1962 by the OBE and for 1929 by a comparable study.[7]

The estimated actual and hypothetical receipts of property income of the top 5 percent of consumer units, stated as percentages of total family personal income, are as follows:

	1929	1960–62 (hypothetical)
Dividends	5.8	2.7
Interest	2.7	1.9
Rent	1.1	0.7
Total property income	9.6	5.3

A lack of comparability arises from the fact that Kuznets' estimates for 1929 relate to individuals whereas the OBE estimates of income distribution are for consumer units. If the average number of individuals per consumer unit were the same at all income levels, the percentage shares for the top groups would be the same regardless of whether the unit was the individual or the consumer unit including single persons and families of two or more. Inasmuch as high-income consumer units tend to have more members on the average than low-income units,[8] the share of the top 5 percent of individuals should be smaller than that of the top 5 percent of consumer units.

Kuznets' estimates of the shares of upper-income groups in various kinds of income are for his "basic variant," which does not include im-

---

7. *Survey of Current Business*, vol. 44 (April 1964), p. 5.

8. U.S. Bureau of Labor Statistics, *Consumer Expenditures and Income, Total United States, Urban and Rural, 1960–61*, Report 237-93 (1965), p. 11; Schultz, *Distribution of Personal Income*, pp. 36, 45.

puted income. The OBE estimates, on the other hand, include imputed income. Thus the ratios for 1929 are between the *money* income from property (excluding capital gains) received by the highest 5 percent and *total family personal* income including imputed income received by all consumer units. Imputed interest and rent increased in relation to money income from property between 1929 and 1960–62. It would have been possible to exclude imputed income, but I did not consider this advisable inasmuch as the shift toward imputed income may have been induced partly by income tax provisions.

Estimates of the shares and amounts of various kinds of income received by the highest 5 percent of consumer units in 1962 can be derived from the Survey of Financial Characteristics of Consumers (SFCC).[9] Comparison with OBE estimates, however, indicates that there was substantial underreporting of property income in the SFCC, even with allowance for imputed interest and rent, which were not covered. The amount of dividends reported by all consumer units in the SFCC is only a little more than half of the OBE-based estimate of the total received by individuals. The 5 percent of consumer units with the highest incomes received approximately 68 percent of the total dividends covered by the SFCC. If the degree of underreporting of dividends in the SFCC was the same for the highest 5 percent as for all units, the dividend receipts of the highest 5 percent would have amounted to about $9.6 billion (about 2.3 percent of total family personal income). An alternative source of information is income tax returns. In 1962 the total amount of dividends, from domestic and foreign corporations, reported on individual income tax returns was equal to 79 percent of the OBE-based estimate of the total received by individuals. The 2.9 million returns with the highest adjusted gross income (equal in number to the top 5 percent of consumer units in the OBE distribution, though not identical units) reported $7.2 billion of dividends,[10] which is equal to 1.7 percent of total family personal income. This makes no allowance for possible underreporting on high-income tax returns. The average of the two estimates is 2 percent, which is the figure mentioned in the text in the section on composition of income in chapter 10.

9. Dorothy S. Projector, Gertrude S. Weiss, and Erling T. Thoresen, "Composition of Income as Shown by the Survey of Financial Characteristics of Consumers," in Lee Soltow, ed., *Six Papers on the Size Distribution of Wealth and Income,* Studies in Income and Wealth, vol. 33 (Columbia University Press for the National Bureau of Economic Research, 1969), pp. 107–56; Dorothy S. Projector and Gertrude S. Weiss, *Survey of Financial Characteristics of Consumers* (Board of Governors of the Federal Reserve System, 1966).

10. Derived by interpolation from U.S. Internal Revenue Service, *Statistics of Income—1962, Individual Income Tax Returns* (1965), pp. 5, 34.

Limitations of the Statistics

Limitations of the available statistics on the distribution of income arise from the omission or incomplete coverage of certain forms of income; from sampling and classification errors; and from social, demographic, and economic changes. On the whole, it seems likely that the income shares of top income groups are understated, and the statistics may exaggerate the reduction over time in the shares received by these groups.[11]

An important shortcoming of the statistics used in chapter 10, except the Pechman-Okner estimates for 1966, is that capital gains and losses are omitted. While comprehensive adjustments of the historical series to take account of capital gains and losses (or net capital gains—that is, gains minus losses) are not available, an impression of the possible importance of this kind of income can be obtained from table D-3. These figures indicate that the inclusion of realized net capital gains would have substantially increased the income share of the top 5 percent in 1929 and would have increased their share by smaller amounts in 1935–36, 1944, and 1958. The pairs of estimates for 1929, 1935–36, and 1944, however, are not fully comparable with the 1958 pair and seem to indicate more difference between the income shares of the top 5 percent, including and excluding realized net capital gains, than would estimates made in the same way as those for 1958.[12]

11. For critiques of the statistics, see George Garvy, "Functional and Size Distributions of Income and Their Meaning," in American Economic Association, *Papers and Proceedings of the Sixty-sixth Annual Meeting, 1953* (*American Economic Review,* vol. 44, May 1954), pp. 242–47; Robert J. Lampman, "Recent Changes in Income Inequality Reconsidered," *American Economic Review,* vol. 44 (June 1954), pp. 254–67; Joseph A. Pechman, "Comment," in *An Appraisal of the 1950 Census Income Data,* Studies in Income and Wealth, by the Conference on Research in Income and Wealth, vol. 23 (Princeton University Press for the NBER, 1958), pp. 107–15; Selma F. Goldsmith, "Changes in the Size Distribution of Income," in AEA, *Papers and Proceedings of the Sixty-ninth Annual Meeting, 1956* (*AER,* vol. 47, May 1957), pp. 511–18; Gabriel Kolko, *Wealth and Power in America: An Analysis of Social Class and Income Distribution* (Praeger, 1962), pp. 13–29; Schultz, *Distribution of Personal Income;* Budd, "Postwar Changes in Size Distribution of Income," pp. 247–60.

12. The 1958 figures are estimates of the Office of Business Economics; they allow for reranking of units when net capital gains are included in income; Kuznets' estimates for the earlier years do not provide for reranking. My own estimate for 1958, which I believe to be comparable to Kuznets' earlier estimates though not identical in technique, indicates that, if realized net capital gains are added to family personal income as estimated by the OBE, the income share of the top 5 percent is raised by 1.6 percentage points rather than 0.4 percentage point. My estimate, derived from *Statistics of Income,* ranks income recipients by adjusted gross income rather than family personal income and does not allow for reranking.

Table D-3. Realized Net Capital Gains and Income Share of Top 5 Percent, 1929, 1935–36, 1944, and 1958

Description	1929	1935–36	1944	1958
1. Net capital gains reported on tax returns (billions of dollars)[a]	2.9	0.2	1.6	8.5
2. Line 1 as percent of total family personal income plus line 1[b]	3.3	0.3	1.1	2.4
3. Income share (percent) of top 5 percent of population, Kuznets[c]				
a. Basic variant	26.4	24.0	16.6	...
b. Basic variant adjusted to include realized net capital gains	30.0	24.6	17.4	...
4. Income share (percent) of top 5 percent of consumer units, OBE[d]				
a. Family personal income	30.0	26.5	20.7	19.9[e]
b. Family personal income plus realized net capital gains	...	...	...	20.3

a. Net gain realized from sales of capital assets and other property, at 100 percent; 1929, 1935–36, and 1944 from Lawrence H. Seltzer, *The Nature and Tax Treatment of Capital Gains and Losses* (National Bureau of Economic Research, 1951), p. 367; 1958, estimate by Seltzer published in National Bureau of Economic Research, *The Uses of Economic Research, Forty-third NBER Annual Report* (1963), p. 89. Taxable fiduciaries are included for all years except 1958.

b. Based on estimates of family personal income from Selma Goldsmith, George Jaszi, Hyman Kaitz, and Maurice Liebenberg, "Size Distribution of Income Since the Mid-Thirties," *Review of Economics and Statistics*, vol. 36 (February 1954), p. 3; *Survey of Current Business*, vol. 43 (April 1963), p. 15.

c. Simon Kuznets, *Shares of Upper Income Groups in Income and Savings* (National Bureau of Economic Research, 1953), p. 599.

d. Except for 1958, from U.S. Bureau of the Census, *Historical Statistics of the United States, Colonial Times to 1957* (1960), p. 166; 1958, from *Survey of Current Business*, vol. 41 (May 1961), p. 14.

e. This estimate was subsequently revised to 20.0 percent (*Survey of Current Business*, April 1963, p. 18); presumably the figure in line 4b would be increased to 20.4 percent if correspondingly revised.

The reliability of the personal income statistics as measures of real income has been progressively impaired by the increasing participation of married women in work outside the home and the decline in the value of home production, which causes measured income to rise more rapidly than real income. On the other hand, the growth of expense accounts and fringe benefits that are not included in current personal income has the opposite effect. Although data are not available on which to base adjustments for these factors, it is apparent that their influence is not confined to either upper or lower incomes. Liberal expense accounts may be mainly a high-income perquisite, but other fringe benefits extend to the lower ranks. Allowance for the earnings of working wives appears to raise the income share of middle and upper-middle income groups but probably does not increase the share of the highest income group.[13] Although it seems likely that the failure to allow for the substitution between measured

13. See James Morgan, "Anatomy of Income Distribution," *Review of Economics and Statistics*, vol. 44 (August 1962), p. 270; Herman P. Miller, *Rich Man, Poor Man* (Crowell, 1964), pp. 188–92.

and unmeasured income causes an overstatement of changes in the degree of inequality, the size of the error is unknown.

Division of property among family members can reduce the apparent concentration of income without equally affecting the distribution of welfare and economic power. In principle, the statistics on which primary reliance has been placed in chapter 10 should not be affected by transfers between husbands and wives or parents and children living in the same household, since an attempt is made to consolidate the incomes of all members of the household. Owing to statistical difficulties, this consolidation may be incomplete or inaccurate. Even with full adjustment for transfers within households, transfers of income-producing property between households, as between parents and married children or between grandparents and grandchildren, will cause a statistical reduction in income inequality which may exaggerate the real change. These transfers may be motivated in considerable part by the desire to avoid income and estate taxes.

In appraising the importance of the various limitations of the statistics, it is well to remember that large dollar corrections would have to be made to have a great effect on income shares. At 1970–71 income levels, a correction of $7.75 billion would be required to change an income share by 1 percentage point. Therefore, in order to show that no reduction occurred in the income share of the top 5 percent of consumer units between 1929 and 1970–71, it would be necessary to demonstrate that at least another $84 billion of economic income should be added to the estimated $149 billion received by the group in 1970–71.[14] This figure is a minimum because it makes no allowance for possible corrections of the 1929 estimates or the estimate for the lower 95 percent in 1970–71.

14. For a similar argument, see Goldsmith, "Changes in the Size Distribution of Income," p. 514. The before-tax share of the top 5 percent fell by 10.8 percentage points between 1929 and 1970–71 (table 10-2).

Estimates Relating to Built-in Flexibility and Elasticity

THIS APPENDIX gives some statistical background for the discussion in chapter 11 of the built-in flexibility and elasticity of the individual income tax and other taxes.

Estimates in the First Edition

In the first edition of this book, published in 1964, I presented an estimate of the relationship between taxable income (TI) and gross national product (GNP) derived from a linear regression covering the period 1950–60:

$$(1) \qquad TI_t - TI_{t-1} = 0.61 + 0.381 \, (GNP_t - GNP_{t-1}).$$
$$(0.049)$$
$$r^2 = 0.845.$$

The subscripts t and $t - 1$ refer to time measured in years; TI and GNP (and other aggregates referred to later in this appendix) are in billions of dollars. The standard error of the regression coefficient is shown in parentheses.

By inspection, I concluded that the marginal tax rate for taxable income was approximately 23.0 percent in the years 1954–60, when the statutory rate schedule was constant.

The built-in flexibility of the individual income tax at 1954–60 rates was computed as follows: $0.38 \times 0.23 = 0.087$. The elasticity of the tax with respect to GNP in 1960 was computed as follows: $0.087/0.079 =$

1.1, where 0.079 is the ratio of federal individual income tax liability to *GNP*. The arithmetic mean of the annual ratios of tax liability to *GNP* in the period 1949–60 was 0.074, which yields an estimate of elasticity for the period as a whole of 1.2.

Pechman's Estimates

Estimates by Pechman of built-in flexibility and elasticity are reported for selected years in table E-1. I find it convenient to relate these to *GNP* and therefore have estimated the relationship between adjusted personal income (*API*) and *GNP* from a linear regression covering the period 1953–71:

$$(2) \qquad API_t - API_{t-1} = 1.635 + 0.715 \,(GNP_t - GNP_{t-1}).$$
$$(0.058)$$
$$\bar{r}^2 = 0.895.$$

The coefficient 0.715 is the built-in flexibility of *API* with respect to *GNP*, shown in column (1) of table E-1. Its use allows Pechman's built-in flexibility and elasticity estimates to be translated into *GNP* terms.

Tanzi's Estimates

The estimates of Tanzi and coworkers of built-in flexibility and elasticity, derived from cross-section data on income and federal income tax liabilities in the fifty states, are given for selected years in table E-2.

Table E-1. Pechman's Estimates of Built-in Flexibility and Elasticity of the Federal Individual Income Tax, Derived from Time Series, Selected Years, 1954–71

Year	Built-in flexibility[a]				Elasticity[a]	
	API to GNP (1)	TI to API (2)	T to TI (3)	T to GNP (4)	T to TI (5)	T to GNP (6)
1954	.715	.589	.230	.097	1.00	1.33
1960	.715	.617	.230	.101	1.00	1.29
1965	.715	.647	.224	.104	1.12	1.44
1970	.715	.665	.237[b]	.113[b]	1.12[b]	1.35[b]
1971	.715	.664	.238	.113	1.12	1.40

Sources: Columns 2, 3, and 5 from Joseph A. Pechman, "Responsiveness of the Federal Individual Income Tax to Changes in Income," *Brookings Papers on Economic Activity, 2:1973*, p. 393. Column 1 is my estimate from equation (2); see text. Column 4 = columns 1 × 2 × 3. Column 6 = column 4 × (GNP/T).

a. Symbols: *API*, adjusted personal income (which is personal income less transfer payments plus personal contributions for social insurance); *GNP*, gross national product; *TI*, taxable income; *T*, federal individual income tax liabilities.

b. Excludes surcharge.

Table E-2. Tanzi's Estimates of Built-in Flexibility and Elasticity of the Federal Individual Income Tax, Derived from Cross-Section Data, Selected Years, 1963–71

	Built-in flexibility			Elasticity	
	TI	T	T	T	T
	to	to	to	to	to
	AGI	TI	AGI	TI	AGI
Year	(1)	(2)	(3)	(4)	(5)
1963	.707	.251	.176	1.08	1.37
1968	...	...	...	1.17	1.42
1970	.755	.238	.179	1.14	1.38
1971	.743	.236	.175	1.15	1.41

Sources: Vito Tanzi and Thomas P. Hart, "The Effect of the 1964 Revenue Act on the Sensitivity of the Federal Income Tax," *Review of Economics and Statistics*, vol. 54 (August 1972), p. 327, and unpublished estimates made by Tanzi with the assistance of Anita Basak. For explanation of symbols, see table E-1.

Owing to lack of *GNP* estimates for the separate states, Tanzi's estimates cannot be converted to a *GNP* basis.[1] It is interesting and reassuring, however, that Pechman's and Tanzi's estimates are close together for the 1970 and 1971 values of the marginal tax rate on taxable income (built-in flexibility of tax liability with respect to taxable income), the elasticity of the tax with respect to taxable income, and the elasticity of the tax with respect to aggregate income (adjusted personal income or *GNP* in Pechman's estimates and adjusted gross income in Tanzi's estimates). They differ considerably in regard to the marginal tax rate for 1963 (Tanzi, 0.251; Pechman, 0.229).

In order to facilitate comparison with Pechman's study, Tanzi, with the assistance of Anita Basak, made estimates of built-in flexibility and elasticity with respect to *API* in 1971 by the cross-section method. Tanzi's estimate of built-in flexibility with respect to *API* in 1971 is 0.153, compared with Pechman's 0.158; Tanzi's estimate of the elasticity of the tax with respect to *API* is 1.50, compared with Pechman's 1.43. Tanzi's elasticity estimates were obtained from regressions in logarithmic form.

Elasticity of a Sales Tax

The elasticity of a broad sales tax or value-added tax would depend to a considerable extent on its coverage. A tax that covered services and exempted food, for example, should have greater income elasticity than one that applied to most commodities but exempted services. Most studies

1. For the statement on page 276, I converted Tanzi's estimate with respect to *API* (reported below) to a *GNP* basis by reference to equation (2), although this involves a departure from the cross-section method.

have estimated the income elasticity of state sales taxes within the range of 0.9 to 1.05; however, a recent study covering fifteen states found that elasticities with respect to per capita personal income fell outside that range, on the lower or upper side, in a number of cases.[2]

As an approximation of the elasticity of a federal retail sales tax, I estimated the elasticity of retail sales (RS) with respect to GNP over the period 1953–71.[3] A value of 0.81 was obtained from the following regression equation:

(3) $\ln RS = -2.131 + 0.810 \ln GNP.$
                              (0.009)
                    $\bar{r}^2 = 0.998.$

A value-added tax might have an elasticity of about 1, provided its base were broadly defined.

Consumption Multiplier

As a first step in estimating the consumption multiplier, I estimated the marginal propensity to consume from a linear regression for the period 1953–71 as follows:

$$C_t - C_{t-1} = 1.86 + 0.760 \, (DI_t - DI_{t-1}),$$
                       (0.117)
$$\bar{r}^2 = 0.697.$$

where C is personal consumption and DI is disposable personal income, both in constant (1958) dollars, and t is time measured in years. Data are estimates of the U.S. Department of Commerce.[4]

The consumption multiplier, on GNP, may be approximated as

(4) $m = \dfrac{1}{1 - c(1 - a - b - d)},$

where m is the multiplier; a is the fraction of a change in GNP that does not enter into personal income; b is the built-in flexibility of the federal individual income tax with respect to GNP; c is the marginal propensity to consume with respect to disposable personal income; and d is the built-in flexibility with respect to GNP of personal tax and nontax receipts

2. Ann F. Friedlaender, Gerald J. Swanson, and John F. Due, "Estimating Sales Tax Revenue Changes in Response to Changes in Personal Income and Sales Tax Rates," *National Tax Journal*, vol. 26 (March 1973), pp. 103–10.

3. The data are estimates of the U.S. Department of Commerce, from *Economic Report of the President, February 1974*, pp. 249, 297. Retail sales are monthly averages for the years.

4. *Economic Report of the President, February 1974*, p. 269.

of the federal, state, and local governments, except the federal individual income tax.

For 1970, the estimated or assumed values are as follows: $c = 0.760$, as estimated above; $a = 0.285$, here approximated as $(1 - p)$, where p is the marginal ratio of adjusted personal income to *GNP,* as estimated above; $b = 0.113$, derived from Pechman's estimate; and $d = 0.029$, which is the ratio of personal tax and nontax receipts other than the federal individual income tax to *GNP* in the year 1970. The numerical estimate of m is 1.77. If the federal individual income tax had been replaced by a tax that was invariant to *GNP,* the multiplier, which may be designated m_r, would have been increased to 2.09.

The change in *GNP* in response to an autonomous change in demand, A, is mA with the federal individual income tax in effect and m_rA with the replacement tax. Thus, the built-in flexibility of the income tax reduces the potential fluctuation in *GNP* by a fraction equal to $(m_rA - mA)/m_rA = 0.15$. This is equal to the index of the "compensatory effectiveness" of built-in flexibility suggested by Musgrave and Miller in 1948, though they stated their measure in a different form.[5]

A tax with an elasticity of 1 (say, a broad-based value-added tax) which yielded the same amount as the individual income tax at 1970 income levels would have built-in flexibility of 0.084, and the multiplier would be 1.84. The index of compensatory effectiveness of this tax would be 0.12. A tax with an elasticity of 0.8 (approximately the estimate for a retail sales tax) and the same yield at 1970 income levels would have built-in flexibility of 0.067; the multiplier would be 1.89 and the index of compensatory effectiveness 0.10.

The index of compensatory effectiveness is rather sensitive to some of the parameters entering into its calculation. In this respect, c, the marginal propensity to consume, is particularly important. To illustrate, if c is assumed to be 0.90, the indexes are 0.21 for the individual income tax, 0.16 for the tax with unitary elasticity, and 0.14 for the tax with elasticity of 0.8.

5. Richard A. Musgrave and Merton H. Miller, "Built-in Flexibility," *American Economic Review,* vol. 38 (March 1948), p. 123. See also Richard A. Musgrave, *The Theory of Public Finance* (McGraw-Hill, 1959), p. 508; Richard A. Musgrave and Peggy B. Musgrave, *Public Finance in Theory and Practice* (McGraw-Hill, 1973), p. 542.

Index